真棒

Zhēn Bàng!

Senior Advisor

王昭華 Margaret M. Wong

Director of International Education / Chinese Instructor

Breck School, Minneapolis, MN

Lead Author

方虹婷 Tiffany Fang

Master of Arts in Teaching Chinese as a Second Language

Contributing Writers

钱玲岑 Chien Ling-Tsen   张静岚 Chang Ching-Nan

EMC
Publishing

ST. PAUL

Editorial Director
Alejandro Vargas

Associate Editors
Lei Han
Hannah Sang
Glenda Kuo
Yu-Han Chang
Danni Wang

Consultant
Ian Burns

English Copy Editors
Jennifer Anderson
Carley Bomstad

Text Designer
Jaana Bykonich

Cover Designer
Leslie Anderson

Production Specialists
Matthias Frasch
Ryan Hamner

Care has been taken to verify the accuracy of information presented in this book. However, the authors, editors, and publisher cannot accept responsibility for Web, e-mail, newsgroup, or chat room subject matter or content, or for consequences from application of the information in this book, and make no warranty, expressed or implied, with respect to its content.

Trademarks: Some of the product names and company names included in this book have been used for identification purposes only and may be trademarks or registered trade names of their respective manufacturers and sellers. The authors, editors, and publisher disclaim any affiliation, association, or connection with, or sponsorship or endorsement by, such owners.

Photo and Realia Credits: See the back of the textbook.

We have made every effort to trace the ownership of all copyrighted material and to secure permission from copyright holders. In the event of any question arising as to the use of any material, we will be pleased to make the necessary corrections in future printings. Thanks are due to the aforementioned authors, publishers, and agents for permission to use the materials indicated.

ISBN 978-0-82194-648-0

© 2012 by EMC Publishing, LLC and LiveABC Interactive Corporation

875 Montreal Way
St. Paul, MN 55102
Email: educate@emcp.com
Website: www.emcschool.com

审阅人员 Reviewers

廖勇红
Shirley Bornstein, MPA
Catholic Central High School
Burlington, Wisconsin

赵喆玄
Sara Bosa
New Trier Township High School
Winnetka, Illinois

高山
Aaron Bray
Sheboygan Falls Middle School /
Sheboygan Falls High School
Sheboygan Falls, Wisconsin

陈琰
Areana Chen, M.S.
San Diego North County Chinese
School / San Diego HuaXia
Chinese School
San Diego, California

陈强
Qiang (John) Chen, M.Ed.
Enloe Magnet High School
Raleigh, North Carolina

竹麗蓮
Lilien Drew, M.A.T.
Franklin High School
Somerset, New Jersey

高微
Wei Gao, M.A.
Manilus Pebble Hill School
DeWitt, New York

何静萍
Jing Ping He
Marvin Ridge High School
Waxhaw, North Carolina

黄霞
Xia Huang
Mingzhou Huaxia Chinese School
Eden Prairie, Minnesota

金晓南
Shannon Jin
Chanhassen High School /
Chaska High School
Chanhassen, Minnesota

谢洪伟
Julia Hongwei Kessel, M.A.
New Trier Township High School
Winnetka, Illinois

李堅惠
Grace Lee, M.A.
Wilson Senior High School
West Lawn, Pennsylvania

周懿
Chloe Lu
Oltman Middle School
Saint Paul Park, Minnesota

吕丽娜
Lina Lu, Ed. D.
Portland State University
Portland, Oregon

吕治萍
ZhiPing Lu
Great Wall Chinese Academy
Denver, Colorado

秦桂敏
Gwen Qin
Denver Language School
Denver, Colorado

鄭金秀
Kiki Scoggins, M.Ed. (candidate)
Clements High School
Sugarland, Texas

徐佳音
Joanne Shang
Durham Academy
Durham, North Carolina

苏纯谊
Chun-Yi Su (Coral)
Nebraska Wesleyan University /
University of Nebraska - Lincoln
Lincoln, Nebraska

田国明
Guo Ming Tian, Ph. D.
Rochester City School District
Rochester, New York

王钧
Jun (John) Wang, M.Ed., M.A.
Lyme Old Lyme High School
Old Lyme, Connecticut

王丽榕
Lirong Wang
Cannon School
Concord, North Carolina

王宇
Yu Wang, Ph.D.
Confucius Institute
Minneapolis, Minnesota

蔡麗莉
Lili Tsai-Wong, M.A.
Clovis West High School /
Buchanan High School
Fresno, California

于军
(Olivia) Jun Yu, M.A. (abd.)
Global Village Academy
Aurora, Colorado

学前寄语 To the Student

真棒！ *Zhēn Bàng!* Congratulations on finishing the first level! We feel very pleased that you are sticking with Chinese and plowing on to the second year of your studies. Having successfully completed the first book, you ought to feel proud of yourself — after all, Chinese isn't an easy language to learn, and as of now you have already cultivated the ability to communicate with other people in Chinese. By virtue of the first book's sequential progression into every facet of the language, whether it be pronunciation, character recognition, writing, or proper usage, be confident that you have already hammered out a solid foundation in this challenging and fascinating language.

Now is the moment for studying Chinese! By linking together the knowledge of characters, vocabulary, and grammar you have accumulated from Level 1, you can formulate even more compound words and phrases out of what you already know. As you move forward, what you study will be more in-depth and challenging, and as a result, you will possess the ability to sufficiently and clearly express yourself and articulate your thoughts. This book covers 6 themes that all pertain to the world around you, facilitating a firm grasp of practical Chinese one will need to tackle everyday life in a Chinese speaking environment. As in Level 1, Level 2 also stresses social interaction and interpersonal relationships, enabling you to put your Chinese to use naturally and consequently absorb it into your permanent working vocabulary.

Level 1 and Level 2 are structurally similar, differing in that the beginning of Level 2 — unlike Level 1 which introduces the fundamentals of Chinese characters, history, and geography — is instead a consummate review of the first level. Before the official start of the new curriculum in Level 2, there is a quick review of the first level's vocabulary and grammar to help you brush up on everything that you've learned so far, getting you nicely warmed-up and 100% ready for the challenges of Level 2.

While Level 2 does not emphasize the foundation of the language as much as Level 1, the 3 lessons per unit will be a more in depth look at the language and culture. In addition to the section entitled Cultural Window, the information on Chinese life and notes on culture interspersed throughout each lesson will assist you even more in understanding the background and setting of this language. At this stage, in order to make you acquainted with even more aspects of Chinese, as well as to push you to take what you've learned and apply it even more smoothly and efficiently, this book has added these two sections — Raising the Bar and Reading Comprehension. The former introduces Chinese proverbs (俗语 *súyǔ*) and idioms (成语 *chéngyǔ*), enabling you to see the beauty of Chinese as well as the potential power and energy inherent in concise language. The latter section, by way of articles and text, trains you in colloquial and spoken Chinese while strengthening reading speed and comprehension.

In recent years, summer study-abroad programs to China and student exchanges between American and Chinese schools are growing more and more popular. What about you— after practicing speaking the language so diligently, do you want to put your plane ticket where your mouth is? Trust that after you finish the second book, no matter if it's living a short period of time in China, or merely interacting with a Chinese-speaking student on your own campus, you'll manage every situation with ease.

Well, a new school year is here, and it's yours to seize and squeeze as much out of as you wish, and to have fun while taking your Chinese up a notch at the same time. But before you undertake any task, however, be sure to keep this Chinese proverb in mind: 一分耕耘，一分收获。(*Yì fēn gēngyún, yì fēn shōuhuò.* Your reward and returns will only be as much as the energy and industry you put into any given task.) Case in point— see how few words Chinese takes to get its point across? The power of brevity, that's Chinese!

Well, enough dilly-dallying here; put your thinking-cap on, forget your native language, loosen your tongue, clear your throat, think like a Chinese, and let's get started! Happy Studies!

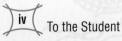

The **Pinyin System** used in
真棒！*Zhēn Bàng!* Level 2

Chinese has both a spoken form and a written form. Standard Spoken Chinese, based on the sounds of Beijing or Northern dialect is called "Putonghua" in Mainland China and "Guoyu" in Taiwan. In English, the term "Mandarin" is used.

Chinese written language is in the form of characters, which convey the meaning, rather than the sound of the language. Since there is no clear relationship between the Chinese sounds and characters, it is more efficient for beginners to learn spoken Chinese via a phonetic transcription system. Although there are many transcription systems, this book has chosen to use Pinyin, the official Romanization of Mainland China.

This book uses the following six rules for Pinyin spelling:

1. A word 词 *cí* should be written together as one word, whether it is one, two, or three syllables.

> Examples: 我 wǒ *I, me*
> 朋友 péngyou *friend*
> 图书馆 túshūguǎn *library*

2. When the word 词 is a Proper Noun, it should be capitalized.

> Examples: 美国 Měiguó *Amecia*
> 星期一 Xīngqīyī *Monday*
> 三月 Sānyuè *March*

3. Number + Measure Word should be written together.

> Examples: 两个 liǎngge *two (people)*
> 三本 sānběn *three (books)*
> 十分钟 shífēn zhōng *ten minutes*

4. Verb-Objects and verb-complements should be written together.

> Examples: 看书 kànshū *to read*   看见 kànjiàn *to see*
> 吃饭 chīfàn *to eat*   睡着 shuìzháo *to fall asleep*
> 写字 xiězì *to write*   听懂 tīngdǒng *to understand*

5. 不 *bù / bú* should be written together with the verb if the verb is one syllable, separated if the verb is two syllables. 没 *méi* is also applicable to this rule.

> Examples: 不要 / 不能 búyào/bùnéng *can't*
> 没有 méiyou *don't have*
> 不喜欢 bù xǐhuan *don't like*
> 没办法 méi bànfǎ *can't help it*

6. If 了 *le*, or 的 *de* after a verb / adjective, it should be written together if the verb / adjective is one syllable and separately if verb / adjective is two syllables. For other final particles like 呢 *ne*, 吗 *ma*, 吧 *ba* and so on, it should be written separately.

> Examples: 累了 lèile *tired*
> 看见了 kànjiàn le *saw already*
> 我的 wǒde *my, mine*
> 你呢? Nǐne? *How about you?*

目录 Table of Contents

Review

Communication

Unit 2 我的一天 *Wǒde Yìtiān* 110

Unit 3 我的朋友真棒
Wǒde Péngyou Zhēn Bàng

Unit 4 欢迎来我家 230
Huānyíng Lái Wǒ Jiā

Unit 5 今天我请客
Jīntiān Wǒ Qǐngkè

Unit 6 夏天到了 *Xiàtiān Dào Le* 356

附录 References

The following reference pages are available in the 真棒！*Zhēn Bàng!*
Internet Resource Center at www.emcschool.net/zhenbang.

Abbreviations for Parts of Speech
Measure Words
Numbers 1 – 100
English Versions of the Dialogues
Chinese to English and Pinyin Vocabulary

Review

Review Basics

发音 **Fāyīn**

Pronunciation

Pinyin Quick Guide

A pinyin syllable can be made up of three parts: an initial, a final, and a tone. Although not every syllable in Chinese has an initial, it must have a final. Initials resemble certain English consonant sounds while finals resemble English vowel sounds. There are 21 initials and 37 finals. There are four tones in Chinese, plus a neutral tone.

Finals → / Initials ↓	Simple Finals 1 a	2 o	3 e	4 -i / yi	5 -u / wu	6 -ü / yu	7 ai	Compound Finals 8 ei	9 ao	10 ou	11 an	Nasal Finals 12 en	13 ang	14 eng	Retroflex 15 er	Group i Finals 16 -ia / ya	17 io / yo
1 b	ba	bo		bi	bu		bai	bei	bao		ban	ben	bang	beng			
2 p	pa	po		pi	pu		pai	pei	pao	pou	pan	pen	pang	peng			
3 m	ma	mo	me	mi	mu		mai	mei	mao	mou	man	men	mang	meng			
4 f	fa	fo			fu			fei		fou	fan	fen	fang	feng			
5 d	da		de	di	du		dai	dei	dao	dou	dan		dang	deng			
6 t	ta		te	ti	tu		tai		tao	tou	tan		tang	teng			
7 n	na		ne	ni	nu	nü	nai	nei	nao	nou	nan	nen	nang	neng			
8 l	la		le	li	lu	lü	lai	lei	lao	lou	lan		lang	leng		lia	
9 g	ga		ge		gu		gai	gei	gao	gou	gan	gen	gang	geng			
10 k	ka		ke		ku		kai		kao	kou	kan	ken	kang	keng			
11 h	ha		he		hu		hai	hei	hao	hou	han	hen	hang	heng			
12 j				ji		ju										jia	
13 q				qi		qu										qia	
14 x				xi		xu										xia	
15 zh(i)	zha		zhe		zhu		zhai	zhei	zhao	zhou	zhan	zhen	zhang	zheng			
16 ch(i)	cha		che		chu		chai		chao	chou	chan	chen	chang	cheng			
17 sh(i)	sha		she		shu		shai	shei	shao	shou	shan	shen	shang	sheng			
18 r(i)			re		ru				rao	rou	ran	ren	rang	reng			
19 z(i)	za		ze		zu		zai	zei	zao	zou	zan	zen	zang	zeng			
20 c(i)	ca		ce		cu		cai		cao	cou	can	cen	cang	ceng			
21 s(i)	sa		se		su		sai		sao	sou	san	sen	sang	seng			

For the sake of economy, some vowels are omitted in pinyin orthography. For example, **iu** is pronounced **iou**, but the **o** is omitted and it is written as **iu**. Also, **ui** and **un** are pronounced **uei** and **uen**, but the **e** is omitted and they are written as **ui** and **un**.

Group i Finals								Group u Finals								Group ü Finals			
⑱	⑲	⑳	㉑	㉒	㉓	㉔	㉕	㉖	㉗	㉘	㉙	㉚	㉛	㉜	㉝	㉞	㉟	㊱	㊲
-ie / ye	iai / yai	-iao / yao	-iu / you	-ian / yan	-in / yin	-iang / yang	-ing / ying	-ua / wa	-uo / wo	-uai / wai	-ui / wei	-uan / wan	-un / wen	-uang / wang	-ong / weng	-üe / yue	-üan / yuan	-ün / yun	-iong / yong
bie		biao		bian	bin		bing												
pie		piao		pian	pin		ping												
mie		miao	miu	mian	min		ming												
die		diao	diu	dian			ding		duo		dui	duan	dun		dong				
tie		tiao		tian			ting		tuo		tui	tuan	tun		tong				
nie		niao	niu	nian	nin	niang	ning		nuo			nuan			nong	nüe			
lie		liao	liu	lian	lin	liang	ling		luo			luan	lun		long	lüe	lüan		
								gua	guo	guai	gui	guan	gun	guang	gong				
								kua	kuo	kuai	kui	kuan	kun	kuang	kong				
								hua	huo	huai	hui	huan	hun	huang	hong				
jie		jiao	jiu	jian	jin	jiang	jing									jue	juan	jun	jiong
qie		qiao	qiu	qian	qin	qiang	qing									que	quan	qun	qiong
xie		xiao	xiu	xian	xin	xiang	xing									xue	xuan	xun	xiong
								zhua	zhuo	zhuai	zhui	zhuan	zhun	zhuang	zhong				
								chua	chuo	chuai	chui	chuan	chun	chuang	chong				
								shua	shuo	shuai	shui	shuan	shun	shuang					
									ruo		rui	ruan	run		rong				
									zuo		zui	zuan	zun		zong				
									cuo		cui	cuan	cun		cong				
									suo		sui	suan	sun		song				

The Structure of Chinese Syllables

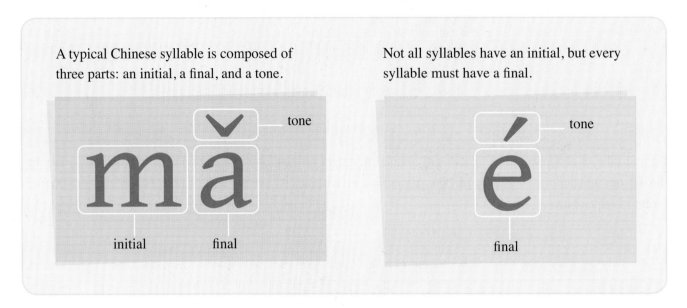

A typical Chinese syllable is composed of three parts: an initial, a final, and a tone.

tone

m a

initial   final

Not all syllables have an initial, but every syllable must have a final.

tone

é

final

The Four Basic Tones

Tones, the pitch of syllables, are an important element of spoken Chinese. The function of tones is to distinguish meaning. Take *shuǐjiǎo* (dumplings) and *shuìjiào* (to sleep), for example. They have the same initials and finals but different tones that result in different meanings. Chinese has four basic tones and one neutral tone. Take a look at the chart below, which shows the four basic tones with examples.

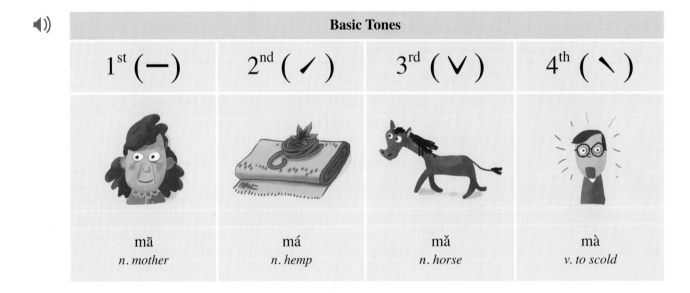

Basic Tones			
1ˢᵗ (—)	2ⁿᵈ (╱)	3ʳᵈ (∨)	4ᵗʰ (╲)
mā *n. mother*	má *n. hemp*	mǎ *n. horse*	mà *v. to scold*

The Neutral Tone

The neutral tone is toneless. It is pronounced softly, and is short, like a staccato. In transcription, the neutral tone does not carry a tone mark. For example:

gēge	háizi	nǎinai	bàba
n. elder brother	n. child	n. grandmother	n. father

Tonal Changes

Every Chinese character is pronounced as a single syllable. However, the tonal value of a syllable changes when pronounced in sequence.

Half-Third Tone

The half-third tone is a variant of the regular third tone. It begins as the full-third does, but, having reached its low point, remains at that level without rising again. As with the first tone, you may check yourself on the half-third tone by seeing whether you can prolong it at a constant pitch.

A third-tone syllable is pronounced in the half-third tone when a syllable in the first, second, or fourth tone immediately follows. A full-third tone is pronounced only when no syllable immediately follows, i.e., only at the end of a phrase, or by itself. When spelling in Pinyin, no distinction is made between a full-third and a half-third tone. Look for examples of half-third tones in the following chart.

简单	女人	跑步	好书	打折	五块
jiǎndān	nǚrén	pǎobù	hǎo shū	dǎzhé	wǔ kuài
simple	woman	to run	good book	discount	five dollars

Transformation of the Third Tone

When a syllable with the third tone is at the end of a sentence or phrase, it remains in the third tone. The third tone transforms, however, when there are more than two third-tone words in sequence.

1. When a third tone syllable is followed by another third tone syllable, the first syllable transforms into the second tone, as in these examples:

	很好	老鼠	表演	语法
	hěn hǎo	lǎoshǔ	biǎoyǎn	yǔfǎ
pronounced as →	╱ ∨	╱ ∨	╱ ∨	╱ ∨
	very good	*mouse*	*performance*	*grammar*

2. When three syllables with the third tone come in sequence, the pronunciation transforms according to context. This usually becomes [third-second-third] or [second-second-third]. Can you find these patterns in the examples below?

	小老板	炒米粉	展览馆	总统府
	xiǎo lǎobǎn	chǎo mǐfěn	zhǎnlǎn guǎn	zǒngtǒng fǔ
pronounced as →	∨ ╱ ∨	∨ ╱ ∨	╱ ╱ ∨	╱ ╱ ∨
	"junior" boss	*stir-fried rice noodles*	*exhibition center*	*presidential palace*

Tone Transformation of 一 *yī*

一 *yī* is pronounced using the first tone, but its tone changes in the following situations:

1. When 一 *yī* is a one-word phrase or at the end of the sentence, it remains in the first tone, as can be seen in these examples:

	十一	第一	万一	星期一
	shíyī	dìyī	wànyī	Xīngqīyī
tones →	╱ —	╲ —	╲ —	— — —
	eleven	*first*	*just in case*	*Monday*

2. When 一 *yī* is followed by another syllable, it is transformed into the second or fourth tone.

◄))	yī + 1ˢᵗ tone	yī + 2ⁿᵈ tone	yī + 3ʳᵈ tone	yī + 4ᵗʰ tone	yī + neutral tone
	一杯	一年	一口	一岁	一个
	yìbēi	yìnián	yìkǒu	yísuì	yíge
tones →	ˋ —	ˋ ／	ˋ ∨	／ ˋ	／
	one cup	*one year*	*one bite*	*one year-old*	*one item*

Tone Transformation of 不 *bù*

不 *bù* is a fourth-tone character. When 不 *bù* is pronounced as a single syllable or at the end of a phrase or clause, it is pronounced in the fourth tone. If it is followed by a first, second, or third-tone syllable, its tone remains as the fourth. If it is followed by another fourth-tone syllable, it then transforms into the second tone. Look at the chart to find examples of the tone transformation of 不 *bù*.

◄))	bù + 1ˢᵗ tone	bù + 2ⁿᵈ tone	bù + 3ʳᵈ tone	bù + 4ᵗʰ tone
	不高	不行	不想	不要
	bù gāo	bù xíng	bù xiǎng	bú yào
tones →	ˋ —	ˋ ／	ˋ ∨	／ ˋ
	not tall	*no way*	*do not want*	*wouldn't like*

Fourth-Tone Sandhi

The modified fourth tone begins where the full fourth tone begins, but in the same amount of time, falls only about half as far as the full fourth.

Some experts believe that this modified fourth tone is in fact better represented as a matter of stress rather than a matter of tone alteration. Since the second syllable of any two-syllable compound—not just fourth-tone compounds—tends to receive slightly more stress than the first, the fourth-plus-fourth phenomenon does not need to be considered a theoretical exception. However, it is still a good idea for beginning language learners to focus on the fourth-plus-fourth combination as a special case. In the chart you will see some examples of the fourth-tone sandhi.

◄))	看报	度假	卖画	大骂	气候	误会
	kàn bào	dù jià	mài huà	dà mà	qìhòu	wùhuì
	to read a newspaper	*to spend one's holidays*	*to sell paintings*	*to scold*	*climate*	*misunderstanding*

Pinyin Spelling Rules

Placement of Tone Marks

Tone marks are written above the main vowel of a syllable. The main vowel is determined by this order of importance: **a – o – e – i – u –ü.**

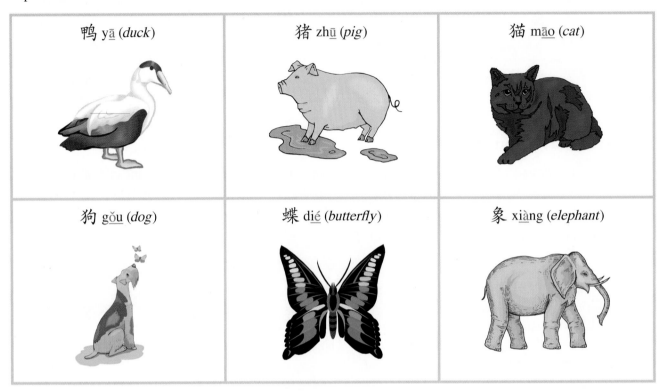

鸭 y<u>a</u> (*duck*)	猪 zh<u>u</u> (*pig*)	猫 m<u>a</u>o (*cat*)
狗 g<u>o</u>u (*dog*)	蝶 di<u>e</u> (*butterfly*)	象 xi<u>a</u>ng (*elephant*)

However, there is an exception with **i** and **u**. That is, when **i** and **u** exist in the same syllable, the tone mark is always placed on the second vowel. For example: 牛 ni<u>ú</u> (*cattle*), 腿 tu<u>ǐ</u> (*leg*)

The dot in the letter **i** is removed when a tone mark is placed over it. For example: 水 shu<u>ǐ</u> (*water*).

Finals for ü Change

-ü, -üē, -üān, -ün		
Remove the two dots when...		Keep the two dots when...
there are no initials.	combined with **j**, **q** and **x**.	combined with **n** and **l**.
月 yuè (*moon*) 圆 yuán (*round*)	橘 jú (*orange*) 裙 qún (*skirt*)	女 nǚ (*girl*) 绿 lǜ (*green*)

Capital Letters

1. Capitalize the first letter of all proper nouns.

孔子 Kǒngzǐ (*Confucius*)

香港 Xiānggǎng (*Hong Kong*)

李先生 Lǐ xiānsheng (*Mr. Li*)

► Confucius was a great teacher and philosopher in China.

2. Capitalize the first letter of the first word in a sentence.

苹果很好吃。 Píngguǒ hěn hǎochī. (*Apples are very delicious.*)

我们去公园吧！ Wǒmen qù gōngyuán ba! (*Let's go to the park!*)

Using an Apostrophe to Divide Syllables

In order to avoid confusion, an apostrophe (') is used to divide two syllables when the combination may cause uncertainty or ambiguity.

饥饿 jī'è (*hunger*)

平安 píng'ān (*safety*)

Tongue Twister

四是四，十是十。

十四是十四，四十是四十。

谁能说准四十四，

就请谁来试一试。

Sì shì sì, shí shì shí.

Shísì shì shísì, sìshí shì sìshí.

Shéi néng shuō zhǔn sìshísì,

Jiù qǐng shéi lái shì yí shì.

Four is four, ten is ten.

Fourteen is fourteen, forty is forty.

If you can say 'forty-four' accurately,

Then give it a try.

Chinese Characters

Pictographs

Pictographs are characters that were originally drawings of objects. For example, the pictograph ☽ is shaped like a crescent moon. The pictograph 龜 looks like the profile of a tortoise with four legs and a shell. Chinese characters have changed their shape considerably over the course of the centuries, becoming much squarer in form. Look at the transformation of the pictograph ☽ (月 yuè) into the modern form:

Generally speaking, pictographs can be divided into four types: the anatomical (body parts and people), the geographical (things in the natural world), the living (animals and plants), and the inanimate (objects). The following are examples of each category.

① The anatomical:

Ancient form	Modern form	Pronunciation	English
𣎼	子	zǐ	*child*
𠙐	口	kǒu	*mouth*

② The geographical:

Ancient form	Modern form	Pronunciation	English
⊖	日	rì	*sun*
⋔	山	shān	*mountain*

3 The living:

Ancient form	Modern form	Pronunciation	English
ψ	牛	niú	*cow*
米	木	mù	*tree*

4 The inanimate:

Ancient form	Modern form	Pronunciation	English
門	门	mén	*door*
册	册	cè	*book*

Ideographs

Ideographs are graphical representations of abstract ideas, such as 一 *yī* (one) and 二 *èr* (two).

Ideographs can be made in two ways. The first way is to portray abstract concepts through symbols only, such as drawing a line to show position, then making a shorter stroke above the longer line to show "up": 上 *shàng*; or one below to show "down": 下 *xià*. The character 三 *sān* is composed of three horizontal lines to represent the number three. The ancient Chinese used the base ten numeral system too, so the number ten would bring the cycle back to the beginning. Thus, to differentiate ten from one (一, *yī*), they added a vertical line to form 十 *shí*; the number ten. The character 大 *dà* shows a man with his arms and legs spread open wide to mean "big." A man with his arms down and his legs together becomes 小 *xiǎo*, meaning "small."

The other way ideographs are formed is to add an abstract symbol to a pictograph; for example, the word 刃 *rèn* (blade) was formed by adding an abstract dot to the pictograph 刀 *dāo* (knife) to show the sharpest point of a knife. Adding a dot to the pictograph 口 *kǒu* (mouth) to show the tongue tasting something makes the word 甘 *gān* (sweet). The ancient Chinese added an abstract sign to the pictograph of a man with his arms and legs spread open wide to form 天 *tiān* to refer to the sky above our heads. The character 寸 *cùn* was formed by adding an abstract sign to the bottom left of the pictograph 手 *shǒu* (hand) to refer to an inch below the palm, the place where traditional Chinese doctors felt to take the pulse of their patients. Use of this character has since evolved to refer to a unit of measurement, the inch.

Combinations of Pictographs and Ideographs

With the development of Chinese civilization, thoughts and ideas that needed to be conveyed became more complex. Thus, when the time came that pictographs and ideographs were not enough, a new type of character appeared that combined the meaning of two or more elements to form a new meaning. For example, the character 日 (*rì*, sun) and the character 月 (*yuè*, moon) were put together to form the character 明 (*míng*), which means "bright." Below you will see some examples of these combinations.

人 (*person*)	+	木 (*tree*)	=	休 (xiū, *to rest*)	
宀 (*roof*)	+	女 (*woman*)	=	安 (ān, *peace*)	
女 (*woman*)	+	子 (*child*)	=	好 (hǎo, *good*)	
亡 (*die*)	+	目 (*eyes*)	=	盲 (máng, *blind*)	
少 (*few*)	+	力 (*strength*)	=	劣 (liè, *inferior*)	
手 (*hand*)	+	目 (*eyes*)	=	看 (kàn, *to see*)	
心 (*heart*)	+	中 (*middle*)	=	忠 (zhōng, *loyalty*)	
日 (*sun*)	+	一 (*one*)	=	旦 (dàn, *dawn*)	

▲ 人 (*person*) + 木 (*tree*) = 休 (*to rest*)

The Basic Strokes

As you learn to write Chinese characters, the first thing to know is how to make the strokes. Strokes are important because they show how the characters are composed and enable you to write the characters more easily. There are eight basic strokes that are commonly used. They are illustrated as follows:

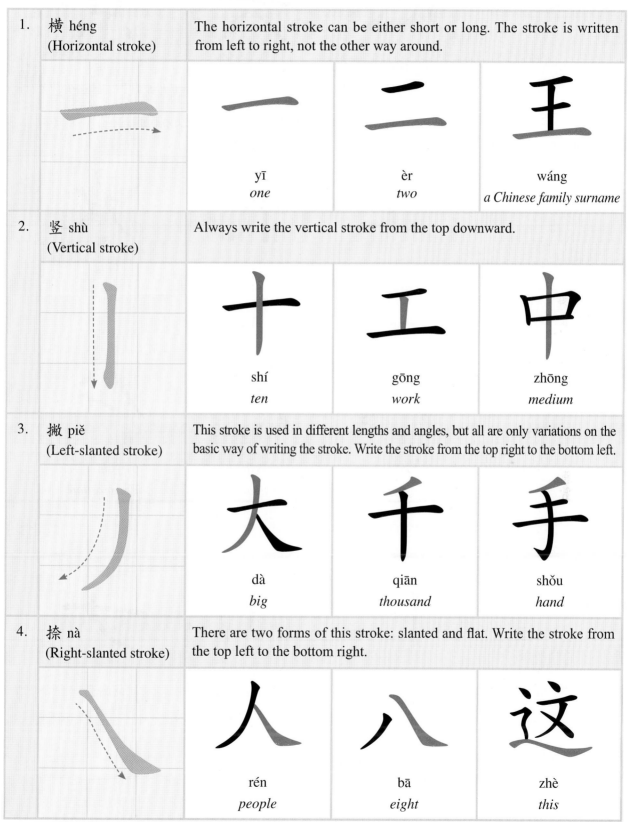

1.	横 héng (Horizontal stroke)	The horizontal stroke can be either short or long. The stroke is written from left to right, not the other way around.		
		一 yī *one*	二 èr *two*	王 wáng *a Chinese family surname*
2.	竖 shù (Vertical stroke)	Always write the vertical stroke from the top downward.		
		十 shí *ten*	工 gōng *work*	中 zhōng *medium*
3.	撇 piě (Left-slanted stroke)	This stroke is used in different lengths and angles, but all are only variations on the basic way of writing the stroke. Write the stroke from the top right to the bottom left.		
		大 dà *big*	千 qiān *thousand*	手 shǒu *hand*
4.	捺 nà (Right-slanted stroke)	There are two forms of this stroke: slanted and flat. Write the stroke from the top left to the bottom right.		
		人 rén *people*	八 bā *eight*	这 zhè *this*

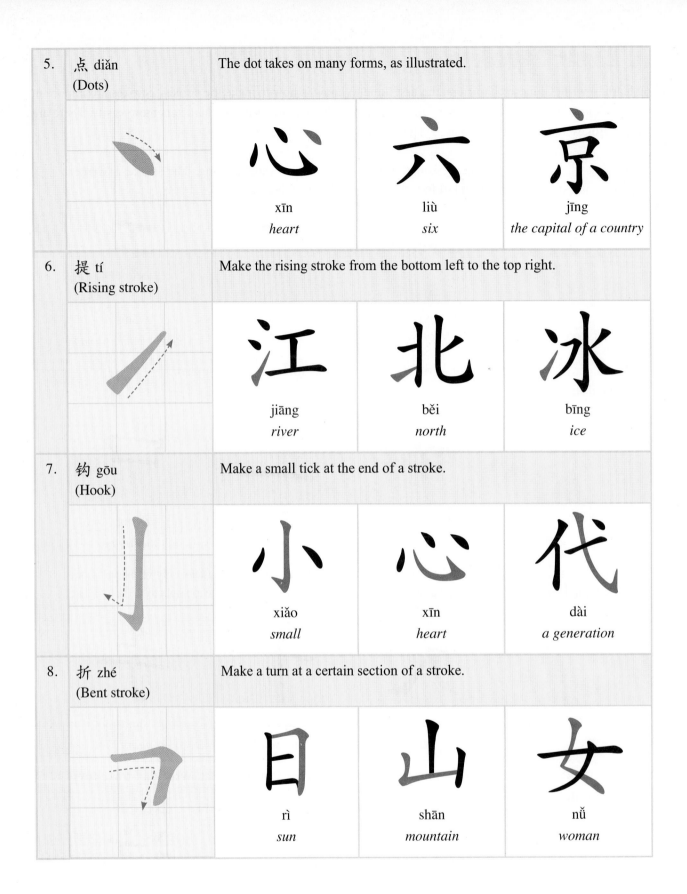

5.	点 diǎn (Dots)	The dot takes on many forms, as illustrated.

心	六	京
xīn	liù	jīng
heart	*six*	*the capital of a country*

6.	提 tí (Rising stroke)	Make the rising stroke from the bottom left to the top right.

江	北	冰
jiāng	běi	bīng
river	*north*	*ice*

7.	钩 gōu (Hook)	Make a small tick at the end of a stroke.

小	心	代
xiǎo	xīn	dài
small	*heart*	*a generation*

8.	折 zhé (Bent stroke)	Make a turn at a certain section of a stroke.

日	山	女
rì	shān	nǚ
sun	*mountain*	*woman*

Stroke Order

When writing Chinese characters, it is important to use the correct stroke order. The following rules for stroke order should be observed.

1.	Horizontal first, then vertical.

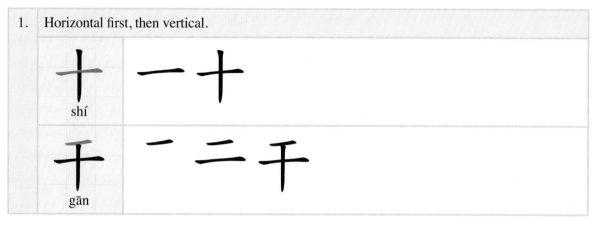

shí

gān

2.	Top first, then bottom.

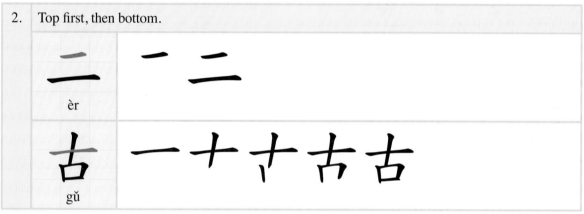

èr

gǔ

3.	Left-slanted first, then right-slanted.

bā

rén

4. Left first, then right.

| 川 <br> chuān | ノ 丿 川 |
| 仁 <br> rén | ノ 亻 仁 仁 |

5. Center first, then both sides.

| 小 <br> xiǎo | 亅 亅 小 |
| 木 <br> mù | 一 十 才 木 |

6. When making aa dot ⟍, write it first if it is positioned on the top or upper-left. When it appears on the upper right or in the middle, write it last.

文 wén	丶 亠 方 文
斗 dǒu	丶 丷 三 斗
犬 quǎn	一 ナ 大 犬
叉 chā	フ 又 叉

7. With "closed" characters, make the outside strokes (left, top, right), then the strokes in the middle, then the bottom stroke that "closes" the character.

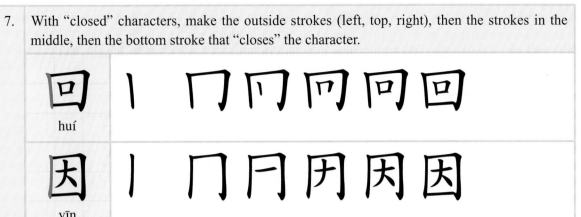

8. With semi-closed characters, there are three different stroke orders:
    ❶ Strokes in the middle before surrounding stroke(s)

    ❷ Surrounding strokes before strokes in the middle

    ❸ Top before middle before lower-left

Simplified Radical Chart

The chart below includes 207 radicals. The most common 50 radicals are in red, followed by the alternative form in parenthesis. The numbers 1 to 12 represent the number of strokes.

1

#		#	
1	丨	2	亅
3	丿	4	一
5	一	6	乙

2

#		#	
7	匕	8	入
9	卜	10	厂
11	冫		
12	儿	13	八
14	讠(言)		
15	匚	16	几
17	冂	18	勹
19	人(亻)		
20	⼍	21	二
22	刀(刂)		
23	厶	24	丷
25	力		
26	十	27	又
28	又		
29	二	30	凵

3

#		#	
31	艹		
32	彡	33	巛
34	饣(食)		
35	彳		
36	巳	37	尢
38	纟		
39	弋	40	幺
41	宀		
42	尸	43	兀
44	广		
45	士	46	马
47	门		
48	川	49	巾
50	辶(辵)		
51	夂	52	夕
53	口		
54	干	55	飞
56	囗		
57	屮	58	寸

#		#	
59	女		
60	廾	61	弓
62	子		
63	大		
64	工	65	尸
66	小		
67	彐	68	己
69	土		
70	山		
71	阝		

4

#		#	
72	礻		
73	贝	74	比
75	爻	76	日
77	歹	78	长
79	心(忄)		
80	方	81	风
82	日		
83	斗	84	厄
85	月		

#		#	
86	水(氵)		
87	廾	88	卅
89	火(灬)		
90	旡	91	见
92	木		
93	斤	94	爿
95	手(扌)		
96	气	97	爿
98	父		
99	片	100	爻
101	户		
102	攵	103	毛
104	牛(牜)		
105	欠	106	氏
107	犬(犭)		
108	爫	109	爪
110	殳	111	瓦
112	王	113	韦
114	止	115	牙
116	文	117	无

#		#	
118	车		

5

#		#	
119	玄	120	疋
121	白	122	癶
123	钅(金)		
124	甘	125	瓜
126	禾	127	业
128	广		
129	矛	130	龙
131	皿		
132	母	133	鸟
134	立		
135	皮	136	生
137	石		
138	矢	139	示
140	目		
141	皿	142	田
143	穴		

6

#		#	
144	羊	145	羽

#		#	
146	虫		
147	臣	148	缶
149	艮	150	虍
151	臼	152	竹
153	页		
154	耒	155	米
156	糸	157	齐
158	衣(衤)		
159	肉	160	色
161	舌	162	网
163	行	164	血
165	西	166	襾
167	聿	168	至

7

#		#	
169	豕	170	辛
171	邑	172	酉
173	足		
174	而	175	辰
176	赤	177	角
178	豆	179	谷

#		#	
180	龟	181	卤
182	麦	183	身
184	走		
185	里	186	豸

8

#		#	
187	鱼	188	隶
189	采	190	齿
191	非	192	阜
193	雨		
194	青	195	隹

9

#		#	
196	骨	197	鬼
198	音	199	革

10

#		#	
200	高	201	髟

11

#		#	
202	麻	203	鹿

12 以上

#		#	
204	黑	205	鼠
206	鼻	207	鼓

Combinations of Radicals and Phonetics

Characters can consist of a radical indicator and a phonetic indicator. Radicals represent a word's meaning or category. The phonetic element gives a word its sound.

Radical		Phonetic		Combinations
女 (woman)	+	马 (mǎ)	=	妈 (mā, mother)
木 (wood)	+	才 (cái)	=	材 (cái, building materials)
水 (water)	+	羊 (yáng)	=	洋 (yáng, ocean)
言 (speech)	+	己 (jǐ)	=	记 (jì, to remember)
心 (heart)	+	相 (xiāng)	=	想 (xiǎng, to think)
人 (people)	+	主 (zhǔ)	=	住 (zhù, to live)

字 zì and 词 cí

The noun 字 zì (character) is comprised of one character and sometimes has an independent meaning. Each 字 zì is one syllable. A 词 cí (word) may be comprised of one or more 字 zì; therefore, 词 cí may be one or more syllables. Most 词 cí in Chinese are composed of two 字 zì.

Here are some examples of 词 cí as one character, two characters, and three characters.

One character	人 (rén, human)	狗 (gǒu, dog)	书 (shū, book)
Two characters	学生 (xué.shēng, student)	冷气 (lěngqì, air conditioner)	早上 (zǎoshang, morning)
Three characters	图书馆 (túshūguǎn, library)	篮球场 (lánqiúchǎng, basketball court)	幼儿园 (yòu'éryuán, kindergarten)

Many of the 25,000 or so individual 字 zì are combined to create compounds perceived as single words; and a 字 zì may or may not retain its original meaning when used in a compound. For example:

中 zhōng (middle)	+	国 guó (kingdom)	→	中国 Zhōngguó (China)
高 gāo (high)	+	兴 xìng (pleasure)	→	高兴 gāoxìng (cheerful)
说 shuō (to speak)	+	话 huà (word)	→	说话 shuōhuà (to speak)
吃 chī (to eat)	+	饭 fàn (rice)	→	吃饭 chīfàn (to eat)
毛 máo (fur)	+	笔 bǐ (pen)	→	毛笔 máobǐ (writing brush made of fur)
天 tiān (sky)	+	气 qì (air)	→	天气 tiānqì (weather)

The Importance of Proportion

Chinese words may look complicated, but in fact, their structures are logical and easy to analyze. Chinese characters are called "square" characters, meaning no matter how simple or complex, each character fits inside a square. They can be divided into four main structures, which are listed below. Once these four structures are mastered, the makeup of Chinese characters will be much more familiar and less intimidating to you. These structures will not only help you memorize characters, but also reduce problems with missing dots or strokes when writing. Understanding these structures will make even complex characters easy to remember.

   Characters should be written with a sense of symmetry and proportion. A character can be formed as a one-picture character, a two-picture character, a three-picture character, or a four-picture character. One-picture characters fit inside a square. There are two possibilities for dividing a square for two-picture characters. Three-picture characters come in five different patterns. The square for four-picture characters can be subdivided in three ways. Understanding how to mentally plot out a character within a square will give you one of the fundamentals needed for effective written communication in Chinese.

	Structure		Examples
1.	One-Picture Character		刀 dāo *knife*
			女 nǚ *female*
2.	Two-Picture Character		叫 jiào *to shout*
			早 zǎo *early*
3.	Three-Picture Character		例 lì *example*
			意 yì *meaning; idea*
			部 bù *part*
			然 rán *really*
			增 zēng *to add*
4.	Four-Picture Character		能 néng *to be able to*
			慢 màn *slow*
			湖 hú *lake*

The Placement of Radicals

Previously, we learned about components of characters and where they are placed. There are rules for where to place radicals, too. Let's look at the table below to learn the rules for placing radicals.

	Placement of Radicals	Radicals	Examples
1.	left of the character	亻 *person*	你 nǐ *you*
		犭 *animal*	狗 gǒu *dog*
		日 *sun*	明 míng *bright*
2.	right of the character	攵 *tap*	故 gù *reason*
		阝 *city*	都 dū *city*
		刂 *knife*	到 dào *to arrive*
3.	top of the character	宀 *roof*	家 jiā *home*
		冖 *cover*	写 xiě *to write*
		艹 *grass*	草 cǎo *grass*
4.	bottom of the character	灬 *fire*	热 rè *hot*
		心 *heart*	想 xiǎng *to think*
5.	whole-word frames	囗 *enclose*	国 guó *country*
		匸 *basket*	区 qū *area*
		冂 *border*	网 wǎng *net*
		凵 *receptacle*	画 huà *painting*
		疒 *disease*	病 bìng *disease*
		辶 *to go*	追 zhuī *to pursue*

Jùxíng Jièshào

Language Patterns

Following is a summary of the language patterns you have already studied in level 1. Each pattern includes an example for your reference.

Unit 1, Lesson A

- Greeting others

  name / title + greeting   老师，您好。

- The Question Word 什么 *shénme* [what]

  什么 *shénme* + Noun？   什么名字？

- Interrogative Particle

  declarative sentence + pronoun + 呢 *ne*   我叫小红，你呢？

Unit 1, Lesson B

- The Question Word 吗 *ma*

  Sentence + 吗 *ma*?   你是王老师吗？

- "How are you?" + Response

  Name / Last name and title + 你好吗 *Nǐ hǎo ma*?   白苹，你好吗？

- The Verb 得 *děi* [must; to have to]

  得 *děi* + Verb Phrase + 了 *le*   我得睡觉了。

Unit 1, Lesson C

- The Particle 的 *de*

  Modifier + 的 *de* + Noun / Pronoun   我的名字。

- The Question Word 哪 *nǎ* [which]

  哪 *nǎ* + Measure Word + Noun？   哪国人？

- The Adverb 也 *yě* [too]

  Subject + 也 *yě* + Negation + Verb   我也是中国人。

- The Negative Adverb 不 *bù* / *bú* [not]

  Noun / Pronoun + 不 *bù* / *bú* + Adjective / Verb   我不饿。

- The Question Word 几 *jǐ* [what; how many]

  Number + Measure Word + Noun　几年级？

- Confirm something by using 对不对 *duì bú duì* [Is that right?]

  Q: Sentence + 对不对 *duì bú duì*?　他是李先生，对不对？

  A: 对 *duì* + Sentence　对，他是李先生。

  　不对 *bú duì* + Sentence　不对，他不是李先生。

Unit 2, Lesson A

- Omitting 的 *de*

  Noun₁ + （的 *de*） + Noun₂　我（的）妈妈。

- The Demonstratives 这 *zhè* [this] and 那 *nà* [that]　这是我（的）哥哥，那是我（的）姐姐

- The Question Word 谁 *shéi* [who]

  谁是 *Shéi shì* + Noun / Pronoun？　谁是王老师？

  Noun / Pronoun + 是谁 *shì shéi*？　他们是谁？

Unit 2, Lesson B

- The Verb 有 *yǒu* [to have]

  （没 *méi*） + 有 *yǒu* + Noun　我有哥哥，没有姐姐。

- Measure Words

  这 *zhèi* / 那 *nèi* + Measure Word + Noun　这 / 那只狗。

  OR Number + Measure Word + Noun　两个人。

- The Question Word 几 *jǐ* [how many]

  几 *jǐ* + Measure Word + Noun？　几双鞋？

Unit 2, Lesson C

- Saying the Date

  年 *nián* + 月 *yuè* + 号 *hào* / 日 *rì*　2002年5月15号 / 日

Unit 2, Lesson D

- "V 不 *bù* / *bú* V" Questions

  Verb + 不 *bù* / *bú* + Verb + Object？　你打不打篮球？

- The Suggestive Particle 吧 *ba*

  Sentence + 吧 *ba*　我们看电影吧。

Unit 3, Lesson A

- The Question Word 哪儿 *nǎr* [where]

  Subject + 在 *zài* + 哪儿 *nǎr* ? 你家在哪儿？

- Place Words and Relative Location

  Subject + 在 *zài* + Place Word 我家在北京。

Unit 3, Lesson B

- The Verb 借 *jiè* [to borrow; to lend]

  Person A + 借给 *jiè gěi* + Person B + Something 我借给你一支笔。

  Person A + 借 *jiè* + Something + 给 *gěi* + Person B 我借一支笔给你。

- The Auxiliary Verb 可以 *kěyǐ* [can; may]

  Q: Subject + 可以 *kěyǐ* + Verb Phrase + 吗 *ma* ? 我可以去你家吗？

  A: YES: 可以 *kěyǐ*。

     NO: 不可以 *bù kěyǐ*。

Unit 3, Lesson C

- Word Order for Time Words

  Time Word + Subject + Verb Phrase 星期天我们去公园。

- The Adverb 还 *hái* [still]

  Subject + Verb Phrase₁ + 还 *hái* + Verb Phrase₂ 我有一个哥哥，还有一个姐姐。

- Adjectives in Chinese

  Subject + Adverb + Adjective 考试很难。

- The Verbs 来 *lái* [to come] and 去 *qù* [to go]

  来 *lái* / 去 *qù* + Place Word 他来 / 去学校。

Unit 3, Lesson D

- The Auxiliary Verb 要 *yào* [to want to]

  要 *yào* + Verb 我要唱歌。

- The Purpose Indicating Pattern: 去 *qù* [to go] / 来 *lái* [to come] + Verb clause

  Subject + 去 *qù* / 来 *lái* + Verb clause 我去看书。

- The Preposition 跟 *gēn* [with]

  Subject₁ + 跟 *gēn* + Subject₂ + Verb Phrase 我跟妈妈去公园。

Unit 4, Lesson A

- The Conjunction 还是 *háishì* [or]

  Choice₁ + 还是 *háishì* + Choice₂   你喝茶还是喝咖啡?

- The Moderating Usage for Verbs: 一下 *yíxià*

  Verb + 一下 *yíxià*   请等一下。

Unit 4, Lesson B

- Asking questions with 有没有 *yǒu méiyǒu* [to have or not]

  有没有 *yǒu méiyǒu* + Noun   你有没有笔?

- Verb+ 的东西 *de dōng xi* [thing]

  Verb + 的东西 *de dōng xi*   吃的东西。

- Answers to 要 *yào* [to want] Questions

  Q: 要不要 *yào bú yào* + Noun / Verb   你要不要吃饭?

  A: YES: 要 *yào*

     NO: 不要 *bú yào*

Unit 4, Lesson C

- The Question Word 多少 *duōshǎo* [how much]

  多少 *duōshǎo* + Noun   这本书多少钱?

- Numbers 100-999

Unit 4, Lesson D

- To express an upcoming action with (快)要了…*(kuài) yào…le* [to be going to]

  (快)要 *(kuài) yào* + Verb Phrase + 了 *le*   我们（快）要点菜了。

- The Negation Adverb 不 *bù* [not]

  Subject + Adjective + 不 *bù* / *bú* + Adjective   酸辣汤酸不酸?

- The Adverb 都 *dōu* [both; all]

  Nouns + 都 *dōu* + Verb Phrase   我们都是美国人。

Unit 5, Lesson A

- 上 *shàng* / 下 *xià* + 个 *ge* + 星期 *xīngqī* / 月 *yuè*   下个星期。

- The Question Word 怎么样 *zěnmeyàng* [how]
  Subject + 怎么样 *zěnmeyàng*？   天气怎么样？

- The Auxiliary Verb 会 *huì* [will]
  Subject + 会 *huì* + Verb Phrase   明天会下雨。

- Time Word + 见 *jiàn* [to see]
  Time Word + 见 *jiàn*   明天见。

Unit 5, Lesson B

- The Pattern 又...又... *yòu…yòu…* [both...and...]
  Subject + 又 *yòu* + Adjective₁ / Verb₁ + 又 *yòu* + Adjective₂ / Verb₂   我又喝茶又喝果汁。

- The Comparative Word 比较 *bǐjiào* [more]
  Subject + 比较 *bǐjiào* + Adjective   昨天比较冷。

- The Pattern 太...了 *tài...le* [too]
  太 *tài* + Adjective + 了 *le*   太甜了。

- Indicating Specific Time with 的时候 *de shíhòu* [when]
  Time Word / Verb Phrase / Clause + 的时候 *de shíhòu*，Sentence   早上的时候, 妈妈去跑步。

Unit 5, Lesson C

- The Verb 看 *kàn* [to depend on]
  看 *kàn* + Noun Phrase   中国节日得看农历。

- The Question Word 为什么 *wèishénme*
  and the Pattern 因为 *yīnwèi*... [because], 所以 *suǒyǐ*... [therefore]
  Q: 为什么 *Wèishénme* + Sentence？   为什么你不喜欢这道菜？
  A: 因为 *Yīnwèi* + the cause, 所以 *suǒyǐ* + the result   因为太咸了，所以我不喜欢吃。

Unit 5, Lesson D

- The Adverb 在 *zài*
  Subject + 在 *zài* + V-ing   我在打球。

- The question particle 吧 *ba*
  Sentence + 吧 *ba*?   考试很难吧？

- Express intensified exclusion with 一点儿也/都不 *yì.diǎnr yě/dōu bù* [not at all]
  Subject + 一点儿 *yìdiǎnr* + 都 *dōu* / 也 *yě* + 不 *bù* + Adjective / Verb   考试一点儿也不难。

- The pattern 除了...以外，也/还... *chú.le... yǐwài, yě / hái...* [in addition to..., also...]
  除了 *chúle* + Verb Phrase₁ / Noun Phrase₁ + 以外 *yǐwài*,
  也 *yě* / 还 *hái* + Verb Phrase₂ / Noun Phrase₂   除了打篮球以外，我还踢足球。

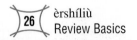

Unit 6, Lesson A

- The Time Words 以前 *yǐqián* [before] and 以后 *yǐhòu* [after]

  以前 *yǐqián* and 以后 *yǐhòu* are Time Words

  Amount of Time + 以前 *yǐqián* / 以后 *yǐhòu* = time ago / after　三个月以前/以后。

  Verbal Clause + 以前 *yǐqián* / 以后 *yǐhòu* = before / after　上课以前 / 以后

- The Numeral 几 *jǐ* [a few]

  几 *jǐ* + Measure Word + Noun　我有几本书给你。

  Number (10, 20, 30,…, 90) + 几 *jǐ* + Measure Word + Noun　十几个学生。

- The Pronoun 自己 *zìjǐ* [oneself]

  Noun / Pronoun + 自己 *zìjǐ*　我自己去图书馆。

Unit 6, Lesson B

- Omission of nouns　这件（衣服）好看吗？
- The Phrase 打#折 *dǎ # zhé* [to have item sold at # percentage of the original price]　打九折

Unit 6, Lesson C

- To express degree using 有点儿 *yǒu diǎnr* [a bit; a little]

  Noun + 有点儿 *yǒu diǎnr* + Adjective　裤子有点儿贵。

- The pattern 不但 *búdàn*…，而且 *érqiě*… [not only…, but also…]

  Subject + 不但 *búdàn* + Verb Clause₁ + 而且 *érqiě* + Verb Clause₂　这件衣服不但便宜而且漂亮。

- Asking about clothing size with 几号 *jǐhào* [what size]　你穿几号衣服？

- The Verb 请 *qǐng* [to request; to invite]

  请 *qǐng* + Somebody + Verb Phrase　我请你去我家。

- To ask for agreement with 好吗 *hǎo ma* [okay]

  Sentence + 好吗 *hǎo ma*？　明天一起打篮球，好吗？

Unit 6, Lesson D

- The Question Pronoun 什么样 *shén meyàng* [what kind]

  什么样 *shén meyàng* + 的 *de* + Object？　什么样的人？

- Moderating Adjectives with 一点儿 *yì.diǎnr* [a little]

  Adjective + 一点儿 *yìdiǎnr*　少一点儿作业。

- The Reduplication of Verbs

  Verb + Verb + (Object)　试试这件衣服。

- The Superlative 最 *zuì* [the most]

  最 *zuì* + Adjective　巧克力最好吃。

Review Unit 1

会话 Huìhuà
Dialogue

🔊 你好! Nǐ hǎo! *Hello!*

王红:	早上好!	Wáng Hóng:	Zǎoshang hǎo!
李刚:	你好!	Lǐ Gāng:	Nǐ hǎo!
王红:	这是我们的新同学，他叫大卫。	Wáng Hóng:	Zhè shì wǒmen de xīn tóngxué, tā jiào Dà Wèi.
大卫:	你好! 你叫什么名字?	Dà Wèi:	Nǐ hǎo! Nǐ jiào shénme míngzi.
李刚:	我叫李刚，很高兴认识你。你是哪国人?	Lǐ Gāng:	Wǒ jiào Lǐ Gāng, hěn gāoxìng rènshi nǐ. Nǐ shì nǎ guó rén?
大卫:	我是美国人。	Dà Wèi:	Wǒ shì Měiguórén.
王红:	今天你们上什么课?	Wáng Hóng:	Jīntiān nǐmen shàng shénme kè?
李刚:	我上午上数学和西班牙语，下午上体育。	Lǐ Gāng:	Wǒ shàngwǔ shàng shùxué hé Xībānyáyǔ, xiàwǔ shàng tǐyù.
大卫:	我上中文、历史，还有体育。	Dà Wèi:	Wǒ shàng Zhōngwén, lìshǐ, háiyǒu tǐyù.
王红:	我得上课了，再见。	Wáng Hóng:	Wǒ děi shàngkè le, zàijiàn.
大卫, 李刚:	再见	Dà Wèi, Lǐ Gāng:	Zàijiàn.

Listen carefully to the dialogue. Then read the dialogue aloud without looking at the Pinyin.

2 | 懂了吗 | **Dǒng le ma?** / *Do you understand?*

Answer the following questions in Chinese.

1. Who introduced Da Wei?
2. What is the nationality of Da Wei?
3. What are the courses Li Gang is taking in the morning?
4. What is the course that both Li Gang and Da Wei are taking?
5. Why does Wang Hong have to leave first?

3 | 听一听 | **Tīng Yì Tīng** / Listening

Select the best response to each sentence you hear.

A. 你好。
   Nǐ hǎo.

B. 我很好。
   Wǒ hěn hǎo.

C. 我叫大卫。
   Wǒ jiào Dà Wèi.

D. 我是中国人。
   Wǒ shì Zhōngguó rén.

E. 我上数学课。
   Wǒ shàng shùxué kè.

F. 我十五岁。
   Wǒ shíwǔsuì.

最近好吗
Zuìjìn hǎo ma?

很好，你呢
Hěn hǎo, nǐ ne?

4 中文怎么说？ | **Zhōngwén zěnme shuō?** / *How would you say it in Chinese?*

Follow the guidelines below to practice Chinese with your classmates.

1. Say "*Hello*."
2. Say "*How are you?*"
3. Say your name.
4. Say "*I am doing well*."
5. Say your nationality.
6. Say your favorite school subjects.
7. Say your grade and age.
8. Say "*Good-bye*."

好久不见！
Hǎo jiǔ bú jiàn!

5 国家 **Guójiā** / *Countries*

Say the name of each country in Chinese based on its flag.

1.

5.

9.

2.

6.

10.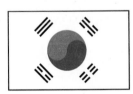

3.

7.

11.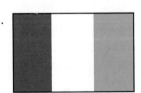

4.

8.

12.

6 写一写 Xiě Yì Xiě / *Writing*

On a separate sheet of paper, write down the Chinese characters according to the Pinyin.

1. nǐ hǎo
2. zǎoshang
3. míngzi
4. wǒmen
5. jǐsuì
6. zhōngwén

7 认字 Rènzì / *Recognize the Characters*

Match the Chinese words on the left with the appropriate English meaning on the right.

1. 中国   A. breakfast
2. 人生   B. good-bye
3. 早上   C. life
4. 早餐   D. superman
5. 超人   E. China
6. 再见   F. morning

▲ 再见

文化复习 Wénhuà Fùxí
Culture Review

- **Chinese Names:** Chinese names are divided into two parts, last names and first names. Unlike Western names, the last name always precedes the first name.

- **Titles:** Titles reflect a person's age, social standing, and gender. For example: 先生，太太。

- **Grade levels in Chinese schools:** The most common educational system used in China is the 6-3-3 system, which describes a format of six years of elementary school, three years of junior high, and three years of senior high.

- **Transportation to school:** Most students in junior and senior high take public transportation, such as buses, the metro, or trains, to get to school.

- **Foreign Languages:** English is the most widely studied foreign language in China.

▲ School students are on their way to school.

Review Unit 2

会话 Huìhuà
Dialogue

🔊 家人 Jiārén *Family*

王红：	明天是我的生日晚会，请你们来我家吃饭。	Wáng Hóng:	Míngtiān shì wǒde shēngrì wǎnhuì, qǐng nǐmen lái wǒjiā chīfàn.
李刚：	你的生日是几月几号？	Lǐ Gāng:	Nǐde shēngrì shì jǐyuè jǐhào?
王红：	八月五号。	Wáng Hóng:	Bāyuè wǔhào.
大卫：	你家有几口人？	Dà Wèi:	Nǐ jiā yǒu jǐkǒu rén?
王红：	我家有四口人，爸爸，妈妈，哥哥和我。你们喜欢做什么？	Wáng Hóng:	Wǒ jiā yǒu sìkǒu rén, bàba, māma, gēge hé wǒ. Nǐmen xǐhuan zuò shénme?
李刚：	我喜欢上网和玩电子游戏。	Lǐ Gāng:	Wǒ xǐhuan shàngwǎng hé wán diànzǐ yóuxì.
大卫：	我喜欢听音乐和唱歌。	Dà Wèi:	Wǒ xǐhuan tīng yīnyuè hé chànggē.
王红：	那我们明天一起玩吧。	Wáng Hóng:	Nà wǒmen míngtiān yìqǐ wán ba.
李刚, 大卫：	好啊，明天见。	Lǐ Gāng, Dà Wèi:	Hǎo a, míngtiān jiàn.

听听读读 Tīngting Dúdu | *Listening and Reading*

🔊 **Listen carefully to the dialogue. Then read the dialogue aloud without looking at the Pinyin.**

懂了吗 **Dǒng le ma?** / *Do you understand?*

Answer the following questions in Chinese.

1. Whose birthday party is tomorrow?
2. What is the date of Wang Hong's birthday?
3. How many people are there in Wang Hong's family?
4. Who are the members of Wang Hong's family?
5. What does Li Gang like to do?
6. What does Da Wei like to do?

听一听 **Tīng Yì Tīng** / *Listening*

Select the best response to each sentence you hear.

A. 我家有三口人。
   Wǒ jiā yǒu sānkǒu rén.

B. 这是我妈妈。
   Zhè shì wǒ māma.

C. 今天是七月十五号。
   Jīntiān shì Qīyuè shíwǔhào.

D. 我的宠物是狗。
   Wǒde chǒngwù shì gǒu.

E. 不是，这是我弟弟。
   Búshì, zhè shì wǒ dìdi.

F. 我的爱好是游泳。
   Wǒde àihào shì yóuyǒng.

▲ 我的宠物是狗。

中文怎么说？ **Zhōngwén zěnme shuō?** / *How would you say it in Chinese?*

Follow the guidelines below to practice Chinese with your classmates.

1. You meet a classmate when you are out walking your dog and you introduce your dog to him or her.
2. You are asked if you have any pets.
3. You ask your mother today's date.
4. You tell your new friend when your birthday is.
5. You ask your classmate for Teacher Lin's telephone number.
6. You tell your classmate that you like playing basketball.

5 休闲活动 **Xiūxián Huódòng** / *Leisure Activities*

Say what each person likes to do according to the photos below.

6 写一写 **Xiě Yì Xiě** / *Writing*

On a separate sheet of paper, write down the Chinese characters according to the Pinyin.

1. xiǎo māo
2. dà gǒu
3. bàba
4. sānkǒu rén
5. jǐ yuè jǐ hào
6. shàngwǎng
7. chīfàn
8. kànshū

▲ xiǎo māo

7 认字 **Rènzì** / *Recognize the Characters*

Match the Chinese words on the left with the appropriate English meaning on the right.

1. 看书
2. 好看
3. 口红
4. 看病
5. 后妈
6. 好吃

A. lipstick
B. stepmother
C. to see a doctor
D. to read
E. delicious
F. good-looking

▲ 好吃

文化复习 Wénhuà Fùxí
Culture Review

- **Pets in China:** Dogs are the most popular pet in China.
- **Birthday Celebration in China:** Noodles and red eggs are often prepared to wish the recipient a long life and good health.
- **Cell Phones in China:** Over half the people in China have cell phones. Chinese cell phone numbers are composed of 11 digits.
- **Sports in China:** Basketball is one of the most popular sports in China.
- **Names for Family Members in Chinese:**

▲ Dogs are popular in China.

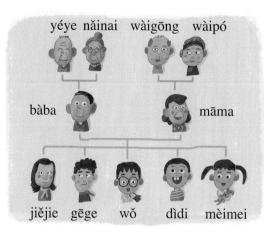

会话 Huìhuà
Dialogue

🔊 学校 Xuéxiào *School*

大卫：下课了，你要做什么？	Dà Wèi: Xiàkè le, nǐ yào zuò shénme?
王红：我觉得数学课很难，我要去图书馆看书。	Wáng Hóng: Wǒ juéde shùxué kè hěn nán, wǒ yào qù túshūguǎn kànshū.
大卫：我也觉得很难，我们可以一起看书吗？	Dà Wèi: Wǒ yě juéde hěn nán, wǒmen kěyǐ yìqǐ kànshū ma?
王红：当然可以！	Wáng Hóng: Dāngrán kěyǐ!

In the library

大卫：奇怪，我的书包不见了。	Dà Wèi: Qíguài, wǒde shūbāo bú jiàn le.
王红：书包里面有什么？	Wáng Hóng: Shūbāo lǐmiàn yǒu shénme?
大卫：纸、铅笔、橡皮和数学课本。你可以借给我一张纸和一支笔吗？	Dà Wèi: Zhǐ, qiānbǐ, xiàngpí hé shùxué kèběn. Nǐ kěyǐ jiè gěi wǒ yìzhāng zhǐ hé yìzhī bǐ ma?
王红：当然可以。	Wáng Hóng: Dāngrán kěyǐ.
大卫：谢谢你。	Dà Wèi: Xièxie nǐ.
王红：现在几点？	Wáng Hóng: Xiànzài jǐ diǎn?
大卫：现在十点二十分。	Dà Wèi: Xiànzài shídiǎn èrshífēn.

1 听听读读 Tīngting Dúdu / Listening and Reading

Listen carefully to the dialogue. Then read the dialogue aloud without looking at the Pinyin.

2 懂了吗 Dǒng le ma? / Do you understand?

Answer the following questions in Chinese.

1. Who is going to the library?
2. What subject is Da Wei going to study?
3. Are Da Wei and Wang Hong going to study together?
4. What is Da Wei looking for?
5. What school supplies does Da Wei borrow?
6. How did Da Wei respond to the question about the time?

3 听一听 Tīng Yì Tīng / Listening

Select the best response to each sentence you hear.

A. 我想去公园。
Wǒ xiǎng qù gōngyuán.

B. 我今天上体育课。
Wǒ jīntiān shàng tǐyù kè.

C. 书在书包里面。
Shū zài shūbāo lǐmiàn.

D. 今天是星期一。
Jīntiān shì Xīngqīyī.

E. 现在八点十分。
Xiànzài bādiǎn shífēn.

F. 请给我纸和笔。
Qǐng gěi wǒ zhǐ hé bǐ.

▲ 我想去公园。

4 中文怎么说? Zhōngwén zěnme shuō? / *How would you say it in Chinese?*

Follow the guidelines below to practice Chinese with your classmates.

1. Ask where the dog is.
2. Ask if the dog is under the table.
3. Ask what time it is.
4. Ask if your classmate needs to borrow a pen.
5. Ask what classes your classmate has today.
6. Ask where your classmate is going for the weekend.

5 文具和运动 Wénjù hé Yùndòng / *School Supplies and Sports*

Identify the school supplies and sports shown in the photos below.

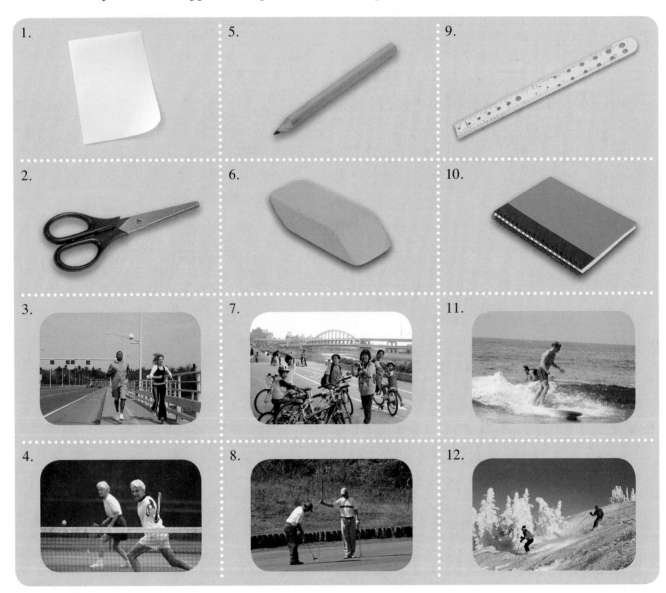

1.
2.
3.
4.
5.
6.
7.
8.
9.
10.
11.
12.

On a separate sheet of paper, write down the Chinese characters according to the Pinyin.

1. diànnǎo
2. zhuōzi
3. shūbāo
4. qiānbǐ
5. báizhǐ
6. Xīngqītiān
7. kuàilè
8. zhōumò

▲ diànnǎo

7 认字 **Rènzì** / *Recognize the Characters*

Match the Chinese words on the left with the appropriate English meaning on the right.

1. 上午   A. to get off work
2. 上班   B. morning
3. 下班   C. furniture
4. 天气   D. heaven
5. 天堂   E. weather
6. 家具   F. to go to work

文化复习 Wénhuà Fùxí

Culture Review

- **Cram Schools:** As competition for admittance into top Chinese universities intensifies, it is more and more common for students to attend cram schools.

- **The Four Treasures of the Study:** Brush, ink, paper and inkstone.

- **At School:** In most schools, a period is 45 minutes long, followed by a 15 minutes break. Chinese students do not switch classroom between classes.

- **Popular Pastimes for Teens in China:** Chinese teens engage in various pastimes such as karaoke and go to night market.

- **Morning in the Park:** Many people like to get in groups to do tai-chi, dance, medication or even bird-walking in the morning in the park. Newcomers are welcome to join in for free.

▲ People do tai-chi in the park.

Review Unit 4

会话 Huìhuà
Dialogue

🔊 餐厅里 Cāntīng Lǐ *In the Restaurant*

服务员： 您好，您要点什么？	Fúwùyuán: Nín hǎo, nín yào diǎn shénme?
李刚： 请给我一个汉堡。	Lǐ Gāng: Qǐng gěi wǒ yíge hànbǎo.
服务员： 好，请问您喝什么？	Fúwùyuán: Hǎo, qǐng wèn nín hē shénme?
李刚： 你们有没有果汁？	Lǐ Gāng: Nǐmen yǒu méiyǒu guǒzhī?
服务员： 有，大杯还是小杯？	Fúwùyuán: Yǒu, dàbēi háishì xiǎobēi?
李刚： 大杯，一共多少钱？	Lǐ Gāng: Dàbēi, yígòng duōshǎo qián?
服务员： 汉堡四块五毛钱，大杯果汁三块五毛钱，一共八块钱。	Fúwùyuán: Hànbǎo sìkuài wǔmáo qián, dàbēi guǒzhī sānkuài wǔmáo qián, yígòng bākuài qián.
李刚： 给你十块钱，谢谢。	Lǐ Gāng: Gěi nǐ shíkuài qián, xièxie.
服务员： 不客气，找您两块。	Fúwùyuán: Bú kèqi, zhǎo nín liǎngkuài.

1 听听读读 Tīngting Dúdu / *Listening and Reading*

🔊 **Listen carefully to the dialogue. Then read the dialogue aloud without looking at the Pinyin.**

2 懂了吗 Dǒng le ma? / *Do you understand?*

Answer the following questions in Chinese.

1. What does Li Gang order to eat?
2. What does Li Gang order to drink?
3. What size drink would Li Gang like?
4. How much does a hamburger cost?
5. How much does a cup of juice cost?
6. How much does Li Gang give to the waiter?

3 听一听 Tīng Yì Tīng / *Listening*

Select the best response to each sentence you hear.

A. 炸鸡两块钱。
   Zhájī liǎngkuài qián.

B. 我要大杯。
   Wǒ yào dà bēi.

C. 鸡汤面不油，很清淡。
   Jītāng miàn bùyóu, hěn qīngdàn.

D. 我要咖啡。
   Wǒ yào kāfēi.

E. 牛肉面很好吃。
   Niúròu miàn hěn hǎochī.

F. 我们有薯条，热狗和三明治。
   Wǒmen yǒu shǔtiáo, règǒu hé sānmíngzhì.

▲ 牛肉面很好吃。

4 中文怎么说? Zhōngwén zěnme shuō? / *How would you say it in Chinese?*

Follow the guidelines below to practice Chinese with your classmates.

1. Ask what your partner would like to drink.
2. Say that you would like to have a cup of tea.
3. Ask what size drink your partner would like.
4. Say that you want a small drink.
5. Ask what your partner had for breakfast.
6. Ask your partner how much each breakfast item costs.

5 食物 **Shíwù** / *Foods*

Identify the foods shown in the photos below.

1.

5.

9.

2.

6.

10.

3.

7.

11.

4.

8.

12.

6 写一写 **Xiě Yì Xiě** / *Writing*

On a separate sheet of paper, write down the Chinese characters according to the Pinyin.

1. sānmíngzhì
2. chá
3. píngguǒ
4. qìshuǐ
5. niúnǎi
6. zhájī
7. ròu
8. mǐfàn

▲ niúnǎi

Match the Chinese words on the left with the appropriate English meaning on the right.

1. 钱包
2. 木材
3. 果酱
4. 菜油
5. 省钱
6. 菜园

A. vegetable oil

B. vegetable garden

C. wallet

D. jam; jelly

E. lumber

F. save money

▲ 钱包

文化复习 Wénhuà Fùxí
Culture Review

- **International Food and Drink Franchises in China:** You can find most popular international restaurant chains in China such as McDonald's, KFC, Starbucks and Subway.

- **Chinese Tea Culture:** Teas are classified as black tea, green tea, white tea, yellow tea and dark tea. When drinking tea, people like to eat certain snacks.

- **Tea House:** The development of a dim sum culture gave birth to a branch of tea house.

- **Lunchtime for Chinese Students:** The schools provide caterers to cook for all the students. At lunchtime, students line up for lunch with their own utensils. The food is diverse and prepared according to nutrition guidelines.

- **The Differences between Chinese and Western Food:** Chinese food is almost never served raw or rare. All ingredients must be fully cooked before they can be Consumed. Chinese eat more vegetables than meat in fact, they eat approximately 600 kinds of vegetables. Chinese cooks can make almost any kind of ingredient into a tasty dish.

Review Unit 5

会话 Huìhuà
Dialogue

◀) 天气 Tiānqì *Weather*

李刚：	今天天气怎么样？	Lǐ Gāng:	Jīntiān tiānqì zěnmeyàng?
大卫：	晴天，气温三十七度。	Dà Wèi:	Qíngtiān, qìwēn sānshíqīdù.
李刚：	真讨厌，太热了。	Lǐ Gāng:	Zhēn tǎoyàn, tài rè le.
大卫：	我们一起去冲浪吧。	Dà Wèi:	Wǒmen yìqǐ qù chōnglàng ba.
李刚：	不行，一点儿风都没有。	Lǐ Gāng:	Bùxíng, yìdiǎnr fēng dōu méiyǒu.
大卫：	那我们去游泳吧？	Dà Wèi:	Nà wǒmen qù yóuyǒng ba?
李刚：	好啊，我们几点到游泳馆？	Lǐ Gāng:	Hǎo a, wǒmen jǐdiǎn dào yóuyǒngguǎn?
大卫：	下午两点怎么样？	Dà Wèi:	Xiàwǔ liǎngdiǎn zěnmeyàng?
李刚：	没问题，下午两点在游泳馆见。	Lǐ Gāng:	Méiwèntí, xiàwǔ liǎngdiǎn zài yóuyǒngguǎn jiàn.

听听读读 Tīngting Dúdu / *Listening and Reading*

◀) **Listen carefully to the dialogue. Then read the dialogue aloud without looking at the Pinyin.**

2 懂了吗 **Dǒng le ma?** / *Do you understand?*

Answer the following questions in Chinese.

1. What is the weather like today?
2. What is the temperature today?
3. Why can't they go surfing?
4. What are they going to do instead?
5. What time will they meet?

3 听一听 **Tīng Yì Tīng** / *Listening*

🔊 **Select the best response to each sentence you hear.**

A. 喝点儿冰水吧。
   Hē diǎnr bīngshuǐ ba.

B. 我在包粽子。
   Wǒ zài bāo zòngzi.

C. 现在五度。
   Xiànzài wǔdù.

D. 明天会下雪。
   Míngtiān huì xiàxuě.

E. 得看农历。
   Děi kàn nónglì.

F. 好吧。
   Hǎo ba.

▲ 粽子

4 中文怎么说? **Zhōngwén zěnme shuō?** / *How would you say it in Chinese?*

👥 **Follow the guidelines below to practice Chinese with your classmates.**

1. Ask about today's weather.
2. Ask for the current temperature.
3. Ask your partner if it will rain next week.
4. Ask your partner about next Sunday's forecast.
5. Tell your partner your favorite weather is a sunny day.
6. Tell your partner you like dragon boats.

5 天气 Tiānqì / Weather

Say what the weather is like in each photo below.

1.

2.

3.

4.

5.

6.

6 四季 Sìjì / Four Seasons

Match each season with the correct illustration below.

1. 夏天 xiàtiān   2. 冬天 dōngtiān   3. 春天 chūntiān   4. 秋天 qiūtiān

A.    B.    C.    D.

7 写一写 Xiě Yì Xiě / Writing

On a separate sheet of paper, write down the Chinese characters according to the Pinyin.

1. xiàxuě
2. míngtiān
3. lěng
4. rè
5. kě
6. è
7. xīnnián
8. jiérì

▲ è

Match the Chinese words on the left with the appropriate English meaning on the right.

1. 雨衣
2. 冰鞋
3. 冰箱
4. 火腿
5. 火车
6. 心情

A. refrigerator
B. raincoat
C. train
D. ham
E. ice skates
F. mood

▲ 火车

文化复习 Wénhuà Fùxí

Culture Review

- **The Metric System in China:** China converted to the metric system from the traditional system in 1957. Most Chinese now use the metric system.

- **Six important Sports in China:** The six most popular sports played in China: basketball, volleyball, soccer, badminton, table tennis and tennis.

- **Chinese New Year:** Also known as the Spring Festival, the New Year is a national holiday in China celebrated on the first day of the first month of the lunar calendar. The lunar new year is also celebrated in many other Asian countries, including Singapore, Korea, Vietnam, and Thailand.

- **The Lunar Calendar:** China was originally an agricultural country, so the lunar calendar was developed in ancient times as a way to track the seasons of the year and to determine the best dates for planting and harvesting crops.

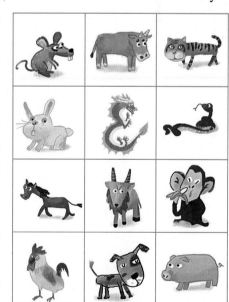

- **Dragon Boat Festival:** The annual Dragon Boat Festival falls on the fifth day of the fifth lunar month. People eat rice dumplings (*zòngzi*) and row dragon boats.

- **The Chinese 12-Animal Zodiac:** rat, ox, tiger, rabbit, dragon, snake, horse, goat, monkey, rooster, dog and pig.

Review Unit 6

会话 Huìhuà
Dialogue

🔊 购物 Gòuwù *Shopping*

王红： 夏天要来了，我想去买衣服。	Wáng Hóng: Xiàtiān yào lái le, wǒ xiǎng qù mǎi yīfu.
李刚： 你想买什么衣服？	Lǐ Gāng: Nǐ xiǎng mǎi shénme yīfu?
王红： 我想买一件T恤和一条裤子。	Wáng Hóng: Wǒ xiǎng mǎi yíjiàn tìxù hé yìtiáo kùzi.

In the shop

李刚： 这件白色的T恤漂亮！	Lǐ Gāng: Zhèijiàn báisè de tìxù piàoliàng!
王红： 好是好，可是四百块太贵了。	Wáng Hóng: Hǎo shì hǎo, kěshì sìbǎikuài tài guì le.
李刚： 现在打六折，打完折以后是两百四十块。	Lǐ Gāng: Xiànzài dǎ liùzhé, dǎ wán zhé yǐhòu shì liǎngbǎi sìshíkuài.
王红： 好吧，我要了。这条牛仔裤时髦吗？	Wáng Hóng: Hǎo ba, wǒ yào le. Zhèitiáo niúzǎikù shímáo ma?
李刚： 不好看，有点儿老。	Lǐ Gāng: Bù hǎokàn, yǒudiǎnr lǎo.

1 听听读读 Tīngtīng Dúdu / *Listening and Reading*

Listen carefully to the dialogue. Then read the dialogue aloud without looking at the Pinyin.

2 懂了吗 Dǒng le ma? / *Do you understand?*

Answer the following questions in Chinese.

1. What season is next?
2. What clothing is Wang Hong going to buy?
3. What color is the shirt that Li Gang likes?
4. What is the original price of the T-shirt?
5. What is the discount?
6. Why does Li Gang not like the jeans?

3 听一听 Tīng Yì Tīng / *Listening*

Select the best response to each sentence you hear.

A. 我穿9号的鞋。
   Wǒ chuān jiǔhào de xié.

B. 我要去逛街。
   Wǒ yào qù guàngjiē.

C. 现在打八折。
   Xiànzài dǎ bāzhé.

D. 我要买裙子。
   Wǒ yào mǎi qúnzi.

E. 我喜欢蓝色。
   Wǒ xǐhuan lánsè.

F. 很好看。
   Hěn hǎokàn.

▲ 我要去逛街。

4 中文怎么说? Zhōngwén zěnme shuō? How would you say it in Chinese?

Follow the guidelines below to practice Chinese with your classmates.

1. Ask what color your partner likes.
2. Say that you like the color red.
3. Ask what clothing your partner wants to buy.
4. Tell your partner that you think what he/she is wearing today suits him/her.
5. Ask what discount you can get for this clothing.
6. Say this clothing is too expensive.

5 颜色 Yánsè Colors

Name the colors you see in the picture below.

1.
2.
3.
4.
5.
6.
7.
8.
9.
10.
11.
12.

6 写一写 Xiě Yì Xiě / Writing

On a separate sheet of paper, write down the Chinese characters according to the Pinyin.

1. yīfu
2. dàyī
3. hóngsè
4. yìqiān
5. lǎorén
6. xié

▲ xié

7 认字 Rènzì / Recognize the Characters

Match the Chinese words on the left with the appropriate English meaning on the right.

1. 衣架   A. elementary school
2. 白宫   B. continent
3. 小学   C. careful
4. 睡衣   D. clothes hanger
5. 大陆   E. the White House
6. 小心   F. pajamas

▲ The White House

文化复习 Wénhuà Fùxí

Culture Review

- **Five Elements:** Traditionally, the Chinese thought that all things in nature were made up of five elements, each with its own representative color. Metal (white), wood (green), water (black), fire (red) and earth (yellow).

- **Chinese Traditional Dress:** The traditional dress of the Han Chinese is called Hanfu. The main garment is a loose-fitting gown with large sleeves, wrapped around the body and secured with a belt or a sash. For women, the traditional Manchu cheongsam, or qipao, is a popular dress.

- **Chinese and American Sizes:** Clothing sizes in China are measured in centimeters, with a 2 cm margin for error. For example, a pair of men's pants with the label 180/100 means that it is suitable for men from 178 cm to 182 cm tall with a waistline between 98 cm to 102 cm.

- **The Story of Silk:** Silk textiles are woven from the protein fibers extracted from the cocoons of silkworm larvae. Silk is not only warm, but also soft to the touch and gives off a pearlescent shine.

▲ A store of silk cloth

Communication

Unit 1

祝你健康 Zhù Nǐ Jiànkāng

In this unit you will be able to:

- ask about and say what you did in the past
- ask about and say how long events took
- inquire and explain how things were done under certain conditions
- express personal feelings about an outcome compared to your expectations
- describe symptoms when seeing a doctor

Lesson A

词汇 Cíhuì
Vocabulary

🔊 身体 Shēntǐ *The Body*

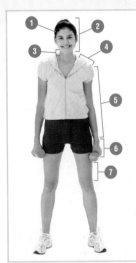

1. 头发 (頭髮) tóufa *n. hair*
2. 头 (頭) tóu *n. head*
3. 脖子 bózi *n. neck*
4. 肩膀 jiānbǎng *n. shoulder*
5. 胳膊 gēbo *n. arm*
6. 手 shǒu *n. hand*
7. 大腿 dàtuǐ *n. thigh*

背
bèi
n. back

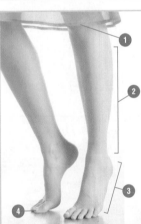

1. 膝盖 (膝蓋) xīgài *n. knee*
2. 小腿 xiǎotuǐ *n. calf*
3. 脚 (腳) jiǎo *n. foot*
4. 脚指 (腳指) jiǎozhǐ *n. toe*

手指
shǒuzhǐ
n. finger

高
gāo
adj. high

低
dī
adj. low

健身房 jiànshēnfáng *n. gym*

他们在健身房运动。
(他們在健身房運動。)
Tāmen zài jiànshēnfáng yùndòng.
They are exercising at the gym.

Time Expressions

You learned how to tell time in Level 1, Unit 3, Lesson B. However, telling the time and counting time are somewhat different.

秒钟 (秒鐘)	分钟 (分鐘)	刻钟 (刻鐘)	小时 (小時) 钟头 (鐘頭)
miǎozhōng	fēnzhōng	kèzhōng	xiǎoshí / zhōngtóu
m.w. second	m.w. minute	m.w. quarter hour	n. hour

我的膝盖好疼，我几乎不能走路。
（我的膝蓋好疼，我幾乎不能走路。）
Wǒde xīgài hǎo téng, wǒ jīhū bùnéng zǒulù.
My knee hurts. I can hardly walk.

我今天不舒服。
Wǒ jīntiān bù shūfu. *I don't feel well today.*

⋯⋯⋯⋯⋯⋯⋯⋯⋯⋯⋯⋯⋯⋯⋯⋯⋯⋯⋯⋯⋯⋯⋯⋯⋯⋯

A: 你周末念书了吗？（你週末念書了嗎？）
Nǐ zhōumò niànshū le ma? *Did you study over the weekend?*

B: 嗯，我念了中文和数学。（嗯，我念了中文和數學。）
Ēn, wǒ niànle Zhōngwén hé shùxué. *Yes, I studied Chinese and math.*

⋯⋯⋯⋯⋯⋯⋯⋯⋯⋯⋯⋯⋯⋯⋯⋯⋯⋯⋯⋯⋯⋯⋯⋯⋯⋯

A: 走路去学校要一个小时。（走路去學校要一個小時。）
Zǒulù qù xuéxiào yào yíge xiǎoshí. *It takes an hour to walk to school.*

B: 怎么那么远！（怎麼那麼遠！）
Zěnme nàme yuǎn! *That's so far!*

⋯⋯⋯⋯⋯⋯⋯⋯⋯⋯⋯⋯⋯⋯⋯⋯⋯⋯⋯⋯⋯⋯⋯⋯⋯⋯

A: 你怎么这么慢？（你怎麼這麼慢？）
Nǐ zěnme zhème màn? *Why are you so slow?*

我游了半个小时。
Wǒ yóule bànge xiǎoshí.
I swam for half an hour.

B: 因为我脚痛。（因為我腳痛。）
Yīnwèi wǒ jiǎo tòng. *Because my feet hurt.*

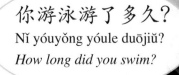

你游泳游了多久？
Nǐ yóuyǒng yóule duōjiǔ?
How long did you swim?

Adjectives

酸	suān	*sore*
疼	téng	*aching; achy*
全	quán	*whole; all over*
舒服	shūfu	*comfortable*
久	jiǔ	*long*

Adverbs

那么 (那麼)	nàme	*that, so*
这么 (這麼)	zhème	*this, so*
总是 (總是)	zǒngshì	*always*
好	hǎo	*so (used before certain adjectives to indicate high degree)*
就	jiù	*just; only*
几乎 (幾乎)	jīhū	*almost*

Auxiliary Verb

能	néng	*can; to be able to; to have the opportunity to*

Measure Word

座	zuò	*(used for mountains or buildings)*

Nouns

路	lù	*road; path; way*
身	shēn	*body*

Particle

了	le	*(used after a verb to indicate completion of action)*

Pronouns

咱们 (咱們)	zánmen	*we; us*
每	měi	*every; each*

Question Words

多久	duōjiǔ	*how long*
怎么 (怎麼)	zěnme	*why; how*

Verbs

戴	dài	to wear; to put on
痛	tòng	to ache
爬	pá	to crawl; to climb
练习 (練習)	liànxí	to practice
确定 (確定)	quèdìng	to determine; to confirm
开始 (開始)	kāishǐ	to begin

Verb-Object

| 走路 | zǒulù | to walk |

---

1 身体部位 **Shēntǐ Bùwèi** / *Body Parts*

 You will hear the names of six body parts. Write the letters A through F according to what you hear.

---

2 穿/戴在哪里? **Chuān / Dài zài nǎlǐ?** / *Where are they worn?*

Look at the photos and determine where each item should be worn.

1.

2.

3.

4.

5.

6.

A. 脚 jiǎo

B. 身体 shēntǐ

C. 头 tóu

D. 手 shǒu

E. 腿 tuǐ

F. 脖子 bózi

3 个人问题 **Gèrén Wèntí** / *Personal Questions*

Answer the following questions in Chinese based on your own experiences and opinions.

1. 你周末做了什么？ Nǐ zhōumò zuòle shénme?

2. 你喜欢爬山吗？ Nǐ xǐhuan páshān ma?

3. 你昨天念书了吗？念了多久？ Nǐ zuótiān niànshū le ma? Niànle duōjiǔ?

4. 你喜欢做什么运动？ Nǐ xǐhuan zuò shénme yùndòng?

5. 运动以后，你总是全身疼吗？ Yùndòng yǐhòu, nǐ zǒngshì quánshēn téng ma?

6. 你去健身房吗？ Nǐ qù jiànshēnfáng ma?

句型介绍 Jùxíng Jièshào
Language Patterns

Completed Action 了 *le*

The particle 了 *le* has many grammatical functions. In this lesson, it indicates that an action has been completed. The completed action 了 *le* is a verb suffix. Therefore, it immediately follows the verb, and verbs can only be action words, such as 吃 *chī*, 喝 *hē*, 听 *tīng*, 玩 *wán*, etc.

Subject + Verb + 了 *le*

他来了。 Tā láile.
林老师到了。 Lín lǎoshī dàole.

Subject + Verb-Object + 了 *le*

他回家了。 Tā huíjiā le.
我们下课了。 Wǒmen xiàkè le.

For the verb plus object pattern, 了 *le* can also be inserted between the two (after the verb).

Subject + Verb + 了 *le* + Object

我吃了饭。 Wǒ chīle fàn.
你买了衣服。 Nǐ mǎile yīfu.

▲ 他回家了。

The Question Word 多久 *duōjiǔ*

The question word 多久 *duōjiǔ* is used to ask "how long" or "how much time."
Remember, in Chinese, the sentence order remains the same even when it is a question.

Q: Subject + Verb + 多久 *duōjiǔ*

A: Subject + Verb + Time Spent

A: 他要去中国多久？ Tā yào qù Zhōngguó duōjiǔ?

B: 他要去半个月。 Tā yào qù bàngè yuè.

A: 你通常每天看书看多久？ Nǐ tōngcháng měitiān kànshū kàn duōjiǔ?

B: 我通常每天看一个小时。 Wǒ tōngcháng měitiān kàn yíge xiǎoshí.

▲ 去中国多久？

Time Words and Time Spent

You learned in Level I Unit 3 Lesson C that time words are movable adverbs which can be placed either before or after the subject, but always in front of the verb. In this case, the time words refer to the time when something happened.

Subject + Time Word + Verb + Object

他昨天吃了中国饭。 Tā zuótian chīle Zhōngguó fàn.

我下个周末要去海边玩。
Wǒ xiàge zhōumò yào qù hǎibiān wán.

Time Word + Subject + Verb + Object

昨天他吃了中国饭。 Zuótian tā chīle Zhōngguó fàn.

下个周末我要去海边玩。
Xiàge zhōumò wǒ yào qù hǎibiān wán.

Time Spent refers to the amount of time spent on one action and is placed AFTER the verb.

Subject + Verb + 了 *le* + Time Spent

A: 他找了多久？ Tā zhǎole duōjiǔ?

B: 他找了十五分钟。 Tā zhǎole shíwǔ fēnzhōng.

▲ 我下个周末要去海边玩。

In the "Verb-Object" structure, the Verb-Object compound needs to remain and the verb needs to repeat before the time spent.

Subject + Verb-Object + Verb + 了 *le* + Time Spent

我看书看了两个小时。 Wǒ kànshū kànle liǎngge xiǎoshí.

他游泳游了半个钟头。 Tā yóuyǒng yóule bàngè zhōngtóu.

The Pattern 怎么这么 *zěnme zhème* / 怎么那么 *zěnme nàme*

The question word 怎么 *zěnme* means "why" or "how." Followed by an adjective, 怎么这么 *zěnme zhème* and 怎么那么 *zěnme nàme* function as either a question or an exclamation, depending on the speaker's tone.

怎么 *zěnme* + 这么 *zhème* / 那么 *nàme* + **Adjective**

这只小狗怎么这么可爱！ Zhèizhī xiǎo gǒu zěnme zhème kě'ài!

A: 你怎么这么累？ Nǐ zěnme zhème lèi?

B: 我看书看了三个小时。 Wǒ kànshū kànle sānge xiǎoshí.

Comparison

The difference between using 这么 *zhème* and 那么 *nàme* depends on the subjective distance, either mentally or physically, felt by the speaker between the object or the event and himself / herself.

俄文怎么这么难！ Éwén zěnme zhème nán!
(*This may be uttered by a student who is learning the Russian language.*)

俄文怎么那么难！ Éwén zěnme nàme nán!
(*This may be uttered by a student who is not taking Russian, but he / she has heard from friends how difficult the Russian language is.*)

The Auxiliary Verb 能 *néng*

The auxiliary verb 能 *néng* means "can," "to be able to do something," or "to have the opportunity to do something."

Subject + 能 *néng* + **Verb Phrase**

我能说中文。 Wǒ néng shuō Zhōngwén.

他能来我的生日晚会。 Tā néng lái wǒde shēngrì wǎnhuì.

我晚上不能喝咖啡。 Wǒ wǎnshang bùnéng hē kāfēi.

▲ 我能说中文。

The Pattern 全...都...quán...dōu...

This pattern expresses wholeness, or entirely, without exception. Note that in Chinese, to refer to the idea of "wholeness," the adverb 都 dōu is always needed after the subject.

> (全 quán) + **Noun** + 都 dōu + **Verb**

我们全家都喜欢跳舞。　Wǒmen quán jiā dōu xǐhuan tiàowǔ.

那个学校，全校都是男生。　Nèige xuéxiào, quánxiào dōu shì nánshēng.

The same meaning can be expressed in some situations by 每 měi.

> 每 měi + **Measure Word** + **Noun** + 都 dōu + **Verb Phrase**

每个学生都喜欢音乐。　Měige xuésheng dōu xǐhuan yīnyuè.

每个学生都不喜欢考试。　Měige xuésheng dōu bù xǐhuan kǎoshì.

会话 Huìhuà
Dialogue

🔊 全身酸痛 Quán Shēn Suān Tòng *Aching All Over*

During their lunch break, Li Yunying and Wu Sen discuss Li Yunying's weekend and the importance of being physically active.

李云英：	我的腿好酸。
吴森：	你周末做了什么？
李云英：	我跟我爸妈去爬山了。
吴森：	你们爬了多久？
李云英：	我们爬了四个小时。
吴森：	怎么那么久？
李云英：	因为那座山很高，路也不好走。今天早上我几乎不能走路。

Lǐ Yúnyīng:	Wǒde tuǐ hǎo suān.
Wú Sēn:	Nǐ zhōumò zuòle shénme?
Lǐ Yúnyīng:	Wǒ gēn wǒ bà-mā qù páshān le.
Wú Sēn:	Nǐmen pále duōjiǔ?
Lǐ Yúnyīng:	Wǒmen pále sìge xiǎoshí.
Wú Sēn:	Zěnme nàme jiǔ?
Lǐ Yúnyīng:	Yīnwèi nàzuò shān hěn gāo, lù yě bùhǎo zǒu. Jīntiān zǎoshang wǒ jīhū bùnéng zǒulù.

吴森：那下午你还来练习篮球吗？	Wú Sēn: Nà xiàwǔ nǐ hái lái liànxí lánqiú ma?
李云英：我不确定。我现在腿酸、脚痛、膝盖疼，全身都不舒服。	Lǐ Yúnyīng: Wǒ bú quèdìng. Wǒ xiànzài tuǐ suān, jiǎo tòng, xīgài téng, quánshēn dōu bù shūfu.
吴森：你啊，总是不运动，平常应该锻炼锻炼。	Wú Sēn: Nǐ a, zǒngshì bú yùndòng, píngcháng yīnggāi duànliàn duànlian.
李云英：我知道，我会开始去健身房。	Lǐ Yúnyīng: Wǒ zhīdào, wǒ huì kāishǐ qù jiànshēnfáng.
吴森：知道就好！快要上课了，咱们走吧！	Wú Sēn: Zhīdào jiù hǎo! Kuài yào shàngkè le, zánmen zǒu ba!

4 她做了什么？ **Tā zuòle shénme?** / *What did she do?*

Identify what Li Yunying did last weekend based on the previous dialogue.

5 懂了吗？ **Dǒngle ma?** / *Do you understand?*

Answer the following questions in Chinese.

1. 李云英怎么了？ Lǐ Yúnyīng zěnme le?

2. 李云英周末做了什么？ Lǐ Yúnyīng zhōumò zuòle shénme?

3. 他们爬山爬了多久？ Tāmen páshān pále duōjiǔ?

4. 为什么他们爬了那么久？ Wèishénme tāmen pále nàme jiǔ?

5. 李云英今天能走路吗？ Lǐ Yúnyīng jīntiān néng zǒulù ma?

6. 李云英下午要去练习篮球吗？ Lǐ Yúnyīng xiàwǔ yào qù liànxí lánqiú ma?

7. 李云英现在觉得怎么样？ Lǐ Yúnyīng xiànzài juéde zěnmeyàng?

8. 李云英平常运动吗？ Lǐ Yúnyīng píngcháng yùndòng ma?

Based on the dialogue, write down the parts of the body in Chinese where Li Yunying is hurting or aching.

文化橱窗 Wénhuà Chúchuāng

Culture Window

Acupuncture and Moxibustion (針灸 *zhēnjiǔ*)

The techniques of acupuncture and moxibustion have been practiced in Chinese medicine since ancient times. Acupuncture involves inserting thin needles (针 *zhēn*) into various points of the body and manipulating the needles to relieve pain. Moxibustion (灸 *jiǔ*) is therapy using mugwort herb (moxa). The burning herb is pressed onto certain points of the body in order to stimulate healing by heat. For thousands of years, people have used metal needles or moxa on various points of a person's body to heal and control pain. These unique methods of healing have led to theories regarding the flow of energy through the human body, and are now practiced all around the world.

▲ *A needle used in acupuncture treatment.*

It is said that acupuncture originated in the days of the first emperors of China and was invented by legendary emperor Fu Xi (伏羲 *Fú Xī*). While this cannot be proven, written records show that acupuncture was a common practice by the second century BCE. Acupuncture has its origins in massage. In ancient times, when people felt discomfort, they would massage, or use stones to press on, parts of the body where they hurt the most. The people then discovered that this led to the lessening or disappearance of symptoms, and thus, the oldest tool used in acupuncture—the needle stone (砭石 *biān shí*)—was introduced. Throughout the ages, the tools used evolved and

▲ *Moxibustion therapy with burning herbs inside*

the needle stone was replaced by copper needles, iron needles, gold needles, silver needles, and today's stainless steel needles.

▲ *Fu Xi*

Acupuncture and moxibustion are unique because they are used to heal internal discomfort from outside the human body without the aid of oral medication—much like physical therapy. A needle or heat is used to stimulate a body part and the nerves nearby to achieve the desired result. After many years of clinical research, acupuncture is now used in many fields of medicine such as dermatology, psychology, immunology, ophthalmology, anti-aging and dietetics.

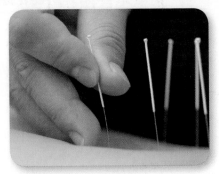

▲ *Acupuncture treatment.*

7 文化动动脑 Wénhuà Dòngdòngnǎo / *Cultural Check-up*

Decide whether each statement is true or false. Correct the false statements.

1. Mugwort herb is used in acupuncture.
2. Acupuncture is said to have been invented by Emperor Fu Xi.
3. The first acupuncture needles were made of iron.
4. The stone needle has been used in acupuncture from ancient times until today.
5. Moxibustion requires people to take oral medication.
6. Acupuncture is now used widely in many fields of medicine.

语言练习 Yǔyán Liànxí
Language Practice

8 做了什么事? Zuòle shénme shì? / *Did these things happen?*

Answer the following questions positively by using the particle 了 *le*.

1. 他来了吗? Tā láile ma?
2. 你吃饭了吗? Nǐ chīfàn le ma?
3. 我们下课了吗? Wǒmen xiàkè le ma?
4. 爸爸回家了吗? Bàba huíjiā le ma?
5. 弟弟去上学了吗? Dìdi qù shàngxué le ma?
6. 你今天练球了吗? Nǐ jīntiān liànqiú le ma?
7. 美美买了大衣吗? Měiměi mǎile dàyī ma?
8. 他们去打球了吗? Tāmen qù dǎqiú le ma?

9 花了多少时间？ Huāle duōshǎo shíjiān? / *How much time was spent?*

With a classmate, take turns asking and answering questions based on the information provided.

Lìzi: 他去英国 / 一个星期 tā qù Yīngguó / yíge xīngqī

A: 他去英国去了多久？ Tā qù Yīngguó qùle duōjiǔ?

B: 他(去英国)去了一个星期。 Tā (qù Yīngguó) qùle yíge xīngqī.

1. 哥哥学音乐 / 两年 gēge xué yīnyuè / liǎngnián
2. 弟弟修日文 / 一个学期 dìdi xiū Rìwén / yíge xuéqī
3. 小狗玩球 / 十分钟 xiǎogǒu wán qiú / shífēnzhōng
4. 你打电子游戏 / 一个小时 nǐ dǎ diànzǐ yóuxì / yíge xiǎoshí
5. 爷爷睡觉 / 一个半小时 yéye shuìjiào / yíge bàn xiǎoshí
6. 姐姐去购物中心 / 一天 jiějie qù gòuwù zhōngxīn / yìtiān
7. 我跟同学打棒球 / 三个钟头 wǒ gēn tóngxué dǎ bàngqiú / sānge zhōngtóu
8. 林先生来美国 / 四个月 Lín xiānsheng lái Měiguó / sìge yuè

10 发出感叹 Fāchū Gǎntàn / *Making an Exclamation*

Look at the following pictures and create an appropriate exclamation for each picture using the pattern 怎么这么 *zěnme zhème* / 怎么那么 *zěnme nàme* and the words provided.

Lìzi: 这只猫 / 可爱 zhèizhī māo / kě'ài

这只猫怎么这么可爱！ Zhèizhī māo zěnme zhème kě'ài!

1.	2.	3.	4.	5.

胖 pàng	大 dà	漂亮 piàoliang	有意思 yǒu yìsi	好玩儿 hǎowánr

11 提出问题 Tíchū Wèntí / Posing a Question

With a classmate, use the words provided and take turns asking questions with the patterns 怎么这么 zěnme zhème / 怎么那么 zěnme nàme and answering questions with 因为 yīnwèi….

Lìzi: 这杯咖啡苦 / 没有加糖(to add sugar) zhèibēi kāfēi kǔ / méiyǒu jiā táng

A: 这杯咖啡怎么这么苦? Zhèibēi kāfēi zěnme zhème kǔ?

B: 因为没有加糖。 Yīnwèi méiyǒu jiā táng.

1. 你累 / 生病了 nǐ lèi / shēngbìng le
2. 你高兴 / 朋友要来我家玩 nǐ gāoxìng / péngyou yào lái wǒ jiā wán
3. 那个汤咸 / 加了太多盐(salt) nèige tāng xián / jiāle tài duō yán
4. 这件大衣贵 / 没有折扣 zhèijiàn dàyī guì / méiyǒu zhékòu
5. 那套西装便宜 / 打了三折 nèitào xīzhuāng piányi / dǎle sānzhé
6. 这条牛仔裤紧 / 太小了 zhèitiáo niúzǎikù jǐn / tài xiǎole

12 一致性 Yízhìxìng / Unity

Use the pattern 全 / 每… 都… quán / měi…dōu… to describe the following pictures.

Lìzi: 全家人都很高。 Quán jiā rén dōu hěn gāo.

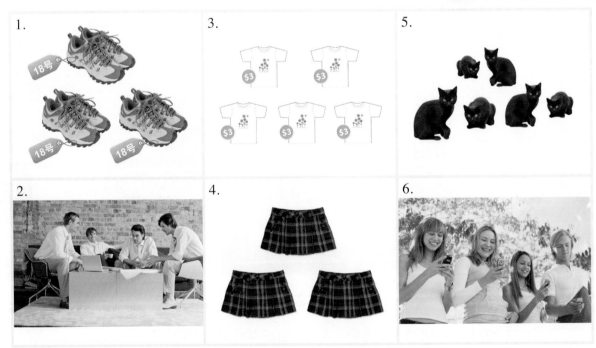

小小调查 Xiǎoxiǎo Diàochá / *A Survey*

Find out what your classmates did last Sunday. Draw a grid like the one shown below. In the grid, write the names of five weekend activities in Chinese. Ask five of your classmates if they participated in any of the activities you listed, and then share the results of your survey with the class.

Lìzi:

A: 你上个星期天做了什么？ Nǐ shàngge Xīngqītiān zuòle shénme?

B: 我看了电影。 Wǒ kànle diànyǐng.

C: 我在家看了书，做了运动。 Wǒ zài jiā kànle shū, zuòle yùndòng.

D: 我去逛了街，打了电子游戏。 Wǒ qù guàngle jiē, dǎle diànzǐ yóuxì.

E: 我也去看了电影。 Wǒ yě qù kànle diànyǐng.

Activity Student	看书 kànshū	做运动 zuò yùndòng	去逛街 qù guàngjiē	看电影 kàn diànyǐng	打电子游戏 dǎ diànzǐ yóuxì
	C	C	D	B, E	D

14 酸痛药膏 Suāntòng Yàogāo / *Ointment for Muscle Pain*

Read the ointment package shown below and answer the questions that follow.

1. 这个药(*medicine*)叫什么名字？ Zhège yào jiào shénme míngzi?

2. 这个药可以擦(*to apply*)在哪里？ Zhège yào kěyǐ cā zài nǎlǐ?

3. 头疼也可以用(*to use*)吗？ Tóu téng yě kěyǐ yòng ma?

自我提升 Zìwǒ Tíshēng

Raising the Bar

Vocabulary

活动	huódòng	*v.*	*to exercise*
		n.	*exercise; activity*
活	huó	*v.*	*to live*
动	dòng	*v.*	*to move*

▲ 活动

活动活动，要活就要动。
Huódòng huódòng, yào huó jiù yào dòng.
Move around and exercise.
To live, you have to move.

Language Note

活动 *huódòng* combines 活 *huó* and 动 *dòng*. In the second half of the sentence, the characters 活 *huó* and 动 *dòng* are separated to form the 要 *yào*…就要 *jiù yào*… sentence pattern that here means "in order to live, one must exercise." Both the first and second half of the sentence end with the word 动 *dòng*, making the sentence easy to remember because it rhymes. This sentence can often be seen in health promotion ads.

"要活就要动，"你整天坐在桌子前不运动，会生病的。
Yào huó jiù yào dòng, nǐ zhěng tiān zuò zài zhuōzi qián bú yùndòng, huì shēngbìng de.
"To live, you must move." If you sit in front of a desk all day without moving, you'll get sick.

"要 *yào*…就要 *jiù yào*…" is a sentence pattern that has an encouraging undertone. Below are some sentences with that contains pattern.

1. A famous quote from Chinese educator and writer Hu Shih:

要这么收获，就要那么栽。
Yào zhème shōuhuò, jiù yào nàme zāi.
To have this harvest, you must sow the seeds. You can only reap what you sow.

2. The following statement is often used by business people:

要做，就要做到最好！
Yào zuò, jiù yào zuò dào zuì hǎo!
If you want to do something, do the best you can!

喜欢运动

　　爸爸和妈妈很喜欢运动，他们每天早上都慢跑。上个星期五晚上，爸爸问[1]我周末要不要跟他们一起去锻炼，所以星期六早上，我跟他们去爬山。那天早上天气不错，二十五度，不热，是爬山的好天气。可是路不好走，所以我们爬了四个小时。回家以后，我全身酸痛。星期天的时候，我不能走路，只能坐在沙发[2]上。我想今天会好一点儿，可是我还是不舒服，所以下午也没去练球。吴森说我平常应该去健身房运动，可是我不想每天都全身疼呀！

[1] 问: to ask　　[2] 沙发: sofa

Xǐhuan Yùndòng

　Bàba hé māma hěn xǐhuan yùndòng, tāmen měitiān zǎoshang dōu mànpǎo. Shàngge Xīngqīwǔ wǎnshang, bàba wèn wǒ zhōumò yào búyào gēn tāmen yìqǐ qù duànliàn, suǒyǐ Xīngqīliù zǎoshang, wǒ gēn tāmen qù páshān. Nèitiān zǎoshang tiānqì búcuò, èrshíwǔdù, búrè, shì páshān de hǎo tiānqì. Kěshì lù bùhǎo zǒu, suǒyǐ wǒmen pále sìge xiǎoshí. Huíjiā yǐhòu, wǒ quánshēn suāntòng. Xīngqītiān de shíhou, wǒ bùnéng zǒulù, zhǐ néng zuò zài shāfā shàng. Wǒ xiǎng jīntiān huì hǎo yìdiǎnr, kěshì wǒ háishì bù shūfu, suǒyǐ xiàwǔ yě méiqù liànqiú. Wú Sēn shuō wǒ píngcháng yīnggāi qù jiànshēnfáng yùndòng, kěshì wǒ bùxiǎng měitiān dōu quánshēn téng ya!

15　通晓文意　Tōngxiǎo Wényì / *Understanding the Passage*

Read the above passage and answer the following questions in Chinese.

1. 她爸妈每天早上做什么运动？ Tā bà-mā měitiān zǎoshang zuò shénme yùndòng?

2. 谁问她要不要一起去锻炼？ Shéi wèn tā yào búyào yìqǐ qù duànliàn?

3. 她星期几去爬山？早上还是下午？ Tā xīngqī jǐ qù páshān? Zǎoshang háishì xiàwǔ?

4. 那天天气怎么样？几度？ Nèitiān tiānqì zěnmeyàng? Jǐdù?

5. 回家以后她觉得怎么样？ Huíjiā yǐhòu tā juéde zěnmeyàng?

6. 星期天的时候，她怎么了？ Xīngqītiān de shíhou, tā zěnme le?

7. 她说的"今天"应该是星期几？ Tā shuōde "jīntiān" yīnggāi shì xīngqī jǐ?

8. 为什么她不去健身房运动？ Wèishénme tā búqù jiànshēnfáng yùndòng?

汉字天地 Hànzì Tiāndì

Chinese Characters

山 ■ shān ■ mountain

The early pictograph of 山 *shān* shows mounds of earth sprouting up above the earth's surface. This later changed into a pictograph of three mountain peaks, the form of which simplified over time until it became the current form for 山 *shān*. It is also a common radical in words related to mountains.

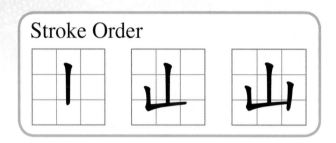

Stroke Order

| 丨 | 山 | 山 |

16 词汇延伸 Cíhuì Yánshēn / *Vocabulary Builder*

Below are characters that can be combined with 山 *shān* to create new words. Match the Chinese words on the left with the appropriate English meanings on the right.

顶 dǐng *n. peak*	水 shuǐ *n. water*	坡 pō *n. slope*	腰 yāo *n. waist*	崩 bēng *v. to collapse*

1. 山顶 shāndǐng   A. hillside

2. 山水 shānshuǐ   B. halfway up a mountain

3. 山坡 shānpō   C. summit; hilltop

4. 山腰 shānyāo   D. landslide

5. 山崩 shānbēng   E. landscape

Can you find 山 in the following pictures?

武陵源·山魂水韵·張家

寄情山水間

冷水器也賣
千山淨水
打動消費

雪山山麓
の
きれいな 水

山寨惹的禍

品市場的老
以鋪天蓋
造成「每個領

地的深夜電視廣告，
商製造的簡單功能，

加二十四

或

健康資料
算在大陸禮品品

山

Lesson B

词汇 Cíhuì
Vocabulary

🔊 **生理感觉 Shēnglǐ Gǎnjué** *Feelings*

精神好

jīngshén hǎo

adj. energetic

精神不好

jīngshén bùhǎo

adj. not energetic

困（睏）

kùn

adj. sleepy

累

lèi

adj. tired

舒服

shūfu

adj. comfortable

不舒服

bù shūfu

adj. uncomfortable

心情好

xīnqíng hǎo

adj. in a good mood

心情不好

xīnqíng bùhǎo

adj. in a bad mood

开心 (開心)

kāixīn

adj. happy

兴奋 (興奮)

xīngfèn

adj. excited

生气 (生氣)

shēngqì

adj./ v.o. angry; to get angry

惊讶 (驚訝)

jīngyà

adj. surprised

担心 (擔心)

dānxīn

adj. / v. worried; to worry

紧张 (緊張)

jǐnzhāng

adj. nervous

难过 (難過)

nánguò

adj. sad

我写博客记录我的心情。

Wǒ xiě bókè jìlù wǒde xīnqíng.

I record my feelings on my blog.

A: 你怎么这么累呢？（你怎麼這麼累呢？）Nǐ zěnme zhème lèi ne? *Why are you so tired?*

B: 我昨天晚上念书念到一点。（我昨天晚上念書念到一點。）

Wǒ zuótiān wǎnshàng niànshū niàn dào yìdiǎn. *Because I studied until one in the morning.*

. . . .

A: 他为什么那么兴奋？（他為什麼那麼興奮？）

Tā wèishénme nàme xīngfèn? *Why is he so excited?*

B: 因为他明天要去旅行。（因為他明天要去旅行。）

Yīnwèi tā míngtiān yào qù lǚxíng. *Because he's going on a trip tomorrow.*

你怎么现在才到？
Nǐ zěnme xiànzài cái dào?
How can you just be getting here?

对不起，你别生气。
Duìbùqǐ, nǐ bié shēngqì.
Sorry. Don't be mad.

我最喜欢的球队今天有比赛。
Wǒ zuì xǐhuan de qiúduì jīntiān yǒu bǐsài.
My favorite team has a game today.

你吃饭了吗？
Nǐ chīfàn le ma?
Have you had your meal?

你一定很兴奋吧。
Nǐ yídìng hěn xīngfèn ba.
You must be very excited.

我吃了。
Wǒ chīle. *I have.*

Adverbs

就	jiù	*(used before a verb to indicate that something happened earlier than was expected)*
一定	yídìng	*must*
才	cái	*(used before a verb to indicate that something happened later than was expected)*
别	bié	*do not (used in imperative sentences)*
好	hǎo	*very*

Common Expression

| 没办法 (沒辦法) | méi bànfǎ | *can not do anything* |

Nouns

精神	jīngshén	*spirit*
心情	xīnqíng	*mood*
话 (話)	huà	*word; remark*
球队 (球隊)	qiúduì	*team*
博客	bókè	*blog*

Particles

呢	ne	*a final particle used at the end of an interrogative sentence*
了	le	*used to indicate a change of status*
喔	o	*a final particle used in imperative sentences to remind the listener to pay attention to what is said*

Time Word

| 一会儿 (一會兒) | yìhuǐr | *a moment* |

Verbs

睡	shuì	*to sleep*
记录 (記錄)	jìlù	*to record*
说 (說)	shuō	*to say; to speak; to talk*
写 (寫)	xiě	*to write*
赢 (贏)	yíng	*to win*
输 (輸)	shū	*to lose*

Verb-Object

| 打瞌睡 | dǎ kēshuì | *to doze; to nod off* |

1 心理反应 **Xīnlǐ Fǎnyìng** / *Mental Reaction*

Choose the appropriate reaction from the box below to match each of the following events.

> A. 开心 kāixīn   B. 惊讶 jīngyà   C. 紧张 jǐnzhāng
>
> D. 生气 shēngqì   E. 担心 dānxīn

1. 你一会儿有一个大考。 Nǐ yìhuǐr yǒu yíge dàkǎo.
2. 晚上十二点，你弟弟还没回家。 Wǎnshang shí'èrdiǎn, nǐ dìdi hái méi huíjiā.
3. 很久不见的朋友给你一个生日礼物。
   Hěnjiǔ bújiàn de péngyou gěi nǐ yíge shēngrì lǐwù.
4. 新年的时候，爸妈要带你去德国旅行。
   Xīnnián de shíhou, bà-mā yào dài nǐ qù Déguó lǚxíng.
5. 你借一百块给一个同学，可是他不还(to return)你。
   Nǐ jiè yībǎikuài gěi yíge tóngxué, kěshì tā bùhuán nǐ.

2 感觉分类 **Gǎnjué Fēnlèi** / *Classifying Feelings*

Organize the following feelings into either the positive or negative column based on whether the feeling is good or bad.

正面 zhèngmiàn (positive)	负面 fùmiàn (negative)	A. 累 lèi B. 兴奋 xīngfèn C. 舒服 shūfu D. 高兴 gāoxìng E. 心情好 xīnqíng hǎo F. 心情不好 xīnqíng bùhǎo

3 个人问题 **Gèrén Wèntí** / *Personal Questions*

Answer the following questions in Chinese based on your own experiences and opinions.

1. 你有博客吗？ Nǐ yǒu bókè ma?
2. 你容易紧张吗？ Nǐ róngyì jǐnzhāng ma?
3. 你上健身房吗？ Nǐ shàng jiànshēnfáng ma?
4. 你常常生气吗？ Nǐ chángcháng shēngqì ma?
5. 上课的时候，你打瞌睡吗？ Shàngkè de shíhou, nǐ dǎ kēshuì ma?
6. 精神不好的时候，你喝咖啡吗？ Jīngshén bùhǎo de shíhou, nǐ hē kāfēi ma?

The Particle 呢 *ne*

The particle 呢 *ne* was introduced in Level 1, Unit 1, Lesson A to form a follow-up question. In this lesson, it is used at the end of an interrogative sentence to soften the tone of the sentence.

Note: 呢 *ne* cannot be used in 吗 *ma* questions.

> **Question** + 呢 *ne*?

他是谁呢？ Tā shì shéi ne?

你在家做什么呢？ Nǐ zài jiā zuò shénme ne ?

▲ 他是谁呢？

The Adverbs 就 *jiù* and 才 *cái*

The adverbs 就 *jiù* and 才 *cái* are used between a time expression and a verb to express the sense of "earlier than expected" (就 *jiù*) and "later than expected" (才 *cái*).

> **Subject** + **Time** + 就 *jiù* + **Verb Phrase**

我今天早上六点就起床了。 Wǒ jīntiān zǎoshang liùdiǎn jiù qǐchuáng le.

他午饭只吃了一个小面包，所以下午三点就饿了。

Tā wǔfàn zhǐ chīle yíge xiǎo miànbāo, suǒyǐ xiàwǔ sāndiǎn jiù èle.

> **Subject** + **Time** + 才 *cái* + **Verb Phrase**

他考试以前才念书。 Tā kǎoshì yǐqián cái niànshū.

我脚痛，走了四十分钟才到家。 Wǒ jiǎo tòng, zǒule sìshífēn zhōng cái dào jiā.

Language Note:

The timing of using 就 *jiù* and 才 *cái* depends a lot on the speaker's expectation toward the time that something happens. For example:

爸爸今天早上七点就回家了。 *Bàba jīntiān zǎoshang qīdiǎn jiù huíjiā le.*

Seven o'clock in the morning is not generally considered an "early" time for a person to return home. However, in this particular case, the father may often work the nightshift and return home after seven o'clock in the morning. Therefore, for the speaker, seeing his / her father return home at seven is considered early.

The Preposition 到 *dào*

The word 到 *dào* can function as a preposition, meaning "until" or "up to." Placed after a verb and followed by a time expression, it means that the action lasts until that particular time.

> **Subject** + **Verb** + **到** *dào* + **Time**

爸爸星期六早上常常睡到十一点。
Bàba Xīngqīliù zǎoshang chángcháng shuì dào shíyīdiǎn.

他明天要比赛了，所以今天会练习到很晚。
Tā míngtiān yào bǐsài le, suǒyǐ jīntiān huì liànxí dào hěn wǎn.

If it is a "verb-object" compound, the verb-object object compound needs to remain and the verb needs to be reduplicated before announcing the time.

> **Subject** + **Verb-Object** + **Verb** + **到** *dào* + **Time**

我今天得上课上到下午五点。 Wǒ jīntiān děi shàngkè shàng dào xiàwǔ wǔdiǎn.

哥哥吃饭吃到晚上十一点才回家。 Gēge chīfàn chī dào wǎnshang shíyīdiǎn cái huíjiā.

The Particle 了 *le*

The particle 了 *le* introduced in Lesson A, was used immediately after a verb to mean that the action of the verb has been completed. Here, 了 *le* is placed at the end of a sentence to indicate a change of situation has occurred.

> **Sentence** + **了** *le*

他今年上高三了。 Tā jīnnián shàng gāosān le.

运动以后，我饿了。 Yùndòng yǐhòu, wǒ èle.

▲ 运动以后，我饿了。

The Adverb 别 *bié*

The adverb 别 *bié* means "do not." It is often used in imperative sentences. The addressee, the person being told not to do something, does not have to be mentioned.

> **(Subject)** + **别** *bié* + **Verb Phrase**

你别那么容易担心。 Nǐ bié nàme róngyì dānxīn.

别在教室里吃东西！ Bié zài jiàoshì lǐ chī dōngxi!

会话 Huìhuà
Dialogue

◀)) 熬夜看球赛 Áoyè Kàn Qiúsài *Late Night Spectator*

Between classes, Qian Yongli and Zhao Mei are sitting in the classroom.

钱永利:	我好想睡觉，你精神怎么这么好呢？	Qián Yǒnglì:	Wǒ hǎo xiǎng shuìjiào, nǐ jīngshén zěnme zhème hǎo ne?
赵梅:	我十点就睡了，精神当然好。你为什么这么困？	Zhào Méi:	Wǒ shídiǎn jiù shuìle, jīngshén dāngrán hǎo. Nǐ wèishénme zhème kùn?
钱永利:	我昨天看足球比赛看到两点钟。我很开心，因为我喜欢的球队赢了。	Qián Yǒnglì:	Wǒ zuótiān kàn zúqiú bǐsài kàn dào liǎngdiǎn zhōng. Wǒ hěn kāixīn, yīnwèi wǒ xǐhuan de qiúduì yíngle.
赵梅:	你一定很兴奋吧！	Zhào Méi:	Nǐ yídìng hěn xīngfèn ba!
钱永利:	是啊，我太兴奋了，所以我四点半才睡。	Qián Yǒnglì:	Shì a, wǒ tài xīngfèn le, suǒyǐ wǒ sìdiǎn bàn cái shuì.
赵梅:	那你在做什么呢？	Zhào Méi:	Nà nǐ zài zuò shénme ne?
钱永利:	我在写博客，我要记录我的心情。	Qián Yǒnglì:	Wǒ zài xiě bókè, wǒ yào jìlù wǒde xīnqíng.
赵梅:	你写了两个半钟头！	Zhào Méi:	Nǐ xiěle liǎngge bàn zhōngtóu!
钱永利:	没办法，我太高兴了，有太多话想说。	Qián Yǒnglì:	Méi bànfǎ, wǒ tài gāoxìng le, yǒu tài duō huà xiǎng shuō.
赵梅:	一会儿上课的时候，别打瞌睡喔！	Zhào Méi:	Yìhuǐr shàngkè de shíhou, bié dǎ kēshuì o!

4 他们的精神怎么样？ Tāmende jīngshén zěnmeyàng? *What are they feeling?*

Match the photos of the two characters (#1 and #2) with the illustrations (A or B) to indicate how they feel according to the dialogue. Say in Chinese each person's feelings.

1.
2.
A.
B.

5 懂了吗？ Dǒngle ma? *Do you understand?*

Answer the following questions in Chinese.

1. 为什么钱永利很困？ Wèishénme Qián Yǒnglì hěn kùn?

2. 赵梅昨天晚上几点睡觉？ Zhào Méi zuótiān wǎnshang jǐdiǎn shuìjiào?

3. 钱永利喜欢的球队赢了还是输了？
   Qián Yǒnglì xǐhuān de qiúduì yíngle háishì shūle?

4. 谁昨天晚上很兴奋？ Shéi zuótiān wǎnshang hěn xīngfèn?

5. 钱永利昨天晚上两点钟才睡吗？
   Qián Yǒnglì zuótiān wǎnshang liǎngdiǎn zhōng cái shuì ma?

6. 足球比赛以后，钱永利在做什么？ Zúqiú bǐsài yǐhòu, Qián Yǒnglì zài zuò shénme?

7. 钱永利写博客写了多久？为什么他写了那么久？
   Qián Yǒnglì xiě bókè xiěle duōjiǔ? Wèishénme tā xiěle nàme jiǔ?

8. 他们一会儿得做什么？ Tāmen yìhuǐr děi zuò shénme?

Language Note

In the United States, people use blogs to record their life and share their thoughts with others. This forum is also popular with Chinese people. However, the word "blog" has different Chinese names in China, Taiwan, and Hong Kong. In China and Taiwan, it is transliterated respectively as 博客 *bókè* and 部落格 *bùluògé*. In Hong Kong, it is called 网志 *wǎngzhì*. In China, the social network Facebook is called 脸书 *liǎnshū*, and the micro blog Twitter is named 推特 *tuītè*.

文化橱窗 Wénhuà Chúchuāng
Culture Window

Social Networking in China

▲ *The icon of QQ.*

With advances in technology and the popularization of computers, high school students in China are spending more and more of their time on the Internet. Perhaps the most common way teens communicate online is through the instant messaging program QQ, represented by a cute penguin icon. QQ supports instant messaging, audio chat, video chat, file transfers, online movies and games with multiple players. With a QQ account, users can add friends to their list and contact them whenever they wish.

In addition to QQ, social networking sites are also widely used in China. The two most popular are 人人网 *rénrénwǎng* and 开心网 *kāixīnwǎng*. The two sites have similar functions, but different target users. Renrenwang is a network for the students in the school, while Kaixinwang is more popular for the students outside school. Both programs allow users to have their own homepage where friends can leave messages and share photos and games.

Blogs and Twitter, both popular in the West, are trendy in China, too. Blogs, or 博客 *bókè* in Chinese, are online journals—spaces where bloggers can record their lives or share stories. Twitter, known in China as 推特 *tuītè*, is used to post one's latest status or thoughts in a short form (140 characters or less). Twitter enables users to share thoughts with large numbers of people all at the same time so that passing on information is quicker and more convenient.

▲ *Renrenwang*

Online games have also taken up a lot of students' time. For example, the fantasy role-playing game World of Warcraft is very popular in China. Internet cafés in China are filled with young gamers. Friends often play side by side, or form a team to complete missions together.

6 文化动动脑 Wénhuà Dòngdòngnǎo / *Cultural Check-up*

Decide whether each statement is true or false. Correct the false statements.

1. Chinese students do not typically chat online.
2. QQ supports video chat.
3. Most Chinese students use Facebook.
4. Kaixinwang is mostly used by students.
5. Blogs, or online journals, are known as 博客 *bókè* in China.
6. Chinese students do not have time for online gaming.

7 舒缓语气 **Shūhuǎn Yǔqì** / *Softening the Tone*

Soften the tone of the following questions by using the particle 呢 *ne*.

1. 你几岁？ Nǐ jǐsuì?
2. 他姓什么？ Tā xìng shénme?
3. 他家有几口人？ Tā jiā yǒu jǐkǒu rén?
4. 你下午上什么课？ Nǐ xiàwǔ shàng shénme kè?
5. 明天天气怎么样？ Míngtiān tiānqì zěnmeyàng?
6. 这条裤子多少钱？ Zhèitiáo kùzi duōshǎo qián?
7. 你周末喜欢去哪儿？ Nǐ zhōumò xǐhuan qù nǎr?
8. 他弟弟打不打篮球？ Tā dìdi dǎ bùdǎ lánqiú?

▲ 你几岁？

8 比较早还是比较晚？ **Bǐjiào Zǎo háishì Bǐjiào Wǎn?** / *Earlier or Later?*

Rewrite the following sentences by determining whether "就 *jiù*" or "才 *cái*" should be used.

1. 我一会儿去健身房。 Wǒ yìhuǐr qù jiànshēnfáng.
2. 他三岁开始打高尔夫。 Tā sānsuì kāishǐ dǎ gāo'ěrfū.
3. 物理课九点开始，他八点到。 Wùlǐkè jiǔdiǎn kāishǐ, tā bādiǎn dào.
4. 功课好难，我写了三个半钟头。 Gōngkè hǎo nán, wǒ xiěle sānge bàn zhōngtóu.
5. 今年天气很奇怪，八月开始下雪。 Jīnnián tiānqì hěn qíguài, Bāyuè kāishǐ xiàxuě.
6. 姐姐昨天很累，她下课以后睡觉。 Jiějie zuótiān hěn lèi, tā xiàkè yǐhòu shuìjiào.
7. 今天有考试，所以我很早到学校。 Jīntiān yǒu kǎoshì, suǒyǐ wǒ hěn zǎo dào xuéxiào.
8. 你怎么现在到？我等你等了两个小时。
   Nǐ zěnme xiànzài dào? Wǒ děng nǐ děngle liǎngge xiǎoshí.
9. 今天好热！早上九点气温三十八度。
   Jīntiān hǎo rè! Zǎoshang jiǔdiǎn qìwēn sānshíbādù.
10. 他弟弟非常聪明，所以十四岁上大学。
    Tā dìdi fēicháng cōngmíng, suǒyǐ shísìsuì shàng dàxué.
11. 她昨天晚上玩电子游戏玩到两点半睡。
    Tā zuótiān wǎnshang wán diànzǐ yóuxì wán dào liǎngdiǎn bàn shuì.
12. 我点的菜在哪里？我半个小时以前点了。
    Wǒ diǎn de cài zài nǎlǐ? Wǒ bànge xiǎoshí yǐqián diǎnle.

▲ 今天好热！

Look at the time or dates in the following images and use the preposition 到 *dào* to accurately describe them.

Lìzi: 她(睡觉)睡到中午十二点。
Tā (shuìjiào) shuì dào zhōngwǔ shí'èr diǎn.

1.

2.

3.

4.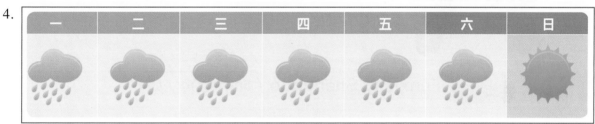

10 不再一样 **Búzài Yíyàng** / *What Changed?*

Look at the following pictures and describe the changes shown using the particle 了 *le*.

Lìzi: 下雨了。 Xiàyǔ le.

1.

3.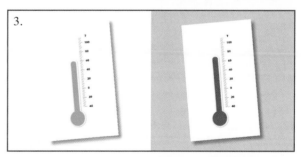

2.

4.

11 有所不为 **Yǒu Suǒ Bù Wéi** / *Don't Do It*

Look at the following signs. Use the adverb 别 *bié* to say what each sign means.

开口说 Kāikǒu Shuō

Communication

12 分享生活 **Fēnxiǎng Shēnghuó** / *Sharing Your Life*

With a classmate, talk about your daily life and say when you do or did certain things. Remember to use the adverbs 就 *jiù* and 才 *cái* when you talk about time. Draw a table like the one below and follow the model.

Lìzi: Amy: 我昨天六点就起床(*to get up*)了。   Wǒ zuótiān liùdiǎn jiù qǐchuáng le.

John: 我八点才起床。   Wǒ bādiǎn cái qǐchuáng.

Student \ Activity	起床 qǐchuáng	吃早饭 chī zǎofàn	去学校 qù xuéxiào	到家 dào jiā	写功课 xiě gōngkè	吃晚饭 chī wǎnfàn	睡觉 shuìjiào
Amy	6:00 A.M.						
John	8:00 A.M.						

Read the following blog entry and answer the questions that follow.

Leo-大干

http://www.emcp.zhenbang.com/leo [订阅] [手机订阅]

首页 | 博文目录 | 图片 | 关于我

个人资料

大干

加好友　发纸条

写留言　加关注

博客等级：12
博客积分：456
博客访问：47,723
关注人气：59

忙！忙！忙！

2013-10-24 18:05

下个星期五有棒球比赛，今天我们练习了一天，现在全身酸痛！小森打球的时候说回家以后要念书，我才记得明天有英文考试。天啊，我怎么这么忙！等一下吃饭以后我要马上读书。喔，我需要帮忙！

阅读(31) | 评论(24) | 转载(5) | 收藏(0)

1. 这个人叫什么名字？他有英文名字吗？
   Zhèige rén jiào shénme míngzi? Tā yǒu Yīngwén míngzi ma?

2. 星期几有棒球比赛？ Xīngqījǐ yǒu bàngqiú bǐsài?

3. 为什么他现在全身酸痛？ Wèishénme tā xiànzài quánshēn suāntòng?

4. 吃饭以后，他要做什么？ Chīfàn yǐhòu, tā yào zuò shénme?

5. 有多少人阅读(to read)过这篇文章？
   Yǒu duōshǎo rén yuèdú guò zhèipiān wénzhāng?

6. 有多少人评论(to comment)了这篇文章？
   Yǒu duōshǎo rén pínglùn le zhèipiān wénzhāng?

7. 一共有多少人访问(to visit)过他的博客？
   Yígòng yǒu duōshǎo rén fǎngwèn guò tāde bókè?

8. 人气(popularity)是多少分？ Rénqì shì duōshǎo fēn?

Vocabulary

废	fèi	v.	to give up
寝	qǐn	v.	to sleep
忘	wàng	v.	to forget
食	shí	v.	to eat

废寝忘食
fèi qǐn wàng shí
forgetting to eat and sleep

▲ 废寝忘食

Language Note

This four-word idiom is used to describe a person who is so absorbed in his / her work that he / she seems to have forgotten the basic necessities of eating and sleeping. This idiom is often used positively to talk about one's work ethic, study habits or hobbies.

小李很喜欢学习，他常常因为念书，所以废寝忘食。
Xiǎo Lǐ hěn xǐhuan xuéxí, tā chángcháng yīnwèi niànshū, suǒyǐ fèi qǐn wàng shí.
Xiao Li loves to learn. He often forgets to eat and sleep due to his studies.

The four-word idioms below mean the same as or the opposite of 废寝忘食 *fèi qǐn wàng shí*.

Same Meaning	夜以继日	yè yǐ jì rì	*night after night*
	发愤忘食	fā fèn wàng shí	*forgetting to eat in one's effort to achieve something.*
Opposite Meaning	无所事事	wú suǒ shì shì	*to do nothing all day long*
	饱食终日	bǎo shí zhōng rì	*too full to do anything*

打瞌睡

今天上英文课以前，我跟钱永利在教室里面聊天[1]。他昨天晚上看足球比赛看到两点钟；球赛以后，他还写博客写到四点半才睡。所以他又累又困，精神很不好。英文老师很认真，也很凶，常常问大家问题，我和钱永利都很紧张。上课以前，他喝了两杯咖啡，可是上课的时候，他还是打瞌睡，老师很生气。老师给钱永利一个功课，要他下次上课的时候说一个科学家[2]的故事。钱永利说他回家以后马上就要做，可是我不确定他要做功课，还是要睡觉。

[1] 聊天: to chat　　[2] 科学家: scientist

Dǎ Kēshuì

Jīntiān shàng Yīngwén kè yǐqián, wǒ gēn Qián Yǒnglì zài jiàoshì lǐmian liáotiān. Tā zuótiān wǎnshang kàn zúqiú bǐsài kàn dào liǎngdiǎn zhōng; qiúsài yǐhòu, tā hái xiě bókè xiě dào sìdiǎn bàn cái shuì. Suǒyǐ tā yòu lèi yòu kùn, jīngshén hěn bùhǎo. Yīngwén lǎoshī hěn rènzhēn, yě hěn xiōng, chángcháng wèn dàjiā wèntí, wǒ hé Qián Yǒnglì dōu hěn jǐnzhāng. Shàngkè yǐqián, tā hēle liǎngbēi kāfēi, kěshì shàngkè de shíhou, tā háishì dǎ kēshuì, lǎoshī hěn shēngqì. Lǎoshī gěi Qián Yǒnglì yíge gōngkè, yào tā xiàcì shàngkè de shíhou shuō yíge kēxuéjiā de gùshi. Qián Yǒnglì shuō tā huíjiā yǐhòu mǎshàng jiù yào zuò, kěshì wǒ bú quèdìng tā yào zuò gōngkè, háishì yào suìjiào.

14 通晓文意 Tōngxiǎo Wényì / *Understanding the Passage*

Read the above passage and answer the following questions in Chinese.

1. 上英文课以前，钱永利的精神怎么样？
   Shàng Yīngwén kè yǐqián, Qián Yǒnglì de jīngshén zěnmeyàng?

2. 钱永利怎么了？ Qián Yǒnglì zěnme le?

3. 他们的英文老师怎么样？ Tāmende Yīngwén lǎoshī zěnmeyàng?

4. 为什么钱永利上课以前很紧张？
   Wèishénme Qián Yǒnglì shàngkè yǐqián hěn jǐnzhāng?

5. 钱永利上课以前喝了什么？ Qián Yǒnglì shàngkè yǐqián hēle shénme?

6. 他喝了几杯？ Tā hēle jǐbēi?

7. 为什么英文老师很生气？ Wèishénme Yīngwén lǎoshī hěn shēngqì?

8. 英文老师给钱永利什么功课？ Yīngwén lǎoshī gěi Qián Yǒnglì shénme gōngkè?

汉字天地 Hànzì Tiāndì

Chinese Characters

情 ■ qíng ■ affections

情 *qíng* means feelings or affections. It is a combination of a radical and a phonetic component. The radical "忄 (心 *xīn*)" on the left means heart, symbolizing that one's emotions have to do with one's heart, and the "青 *qīng*" on the right is the phonetic component that gives the character 情 *qíng* at least some of its pronunciation.

Stroke Order

15 词汇延伸 Cíhuì Yánshēn / Vocabulary Builder

Below are characters that can be combined with 情 *qíng* to create new words. Match the Chinese words on the left with the appropriate English meanings on the right.

人 *rén* n. people	义 *yì* n. human relationship	书 *shū* n. book	歌 *gē* n. song	感 *gǎn* n. feeling

1. 情人 qíngrén   A. love song
2. 情义 qíngyì   B. comradeship
3. 情书 qíngshū   C. lover
4. 情歌 qínggē   D. emotion
5. 情感 qínggǎn   E. love letter

Can you find 情 in the following pictures?

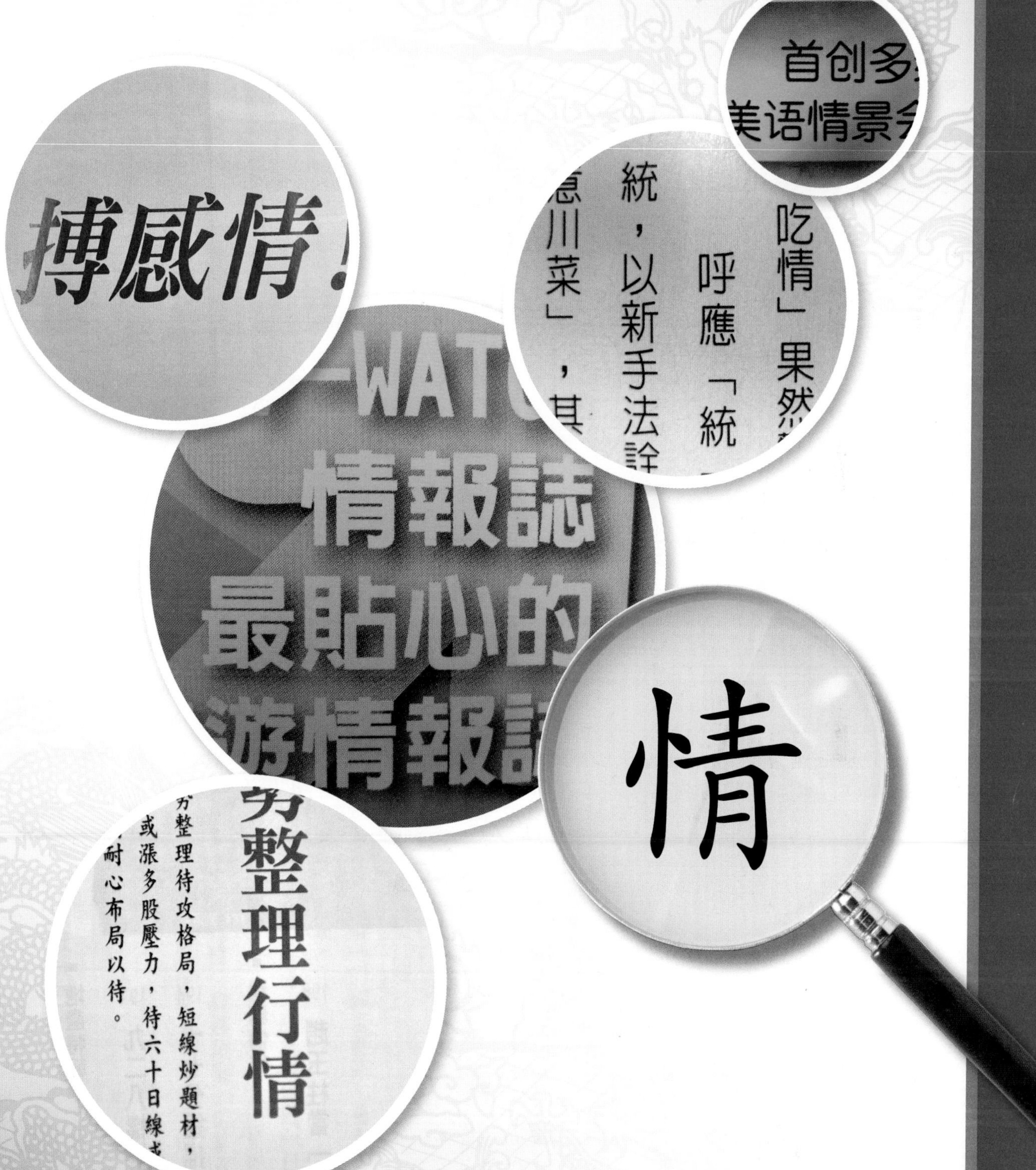

搏感情！

首创多
美语情景会

吃情」果然

呼應「統
統，以新手法詮
惡川菜」，其

-WATC
情報誌
最貼心的
游情報誌

方整理待攻格局，短線炒題材，
或漲多股壓力，待六十日線書
耐心布局以待。

为整理行情

情

Lesson C

词汇 Cíhuì
Vocabulary

🔊 看病 Kànbìng *See a Doctor*

医生 (醫生)

yīshēng

n. doctor

护士 (護士)

hùshi

n. nurse

病人

bìngrén

n. patient

医院 (醫院)

yīyuàn

n. hospital

诊所 (診所)

zhěnsuǒ

n. clinic

体温 (體溫)

tǐwēn

n. body temperature

体温计 (體溫計)

tǐwēnjì

n. thermometer

药 (藥)

yào

n. medicine; medication

水果

shuǐguǒ

n. fruit

生病
shēngbìng
v. to be sick

感冒
gǎnmào
v. to have a cold

休息
xiūxi
v. to rest

症状 Zhèngzhuàng *Symptoms*

发烧 (發燒)
fāshāo
v.o. to have a fever

流鼻涕
liú bítì
v.o. to have a runny nose

咳嗽
késòu
v. to cough

打喷嚏 (打噴嚏)
dǎ pēntì
v.o. to sneeze

头晕 (頭暈)
tóuyūn
adj. dizzy

头痛 (頭痛)
tóutòng
n. headache

鼻塞
bísāi
adj. (a) stuffed nose

喉咙痛 (喉嚨痛)
hóulóng tòng
n. (a) sore throat

拉肚子
lā dùzi
v.o. to suffer from diarrhea

全身无力（全身無力）

quánshēn wúlì

adj. to feel weak all over

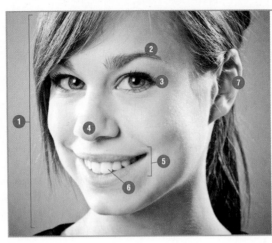

1. 脸（臉）liǎn *n. face*
2. 眉毛 méimáo *n. eyebrow*
3. 眼睛 yǎnjīng *n. eye*
4. 鼻子 bízi *n. nose*
5. 嘴巴 zuǐba *n. mouth*
6. 牙齿（牙齒）yáchǐ *n. tooth*
7. 耳朵 ěrduo *n. ear*

A: 你哪里不舒服？（你哪裡不舒服？）

Nǐ nǎlǐ bù shūfu? *Where do you feel discomfort?*

B: 我咳嗽、喉咙痛。（我咳嗽、喉嚨痛。）

Wǒ késòu, hóulóng tòng. *I'm coughing and my throat hurts.*

A: 他生病了。

Tā shēngbìng le. *He's ill.*

B: 那我们带他去医院吧。（那我們帶他去醫院吧。）

Nà wǒmen dài tā qù yīyuàn ba. *Then let's take him to the hospital.*

A: 爷爷一天要吃几次药？（爺爺一天要吃幾次藥？）

Yéye yìtiān yào chī jǐcì yào? *How many times does grandpa have to take his medicine a day.*

B: 一天一次，一次一包。除了吃药以外，他一天还要量一次体温。

（一天一次，一次一包。除了吃藥以外，他一天還要量一次體溫。）

Yìtiān yícì, yícì yìbāo. Chúle chīyào yǐwài, tā yìtiān háiyào liáng yícì tǐwēn.

Once a day, and one packet a time. Apart from that, he also has to have his temperature taken once a day.

我发烧了，得在家休息。（我發燒了，得在家休息。）

Wǒ fāshāo le, děi zài jiā xiūxi. *I have a fever, so I have to stay at home and rest.*

医生，我需要吃药吗？

Yīshēng, wǒ xūyào chīyào ma?

Doctor, do I have to take any medicine?

不用，多喝水、多休息就可以了。

Búyòng, duō hēshuǐ, duō xiūxi jiù kěyǐ le.

No, just drink lots of water and take a lot of rest.

A: 我怕打针。（我怕打針。）

Wǒ pà dǎzhēn. *I'm scared of shots.*

B: 不用怕。

Búyòng pà. *Don't be.*

- -

A: 护士小姐，我应该注意什么？（護士小姐，我應該注意什麼？）

Hùshì xiǎojiě, wǒ yīnggāi zhùyì shénme? *Nurse, what things should I be aware of?*

B: 吃药的时候，不可以喝茶或咖啡。（吃藥的時候，不可以喝茶或咖啡。）

Chīyào de shíhou, bù kěyǐ hēchá huò kāfēi. *You can't take your medicine with tea or coffee.*

Adjectives

严重（嚴重）	yánzhòng	*serious*
好	hǎo	*in good health; to get well*
健康	jiànkāng	*healthy*

Adverbs

最好	zuìhǎo	*had better; it would be best if*
多	duō	*more; a lot*

Measure Words

次	cì	*times*
粒	lì	*pill*

Noun

健康	jiànkāng	*health*

Verbs

晕（暈）	yūn	*to feel dizzy; to faint*
量	liáng	*to measure*
注意	zhùyì	*to pay attention to*
过（過）	guò	*to pass; to go through*
怕	pà	*to be afraid of*

Verb-Object

看病	kànbìng	*(of a patient) to see a doctor; (of a doctor) to see a patient*

脸部特征 Liǎnbù Tèzhēng / *Facial Characteristics*

Look at the face below and fill in the blanks in the paragraph using the words provided. Not all the words will be used.

A. 大 dà

B. 小 xiǎo

C. 女生 nǚshēng

D. 黑色 hēisè

E. 蓝色 lánsè

F. 男生 nánshēng

这是一张 1.___ 的脸。她的眉毛是 2.___ 的，眼睛是 3.___ 的。她的鼻子很 4.___，嘴巴很 5.___，她的两个耳朵也很小。

Zhè shì yìzhāng 1.____ de liǎn. Tāde méimáo shì 2.____ de, yǎnjīng shì 3.____ de. Tāde bízi hěn 4.____, zuǐba hěn 5.____, tāde liǎngge ěrduo yě hěn xiǎo.

感冒症状 Gǎnmào Zhèngzhuàng / *Symptoms of a Cold*

Feng is feeling sick. Look at the drawing below and listen carefully as she describes the symptoms she has. In a separate sheet of paper, write the letter of the parts of the body that are affected.

Answer the following questions in Chinese based on your own experiences and opinions.

1. 你容易生病吗？ Nǐ róngyì shēngbìng ma?

2. 你怕打针吗？ Nǐ pà dǎzhēn ma?

3. 你家有体温计吗？ Nǐ jiā yǒu tǐwēnjì ma?

4. 感冒的时候，最好别吃什么东西？
   Gǎnmào de shíhou, zuìhǎo bié chī shénme dōngxi?

5. 感冒的时候，你去看医生吗？如果*(if)*你不看医生，你做什么？
   Gǎnmào de shíhou, nǐ qù kàn yīshēng ma? Rúguǒ nǐ búkàn yīshēng, nǐ zuò shénme?

句型介绍 Jùxíng Jièshào
Language Patterns

Reduplication of Adjectives

Adjectives are used to describe things, and the reduplication of adjectives makes the description more vivid. Reduplication means that the root or stem of the word is repeated.

她有双大眼睛。 Tā yǒu shuāng dà yǎnjīng.

她有双大大的眼睛。 Tā yǒu shuāng dàdà de yǎnjīng.

弟弟喜欢穿松松的衣服。 Dìdi xǐhuan chuān sōngsōng de yīfu.

那只白白胖胖的猫是我的宠物。 Nèizhī báibái pàngpàng de māo shì wǒde chǒngwù.

To reduplicate adjectives that are monosyllabic, repeat the word one more time and add 的 *de* at the end.

热热的 rèrè de, 痛痛的 tòngtòng de, 胖胖的 pàngpàng de

When the adjectives are disyllabic, repeat each character.

高兴 gāoxìng → 高高兴兴的 gāogaoxìngxing de

健康 jiànkāng → 健健康康的 jiànjiankāngkang de

These forms can also be used to comment on the subject.

▲ 高兴

宫保鸡丁辣辣的。 Gōngbǎo jīdīng làlà de.

这个餐厅的服务生都客客气气的。 Zhèige cāntīng de fúwùshēng dōu kèkeqìqi de.

In addition when these forms are followed by 地 *de*, they become adverbs and can be used to modify a verb phrase.

今天是星期天，他慢慢地吃早餐。 Jīntiān shì Xīngqītiān, tā mànmàn de chī zǎocān.

学生们高高兴兴地来学校。 Xuéshengmen gāogaoxìngxing de lái xuéxiào.

The Adverb 最好 *zuìhǎo*

The adverb 最好 *zuìhǎo* means "had better; it would be best to…if." It is used when giving suggestions or advice to others.

Subject + 最好 *zuìhǎo* + **Verb Phrase**

生病的时候，最好多睡一点儿。
Shēngbìng de shíhou, zuìhǎo duō shuì yìdiǎnr.

想要身体健康，你最好每天运动。
Xiǎng yào shēntǐ jiànkāng, nǐ zuìhǎo měitiān yùndòng.

▲ 身体健康

The Adverb 就 *jiù*

The adverb 就 *jiù* means "then", and it indicates the consequence of the previous statement. The phrase 就…了 *jiù… le* can be translated as "then it will be…."

小感冒不用去医院，在家休息就行了。
Xiǎo gǎnmào búyòng qù yīyuàn, zài jiā xiūxi jiù xíng le.

or 小感冒就不用去医院了。 Xiǎo gǎnmào jiù búyòng qù yīyuàn le.

你的病不严重，过两三天就好了。
Nǐde bìng bù yánzhòng, guò liǎng sān tiān jiù hǎole.

A: 我今天应该怎么穿？ Wǒ jīntiān yīnggāi zěnme chuān?
B: 外面很热，你穿吊带衫就可以了。
Wàimiàn hěn rè, nǐ chuān diàodàishān jiù kěyǐ le.

▲ 我今天应该怎么穿？

The Frequency of an Action

To give the frequency of an action, first define the time period in which the action takes place, and then say the verb and the number of times the action is carried out. To ask "how often," use the question word 多久 *duōjiǔ* to replace the time period.

Subject + Time Period + Verb + number of times

弟弟喜欢吃快餐，他一个星期吃五次。
Dìdi xǐhuan chī kuàicān, tā yíge xīngqī chī wǔcì.

A: 那家书店，你多久去一次？
Nèijiā shūdiàn, nǐ duōjiǔ qù yícì?

B: 一个月去一次。 Yíge yuè qù yícì.

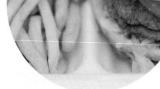
▲ 快餐

In sentences containing verb-object compounds, the verb-object compound needs to be split and the number of times needs to be inserted between the verb and the object.

Subject + Time Period + Verb + number of times + (的 *de*) + Object

她一个星期跳三次舞。 Tā yíge xīngqī tiào sāncì wǔ.

我昨天晚上看了三个钟头的书。 Wǒ zuótiān wǎnshang kànle sānge zhōngtóu de shū.

The same rule also applies to sentences with a verb and an object.

我一个星期上三次中文课。 Wǒ yíge xīngqī shàng sāncì Zhōngwén kè.

他吃了坏东西，昨天拉了好几次肚子。
Tā chīle huài dōngxi, zuótiān lāle hǎojǐcì dùzi.

The Adverbs 多 *duō* and 少 *shǎo*

The adverb 多 *duō* is placed before the verb and means "to do something more often." The opposite is 少 *shǎo*, which means "to do something less often."

(Subject) + 多 *duō* / 少 *shǎo* + Verb Phrase

你太累了，应该多休息。 Nǐ tài lèile, yīnggāi duō xiūxi.

炸的东西不健康，你少吃一点。 Zháde dōngxi bú jiànkāng, nǐ shǎo chī yìdiǎn.

▲ 太累了

🔊 我生病了 Wǒ Shēngbìng Le *I Came Down With Something*

At the clinic, Wu Sen is talking to the doctor.

医生：	你哪里不舒服？	yīshēng:	Nǐ nǎlǐ bù shūfu?
吴森：	我鼻塞、喉咙疼，头也晕晕的。	Wú Sēn:	Wǒ bí sāi, hóulóng téng, tóu yě yūnyūn de.
医生：	我来量量你的体温。三十九度，你发烧了。	yīshēng:	Wǒ lái liángliang nǐde tǐwēn. Sānshíjiǔdù, nǐ fāshāo le.
吴森：	很严重吗？	Wú Sēn:	Hěn yánzhòng ma?
医生：	不严重，只是感冒。你最好在家休息几天。	yīshēng:	Bù yánzhòng, zhǐshì gǎnmào. Nǐ zuìhǎo zài jiā xiūxi jǐtiān.
吴森：	需要打针吗？	Wú Sēn:	Xūyào dǎzhēn ma?
医生：	不用打针，吃药就行了。	yīshēng:	Búyòng dǎzhēn, chīyào jiù xíngle.
吴森：	一天要吃几次药？	Wú Sēn:	Yìtiān yào chī jǐcì yào?
医生：	一天三次，一次两粒。	yīshēng:	Yìtiān sāncì, yícì liǎnglì.
吴森：	我还应该注意什么？	Wú Sēn:	Wǒ hái yīnggāi zhùyì shénme?
医生：	多喝水，多吃点水果，过几天就好了。	yīshēng:	Duō hēshuǐ, duō chī diǎn shuǐguǒ, guò jǐtiān jiù hǎole.

4 吴森的治疗方法 Wú Sēn de Zhìliáo Fāngfǎ / *Wu Sen's Treatment*

Choose the letters of the pictures that best describe the treatment and/or suggestions that the doctor gave Wu Sen in the dialogue.

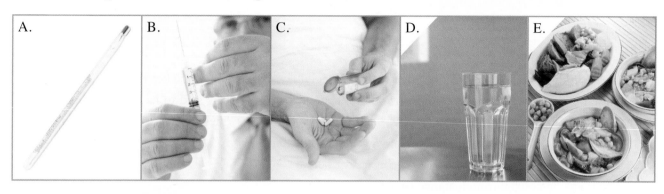

5 懂了吗? Dǒngle ma? / *Do you understand?*

Answer the following questions in Chinese.

1. 吴森在跟谁说话(*to talk*)? Wú Sēn zài gēn shéi shuōhuà?
2. 吴森的鼻子怎么了? 喉咙呢? 头呢? Wú Sēn de bízi zěnme le? hóulóng ne? tóu ne?
3. 吴森的体温多少度? 他发烧了吗? Wú Sēn de tǐwēn duōshǎo dù? Tā fāshāo le ma?
4. 吴森的感冒严重吗? Wú Sēn de gǎnmào yánzhòng ma?
5. 吴森得在家休息吗? Wú Sēn děi zài jiā xiūxi ma?
6. 吴森需不需要打针? Wú Sēn xū bù xūyào dǎzhēn?
7. 吴森一天要吃几次药? Wú Sēn yìtiān yào chī jǐcì yào?
8. 医生说吴森的感冒多久才会好? Yīshēng shuō Wú Sēn de gǎnmào duōjiǔ cái huì hǎo?

6 哪里不舒服? Nǎlǐ bù shūfu? / *Where do you feel discomfort?*

Write down the parts of the body where Wu Sen does not feel well and describe his symptoms aloud.

◀嗨，我是吴森。

Wénhuà Chúchuāng
Culture Window

Chinese Traditional Medicine

Chinese traditional medicine, unlike other medical specialties, uses natural remedies to heal sickness. The Chinese have practiced their traditional medicine since ancient times. It is said to have been invented by the mythological emperor Shennong (神农 *Shénnóng*), also known as "the emperor of medicine," after he tasted a hundred different herbs in search of ways to heal the human body.

Chinese traditional medicine, or CTM, consists of herbal (roots, stems, juices and fruits), animal (innards, skin, bones and organs), and mineral treatments. Because the herbal element is the most prominent, Chinese traditional medicine is also known as herbal medicine. Nowadays, there are thousands of ingredients used in Chinese traditional medicine, and the mixing and matching of ingredients results in countless different prescriptions.

The ancient Chinese did extensive research on Chinese traditional medicine, paving the way for wide acceptance

▲ *Chinese herbs*

today. There are many ways that Chinese traditional medicine may be taken. Some remedies need to be boiled and then drunk as tea, while others might be ground into powder or mixed with water or alcohol. Medicines may also be administered in the form of pills, ointments, patches, or injections.

The skills involved in making Chinese traditional medicine are extensive. The process includes removing weeds, sand, and parts not used, cutting or slicing according to need, and then drying under the sun or in ovens for

▲ *mortar and pestle*

preservation. Additional work is done to the ingredients while keeping their appearance, fragrance, and nutrients intact. Chinese traditional medicine stresses the four *qi* and five tastes. The four *qi* are also known as the four characteristics of the ingredients: cold, heat, warmth and coolness. The five tastes are spicy, sour, sweet, bitter and salty. The differences in the four *qi* and five tastes result in different remedies for different ailments.

▲ *Chinese traditional pharmacy*

7 文化动动脑 **Wénhuà Dòngdòngnǎo** / *Cultural Check-up*

Decide whether each statement is true or false. Correct the false statements.

1. The emperor Shennong was known as the "emperor of medicine."
2. Chinese traditional medicine uses only herbal, not animal, ingredients.
3. There are only a handful of ingredients used in Chinese medicine.
4. Some Chinese medicines may be drunk as tea.
5. The four *qi* are spicy, sour, sweet, and bitter.

 语言练习 **Yǔyán Liànxí**

Language Practice

8 形容东西 **Xíngróng Dōngxi** / *Describing Objects*

Use reduplication of the adjectives provided to describe the following pictures.

1. 胖 pàng	3. 丑 chǒu	5. 健康 jiànkāng

2. 红 hóng	4. 小 xiǎo	6. 漂亮 piàoliang

叙述句子 Xùshù Jùzi / *Recount the Sentences*

Create vivid sentences using the words provided and by reduplicating the adjective or adverb.

1. 我的肩膀 / 痛 wǒde jiānbǎng / tòng
2. 这几道菜 / 油 zhè jǐdào cài / yóu
3. 黑巧克力 / 苦 hēi qiǎokèlì / kǔ
4. 他们 / 喝茶 / 慢 tāmen / hēchá / màn
5. 妹妹 / 睡觉 / 舒服 mèimei / shuìjiào / shūfu
6. 今年有很多事 / 奇怪 jīnnián yǒu hěnduō shì / qíguài
7. 大家 / 去旅行 / 快乐 dàjiā / qù lǚxíng / kuàilè

▲ 快乐

给个建议 Gěi Ge Jiànyì / *Give A Suggestion*

Read the following situations and offer suggestions by using the adverb 最好 *zuìhǎo*.

1. 他们又累又困。 Tāmen yòu lèi yòu kùn.
2. 我下个星期有三个考试。 Wǒ xiàge xīngqī yǒu sānge kǎoshì.
3. 肉的味道酸酸的，很奇怪。 Ròu de wèidào suānsuan de, hěn qíguài.
4. 我全身热热的，不太舒服。 Wǒ quánshēn rèrè de, bú tài shūfu.
5. 咳嗽的时候，可以吃冰淇淋吗？ Késòu de shíhou, kěyǐ chī bīngqílín ma?
6. 我的腿好疼。我明天应该去爬山吗？
   Wǒde tuǐ hǎo téng. Wǒ míngtiān yīnggāi qù páshān ma?

解决方法 Jiějué Fāngfǎ / *Solutions*

Read the following situation and use the phrase 就…了 *jiù…le* (就行了 *jiù xíngle*; 就好了 *jiù hǎole*; 就可以了 *jiù kěyǐ le*; 就对了 *jiù duìle*) to give a possible solution. Use the words provided in your response.

1. 我感冒了，要去看医生吗？ (多休息)
   Wǒ gǎnmào le, yào qù kàn yīshēng ma? (duō xiūxi)
2. 我应该给一个月的孩子(child)吃什么？ (牛奶)
   Wǒ yīnggāi gěi yíge yuède háizi chī shénme? (niúnǎi)
3. 我不知道中国新年是哪一天。 (看农历)
   Wǒ bù zhīdào Zhōngguó xīnnián shì nǎ yìtiān. (kàn nónglì)
4. 朋友的生日晚会，我得穿连衣裙吗？ (好看的衣服)
   Péngyou de shēngrì wǎnhuì, wǒ děi chuān liányīqún ma? (hǎokàn de yīfu)

5. 十二月去北京旅行，应该带什么衣服？（大衣）
   Shí'èryuè qù Běijīng lǚxíng, yīnggāi dài shénme yīfu? (dàyī)

6. 我的中文课本在家，要上课了，怎么办(what should I do)？（跟同学一起看）
   Wǒde Zhōngwén kèběn zài jiā, yào shàngkè le, zěnme bàn? (gēn tóngxué yìqǐ kàn)

12 多常？ Duō Cháng? / How Often?

Create a sentence that describes the frequency of each action.

1. 李小姐去英国 / 两个月一次
   Lǐ xiǎojiě qù Yīngguó / liǎngge yuè yícì

2. 王先生打高尔夫 / 一个星期一次
   Wáng xiānsheng dǎ gāo'ěrfū / yíge xīngqī yícì

3. 妈妈给外公外婆打电话 / 三天一次
   māma gěi wàigōng wàipó dǎ diànhuà / sāntiān yícì

4. 吴老师旅行 / 一年四次
   Wú lǎoshī lǚxíng / yìnián sìcì

5. 这家百货商店打折 / 一年两次
   zhèijiā bǎihuò shāngdiàn dǎzhé / yìnián liǎngcì

6. 爸爸上电脑课 / 两天一次 bàba shàng diànnǎokè / liǎngtiān yícì

▲ 王先生打高尔夫。

13 劝说 Quànshuō / Suggestions

Look at the pictures and give suggestions by using the adverbs 多 duō or 少 shǎo.

Kāikǒu Shuō

开口说

Communication

---

14 生活频率 **Shēnghuó Pínlǜ** / *Frequencies of Life*

Working in groups of three, take turns asking each other about the frequency of the following things you do in life. Draw a table like the one below and write down the frequencies in Chinese. Mark the most frequent activity and report your findings to the class.

> **Lìzi:** **A:** 你多久运动一次？ Nǐ duōjiǔ yùndòng yícì?
>
> **B:** 我两天运动一次。 Wǒ liǎngtiān yùndòng yícì.
>
> **C:** 我每天运动。 Wǒ měitiān yùndòng.

Activity / Student	运动 yùndòng	逛街 guàngjiē	去图书馆 qù túshūguǎn	看爷爷奶奶 kàn yéye nǎinai	打电子游戏 dǎ diànzǐ yóuxì
A					
B	两天一次 liǎngtiān yícì				
C	每天 měitiān				

---

15 药袋 **Yàodài** / *Medicine Bag*

Refer to the medicine bag and answer the following questions in Chinese.

1. 这是什么诊所？ Zhè shì shénme zhěnsuǒ?

2. 谁生病了？ Shéi shēngbìng le?

3. 哪个眼睛有问题(*problem*)？
   Něige yǎnjīng yǒu wèntí?

4. 他应该多久点(*to drip*)一次药？
   Tā yīnggāi duōjiǔ diǎn yícì yào?

5. 一次点几滴(*drop*)？ Yícì diǎn jǐdī?

6. 这个处方，他应该用多久？
   Zhège chǔfāng, tā yīnggāi yòng duōjiǔ?

健康眼科诊所

挂号电话: 021-6688-1111

病历号：AAR002

姓名：王明

性别：男

年龄：15

用法与用量：
右眼用，每次一滴，每日四次
（建议于开方30天内使用）

Vocabulary

对	duì	v.	*to aim at*
症	zhèng	n.	*symptom*
下	xià	v.	*to issue; to prescribe*

对症下药
duì zhèng xià yào
Let the remedy fit the disease

▲ 对症下药

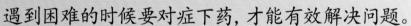

Language Note

The original sentence means to suit the medicine to the illness. This idiom is used metaphorically to say that people should find out the cause of a problem in order to fix it properly.

中文

遇到困难的时候要对症下药，才能有效解决问题。

Yù dào kùnnán de shíhòu yào duì zhèng xià yào, cái néng yǒuxiào jiějué wèntí.

When you are having difficulty resolving a problem, you should take care of whatever caused the problem in order to solve it effectively.

This idiom is formed by connecting two consequential actions: 对症 *duì zhèng* then 下药 *xià yào*. This is a classic form of four-word idioms. Other examples are 成家立业 *chéng jiā lì yè*, meaning to first have a family before one establishes a business (which is a traditional Chinese point of view); and 举一反三 *jǔ yī fǎn sān*, meaning to give one example and use it in other similar situations, and is used to say that a person has great comprehension or practical skills.

身体不舒服

　　我前天精神不好，身体也不舒服。我想我可能[1]太累，所以我早一点回家。我睡了十几个小时，可是昨天起床以后还是发烧，而且[2]全身酸痛无力。妈妈很紧张，马上带我去诊所。医生说我的感冒有点儿严重，因为我又咳嗽又鼻塞，所以需要吃药。医生要妈妈别担心，他说我的病应该一个星期就会好了。我一天得吃四次药，三餐以后和睡觉以前。因为药很苦，所以我吃药以后，就想吃甜甜的东西。我请妈妈买巧克力给我，可是妈妈说我应该少吃甜的，所以她只给我小小的一块。现在我身体不舒服，心情也不好了。

[1] 可能: probably　　[2] 而且: moreover

Shēntǐ Bù Shūfu

Wǒ qiántiān jīngshén bùhǎo, shēntǐ yě bù shūfu. Wǒ xiǎng wǒ kěnéng tài lèi, suǒyǐ wǒ zǎo yìdiǎn huíjiā. Wǒ shuìle shíjǐge xiǎoshí, kěshì zuótiān qǐchuáng yǐhòu háishì fāshāo, érqiě quánshēn suāntòng wúlì. Māma hěn jǐnzhāng, mǎshàng dài wǒ qù zhěnsuǒ. Yīshēng shuō wǒde gǎnmào yǒudiǎnr yánzhòng, yīnwèi wǒ yòu késòu yòu bí sāi, suǒyǐ xūyào chī yào. Yīshēng yào māma bié dānxīn, tā shuō wǒde bìng yīnggāi yíge xīngqī jiù huì hǎole. Wǒ yìtiān děi chī sìcì yào, sāncān yǐhòu hé shuìjiào yǐqián. Yīnwèi yào hěn kǔ, suǒyǐ wǒ chī yào yǐhòu, jiù xiǎng chī tiántián de dōngxi. Wǒ qǐng māma mǎi qiǎokèlì gěi wǒ, kěshì māma shuō wǒ yīnggāi shǎo chī tiánde, suǒyǐ tā zhǐ gěi wǒ xiǎoxiao de yíkuài. Xiànzài wǒ shēntǐ bù shūfu, xīnqíng yě bù hǎole.

16 通晓文意 Tōngxiǎo Wényì / *Understanding the Passage.*

Read the above passage and answer the following questions in Chinese.

1. 他昨天开始不舒服吗？　Tā zuótiān kāishǐ bù shūfu ma?

2. 他睡了多少小时？　Tā shuìle duōshǎo xiǎoshí?

3. 他发烧吗？什么时候(*when*)？　Tā fāshāo ma? Shénme shíhou?

4. 他去了诊所吗？　Tā qùle zhěnsuǒ ma?

5. 为什么他得吃药？他有什么症状？
　Wèishénme tā děi chīyào? Tā yǒu shénme zhèngzhuàng?

6. 他一天得吃几次药？什么时候吃？　Tāyìtiān děi chī jǐcì yào? Shénme shíhou chī?

7. 医生说他的病多久可以好？　Yīshēng shuō tāde bìng duōjiǔ kěyǐ hǎo?

8. 妈妈给他很多巧克力吗？为什么？　Māma gěi tā hěnduō qiǎokèlì ma? Wèishénme?

汉字天地 Hànzì Tiāndì

Chinese Characters

休 ■ xiū ■ to rest

The character 休 *xiū* is a combination of two pictographs. The left side is 人 *rén*, which means "people." The right side is 木 *mù*, which means "tree." The two pictographs combined represent a man leaning against a tree, and the character formed means to rest and to cease.

Stroke Order

ノ	イ	仁	什	休	休

17 词汇延伸 Cíhuì Yánshēn / *Vocabulary Builder*

Below are characters that combine with 休 *xiū* to create new words. Match the Chinese words on the left with the appropriate English meanings on the right.

假 jià	养 yǎng	息 xī	学 xué	市 shì
n. holiday	*v. to feed*	*n. rest*	*v. to learn*	*n. market*

1. 休假 xiūjià   A. to rest
2. 休养 xiūyǎng   B. to take a vacation
3. 休息 xiūxi   C. market closed
4. 休学 xiūxué   D. to recuperate
5. 休市 xiūshì   E. to suspend one's study

18 汉字侦探 Hànzì Zhēntàn / *Visual Detective*

Can you find 休 in the following pictures?

您的豪宅休閒行館

風靡全球 Golf 運動在台灣，行之經年
跨國企業主與政商名流
無不往返於這美麗的小白球故鄉——
國際化最深的林口

關於休旅車‧‧‧‧

隨著週休二日的普及
假風潮的盛行，SUV (S
Vehicle) 的熱潮不斷在台
燒，不論在大街上或各
點，隨處可見 SUV 的蹤

Unit 2

我的一天 Wǒde Yìtiān

In this unit you will be able to:

- express personal moods and interests
- give a compliment
- talk about the amount of time spent on an activity
- give and respond to suggestions
- express alternatives and exclamations
- make a phone call
- express comments and opinions
- describe daily life

Lesson A

Vocabulary

🔊 日常生活 Rìcháng Shēnghuó *Daily Life*

醒
xǐng

v. to wake up

起床
qǐchuáng

v. to get up

刷牙
shuāyá

v.o. to brush one's teeth

洗脸 (洗臉)
xǐliǎn

v.o. to wash one's face

上厕所 (上廁所)
shàng cèsuǒ

v.o. to use the toilet

化妆 (化妝)
huàzhuāng

v. to put on makeup

换衣服 (換衣服)
huàn yīfu

v.o. to change clothes

出门 (出門)
chūmén

v. to go out

做功课 (做功課)
zuò gōngkè

v.o. to do homework

洗澡

xǐzǎo

v.o. to take a shower;
to take a bath

泡澡

pào zǎo

v.o. to take a soak in the tub

吹头发 (吹頭髮)

chuī tóufa

v.o. to blow-dry hair

吃早饭 (吃早飯)

chī zǎofàn

v.o. to have breakfast

午饭 (午飯)	wǔfàn	*n. lunch*
中饭 (中飯)	zhōngfàn	*n. lunch*
晚饭 (晚飯)	wǎnfàn	*n. dinner*
点心 (點心)	diǎnxīn	*n. snack*
夜宵	yèxiāo	*n. late-night snack*

Language Note

For 早饭 *zǎofàn* / 午饭 *wǔfàn* / 中饭 *zhōngfàn* / 晚饭 *wǎnfàn*, you can also replace 饭 *fàn* with 餐 *cān* to form 早餐 *zǎocān* / 午餐 *wǔcān* / 中餐 *zhōngcān* / 晚餐 *wǎncān*.

中文

◀)) 交通工具 Jiāotōng Gōngjù *Transportation*

校车 (校車)

xiàochē

n. school bus

公交车 (公交车)

gōngjiāochē

n. bus

出租车 (出租车)

chūzūchē

n. taxi; cab

火车 (火車)

huǒchē

n. train

船

chuán

n. boat; ship

飞机 (飛機)

fēijī

n. plane

骑自行车(騎自行車)

qí zìxíngchē

v.o. to ride a bicycle

骑摩托车(騎摩托車)

qí mótuōchē

v.o. to ride a motorcycle

开车 (開車)

kāichē

v.o. to drive a car

我坐校车去学校。(我坐校車去學校。)

Wǒ zuò xiàochē qù xuéxiào. *I take the school bus to school.*

....

困死我了！(睏死我了！)

Kùn sǐ wǒ le! *I'm so sleepy!*

....

A: 我今天有三个考试。(我今天有三個考試。)

Wǒ jīntiān yǒu sānge kǎoshì. *I have three tests today.*

B: 难怪你那么紧张。(難怪你那麼緊張。)

Nánguài nǐ nàme jǐnzhāng. *No wonder you're so nervous.*

....

李先生很忙，连吃饭的时间都没有。(李先生很忙，連吃飯的時間都沒有。)

Lǐ xiānsheng hěn máng, lián chīfàn de shíjiān dōu méiyǒu. *Mr. Li is so busy and he doesn't even have time to eat.*

....

A: 星期六的晚会，我应该穿西装吗？(星期六的晚會，我應該穿西裝嗎？)

Xīngqīliù de wǎnhuì, wǒ yīnggāi chuān xīzhuāng ma? *Should I wear a suit for the party on Saturday?*

B: 不用，你穿不穿西装都帅。(不用，你穿不穿西裝都帥。)

Búyòng, nǐ chuān bùchuān xīzhuāng dōu shuài. *No. You look very handsome with or without a suit.*

Adjectives

晚	wǎn	*late*
早	zǎo	*early*
急	jí	*anxious; in a hurry*
湿 (濕)	shī	*wet*

Adverbs

死	sǐ	*extremely*
就要	jiùyào	*be about to; be going to*

Conjunctions

难怪 (難怪)	nánguài	*no wonder*
连 (連)	lián	*even*

Common Expression

没关系 (沒關係)	méiguānxi	*it's okay*

Interjection

咦	yí	*(indicating surprise) well; why; what*

Nouns

时间 (時間)	shíjiān	*time*
车 (車)	chē	*car; vehicle*
学校 (學校)	xuéxiào	*school*

Verbs

等	děng	*to wait*
搭	dā	*to take a ride from someone; to travel by; to go by*
坐	zuò	*to go by; to travel by*
迟到 (遲到)	chídào	*to arrive late; to be late*

Language Note

The verbs 坐 *zuò* and 搭 *dā* both mean of "to travel by." Therefore, 坐飞机 *zuò fēijī* is the same as 搭飞机 *dā fēijī*, and 坐船 *zuò chuán* is the same as 搭船 *dā chuán*. However, when one says 坐车 *zuò chē*, it means "to take transportation," but 搭车 *dā chē* means "to get a ride from someone."

1 交通工具 | Jiāotōng Gōngjù / Transportation

🔊 **You will hear six sentences. Match the person to the type of transportation he or she uses.**

A.

C.

E.

B.

D.

F.

2 用哪个部位? | Yòng něige bùwèi? / *What part of the body is working?*

Identify the activities shown in each of the following images, then decide which of the body parts listed on the right are involved in these actions. Match the correct body part or parts to their corresponding actions.

Lìzi: 吃早饭 *chī zǎofàn* — I.(嘴巴 *zuǐba*)、D.(手 *shǒu*)

A. 腿 *tuǐ*
B. 脸 *liǎn*
C. 头 *tóu*
D. 手 *shǒu*
E. 手指 *shǒuzhǐ*
F. 身体 *shēntǐ*
G. 头发 *tóufa*
H. 牙齿 *yáchǐ*
I. 嘴巴 *zuǐba*

Answer the following questions in Chinese based on your own experiences and opinions.

1. 你今天几点起床？ Nǐ jīntiān jǐdiǎn qǐchuáng?

2. 你起床以后洗澡，还是睡觉以前洗澡？
   Nǐ qǐchuáng yǐhòu xǐzǎo, háishì shuìjiào yǐqián xǐzǎo?

3. 洗头发以后，你吹头发吗？ Xǐ tóufa yǐhòu, nǐ chuī tóufa ma?

4. 你平常化妆吗？ Nǐ píngcháng huàzhuāng ma?

5. 你怎么来学校？ Nǐ zěnme lái xuéxiào?

句型介绍 Jùxíng Jièshào
Language Patterns

The Pattern "Adj 死了 *sǐle*"

This pattern uses an exaggeration to describe that, for someone, something has reached an extreme level.

Adjective + 死了 *sǐle*

我累死了，事情怎么那么多！
Wǒ lèi sǐle, shìqíng zěnme nàme duō!

妹妹八点才回家，爸爸紧张死了。
Mèimei bādiǎn cái huíjiā, bàba jǐnzhāng sǐle.

A few adjectives can also be used in the following pattern, usually with 我 *wǒ* as the object . For example, 饿 *è*, 渴 *kě*, 累 *lèi*, 困 *kùn*, 气 *qì*, 疼 *téng*, etc.

Verb + 死 *sǐ* + **Object** + 了 *le*

我昨天只睡了三个小时，困死我了。
Wǒ zuótiān zhǐ shuì le sānge xiǎoshí, kùn sǐ wǒ le.

饿死我了！我们几点可以吃晚饭？
È sǐ wǒ le! Wǒmen jǐdiǎn chī wǎnfàn?

▲ 妹妹八点才回家，爸爸紧张死了。

The Conjunction 难怪 *nánguài*

The conjunction 难怪 *nánguài* means "no wonder." It is used when the speaker reaches a conclusion after comparing the current situation with a preceding one. It is followed or preceded with an explanation.

A: 你发烧了。 Nǐ fāshāo le.

B: 难怪我全身热热的。 Nánguài wǒ quán shēn rèrè de.

A: 我下个星期要去旅行！ Wǒ xiàge xīngqī yào qù lǚxíng!

B: 难怪你心情这么好。 Nánguài nǐ xīnqíng zhème hǎo.

The Pattern "V 不 *bù* / *bú* V (O) 都 *dōu*"

This pattern is used to indicate that whether something is done or not, the result will be the same. For verbs with negative objects, only the repeating verb has the object attached. Sometimes, to put emphasis on the object, the object is moved to the front of the sentence.

> **Subject** + **Verb** + **不 *bù* / *bú*** + **Verb** + **(Object)** + **都 *dōu*** + **result**

你的病不严重，看不看医生都没关系。

Nǐde bìng bù yánzhòng, kàn búkàn yīshēng dōu méi guānxi.

> **Object**, **Subject** + **Verb** + **不 *bù* / *bú*** + **Verb** + **都 *dōu*** + **result**

李文的生日晚会，你去不去都可以。 Lǐ Wén de shēngrì wǎnhuì, nǐ qù búqù dōu kěyǐ.

When the verb is 有 *yǒu*, the pattern should be 有没有 *yǒu méiyǒu*.

我们已经有很多种水果了，
所以有没有果汁都行吧。

Wǒmen yǐjīng yǒu hěn duō zhǒng shuǐguǒ le,
suǒyǐ yǒu méiyǒu guǒzhī dōu xíng ba.

Other adjectives can also be used in this pattern. If it is a disyllabic word, one can omit the second character of the second adjective.

▲ 很多种水果

> **Subject** + **Adjective** + **不 *bù* / *bú*** + **Adjective** + **都 *dōu*** + **result**

你累不累都得做功课。 Nǐ lèi búlèi dōu děi zuò gōngkè.

这道菜好不好吃你都得吃。 Zhèidào cài hǎo bù hǎochī nǐ dōu děi chī.

The use of 了 *le* to indicate time spent on an ongoing action

We learned how to express time spent performing an action in Unit 1, Lesson A. In that lesson, the action was already complete when the speaker spoke about it. In this lesson, we are talking about an action that has already begun but is still ongoing.

Subject + **Verb** + 了 *le* + **Time Spent** + 了 *le*

妹妹玩了半个小时了。 Mèimei wánle bàngè xiǎoshí le.

他们已经走了四十分钟了。 Tāmen yǐjīng zǒule sìshífēn zhōng le.

When the sentence contains a verb with an object and the action involved is being mentioned for the first time, we first state the complete verb plus object action, so that our audience knows what we are going to be talking about, and then repeat the verb with 了 *le*, before announcing the time.

Subject + **Verb-Object** + **Verb** + 了 *le* + **Time Spent** + 了 *le*

我们学中文学了一年了。 Wǒmen xué Zhōngwén xuéle yìnián le.

姐姐洗澡已经洗了一个钟头了。 Jiějie xǐzǎo yǐjīng xǐle yíge zhōngtóu le.

Another way to say it is to put the object between the time spent and the final 了 *le*.

Subject + **Verb** + 了 *le* + **Time Spent** + **Object** + 了 *le*

我们学了一年中文了。 Wǒmen xuéle yìnián Zhōngwén le.

姐姐已经洗了一个钟头澡了。 Jiějie yǐjīng xǐle yíge zhōngtóu zǎo le.

To Express an Imminent Action with the Pattern 就要…了 *jiùyào… le*

You learned the pattern (快)要…了 *(kuài) yào… le* in Level 1, Unit 4, Lesson D. The pattern 就要…了 *jiùyào… le* is similar, but the meaning of the adverb 就要 *jiùyào* is stronger than 快要 *kuài yào* and 要 *yào*. The adverb 就要 *jiùyào* means "to be about to," which indicates that the action is likely to happen in the next few moments.

▲ 十二点就要到了

Subject + 就要 *jiùyào* + **Verb Phrase** + 了 *le*

公交车就要走了。 Gōngjiāochē jiùyào zǒule.

你就要睡了，别吃太多东西。 Nǐ jiùyào shuìle, bié chī tài duō dōngxi.

十二点就要到了。 Shí'èrdiǎn jiùyào dàole.

🔊 快迟到了 Kuài Chídào Le *Running Late*

Qian Yongli is waiting for the bus at the bus stop. Li Yunying is running towards the bus stop.

钱永利:	你今天晚了!	Qián Yǒnglì:	Nǐ jīntiān wǎnle!
李云英:	我七点才起床,刷牙洗脸,还得洗澡,急死我了!	Lǐ Yúnyīng:	Wǒ qīdiǎn cái qǐchuáng, shuāyá xǐliǎn, hái děi xǐzǎo, jí sǐ wǒ le!
钱永利:	难怪你的头发湿湿的。	Qián Yǒnglì:	Nánguài nǐde tóufa shīshī de.
李云英:	看,我也没有时间化妆。	Lǐ Yúnyīng:	Kàn, wǒ yě méiyǒu shíjiān huàzhuāng.
钱永利:	没关系,你化不化妆都很漂亮。	Qián Yǒnglì:	Méi guānxi, nǐ huà bú huàzhuāng dōu hěn piàoliang.
李云英:	你等车等了多久了?	Lǐ Yúnyīng:	Nǐ děng chē děngle duōjiǔ le?
钱永利:	我等了二十分钟了。	Qián Yǒnglì:	Wǒ děngle èrshífēn zhōng le.
李云英:	二十分钟?现在几点了?	Lǐ Yúnyīng:	Èrshífēn zhōng? Xiànzài jǐdiǎn le?
钱永利:	七点半,我们就要迟到了。	Qián Yǒnglì:	Qīdiǎn bàn, wǒmen jiùyào chídào le.
李云英:	是啊。	Lǐ Yúnyīng:	Shì a.
钱永利:	咦,那不是林老师的车吗?	Qián Yǒnglì:	Yí, nà búshì Lín lǎoshī de chē ma?
李云英:	太好了,我们搭林老师的车去学校吧!	Lǐ Yúnyīng:	Tài hǎole, wǒmen dā Lín lǎoshī de chē qù xuéxiào ba!

4 她做了什么？ **Tā zuò le shénme?** / *What did she do?*

Based on the dialogue, identify which of the following activities Li Yunying did before going to the bus stop.

A.

C.

E.

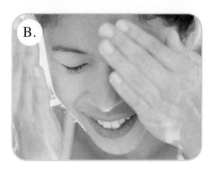

B.

D.

F.

5 关键词 **Guānjiàncí** / *Keywords*

Complete the following sentences according to the information provided in the dialogue.

1. ___ 今天晚了。 ___ jīntiān wǎnle.

2. 李云英 ___ 点起床。 Lǐ Yúnyīng ___ diǎn qǐchuáng.

3. 起床以后，李云英 ___、 ___，还要 ___。
   Qǐchuáng yǐhòu, Lǐ Yúnyīng ___, ___ hái yào ___.

4. 李云英很 ___，因为她太晚起床了。
   Lǐ Yúnyīng hěn ___, yīnwèi tā tài wǎn qǐchuáng le.

5. 李云英的头发 ___，因为她没有时间吹头发。
   Lǐ Yúnyīng de tóufa ___, yīnwèi tā méiyǒu shíjiān chuī tóufa.

6. 李云英也没有时间 ___，可是钱永利说她化不化妆都很 ___。
   Lǐ Yúnyīng yě méiyǒu shíjiān ___, kěshì Qián Yǒnglì shuō tā huà bú huàzhuāng dōu hěn ___.

7. 钱永利等车等了 ___ 分钟了。 Qián Yǒnglì děng chē děngle ___ fēn zhōng le.

8. 他们看到(*saw*) ___ 的车。 Tāmen kàndào ___ de chē.

Review the times shown on the clocks below and identify what Li Yunying and Qian Yongli were doing at each particular time.

1.

2.

3.

文化橱窗 Wénhuà Chúchuāng

Culture Window

Dress Code and Etiquette in Chinese Schools

In most Chinese elementary and middle schools, there are strict regulations regarding the dress code and manners. Students are required to wear uniforms (校服 *xiàofú* or 制服 *zhìfú*). Typically, there will also be a gym uniform for students to wear when doing sports. Each student will have two sets of uniforms: a summer uniform and a winter uniform. Having students wear the same clothes not only strengthens their sense of belonging and school pride, but more importantly, it eliminates the chance for students to compare each other's clothing. No matter what their family's income level, all students look the same.

▲ *Some Chinese students wear the uniforms.*

In addition to wearing uniforms, students must follow strict rules regarding hairstyles, makeup, and accessories. Boys must wear their hair short and cannot wear hairstyles that may be considered offbeat or unusual. Both girls and boys are forbidden to perm or dye their hair. Students are also forbidden to use makeup, wear flip-flops or high-heels, or have piercings or tattoos.

Schools also place great emphasis on students' manners. Students are required to show respect to teachers and peers and to follow the rules of the classroom. When class begins and the teacher enters the room, students rise to their feet and

▲ *Chinese high school students*

greet the teacher. The students may be seated after the teacher answers their greeting. If a student is late to class and the teacher is already in the classroom, the student must call out "报告 *bàogào*" at the doorway and wait for the teacher's permission to enter.

During class, Chinese students silently listen and take notes while the teacher is speaking. They may raise their hands if they have questions. When speaking in class, students must stand up and speak Mandarin clearly. At the end of class, students again stand and bid the teacher "再见

▲ *The students greet the teacher in the beginning of a class.*

zàijiàn" before following the teacher out of the classroom. When students meet a teacher outside of the classroom, they must also greet the teacher, and when visiting a teacher's or administrator's office, they must knock and receive permission before entering.

7 文化动动脑 Wénhuà Dòngdòngnǎo / Cultural Check-up

On a separate sheet of paper, write a short answer in English for each question.

1. What do Chinese students wear to school?
2. What sorts of footwear are forbidden in Chinese schools?
3. What are two advantages of uniforms?
4. What should students do to show respect when a teacher enters the classroom at the beginning of class?
5. If a student is late, what must the student say in order to be allowed into the classroom?
6. What should students do when they wish to speak in class?

▲ *Do you like our uniforms?*

语言练习 Yǔyán Liànxí
Language Practice

8 夸张一点儿 Kuāzhāng Yìdiǎnr / *Exaggerate a Little*

Complete the following sentences using the provided words and the pattern "Adj. 死了 sǐ le."

1. 爸爸上班迟到了，他 __ 了。(急) Bàba shàngban chídào le, tā ___ le. (jí)

2. 公交车现在才来，__。(急) Gōngjiāochē xiànzài cái lái, ___. (jí)

3. 我跌倒(to fall)了，膝盖 __。(痛) Wǒ diēdǎo le, xīgài ___. (tòng)

4. 我昨天慢跑跑了三个小时，腿 __。(酸)
   Wǒ zuótiān mànpǎo pǎole sānge xiǎoshí, tuǐ ___. (suān)

5. 他最喜欢的背包不见了，他 __。(难过)
   Tā zuì xǐhuan de beibāo bú jiàn le, tā ___. (nánguò)

6. 昨天二十五度，今天突然十二度，__。(冷)
   Zuótiān èrshíwǔ dù, jīntiān tūrán shí'èr dù, ___. (lěng)

▲ 上班迟到了

7. 吴森上个星期一考试，打篮球比赛，去合唱团练习，__。(忙)
   Wú Sēn shàngge Xīngqīyī kǎoshì, dǎ lánqiú bǐsài, qù héchàngtuán liànxí, ___. (máng)

9 恍然大悟 Huǎngrán-dàwù / *Sudden Realizations*

With a classmate, take turns reading from column A and commenting on the statements by using a corresponding response from column B with the adverb 难怪 *nánguài* placed at the beginning.

Person A	Person B
1. 我弟弟生病了。 Wǒ dìdi shēngbìng le.	A. 他坐出租车来。 Tā zuò chūzūchē lái.
2. 李先生今天迟到。 Lǐ xiānsheng jīntiān chídào.	B. 你今天精神很好。 Nǐ jīntiān jīngshén hěn hǎo.
3. 我不知道要穿什么。 Wǒ bù zhīdào yào chuān shénme.	C. 你爸妈那么担心。 Nǐ bà-mā nàme dānxīn.
4. 我昨天睡了十个小时。 Wǒ zuótiān shuìle shíge xiǎoshí.	D. 你换衣服换那么久。 Nǐ huàn yīfu huàn nàme jiǔ.
5. 他写功课写到十二点。 Tā xiě gōngkè xiědào shí'èr diǎn.	E. 他今天上课打瞌睡。 Tā jīntiān shàngkè dǎ kēshuì.
6. 爸爸中饭只吃了一个面包。 Bàba zhōngfàn zhǐ chīle yíge miànbāo.	F. 他六点就想吃晚饭了。 Tā liùdiǎn jiù xiǎng chī wǎnfàn le.

10 什么都可以 **Shénme dōu kěyǐ.** / *Whatever works.*

Read the following sentences and paraphrase them using the pattern "V 不 *bù* / *bú* V (O) 都 *dōu*."

1. 你去也可以，不去也可以。
   Nǐ qù yě kěyǐ, búqù yě kěyǐ.

2. 他喜欢，我要买。他不喜欢，我也要买。
   Tā xǐhuan, wǒ yào mǎi. Tā bù xǐhuan, wǒ yě yào mǎi.

3. 早上你饿，要吃早餐。你不饿，也要吃早餐。
   Zǎoshang nǐ è, yào chī zǎocān. Nǐ bú'è, yě yào chī zǎocān.

4. 考试的时候，我念书。不考试的时候，我也念书。
   Kǎoshì de shíhou, wǒ niànshū. Bù kǎoshì de shíhou, wǒ yě niànshū.

5. 天气好的时候，妈妈慢跑。天气不好的时候，妈妈也慢跑。
   Tiānqì hǎo de shíhou, māma mànpǎo. Tiānqì bùhǎo de shíhou, māma yě mànpǎo.

6. 上课的时候，我精神好，不打瞌睡。精神不好，也不打瞌睡。
   Shàngkè de shíhou, wǒ jīngshén hǎo, bùdǎ kēshuì. Jīngshén bùhǎo, yě bùdǎ kēshuì.

11 持续的时间 **Chíxù de Shíjiān** / *Duration*

With a classmate, look at the following visuals and take turns asking each other how long each action has lasted.

Lìzi: A: 他在中国玩了多久了？ Tā zài Zhōngguó wánle duōjiǔ le?
　　　　 B: 他在中国玩了十天了。 Tā zài Zhōngguó wánle shítiān le.

1.

2.

3.

4.

5.

6.

就要发生了 **Jiùyào Fāshēng le** / *About to Happen*

Look at the following images and describe each one using the pattern "就要…了 *jiùyào… le.*"

1.

3.

2.

4.

开口说 Kāikǒu Shuō

Communication

13 **小小调查** **Xiǎoxiǎo Diàochá** / *A Survey*

 Find out how much time your classmates spend on specific activities each day. Draw a table like the one shown below. In the table, write the names of five daily routines in Chinese, and then ask five of your classmates how long they spend on these activities. Record their responses in the chart below and then circle the most time (最 *zuì*) spent on each activity.

Lìzi: A: 你每天洗澡洗多久？ Nǐ měitiān xǐzǎo xǐ duōjiǔ?

B: 我每天洗二十分钟。 Wǒ měitiān xǐ èrshífēn zhōng.

Activity / Student	洗澡 xǐzǎo	吃晚饭 chī wǎnfàn	锻炼 duànliàn	念书 niànshū	睡觉 shuìjiào
B	20分钟				

14 上学路上 Shàngxué Lù shàng / The Way to School

With a partner, make up a conversation that might occur while waiting for a bus to arrive or while riding on a bus. Write the conversation down and submit it to your teacher for correction. The teacher may choose to select a few pairs to perform their created conversations for the class.

15 周末活动 Zhōumò Huódòng / Weekend Activities

The following is a survey that shows the top three weekend activities of senior high school students from four different countries. Review the information provided and answer the questions that follow.

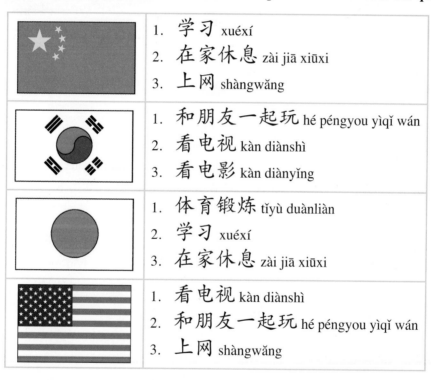

	1. 学习 xuéxí
	2. 在家休息 zài jiā xiūxi
	3. 上网 shàngwǎng
	1. 和朋友一起玩 hé péngyou yìqǐ wán
	2. 看电视 kàn diànshì
	3. 看电影 kàn diànyǐng
	1. 体育锻炼 tǐyù duànliàn
	2. 学习 xuéxí
	3. 在家休息 zài jiā xiūxi
	1. 看电视 kàn diànshì
	2. 和朋友一起玩 hé péngyou yìqǐ wán
	3. 上网 shàngwǎng

1. 哪些国家的高中生周末学习?
   Něixiē guójiā de gāozhōngshēng zhōumò xuéxí?

2. 哪些国家的高中生周末常常和朋友一起玩?
   Něixiē guójiā de gāozhōngshēng zhōumò chángcháng hé péngyou yìqǐ wán?

3. 每个国家的高中生周末都想在家休息,对不对?
   Měige guójiā de gāozhōngshēng zhōumò dōu xiǎng zài jiā xiūxi, duì búduì?

4. 美国的高中生周末最喜欢做什么?
   Měiguó de gāozhōngshēng zhōumò zuì xǐhuan zuò shénme?

5. 日本的高中生周末最喜欢做什么?
   Rìběn de gāozhōngshēng zhōumò zuì xǐhuan zuò shénme?

Zìwǒ Tíshēng

Raising the Bar

Vocabulary

惊	jīng	*n.*	*fright*
无	wú	*v.*	*to not have*
险	xiǎn	*n.*	*danger*

▲ 有惊无险

有惊无险
yǒujīng-wúxiǎn
A scare without danger

Language Note

This means that a situation that looks frightening may not be dangerous at all. The phrase is used to acknowledge that although there seemed to be many obstacles to overcome, everything eventually worked out.

这场地震很大，但没有人受伤，可以说是有惊无险。

Zhèchǎng dìzhèn hěn dà, dàn méiyǒu rén shòushāng, kěyǐ shuō shì yǒujīng-wúxiǎn

The earthquake was a big one, but there were no injuries. It was a scare without any danger.

Below are some idioms that also use the pattern "有 *yǒu* …无 *wú* …"

1. "有口无心 *yǒukǒu-wúxīn*": This idiom is used to describe a person who says things he or she might not mean.

   他说话有口无心，你别生气。

   Tā shuōhuà yǒukǒu-wúxīn, nǐ bié shēngqì.

   He speaks without thinking first. Don't be upset.

2. "有眼无珠 *yǒuyǎn-wúzhū*" 珠 *zhū* is 眼珠 *yǎnzhū* (eyeball): This is a negative phrase used to say that a person cannot tell right from wrong, and is often used to scold oneself or others.

   你真是有眼无珠，不知道他是校长。

   Nǐ zhēnshì yǒuyǎn-wúzhū, bù zhīdào tā shì xiàozhǎng.

   You have to really be blind to not know that he's the principal.

迟到

最近天气比较冷，所以我常常赖床¹。我几乎每天都迟到，妈妈很生气。她要我晚上早一点睡觉，看电视只能看到十点半。我很不高兴，可是也没办法。昨天我练习棒球，很累，所以很早就睡了。今天早上起床的时候，我看到时间是八点五十，我吓²死了！我马上刷牙洗脸，可是我想我没有时间洗澡，所以只换了衣服，我很担心我会臭³臭的。我请妈妈开车带我去学校，妈妈觉得很奇怪，她问我："为什么你星期六要去学校？"天啊，我太紧张了！

¹赖床: to linger in one's bed   ²吓: to scare   ³臭: to smell bad

Chídào

Zuìjìn tiānqi bǐjiào lěng, suǒyǐ wǒ chángcháng lài chuáng. Wǒ jīhū měitiān dōu chídào, māma hěn shēngqì. Tā yào wǒ wǎnshang zǎo yìdiǎn shuìjiào, kàn diànshì zhǐnéng kàn dào shídiǎn bàn. Wǒ hěn bù gāoxìng, kěshì yě méi bànfǎ. Zuótiān wǒ liànxí bàngqiú, hěn lèi, suǒyǐ hěn zǎo jiù shuìle. Jīntiān zǎoshang qǐchuáng de shíhou, wǒ kàndào shíjiān shì bādiǎn wǔshí, wǒ xià sǐle! Wǒ mǎshàng shuāyá xǐliǎn, kěshì wǒ xiǎng wǒ méiyǒu shíjiān xǐzǎo, suǒyǐ zhǐ huànle yīfu, wǒ hěn dānxīn wǒ huì chòuchòu de. Wǒ qǐng māma kāichē dài wǒ qù xuéxiào, māma juéde hěn qíguài, tā wèn wǒ: "Wèishénme nǐ Xīngqīliù yào qù xuéxiào?" Tiān a, wǒ tài jǐnzhāng le!

---

16 通晓文意 Tōngxiǎo Wényì / *Understanding the Passage*

Read the above passage and decide if the statements are true or false. Correct any false statements.

1. 因为他最近练习棒球，所以常常赖床。
   Yīnwèi tā zuìjìn liànxí bàngqiú, suǒyǐ chángcháng lài chuáng.

2. 他几乎每天都迟到，所以他妈妈很生气。
   Tā jīhū měitiān dōu chídào, suǒyǐ tā māma hěn shēngqì.

3. 他很喜欢看电视，所以他不听妈妈的话，每天还是看到十二点。
   Tā hěn xǐhuan kàn diànshì, suǒyǐ tā bùtīng māma de huà, měitiān háishì kàndào shí'èrdiǎn.

4. 他昨天很累，所以很早就睡了。 Tā zuótiān hěn lèi, suǒyǐ hěn zǎojiù shuìle.

5. 他今天早上八点五十分起床。 Tā jīntiān zǎoshang bādiǎn wǔshífēn qǐchuáng.

6. 因为天气很冷，所以他早上不想洗澡。
   Yīnwèi tiānqì hěn lěng, suǒyǐ tā zǎoshang bù xiǎng xǐzǎo.

7. 他妈妈觉得他臭臭的很奇怪。 Tā māma juéde tā chòuchòu de hěn qíguài.

汉字天地　Hànzì Tiāndì

Chinese Characters

车 / 車 ■ chē ■ vehicle

The character 车 *chē* is a pictograph. In ancient times, the chariot had spokes, a shaft, and yokes. People wrote 車 *chē* based on a bird's eye view of a car. The yoke was depicted in the front, with the two wheels in the back. It was then simplified to a wheel with an axle in the middle. 車 *chē* is also a common radical in words related to vehicles. Knowing this can help us better understand the meaning of some Chinese words.

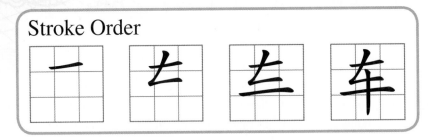

Stroke Order

17 词汇延伸　Cíhuì Yánshēn / Vocabulary Builder

Below are characters that combine with 车 *chē* to create new words. Match the Chinese words on the left with the appropriate English meanings on the right.

票 piào	库 kù	费 fèi	厢 xiāng	祸 huò
n. ticket	*n. warehouse*	*n. fee*	*n. compartment*	*n. misfortune*

1. 车票 chēpiào   A. fare
2. 车库 chēkù   B. traffic accident
3. 车费 chēfèi   C. train or bus ticket
4. 车厢 chēxiāng   D. garage
5. 车祸 chēhuò   E. railway carriage

18 汉字侦探 Hànzì Zhēntàn / *Visual Detective*

Can you find 车 in the following pictures?

沪售
12车043号
二等座

中途下车失效
26A0-0828-9

馆   39、售票厅
40、市场
41、停车场
42、停车场
43、寄存处

上海公交汽电车乘

车

号
证号
日期
上/下车
单价(元)
里程(km)
等候

手写无效

Lesson B

🔊 课外活动 Kèwài Huódòng *Extracurricular Activities*

话剧 (話劇)

huàjù

n. drama

艺术 (藝術)

yìshù

n. art

舞蹈

wǔdǎo

n. dance

童子军 (童子軍)

tóngzǐjūn

n. scouts

摄影 (攝影)

shèyǐng

n. photography

校刊

xiàokān

n. school paper

运动 (運動)

yùndòng

n. sports

志愿者 (志願者)

zhìyuànzhě

n. volunteer

乐团 (樂團)

yuètuán

n. band

合唱团 (合唱團)
héchàngtuán
n. chorus, choir

社团 (社團)
shètuán
n. club

打工
dǎgōng
vo. to have a part-time job

Language Note

To say what activities you participate in, just say the category plus 社 *shè*.
For example, 话剧社 *huàjù shè*, 舞蹈社 *wǔdǎo shè*, 校刊社 *xiàokān shè*, etc.

打工选择 (打工選擇) Dǎgōng Xuǎnzé *Choices of Part-time Jobs*

家教	jiājiào	*n. tutor*
保姆	bǎomǔ	*n. baby-sitter*
店员 (店員)	diànyuán	*n. sales clerk*
服务员 (服務員)	fúwùyuán	*n. waiter / waitress*

Language Note

In Chinese, we usually use 服务员 *fúwùyuán* to cover both male and female
ones. Therefore, when we need to call for the waiter / waitress' attention,
just say 服务员 *fúwùyuán*.

我明天要去一个晚会，你可以帮我化妆吗？

Wǒ míngtiān yào qù yíge wǎnhuì, nǐ kěyǐ bāng wǒ huàzhuāng ma?

I'm going to a party tomorrow, can you do my makeup for me?

放学以后，来我家玩电子游戏吧！

Fàngxué yǐhòu, lái wǒ jiā wán diànzǐ yóuxì ba!

Come to my house to play video games after school!

虽然我很想去，但是不行，我得打工。

Suīrán wǒ hěn xiǎng qù, dànshì bù xíng, wǒ děi dǎgōng.

Although I really want to go, I can't. I have to work part-time.

要是你累了，就去睡觉，别看书了。

（要是你累了，就去睡覺，別看書了。）

Yàoshì nǐ lèile, jiù qù shuìjiào, bié kànshū le.

If you're tired, go to bed. Stop reading.

· ·

A: 这本书可以借给我吗？

（這本書可以借給我嗎？）

Zhèi běn shū kěyǐ jiè gěi wǒ ma?

Can you lend me this book?

B: 可以是可以，可是只能借你一天。

（可以是可以，可是只能借你一天。）

Kěyǐ shì kěyǐ, kěshì zhǐnéng jiè nǐ yìtiān.

I can, but only for one day.

Adjective

忙	máng	busy

Adverbs

的确 (的確)	díquè	indeed; really
又	yòu	again

Conjunctions

虽然 (雖然)	suīrán	although
但是	dànshì	but
要是 ...	yàoshì	if
如果 ...	rúguǒ	if

Nouns

功课 (功課)	gōngkè	homework
空	kòng	free time

Particle

吧	ba	used at the end of a sentence to indicate doubt or conjecture

Preposition

给 (給)	gěi	for

Verbs

帮 (幫)	bāng	to help
让 (讓)	ràng	to let; to allow
是	shì	used to express emphasis and to indicate certainty
忘记 (忘記)	wàngjì	to forget
记得 (記得)	jìde	to remember
上学 (上學)	shàngxué	to go to school
放学 (放學)	fàngxué	to finish school
照顾 (照顧)	zhàogù	to take care (of sb.)
学习 (學習)	xuéxí	to study

Verb-Complement

出去	chūqù	to go out

Verb-Object

打电话 (打電話)	dǎ diànhuà	to make a phone call

1 课外活动 Kèwài Huódòng / Extracurricular Activities

🔊 **You will hear six activities. Match each activity with the appropriate illustration.**

2 兼职工作 Jiānzhí Gōngzuò / Part-time Jobs

🔊 **You will hear four sentences. Based on the sentences, identify the appropriate job title for each.**

A. 家教 jiājiào   B. 保姆 bǎomǔ   C. 店员 diànyuán   D. 服务员 fúwùyuán

3 个人问题 Gèrén Wèntí / Personal Questions

Answer the following questions in Chinese based on your own experiences and opinions.

1. 你打工吗？你做什么？一个星期做几个小时？
   Nǐ dǎgōng ma? Nǐ zuò shénme? Yíge xīngqī zuò jǐge xiǎoshí?

2. 你喜欢照顾人吗？动物呢？ Nǐ xǐhuan zhàogù rén ma? Dòngwù ne?

3. 你有空的时候，喜欢做什么？ Nǐ yǒukòng de shíhou, xǐhuan zuò shénme?

4. 晚上十一点，你爸妈还让你出去吗？
   Wǎnshang shíyì diǎn, nǐ bà-mā hái ràng nǐ chūqù ma?

5. 你常常忘记事情(things)吗？ Nǐ chángcháng wàngjì shìqíng ma?

6. 你喜欢给朋友打电话吗？ Nǐ xǐhuan gěi péngyou dǎ diànhuà ma?

7. 你记得全家人的生日吗？ Nǐ jìde quán jiārén de shēngrì ma?

句型介绍 Jùxíng Jièshào

Language Patterns

The Pattern "虽然…，但是… *suīrán…, dànshì…*"

The pattern 虽然…，但是… *suīrán…, dànshì…* is formed from a pair of conjunctions that show concession. It is similar to the English pattern "although…" The word 但是 *dànshì* can be replaced with 可是 *kěshì*. The word 虽然 *suīrán* is optional and can be placed either before or after the subject, but 但是 *dànshì* cannot be omitted.

虽然 *suīrán* + Sentence 1 , 但是 *dànshì* /可是 *kěshì* +

Sentence 2

虽然中文不容易，但是弟弟还是想学。
Suīrán Zhōngwén bù róngyì, dànshì dìdi háishì xiǎng xué.

虽然我周末有空，可是我得在家照顾妹妹。
Suīrán wǒ zhōumò yǒu kòng, kěshì wǒ děi zài jiā zhàogù mèimei.

▲ 中文不容易

The Pattern "…是…，可是… *…shì…, kěshì…*"

This pattern is used to express the speaker's opinions in an indirect manner. The front half "…是 *shì*…" repeats an existing situation of which the speaker concedes the truth. The latter half is introduced with 可是 *kěshì*, where the speaker states his opinions or feelings. The word 可是 *kěshì* can be replaced with 但是 *dànshì*.

(Something) + Verb / Adjective + 是 *shì* + Verb / Adjective , 可是 *kěshì* + Sentence

A: 这件衬衫真好看，你应该买。 Zhèjiàn chènshān zhēn hǎokàn, nǐ yīnggāi mǎi.
B: 好看是好看，但是我觉得太贵了。 Hǎokān shì hǎokān, dànshì wǒ juédé tài guì le.

A: 这个药好苦，我不要吃。 Zhèige yào hǎo kǔ, wǒ búyào chī.
B: 药苦是苦，可是你生病了就得吃。 Yào kǔ shì kǔ, kěshì nǐ shēngbìng le jiù děi chī.

The Pattern "要是…就… *yàoshì…jiù…*"

This pattern is used for hypothetical situations, and is similar to the English pattern "if…then…." The word 要是 *yàoshì* can be replaced with 如果 *rúguǒ*.

要是 *yàoshì* /如果 *rúguǒ* + Sentence 1 , 就 *jiù* + Sentence 2

要是你可以来，就给我打电话。 Yàoshì nǐ kěyǐ lái, jiù gěi wǒ dǎ diànhuà.
要是你每天运动，就会比较健康。 Yàoshì nǐ měitiān yùndòng, jiù huì bǐjiào jiànkāng.

Language Note

The structure 的话 *dehuà* also means "if", but unlike the two conjunctions 要是 *yàoshì* and 如果 *rúguǒ*, it is placed at the end of the hypothetical clause.

Sentence 1 + 的话 *dehuà*, 就 *jiù* + Sentence 2

明天天气好的话，我们就出去玩。
Míngtiān tiānqì hǎo dehuà, wǒmen jiù chūqù wán.

The word 的话 *dehuà* can even be combined with 要是 *yàoshì* and 如果 *rúguǒ* to form the pattern below. However, this pattern is only used when the hypothetical sentence is not too long.

要是 *yàoshì* / 如果 *rúguǒ* + Sentence 1 + 的话 *dehuà*, 就 *jiù* + Sentence 2

如果你喜欢唱歌的话，就去合唱团吧。
Rúguǒ nǐ xǐhuan chànggē dehuà, jiù qù héchàngtuán ba.

The Pattern 是... *shì*... used for Emphasis

You learned in Level 1 text adjectives in Chinese sometimes function as verbs so a verb is not always necessary in a sentence. However, if you want to express emphatic agreement or approval to a statement heard, you can place the verb 是 *shì* in front of the content you would like to emphasize. Note that the word 是 *shì* is usually pronounced emphatically.

Subject + 是 *shì* + (Adverb) + Adjective / Verb Phrase

A: 这件外套很漂亮。 Zhèijiàn wàitào hěn piàoliang.

B: 是很漂亮呀！我很喜欢。 Shì hěn piàoliang ya! Wǒ hěn xǐhuan.

A: 你不喜欢这道菜，对不对？ Nǐ bù xǐhuan zhèidào cài, duì búduì?

B: 嗯，我是不喜欢，这道菜太辣了。 Èn, wǒ shì bù xǐhuan, zhèidào cài tài là le.

The Pattern "又 *yòu*"

"又 *yòu*" means "again," but unlike "again" in English which can refer to something in both the past and the future, it refers to something which has happened in the past and that the speaker does not want to see repeated in the future. It cannot refer to something which is going to happen again in the future.

Subject + 又 *yòu* + Verb Phrase + 了 *le*

你今天又迟到了！ Nǐ jīntiān yòu chídào le!
我上个月感冒，这个月又感冒了。
Wǒ shàngge yuè gǎnmào, zhèige yuè yòu gǎnmào le.

▲ 你今天又迟到了！

🔊 忙碌的生活 Mánglù de Shēnghuó *Busy Life*

Four friends are chatting about what they are planning to do after school.

吴森:	放学了！我们要不要去打网球？	Wú Sēn:	Fàngxué le! Wǒmen yào búyào qù dǎ wǎngqiú?
钱永利:	不行，我得去图书馆打工。	Qián Yǒnglì:	Bùxíng, wǒ děi qù túshūguǎn dǎgōng.
李云英:	我要回家帮我妈照顾我弟弟妹妹。	Lǐ Yúnyīng:	Wǒ yào huíjiā bāng wǒ mā zhàogù wǒ dìdi mèimei.
赵梅:	别看我，我要做功课。	Zhào Méi:	Bié kàn wǒ, wǒ yào zuò gōngkè.
吴森:	晚饭以后，你们有没有空？	Wú Sēn:	Wǎnfàn yǐhòu, nǐmen yǒu méiyǒu kòng?
钱永利:	虽然有空，但是我爸妈不让我出去玩儿。	Qián Yǒnglì:	Suīrán yǒu kòng, dànshì wǒ bà-mā búràng wǒ chūqù wánr.
李云英:	我有是有空，可是我要学习。	Lǐ Yúnyīng:	Wǒ yǒu shì yǒu kòng, kěshì wǒ yào xuéxí.
赵梅:	要是我没事，我就给你打电话。	Zhào Méi:	Yàoshì wǒ méishì, wǒ jiù gěi nǐ dǎ diànhuà
吴森:	你们怎么都那么忙？	Wú Sēn:	Nǐmen zěnme dōu nàme máng?
李云英:	的确是很忙啊！明天有数学和化学的考试呢！	Lǐ Yúnyīng:	Díquè shì hěn máng a! Míngtiān yǒu shùxué hé huàxué de kǎoshì ne!
赵梅:	你一定又忘记了吧？	Zhào Méi:	Nǐ yídìng yòu wàngjì le ba?
吴森:	为什么我总是不记得考试这件事！	Wú Sēn:	Wèishéme wǒ zǒngshì bú jìde kǎoshì zhèijiàn shì!

4 他们要做什么? Tāmen yào zuò shénme? *What will they do?*

Say what each of the following people plans to do based on the previous dialogue.

1.
吴森

2.
钱永利

3.
李云英

4.
赵梅

5 关键词 Guānjiàncí *Keywords*

Complete each statement according to the dialogue.

1. 他们已经 ___ 了。 Tāmen yǐjīng ___ le.

2. 吴森想去 ___。 Wú Sēn xiǎng qù ___.

3. 李云英得回家 ___ 弟弟和妹妹。 Lǐ Yúnyīng děi huíjiā ___ dìdi hé mèimei.

4. 赵梅要做 ___。 Zhào Méi yào zuò ___.

5. 钱永利要去图书馆 ___。 Qián Yǒnglì yào qù túshūguǎn ___.

6. ___ 的爸妈不让他出去玩儿。 ___ de bà-mā búràng tā chūqù wánr.

7. 晚饭以后, 李云英有空, 可是她要 ___。
   Wǎnfàn yǐhòu, Lǐ Yúnyīng yǒu kòng, kěshì tā yào ___.

8. 赵梅说, 要是她 ___, 就给 ___ 打电话。
   Zhào Méi shuō yàoshì tā ___, jiù gěi ___ dǎ diànhuà.

9. 大家都很忙, 因为明天有 ___ 和 ___ 考试。
   Dàjiā dōu hěn máng, yīnwèi míngtiān yǒu ___ hé ___ kǎoshì.

10. ___ 又忘了明天有考试。 ___ yòu wàngle míngtiān yǒu kǎoshì.

6 考什么? Kǎo shénme? *What subjects?*

Based on the dialogue, identify the subjects that the friends will be tested on tomorrow.

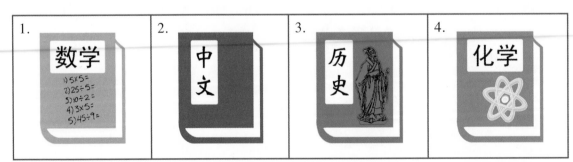

The National Higher Education Entrance Examination (NHEEE)

The NHEEE (高考 *gāokǎo* for short) is the college entrance exam for high school students in China, and is equivalent to the SAT in the US. The results of the exam directly affect a student's chances of entering the type of college he or she might select. There are two main categories in the NHEEE: the humanities and the sciences. Students can take either one according to their interests. The humanities category includes geography, history and politics, and the sciences category includes physics, chemistry, and biology. Both include Chinese languages, math and English.

Categories	Testing Subjects	
	Common Subjects	**Special Subjects**
the Humanities	Chinese languages, math, English	geography, history and politics
the Sciences		physics, chemistry, and biology

Usually, the Chinese languages, math and English exams are separate, and each lasts two to two and a half hours. The maximum score for each of these subjects is 150. The other three subjects are combined into one exam. In the humanities category, geography, history and politics are grouped together into a combined humanities exam (文综 *wénzōng*); in the sciences category, physics, chemistry and biology are the combined sciences (理综 *lǐzōng*). The exams for these combined subjects last 2.5 hours and have a maximum score of 300 points, making 750 the total maximum score of the NHEEE.

▲ *Students study diligently for the tests.*

There are two main types of Chinese colleges: regular colleges or 本科 *běnkē*, and colleges for professional training, known as 专科 *zhuānkē*. Regular colleges are equivalent to four-year colleges and universities in the US, and colleges for professional training are equivalent to technical or community colleges. Chinese universities are ranked according to prestige. The most prestigious are first-tier universities, while second-tier and third-tier universities are less prestigious.

Generally, students will be accepted into a regular college with scores over 500. Second-tier universities require a score above 550, and a score of above 600 will gain students entrance to a first-tier university. A score between 300 and 500 will qualify a student for admission to a college for professional training.

The exams are always held on the seventh and eighth of June each year, and the schedule is as follows:

	June 7th	June 8th
9:00-11:30	Chinese Languages	Combined (humanities/sciences)
15:00-17:00	Math	Foreign Languages

The exams are written exams, and students will usually be able to check their scores on the Internet two months after the exam is held.

Exam time is extremely stressful for Chinese students. Only students with the highest scores can apply to top-tier universities, and the pressure to get into a top university is high. In China, attending a prestigious university greatly influences the rest of a person's life. It has always been the Chinese tradition to place a lot of emphasis on studies, and with the competition in the workplace getting stiffer year after year, having a degree from the right university opens doors. In addition to the students themselves, the parents also hope their children can get good scores. In fact, often the parents are more nervous than their children before the exam.

▲ *Students walk into examination hall and anxious parents are waiting outside.*

7 文化动动脑 Wénhuà Dòngdòngnǎo / *Cultural Check-up*

Write a short answer in English for each question.

1. What is the NHEEE?
2. What are the two main categories of the NHEEE?
3. What is the highest possible total score on the NHEEE?
4. When does the NHEEE take place each year?
5 What subjects are tested on the first day?
6. How long after the exams can students find out their scores?
7. What is the minimum score require to get into a first-tier university?

语言练习 Yǔyán Liànxí
Language Practice

8 说明理由 **Shuōmíng Lǐyóu** / *Explaining Why*

With a classmate, take turns asking and answering the following questions using the pattern "虽然…，但是… *suīrán…, dànshì….*"

1. 中文那么难，你为什么想学？ Zhōngwén nàme nán, nǐ wèishénme xiǎng xué?

2. 你发烧了，为什么不去看病？ Nǐ fāshāo le, wèishénme búqù kànbìng?

3. 下雨了，为什么你还去慢跑？ Xiàyǔ le, wèishénme nǐ hái qù mànpǎo?

4. 你周末有空，为什么不去打工？ Nǐ zhōumò yǒukòng, wèishénme bú qù dǎgōng?

5. 你的头发很长了，为什么不剪？ Nǐde tóufa hěn chángle, wèishénme bùjiǎn?

6. 这件大衣很好看，你为什么不买？ Zhèijiàn dàyī hěn hǎokàn, nǐ wèishénme bùmǎi?

7. 现在已经十二点了，你为什么不睡觉？
Xiànzài yǐjīng shí'èr diǎn le, nǐ wèishénme bú shuìjiào?

8. 你喜欢唱歌，为什么不参加(to join)合唱团？
Nǐ xǐhuan chànggē, wèishénme bù cānjiā héchàngtuán?

9 尽管如此 **Jǐnguǎn rúcǐ** / *For All That*

With a classmate, take turns asking and answering the following questions by using the pattern "…是…，可是… *…shì…, kěshì…*" and the words provided.

1. 你醒了吗？(不想起床) Nǐ xǐngle ma? (bùxiǎng qǐchuáng)

2. 那本书好贵呀！(是课本) Nèiběn shū hǎo guì ya! (shì kèběn)

3. 这件红裤子真时髦。(红色的裤子很奇怪)
Zhèijiàn hóng kùzi zhēn shímáo. (hóngsè de kùzi hěn qíguài)

4. 昨天是他的生日，你记得吗？(忘记买礼物)
Zúotiān shì tāde shēngrì, nǐ jìde ma? (wàngjì mǎi lǐwù)

5. 你星期天有空吗？一起去逛街吧！(看爷爷奶奶)
Nǐ Xīngqītiān yǒu kòng ma? Yìqǐ qù guàngjiē ba! (kàn yéye nǎinai)

6. 你给李明打电话了吗？他要不要去？(有事不能去)
Nǐ gěi Lǐ Míng dǎ diànhuà le ma? Tā yào búyào qù? (yǒu shì bùnéng qù)

7. 你每天锻炼，怎么身体还是不好？(每天只锻炼十几分钟)
Nǐ měitiān duànliàn, zěnme shēntǐ háishì bùhǎo? (měitiān zhǐ duànliàn shí jǐ fēn zhōng)

8. 这双运动鞋只要十块，真便宜，你应该买。(已经有很多运动鞋了)
Zhèishuāng yùndòngxié zhǐyào shíkuài, zhēn piányi, nǐ yīnggāi mǎi. (yǐjīng yǒu hěn duō yùndòngxié le)

Look at the following images and describe what they illustrate using the pattern "如果 / 要是...就...
rúguǒ / yàoshì...jiù...."

1.

3.

5.

2.

4.

6.

---

11 加强语气 **Jiāqiáng Yǔqì** / *Making Emphasis*

With a classmate, take turns giving an emphatic response to the following statements. Follow the model.

Lizi: 他一定很难过。(他的钱不见了) Tā yídìng hěn nánguò. (tāde qián bú jiàn le)

A: 他一定很难过。 Tā yídìng hěn nánguò.

B: 他的钱不见了，他是很难过。 Tāde qián bújiàn le, tā shì hěn nánguò.

1. 他真忙。(每天都要打工) Tā zhēn máng. (měitiān dōu yào dǎgōng)

2. 数学好难。(我得每天练习) Shùxué hǎo nán. (wǒ děi měitiān liànxí)

3. 这个汤好咸。(我不想喝了) Zhèige tāng hǎo xián. (wǒ bùxiǎng hēle)

4. 你不常常打球。(我不喜欢运动) Nǐ bù chángcháng dǎqiú. (wǒ bù xǐhuan yùndòng)

5. 今天功课好多。(我已经写了两个小时了)
Jīntiān gōngkè hǎo duō. (wǒ yǐjīng xiěle liǎngge xiǎoshí le)

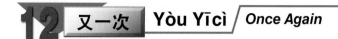

12 又一次 Yòu Yīcì / *Once Again*

Read the following sentences and combine them together using the adverb 又 *yòu*.

Lìzi: 她昨天去逛街。她今天去逛街。 Tā zuótiān qù guàngjiē. Tā jīntiān qù guàngjiē.
她昨天去逛街，今天又去逛街。 Tā zuótiān qù guàngjiē, jīntiān yòu qù guàngjiē.

1. 他昨天忘记带课本。他今天忘记带课本。
Tā zuótiān wàngjì dài kèběn. Tā jīntiān wàngjì dài kèběn.
2. 他们上个学期去了乐团。他们这个学期去乐团。
Tāmen shàngge xuéqī qùle yuètuán. Tāmen zhèige xuéqī qù yuètuán.
3. 弟弟前天发烧。弟弟今天发烧。 Dìdi qiántiān fāshāo. Dìdi jīntiān fāshāo.
4. 李晴化学课打瞌睡。李晴音乐课打瞌睡。
Lǐ Qíng huàxué kè dǎ kēshuì. Lǐ Qíng yīnyuè kè dǎ kēshuì.
5. 她下午三点吃了点心。她现在在吃点心。
Tā xiàwǔ sāndiǎn chīle diǎnxīn. Tā xiànzài zài chī diǎnxīn.

开口说 Kāikǒu Shuō
Communication

13 小小调查 Xiǎoxiǎo Diàochá / *A Survey*

Find out what your classmates usually do after school. Draw a table like the one shown below. In the table, write the names of five classmates, and ask them the top three things they do after school. The top activity gets three points, the second one two points, and the third one point. Calculate to get the top three activities in your table, and share it with the class. An example is provided below.

Lìzi: A: 你放学以后做什么？ Nǐ fàngxué yǐhòu zuò shénme?
B: 我去运动、做功课、吃晚饭。 Wǒ qù yùndòng, zuò gōngkè, chī wǎnfàn.

Student / Activity	B				
1	运动 yùndòng				
2	写功课 xiě gōngkè				
3	吃晚饭 chī wǎnfàn				

Read the following advertisement for a cram school, and answer the questions that follow.

教育 英数理化
补习班

暑期班七月开课
名师芸集

今年更推出"一对一辅导"加强班
个性化教学　小班授课

报名 / 试听 垂询电话: 5560789
地址: 淮北市黄浦路七号

一科1000元，报名两科或三科另有优惠

1. 这家补习班有几个科目(subject)？ 哪几个？ Zhèijiā bǔxíbān yǒu jǐge kēmù? Nǎ jǐge?

2. 他们的暑期班几月开始上课？ Tāmende shǔqībān jǐyuè kāishǐ shàngkè?

3. 你想什么是"一对一"？ Nǐ xiǎng shénme shì "yī duì yī"?

4. 上一科多少钱？ 上两科或三科比较便宜吗？
   Shàng yìkē duō shǎo qián? Shàng liǎngkē huò sānkē bǐjiào piányi ma?

Culture Note

In China, parents hate for their kids to not do as well as they expected, and so apart from talent classes and academic cram schools, there are also cram schools that exist purely to help kids ace the NHEEE called "复读班 *fùdúbān* (re-take classes)." These cram schools are filled with students who did not get into their ideal schools or departments the first time around and would rather put aside a year to retake the exam than accept their original scores. Because of this demand, most re-take classes require that students are good candidates for the course and meet certain prerequisites. These might include obtaining a particular score in the previous test. This helps to increase the percentage of students that receive their ideal score the following year and build the cram school's reputation. In addition, students who do well on the exam will also be awarded with scholarships or waivers. The schools will typically ask teachers who are teaching seniors in high school to teach these students in hopes that they will achieve a better exam score.

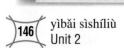

Zìwǒ Tíshēng

Raising the Bar

Vocabulary

贵	guì	*adj.*	*honored*
多	duō	*adv.*	*often*
忘	wàng	*v.*	*to forget*
事	shì	*n.*	*matter*

贵人多忘事
guì rén duō wàng shì
People in high places forget things easily

▲ 贵人多忘事

Language Note

This idiom originally means that people in position of power are often prone to forgetting things because of how busy they are. Here, the word 贵人 *guì rén* beautifies the flaw of forgetting things and does not place the other person in an awkward spot, which is why this idiom is often used as an excuse for forgetting things. However, there is still some sarcasm embedded in the phrase, so one should be careful when and where one uses it.

A: 昨天你借给我的书，我忘记带了。

Zuótiān nǐ jiègěi wǒ de shū, wǒ wàngjì dài le.

I forgot to bring the book you lent me yesterday.

B: 你贵人多忘事，没关系，明天还我就好了！

Nǐ guì rén duō wàng shì, méiguānxi, míngtiān huán wǒ jiù hǎo le!

People in high places often forget things. It's okay. Just give it back to me tomorrow.

Some people have a bad memory and are prone to forgetting things, but others do not have this problem. Here are some four-word idioms related to memory:

1. 过目不忘 *guòmù búwàng*: 目 *mù* means "eyes." This idiom is used to say that a person has a photographic memory.

2. 丢三忘四 *diū sān wàng sì*: This idiom is used to describe a careless person who continually forgets things.

社团活动

　　我的学校社团很多，我去年参加[1]了合唱团和排球队。今年我想写写东西，所以我就参加了校刊社。因为校刊社需要照片，所以我也参加摄影社。新年以后我们得出[2]一本校刊，大家都紧张死了，因为我们才刚刚开始做。要是我们早一点做，现在就不会这么担心了。参加了校刊社以后，我才知道做一本书不容易。我们一个星期见两次，每次两个小时。很忙的时候，一个星期会见三次。虽然很累，但是我很喜欢。明天我要给一篇报导[3]，我写是写了，可是我觉得不是很好，我想一会儿请妈妈帮我看看吧。

[1]参加: to join　　[2]出: to publish　　[3]报导: report

Shètuán Huódòng

　Wǒde xuéxiào shètuán hěn duō, wǒ qùnián cānjiā le héchàngtuán hé páiqiúduì. Jīnnián wǒ xiǎng xiěxie dōngxi, suǒyǐ wǒ jiù cānjiā xiàokānshè. Yīnwèi xiàokānshè xūyào zhàopiàn, suǒyǐ wǒ yě cānjiā le shèyǐngshè. Xīnnián yǐhòu wǒmen děi chū yìběn xiàokān, dàjiā dōu jǐnzhāng sǐ le, yīnwèi wǒmen cái gānggāng kāishǐ zuò. Yàoshì wǒmen zǎo yìdiǎn zuò, xiànzài jiù búhuì zhème dānxīn le. Cānjiā le xiàokānshè yǐhòu, wǒ cái zhīdào zuò yìběn shū bù róngyì. Wǒmen yíge xīngqī jiàn liǎngcì, měicì liǎngge xiǎoshí. Hěn mángde shíhou, yíge xīngqī huì jiàn sāncì. Suīrán hěn lèi, dànshì wǒ hěn xǐhuan. Míngtiān wǒ yào gěi yìpiān bàodǎo, wǒ xiě shì xiěle, kěshì wǒ juéde búshì hěn hǎo, wǒ xiǎng yìhuǐr qǐng māma bāng wǒ kànkan ba.

14 通晓文意 Tōngxiǎo Wényì / Understanding the Passage

Read the above passage and decide if the statements are true or false. Correct any false statements.

1. 他去年只参加了一个社团。　Tā qùnián zhǐ cānjiā le yíge shètuán.

2. 他今年参加两个社团。　Tā jīnnián cānjiā liǎngge shètuán.

3. 他参加摄影社是因为他喜欢摄影。
   Tā cānjiā shèyǐngshè shì yīnwèi tā xǐhuan shèyǐng.

4. 新年以后才出校刊，所以他们不紧张。
   Xīnnián yǐhòu cái chū xiàokān, suǒyǐ tāmen bù jǐnzhāng.

5. 他们一个星期见四个小时，很忙的时候会见到六个小时。
   Tāmen yíge xīngqī jiàn sìge xiǎoshí, hěn mángde shíhou huì jiàn dào liùge xiǎoshí.

6. 他喜欢是喜欢，可是太累了，所以他不想做了。
   Tā xǐhuan shì xǐhuan, kěshì tài lèile, suǒyǐ tā bùxiǎng zuò le.

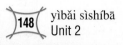

汉字天地 Hànzì Tiāndì
Chinese Characters

明 ■ míng ■ clear

The character 明 *míng* is a combination of two pictographs. The left side is 日 *rì* which represents "sun," and the right side is 月 *yuè* which represents "moon." The two pictographs combined indicate "brightness." The extended meanings of 明 *míng* are "clear" or "distinct."

Stroke Order

16 词汇延伸 Cíhuì Yánshēn / Vocabulary Builder

Below are characters that combine with 明 *míng* to create new words. Match the Chinese words on the left with the appropriate English meanings on the right.

显 xiǎn	星 xīng	白 bái	亮 liàng	智 zhì
adj. noticeable	*n.* star	*n.* white	*adj.* bright	*n.* wisdom

1. 明显 míngxiǎn   A. clear
2. 明星 míngxīng   B. wise
3. 明白 míngbái   C. star

4. 明亮 míngliàng   D. bright
5. 明智 míngzhì   E. obvious

17 汉字侦探 Hànzì Zhēntàn / Visual Detective

Can you find 明 in the following pictures?

Lesson C

🔊 电影分类 **Diànyǐng Fēnlèi** *Film Genres*

喜剧片（喜劇片）
xǐjùpiàn
n. comedy

悲剧片（悲劇片）
bēijùpiàn
n. tragedy drama

功夫片
gōngfupiàn
n. kung-fu

恐怖片
kǒngbùpiàn
n. horror

科幻片
kēhuànpiàn
n. sci-fi

动作片（動作片）
dòngzuòpiàn
n. action & adventure

剧情片（劇情片）
jùqíngpiàn
n. drama

记录片（記錄片）
jìlùpiàn
n. documentary

浪漫爱情片
（浪漫愛情片）
làngmàn àiqíngpiàn
n. romance

卡通片
kǎtōngpiàn
n. animation; cartoon

联络工具 Liánluò Gōngjù *Communication Tools*

短信
duǎnxìn
n. text message

电邮（電郵）
diànyóu
n. email
(the short form of
电子邮件
diànzǐ yóujiàn)

视频（視頻）
shìpín
n. video chat

聊天室
liáotiānshì
n. chat room

论坛（論壇）
lùntán
n. bulletin board system (BBS)

A: 喂，美美。
　Wéi, Měiměi. *Hello, Meimei.*

B: 嗨，小兰，有什么事？（嗨，小蘭，有什麼事？）
　Hāi, Xiǎolán, yǒu shénme shì? *Hello, Xiaolan. What's up?*

你没收到我的电邮吗？
Nǐ méi shōudào wǒde diànyóu ma?
Didn't you get my email?

对不起，我最近没有上网。
Duìbùqǐ, wǒ zuìjìn méiyǒu shàngwǎng.
Sorry, I haven't been online lately.

A: 嘿，大山，有什么事？（嘿，大山，有什麼事？）
　Hēi, Dàshān, yǒu shénme shì? *Hey, Dashan, what's up?*

B: 我想问你周末要不要去打冰球。（我想問你週末要不要去打冰球。）
　Wǒ xiǎng wèn nǐ zhōumò yào búyào qù dǎ bīngqiú. *I wanted to ask if you want to play hockey this weekend.*

A: 我哪里都不想去。
　Wǒ nǎlǐ dōu bùxiǎng qù. *I don't want to go anywhere.*

- -

A: 你喜欢吃什么菜？（你喜歡吃什麼菜？）
　Nǐ xǐhuan chī shénme cài? *What do you like to eat?*

B: 什么菜我都喜欢吃。（什麼菜我都喜歡吃。）
　Shénme cài wǒ dōu xǐhuan chī. *I like to eat anything.*

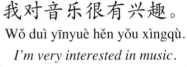

我对音乐很有兴趣。
Wǒ duì yīnyuè hěn yǒu xìngqù.
I'm very interested in music.

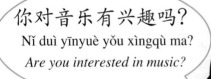

你对音乐有兴趣吗？
Nǐ duì yīnyuè yǒu xìngqù ma?
Are you interested in music?

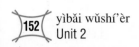

Adjective

肉麻	ròumá	*disgusting*

Adverbs

没有 (沒有)	méiyǒu	*did not; have not*
最近	zuìjìn	*recently; lately*
只是	zhǐshì	*merely; simply; just; only*
其实 (其實)	qíshí	*in fact; actually*

Common Expressions

除了...以外, 都 / 也...	chúle...yǐwài, dōu / yě	*except for; besides*
怎么了 (怎麼了)	zěnme le	*What's up? What's wrong?*
没什么 (沒什麼)	méi shénme	*nothing; don't mention it;*

Measure Words

部	bù	*used for films or a volume of books*
封	fēng	*used for letters, emails*
条 (條)	tiáo	*used for text messages*

Nouns

问题 (問題)	wèntí	*problem; question*
兴趣 (興趣)	xìngqù	*interest*

Preposition

对 (對)	duì	*to; toward*

Verb

发 (發)	fā	*to send; to distribute*

Verb-Complement

收到	shōudào	*to receive; to get*

1 看电影 **Kàn Diànyǐng** / *Watching Movies*

Listen carefully as Chéng describes the emotions he feels when he watches different types of movies. Choose the letter of the photo that matches his emotions for each type of movie you hear.

A.

难过
nánguò

B.

兴奋
xīngfèn

C.

紧张
jǐnzhāng

D.

心情好
xīnqíng hǎo

2 现代人的生活 **Xiàndàirén de Shēnghuó** / *Modern Living*

You will hear a paragraph in which Meimei discusses the tools she uses to communicate with others. These tools are depicted in the images below. Organize the tools she mentions by writing down the corresponding letters in the order that they are mentioned in the dialogue.

A.

B.

C.

D.

E.

Answer the following questions in Chinese based on your own experiences and opinions.

1. 你常常给朋友发短信吗？ Nǐ chángcháng gěi péngyou fā duǎnxìn ma?

2. 你的学校有论坛吗？ Nǐde xuéxiào yǒu lùntán ma?

3. 你喜欢什么电影？ Nǐ xǐhuan shénme diànyǐng?

4. 你最近想看哪部电影？ Nǐ zuìjìn xiǎng kàn něibù diànyǐng?

5. 你看过中国的功夫片吗？ Nǐ kànguo Zhōngguó de gōngfupiàn ma?

6. 你对什么事情有兴趣？ Nǐ duì shénme shìqing yǒu xìngqù?

句型介绍 Jùxíng Jièshào

Language Patterns

The Negative Question Pattern "没(有)...吗? *méi(yǒu)...ma?*"

This pattern is used to ask about something that the speaker is unsure, but might not have happened in the past. The adverb 没(有) *méi(yǒu)* expressed "not" and is used to form the negation of a completed action.

Subject + 没(有) *méi(yǒu)* + **Verb Phrase** + 吗 *ma*?

A: 我好饿。 Wǒ hǎo è.

B: 你没有吃晚饭吗？ Nǐ méiyǒu chī wǎnfàn ma?

他今天没有来上课吗？
Tā jīntiān méiyǒu lái shàngkè ma?

To ask about things that have not happened yet, and about which you, the speaker, are unsure, the same pattern, but with the non-past negative "不 *bù/ bú*", can be used.

Subject + 不 *bù / bú* + **Verb Phrase** + 吗 *ma*?

放学了！你不马上回家吗？
Fàngxué le! Nǐ bù mǎshàng huíjiā ma?

明天要考试，你今天晚上不念书吗？
Míngtiān yào kǎoshì, nǐ jīntiān wǎnshang bú niànshū ma?

▲ 放学回家！

The Question Word 什么时候 *shénme shíhou*

You learned in Level 1, Unit 3 Lesson C, about the word order for words that describe time. The question word 什么时候 *shénme shíhou* is another time word, and it is usually placed after the subject.

> Subject + 什么时候 *shénme shíhou* + Verb Phrase?

A: 你明天什么时候来我家？ Nǐ míngtiān shénme shíhou lái wǒ jiā?

B: 下午三点。 Xiàwǔ sāndiǎn.

A: 你要什么时候学中文？ Nǐ yào shénme shíhou xué Zhōngwén?

B: 我要下个学期学。 Wǒ yào xiàge xuéqī xué.

The Pattern of "V + 不 *bù* / *bú* V"

In English, to phrase a "one-or-the-other" question as a statement, just add a "if" to connect the choices to the statement. In Chinese, however, the conjunctions 要是 *yàoshì* or 如果 *rúguǒ* do not have the same function. For sentences like those mentioned above, use the "V不 *bù* / *bú* V" question form since it offers a choice between either doing or not doing an action.

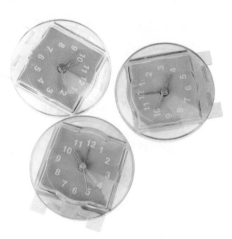

我想知道他去不去。 Wǒ xiǎng zhīdào tā qù bú qù.

他不知道你喜不喜欢这本书。

Tā bù zhīdào nǐ xǐ bù xǐhuan zhèiběn shū.

The same pattern can apply to auxiliary verbs and adjectives.

请问你明天能不能来。

Qǐngwèn nǐ míngtiān néng bùnéng lái.

他不确定这部电影好不好看。

Tā bú quèdìng zhèibù diànyǐng hǎo bù hǎokàn.

▲ 什么时候？

The Pattern "对…(没)有兴趣 *duì…(méi)yǒu xìngqù*"

This pattern means "to be interested in…." The preposition 对 *duì* is used to introduce the object and must be placed after the subject.

> Subject + 对 *duì* + something + (没)有兴趣 *(méi)yǒu xìngqù*

你对什么运动有兴趣？ Nǐ duì shénme yùndòng yǒu xìngqù?

我对唱歌很有兴趣，所以这个学期我想参加合唱团。

Wǒ duì chànggē hěn yǒu xìngqù, suǒyǐ zhèige xuéqī wǒ xiǎng cānjiā héchàngtuán.

Question Words followed by 都 *dōu* / 也 *yě* to Express Inclusiveness or Exclusiveness

As in the English language words like whoever, whatever, wherever, 都 *dōu* follows a question word such as 谁 *shéi*, 什么 *shénme*, 哪 *nǎ*, the meaning becomes "every" or "any" to express inclusiveness.

> **Subject** + **Question Word** + **都 *dōu* / 也 *yě*** + **Verb**
>
> 你什么时候都可以来我家。
> Nǐ shénme shíhou dōu kěyǐ lái wǒ jiā.
>
> **A:** 你想吃什么菜？ Nǐ xiǎng chī shénme cài?
> **B:** 我什么菜都想吃。 Wǒ shénme cài dōu xiǎng chī.

▲ 什么菜？

To express exclusiveness, add a 不 *bù* / *bú* or 没 *méi* after the 都 *dōu* or 也 *yě* and the meaning becomes "nothing," "no one," "nowhere." 也 *yě* often substitutes for 都 *dōu* in this pattern, especially when the verb is negative.

> 他心情不好，谁都不想见。
> Tā xīnqíng bù hǎo, shéi dōu bù xiǎng jiàn.
>
> 我今天哪里都不想去，我想在家。 Wǒ jīntiān nǎlǐ dōu bù xiǎng qù, wǒ xiǎng zài jiā.

The Pattern 除了...以外, 都 / 也... *chúle...yǐwài, dōu / yě* ... to Indicate Inclusiveness and Exclusiveness

除了 *chúle* expresses exclusiveness. In the pattern "除了...以外, 都... *chúle...yǐwài, dōu*...," the first clause indicates an exception, and 都 *dōu* is placed in the second clause to refer to the rest. It means "besides" when followed by a positive statement.

> **除了 *chúle*** + **Noun Phrase** + **以外 *yǐwài***, **Subject** + **Question Word** + **(Noun)** + **都 *dōu*** + **Verb**
>
> 除了猪肉以外，我什么都吃。 Chúle zhūròu yǐwài, wǒ shénme dōu chī.
> 除了滑雪以外，我什么运动都喜欢。
> Chúle huáxuě yǐwài, wǒ shénme yùndòng dōu xǐhuan.

When followed by a negative statement, it means "except for, apart from".

> **除了 *chúle*** + **Noun Phrase** + **以外 *yǐwài***, **Subject** + **Question Word** + **Noun** + **都 *dōu* / 也 *yě*** + **不 *bù* / 没 *méi*** + **Verb**
>
> 除了猪肉以外，我什么肉也不吃。 Chúle zhūròu yǐwài, wǒ shénme ròu yě bùchī.
> 除了滑雪以外，我什么运动都不喜欢。
> Chúle huáxuě yǐwài, wǒ shénme yùndòng dōu bù xǐhuan.

🔊 **讨论电影 Tǎolùn Diànyǐng** *Discussing Movies*

Qian Yongli is calling Wu Sen from home.

钱永利：	喂，吴森，我是钱永利。
吴森：	嘿，永利，有什么事？
钱永利：	你没收到我发的短信吗？
吴森：	没有，我的手机最近有点儿问题。怎么了？
钱永利：	没什么，我只是要问你明天想不想去看电影。
吴森：	你想看哪部电影？
钱永利：	我不知道。你对什么电影有兴趣？
吴森：	什么电影我都喜欢，你呢？
钱永利：	我喜欢恐怖片。
吴森：	喔，除了恐怖片，什么电影我都看。
钱永利：	浪漫爱情片呢？
吴森：	那个太肉麻了，我不看。
钱永利：	那喜剧片呢？
吴森：	我也不看。
钱永利：	其实你什么电影都不喜欢。

Qián Yǒnglì: Wéi, Wú Sēn, Wǒ shì Qián Yǒnglì.

Wú Sēn: Hēi, Yǒnglì, yǒu shénme shì?

Qián Yǒnglì: Nǐ méi shōudào wǒ fāde duǎnxìn ma?

Wú Sēn: Méiyǒu, wǒde shǒujī zuìjìn yǒudiǎnr wèntí. Zěnme le?

Qián Yǒnglì: Méi shénme, wǒ zhǐshì yào wèn nǐ míngtiān xiǎng bùxiǎng qù kàn diànyǐng.

Wú Sēn: Nǐ xiǎng kàn něibù diànyǐng?

Qián Yǒnglì: Wǒ bù zhīdào. Nǐ duì shénme diànyǐng yǒu xìngqù?

Wú Sēn: Shénme diànyǐng wǒ dōu xǐhuan, nǐ ne?

Qián Yǒnglì: Wǒ xǐhuan kǒngbùpiàn.

Wú Sēn: Ō, chúle kǒngbùpiàn, shénme diànyǐng wǒ dōu kàn.

Qián Yǒnglì: Làngmàn àiqíngpiàn ne?

Wú Sēn: Nèige tài ròumá le, wǒ búkàn.

Qián Yǒnglì: Nà xǐjùpiàn ne?

Wú Sēn: Wǒ yě búkàn.

Qián Yǒnglì: Qíshí nǐ shénme diànyǐng dōu bù xǐhuan.

4 他喜欢的电影 Tā xǐhuan de diànyǐng *The Movies He Likes*

Based on the dialogue, identify which of the following types of movies Qian Yongli prefers.

A.

B.

C.

5 联络方法 Liánluò Fāngfǎ *How to Keep in Touch*

Based on the dialogue, choose the method Qian Yongli used to contact Wu Sen.

A.    B.   C.

6 关键词 Guānjiàncí *Keywords*

Complete each statement according to the information in the dialogue.

1. 吴森给钱永利打 ___。 Wú Sēn gěi Qián Yǒnglì dǎ ___.

2. 吴森没有收到钱永利的 ___。 Wú Sēn méiyǒu shōudào Qián Yǒnglì de ___.

3. 吴森的 ___ 最近有点儿问题。 Wú Sēn de ___ zuìjìn yǒu diǎnr wèntí.

4. 钱永利问吴森明天想不想去 ___。
   Qián Yǒnglì wèn Wú Sēn míngtiān xiǎng bùxiǎng qù ___.

5 ___ 不知道他要看哪部电影。 ___ bù zhīdào tā yào kàn něibù diànyǐng.

6. 吴森说 ___ 电影他都喜欢，钱永利说他喜欢 ___。
   Wú Sēn shuō ___ diànyǐng tā dōu xǐhuan, Qián Yǒnglì shuō tā xǐhuan ___.

7. 吴森觉得浪漫爱情片太 ___ 了，所以他不看。
   Wú Sēn juéde làngmàn àiqíngpiàn tài ___ le, suǒyǐ tā búkàn.

Wénhuà Chúchuāng

文化橱窗

Culture Window

Cultural Activities in China

In China, there are a variety of cultural activities for people to enjoy—from traditional Chinese performances such as the Chinese opera, comedic "cross-talk" routines, and plays to relatively newer, Western forms of entertainment such as movies, rock concerts, musicals, and talk shows. Traditional Chinese forms of entertainment are popular with the older generation, while young people tend to be more appreciative of newer things.

▲ *movie theater*

Until a few decades ago, China did not have movie theaters. To watch movies, people would set up a screen outdoors and watch. Nowadays, movie theaters are extremely popular and getting fancier, with 3D and IMAX technology and screenings of Chinese, Japanese, and Korean films as well as the newest blockbusters from Europe and the US.

▲ *acrobatics*

In recent years, more Chinese films are being produced than ever before, and many are being seen around the world. This has allowed more Westerners to understand Chinese culture and philosophy through Chinese movies, and has provided more opportunities for Chinese actors to make the move to Hollywood. Some of the biggest stars are kung fu action heroes like Jackie Chan and Jet Li. Chinese leading ladies Zhang Ziyi, Gong Li, and Bai Ling have also become famous internationally. Chinese directors such as Zhang Yimou, who directed *Curse of the Golden Flower*, and Feng Xiaogang, director of *Aftershock*, have won accolades and awards at home and abroad.

The China National Acrobatics Troupe, famous for their incredible acrobatics, has also won numerous international awards and represented China in various international cultural events with shows such as "Bicycle Skill," "Diabolo," "Plate Spinning" and "Umbrella Juggling."

Concerts are very popular with the younger generation. They love to watch their favorite stars performing live onstage in stadium shows. Nowadays, many famous international performers such as Avril Lavigne, Beyoncé, the Black Eyed Peas, the Backstreet Boys, and Christina Aguilera, hold concerts in China.

▲ *concert*

7 文化动动脑 **Wénhuà Dòngdòngnǎo** / *Culture Check-up*

On your own paper, write a short answer in English for each question.

1. What are some traditional forms of entertainment in China?
2. Before movie theaters became popular, how did people watch movies?
3. Name some famous Chinese directors.
4. Chinese movie stars are often well-known for what kind of movies?
5. What are some shows performed by the China National Acrobatics Troupe?
6. Name two international performers that have held concerts in China.

语言练习 Yǔyán Liànxí
Language Practice

8 没有…吗? **Méiyǒu...ma?** / *Didn't you?*

 With a classmate, take turns reading from column A and responding by selecting a logical response from column B.

Person A	Person B
1. 我好困。 Wǒ hǎo kùn.	A. 你不紧张吗? Nǐ bù jǐnzhāng ma?
2. 我不想吃东西。 Wǒ bùxiǎng chī dōngxi.	B. 你没有念书吗? Nǐ méiyǒu niànshū ma?
3. 我的电脑不见了。 Wǒde diànnǎo bújiàn le.	C. 你还没有结束吗? Nǐ hái méiyǒu jiéshù ma?
4. 请你帮我送礼物给他。 Qǐng nǐ bāng wǒ sòng lǐwù gěi tā.	D. 你昨天没有睡好觉吗? Nǐ zuótiān méiyǒu shuì hǎo jiào ma?
5. 不好意思,请再等我一下。 Bù hǎoyìsi, qǐng zài děng wǒ yíxià.	E. 你不去他的生日会吗? Nǐ búqù tāde shēngrìhuì ma?
6. 今天的考试,我只考了六十分。 Jīntiān de kǎoshì, wǒ zhǐ kǎole liùshífēn.	F. 你不饿吗? Nǐ bú'è ma?

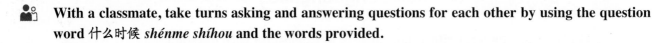

9 | 询问时间 | **Xúnwèn Shíjiān** / *Asking the Time*

👥 With a classmate, take turns asking and answering questions for each other by using the question word 什么时候 *shénme shíhou* and the words provided.

Lìzi: 你上聊天室。(每天晚上九点) Nǐ shàng liáotiānshì. (měitiān wǎnshang jiǔdiǎn)

A: 你什么时候上聊天室？ Nǐ shénme shíhou shàng liáotiānshì?

B: 我每天晚上九点上聊天室。 Wǒ měitiān wǎnshang jiǔdiǎn shàng liáotiānshì.

1. 爸爸到家。(八点) Bàba dào jiā. (bādiǎn)
2. 他要去看病。(早上) Tā yào qù kànbìng. (zǎoshang)
3. 李英开始打工。(上上个月) Lǐ Yīng kāishǐ dǎgōng. (shàng shàngge yuè)
4. 你去健身房锻炼。(每天晚上) Nǐ qù jiànshēnfáng duànliàn. (měitiān wǎnshang)
5. 我们去墨西哥旅行。(下个月) Wǒmen qù Mòxīgē lǚxíng. (xiàge yuè)
6. 妈妈会给李太太打电话。(等一下) Māma huì gěi Lǐ tàitai dǎ diànhuà. (děng yíxià)

10 | 不确定 | **Bú Quèdìng** / *Uncertainty*

👥 With a classmate, take turns asking and answering the following questions in the manner of the example and using 我不知道 *wǒ bù zhīdào* to begin your answers.

Lìzi: 他来吗？ Tā lái ma?

A: 他来吗？ Tā lái ma?

B: 我不知道他来不来。
Wǒ bù zhīdào tā lái bùlái.

1. 他们明天有空吗？
Tāmen míngtiān yǒu kòng ma?

2. 他有兄弟姐妹吗？
Tā yǒu xiōngdì-jiěmèi ma?

3. 这是王校长的猫吗？
Zhè shì Wáng xiàozhǎng de māo ma?

4. 董先生喜欢张小姐吗？
Dǒng xiānsheng xǐhuan Zhāng xiǎojiě ma?

5. 他可以借给我他的电脑吗？
Tā kěyǐ jiè gěi wǒ tāde diànnǎo ma?

6. 那位先生是你弟弟的老师吗？
Nèiwèi xiānsheng shì nǐ dìdi de lǎoshī ma?

▲ 我不知道。

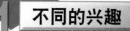

11 不同的兴趣 **Bùtóng de Xìngqù** / *Different Interests*

Say what everyone is interested in using the pattern "对…(没)有兴趣 *duì…(méi) yǒu xìngqù*." Follow the model.

Lìzi: Helen对音乐有兴趣，Mathew对音乐没有兴趣。
Helen duì yīnyuè yǒu xìngqù, Mathew duì yīnyuè méiyǒu xìngqù.

| ✓ Helen | ✗ Mathew |

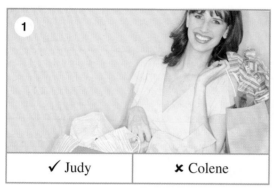

| ✓ Judy | ✗ Colene |

| ✓ 吴均 Wú Jūn | ✗ 李德 Lǐ Dé |

| ✓ Thai | ✗ Jung |

| ✓ 林美华 Lín Měihuá | ✗ 王健 Wáng Jiàn |

12 没有问题 **Méiyǒu Wèntí** / *No Problem*

With a classmate, take turns asking and answering the following questions by using question words to show inclusiveness and exclusiveness.

1. 你想喝什么？ Nǐ xiǎng hē shénme?
2. 你喜欢哪个国家？ Nǐ xǐhuan něige guójiā?
3. 你想去哪里旅行？ Nǐ xiǎng qù nǎlǐ lǚxíng?
4. 你喜欢什么运动？ Nǐ xǐhuan shénme yùndòng?
5. 你想跟谁去打球？ Nǐ xiǎng gēn shéi qù dǎqiú?
6. 我什么时候能去你家？ Wǒ shénme shíhou néng qù nǐ jiā?
7. 你想买什么颜色的T恤？ Nǐ xiǎng mǎi shénme yánsè de T-xù?
8. 我什么时候可以给你打电话？ Wǒ shénme shíhou kěyǐ gěi nǐ dǎ diànhuà?

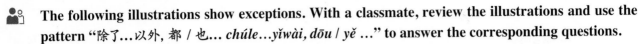

13 凡事都有例外　Fán shì dōu yǒu lìwài.　*Everything has an exception.*

The following illustrations show exceptions. With a classmate, review the illustrations and use the pattern "除了…以外, 都 / 也… *chúle…yǐwài, dōu / yě …*" to answer the corresponding questions.

Lìzi:　A: 你不吃什么肉？　Nǐ bùchī shénme ròu?

　　　　B: 除了牛肉, 什么肉我都不吃。
　　　　Chúle niúròu, shénme ròu wǒ dōu bùchī.

1.

数学

你喜欢哪个科目？
Nǐ xǐhuan něige kēmù?

3.

你喜欢吃什么？
Nǐ xǐhuan chī shénme?

5.

你喜欢什么季节？
Nǐ xǐhuan shénme jìjié?

2.

你喝什么？
Nǐ hē shénme?

4.

早上	下午	晚上
		X

你什么时候有空？
Nǐ shénme shíhou yǒu kòng?

6.

你哪里不舒服？
Nǐ nǎlǐ bù shūfu?

开口说　Kāikǒu Shuō

Communication

14 喜欢的电影　Xǐhuan de Diànyǐng　*A Movie You Like*

With a classmate, talk about a movie you like.

1. Ask your classmate what type(s) of movie he or she likes and say what you like in return.
2. Ask your classmate what movie he or she considers his or her favorite and provide your own answer.
3. Ask your classmate what recently released movie he or she wants to see and provide your own answer.
4. Make plans to see a movie together.

电子邮件 **Diànzǐ Yóujiàn** / *Email*

Read the following email and use it to choose the correct answers to the questions that follow.

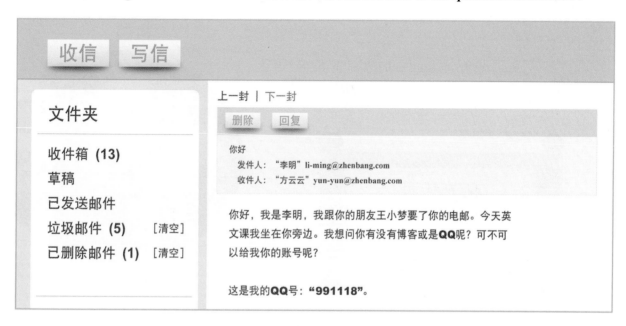

1. 写信的人是谁？ Xiěxìn de rén shì shéi?

    A. 李明 Lǐ Míng

    B. 方云云 Fāng Yúnyún

    C. 王小梦 Wáng Xiǎomèng

2. 写信的人想要做什么？ Xiěxìn de rén xiǎng yào zuò shénme?

    A. 问英文问题 wèn Yīngwén wèntí

    B. 要博客和QQ号 yào bókè hé QQ hào

    C. 给朋友账号 gěi péngyou zhànghào

3. 哪个是李明的邮箱地址(email address)？ Něige shì Lǐ Míng de yóuxiāng dìzhǐ?

    A. ming991118@zhenbang.com

    B. li-ming@zhenbang.com

    C. 他没有邮箱地址。Tā méiyǒu yóuxiāng dìzhǐ.

4. 如果想看新的电邮，得按(to click)哪个键(key)？
    Rúguǒ xiǎng kàn xīn de dianyou, děi àn něi ge jiàn?

    A. 收信shōu xìn   B. 写信xiě xìn   C. 回复huífù

Vocabulary

| 挑 | tiāo | *v.* | *to choose; to select* |
| 拣 | jiǎn | *v.* | *to pick* |

挑三拣四
tiāosān-jiǎnsì
To be very picky

▲ 挑三拣四

Language Note

This means that a person is extremely picky.

你每次买东西都挑三拣四，我不想跟你去逛街了。

Nǐ měicì mǎi dōngxi dōu tiāosān-jiǎnsì, wǒ bùxiǎng gēn nǐ qù guàngjiē le.

You are always so picky when you buy things. I don't want to go shopping with you.

These idioms place emphasis on the verbs by adding some numbers in between the verbs. The two verbs in these idioms are often either synonyms or very similar in meaning. Below are some examples:

1. 接二连三 *jiē'èr-liánsān*: One after the other. This is used to describe things that happen consecutively.

   最近接二连三地发生地震，真可怕！

   Zuìjìn jiē'èr-liánsān de fāshēng dìzhèn, zhēn kěpà!

   Recently, earthquakes have happened one after the other. It's very frightening!

2. 丢三落四 *diūsān-làsì*: To leave things out. This is used to say that a person is careless and often forgets things.

   你要细心一点，不要丢三落四。

   Nǐ yào xìxīn yìdiǎn, búyào diūsān-làsì.

   You should pay more attention to detail and not leave things out.

看电影

　　我的好朋友张舒对电影很有兴趣，他常常找我跟他一起去看电影。他几乎什么电影都看，我觉得最没有意思的记录片，他也看。不过大家都喜欢的卡通片，他一点儿也不喜欢，他说卡通片太可爱了。他昨天晚上发了一封电邮给我，我今天早上才看到。他问我今天有没有空，他想去看一部中国的功夫片，而且他已经买了两张票[1]。我很喜欢功夫片，所以就马上给他发短信。可是他说我太晚告诉[2]他了，董真真昨晚就给他回信[3]了。唉，下次吧！

[1]票: ticket　　[2]告诉: to tell　　[3]回信: to reply

Kàn Diànyǐng

　　Wǒde hǎo péngyou Zhāng Shū duì diànyǐng hěn yǒu xìngqù, tā chángcháng zhǎo wǒ gēn tā yìqǐ qù kàn diànyǐng. Tā jīhū shénme diànyǐng dōu kàn, wǒ juéde zuì méiyǒu yìsi de jìlùpiàn, tā yě kàn. Búguò dàjiā dōu xǐhuan de kǎtōngpiàn, tā yìdiǎnr yě bù xǐhuan, tā shuō kǎtōngpiàn tài kě'ài le. Tā zuótiān wǎnshang fāle yìfēng dianyou gěi wǒ, wǒ jīntiān zǎoshang cái kàndào. Tā wèn wǒ jīntiān yǒu méiyǒu kòng, tā xiǎng qù kàn yíbù Zhōngguó de gōngfupiàn, érqiě tā yǐjīng mǎile liǎngzhāng piào. Wǒ hěn xǐhuan gōngfupiàn, suǒyǐ jiù mǎshàng gěi tā fā duǎnxìn. Kěshì tā shuō wǒ tài wǎn gàosù tā le, Dǒng Zhēnzhēn zuó wǎn jiù gěi tā huíxìn le. Ài, xiàcì ba!

16 通晓文意 Tōngxiǎo Wényì / *Understanding the Passage*

Read the above passage and decide if the statements are true or false. Correct any false statements.

1. 张舒对电影很有兴趣。　Zhāng Shū duì diànyǐng hěn yǒu xìngqù.

2. 张舒什么电影都看。　Zhāng Shū shénme diànyǐng dōu kàn.

3. 他觉得记录片很没有意思。　Tā juéde jìlùpiàn hěn méiyǒu yìsi.

4. 张舒很喜欢卡通片，因为卡通片太可爱了。
Zhāng Shū hěn xǐhuan kǎtōngpiàn, yīnwèi kǎtōngpiàn tài kě'ài le.

5. 他昨天晚上发了一封电邮给张舒。
Tā zuótiān wǎnshang fāle yìfēng diànyóu gěi Zhāng Shū.

6. 张舒买了两张电影票。　Zhāng Shū mǎile liǎngzhāng diànyǐng piào.

7. 他很喜欢功夫片，可是他今天很晚才有空，所以不能去。
Tā hěn xǐhuan gōngfupiàn, kěshì tā jīntiān hěn wǎn cái yǒu kòng, suǒyǐ bùnéng qù.

8. 张舒要跟董真真去看电影。　Zhāng Shū yào gēn Dǒng Zhēnzhēn qù kàn diànyǐng.

汉字天地 Hànzì Tiāndì
Chinese Characters

信 ■ xìn ■ letter

The character 信 *xìn* is a combination of two pictographs. The left side is 人 *rén* which represents "people," and the right side is 言 *yán* which means "to speak." When these two are combined, they become 信 *xìn*, which indicates "belief" and "trust." In addition, 信 *xìn* also has other meanings such as "letter," "message" and "information," etc.

Stroke Order

17 词汇延伸 Cíhuì Yánshēn / *Vocabulary Builder*

Below are characters that combine with 信 *xìn* to create words. Match the Chinese words on the left with the appropriate English meanings on the right.

心 xīn	用 yòng	封 fēng	号 hào	仰 yǎng
n. heart	*v. to use*	*v. to seal*	*n. number*	*v. to admire*

1. 信心 xìnxīn   A. envelope
2. 信用 xìnyòng   B. confidence
3. 信封 xìnfēng   C. faith
4. 信号 xìnhào   D. credit
5. 信仰 xìnyǎng   E. signal

Can you find 信 in the following pictures?

信

Unit 3

我的朋友真棒

Wǒde Péngyou Zhēn Bàng

In this unit you will be able to:

- describe a person's feelings
- suggest interesting things to do with friends
- make comparisons
- ask and explain how things are going
- ask for and provide reasons
- make invitations
- describe one's or someone else's life

Lesson A

词汇 Cíhuì
Vocabulary

🔊 身材 Shēncái *Figure*

高 gāo   矮 ǎi
adj. tall   *adj. short*

胖 pàng
adj. fat

瘦 shòu
adj. thin

壮（壯）zhuàng
adj. strong

结实（結實）jiēshi
adj. fit; firm

苗条（苗條）miáotiáo
adj. slender; slim

🔊 个性 Gèxìng *Personality*

害羞 hàixiū
adj. shy

热情（熱情）rèqíng
adj. passionate

冷淡 lěngdàn
adj. aloof

开朗 (開朗) kāilǎng
adj. out-going

善变 (善變) shànbiàn
adj. fickle

固执 (固執) gùzhí
adj. stubborn

随和 (隨和) suíhé
adj. easy-going

大方 dàfāng
adj. natural and poised

内向 nèixiàng
adj. introverted

外向 wàixiàng
adj. extroverted

男 nán *adj./n. male*
男的 nánde *n. male*
男生 nánshēng *n. boy*
男人 nánrén *n. man*

女 nǚ *adj./n. female*
女的 nǚde *n. female*
女生 nǚshēng *n. girl*
女人 nǚrén *n. woman*

A: 这个学期你们班来了新同学吗？（這個學期你們班來了新同學嗎？）
Zhège xuéqī nǐmen bān láile xīn tóngxué ma?
Do you have any new classmates this semester?

B: 是呀，这个学期来了一个男生，一个女生。（是呀，這學期來了一個
男生，一個女生。）Shì ya, zhège xuéqī láile yíge nánshēng, yíge nǚshēng.
Yes, a boy and a girl.

A: 你会做汉堡包吗？（你會做漢堡包嗎？）
Nǐ huì zuò hànbǎobāo ma? *Can you make burgers?*

B: 当然会，做汉堡包一点儿也不难。（當然會，做漢堡包一點兒也不難。）
Dāngrán huì, zuò hànbǎobāo yìdiǎnr yě bùnán. *Of course, making burgers is not hard at all.*

C: 我会，可是我做得不好。（我會，可是我做得不好。）
Wǒ huì, kěshì wǒ zuòde bùhǎo. *Yes, but I can't make them well.*

他哥哥长得怎么样？
Tā gēge zhǎng de zěnmeyàng?
What does his big brother look like?

他哥哥长得很帅，而且又高又壮。
Tā gēge zhǎng de hěn shuài, érqiě yòu gāo yòu zhuàng.
He's very good-looking, and he's tall and well-built too.

A: 吴小姐的个性怎么样？（吳小姐的個性怎麼樣？）Wú xiǎojiě de gèxìng zěnmeyàng?
What's Miss Wu's personality like?

B: 她很开朗，也很大方。（她很開朗，也很大方。）Tā hěn kāilǎng, yě hěn dàfāng.
She is very easy-going, and very natural.

我跟孙大成很熟，他是我的好朋友。
Wǒ gēn Sūn Dàchéng hěn shú, tā shì wǒde hǎo péngyou.
I know Sun Dacheng very well,
he's a good friend of mine.

改天一起打球吧！
Gǎitiān yìqǐ dǎqiú ba! *Let's play ball together some day!*

Adjectives

国际（國際）	guójì	*international*
一样（一樣）	yíyàng	*the same*
大	dà	*old (age-wise)*
熟	shú	*familiar*

Adverb

改天	gǎitiān	*another day; some other day*

Auxiliary Verb

会（會）	huì	*can; to know how to; to be able to*

Nouns

班	bān	*class*
人	rén	*person*
心地	xīndì	*heart (metaphorical)*
男朋友	nánpéngyou	*boyfriend*
女朋友	nǚpéngyou	*girlfriend*

Particles

得	de	*used between a verb or an adjective and its complement to indicate degree*
呀	ya	*used after short answers to soften the tone*

Preposition

比	bǐ	*used to indicate a difference in manner or degree through comparison*

Verbs

长（長）	zhǎng	*to grow*
找	zhǎo	*to call on; to invite; to look for*

1 他们的身材 Tāmen de Shēncái / *Their Stature*

🔊 **You will hear four descriptions. Match each description to the image that it describes.**

A.　　　　B.　　　　C.　　　　D.

2 性格特征 Xìnggé Tèzhēng / *Personality*

Match each of the following personalities with their corresponding description.

1. 害羞 hàixiū
2. 热情 rèqíng
3. 冷淡 lěngdàn
4. 善变 shànbiàn
5. 随和 suíhé

A. 喜欢帮助人 xǐhuan bāngzhù rén
B. 不想跟人说话 bù xiǎng gēn rén shuōhuà
C. 不好意思跟人说话 bù hǎoyìsi gēn rén shuōhuà
D. 大家说什么都可以 dàjiā shuō shénme dōu kěyǐ
E. 这一分钟和下一分钟不一样
　 zhè yìfēn zhōng gēn xià yìfēn zhōng bù yíyàng

3 个人问题 Gèrén Wèntí / *Personal Questions*

Answer the following questions in Chinese based on your own experiences and opinions.

1. 你的个性内向还是外向?　Nǐde gèxìng nèixiàng háishì wàixiàng?

2. 你随和吗?　Nǐ suíhé ma?

3. 你的中文班里有多少男生? 多少女生?
　 Nǐde Zhōngwén bān lǐ yǒu duōshao nánshēng? Duōshao nǚshēng?

4. 你的中文班的同学都一样大吗?
　 Nǐde Zhōngwén bān de tóngxué dōu yíyàng dà ma?

5. 除了中文和英文以外, 你还会说什么语言(*language*)?
　 Chúle Zhōngwén hé Yīngwén yǐwài, nǐ hái huì shuō shénme yǔyán?

The Auxiliary Verb 会 *huì*

You first met 会 *huì* in level 1, Unit 5, Lesson A. In this lesson you will work with 会 *huì* again as the auxiliary verb with another of its many meanings: "to know how to do something; to have the skill or ability to do something."

Subject + 会 *huì* + **Verb Phrase**

你会游泳吗？ Nǐ huì yóuyǒng ma?

我学中文学了一个学期了，我现在会说中文了。
Wǒ xué Zhōngwén xuéle yíge xuéqī le, wǒ xiànzài huì shuō Zhòngwén le.

Language Note

能 *néng*	(1)	can, to be physically capable of
		我的手很痛，所以今天不能打篮球。
		Wǒde shǒu hěn tòng, suǒyǐ jīntiān bùnéng dǎ lánqiú.
	(2)	indicates having the opportunity or permission to (same as 可以 *kěyǐ*)
		我能跟你去看电影。 *Wǒ néng gēn nǐ qù kàn diànyǐng.*

会 *huì*	(1)	can, know how to
		我会说中文。 *Wǒ huì shuō Zhòngwén.*
	(2)	It appears to be a main verb if one is speaking about knowledge of a language, but the main verb 说 *shuō* is usually omitted.
		我会德文。 *Wǒ huì Déwén.*
	(3)	possibility
		明天会下雨。 *Míngtiān huì xiàyǔ.*

可以 *kěyǐ*	(1)	can, may
		你可以来我家。 *Nǐ kěyǐ lái wǒ jiā.*
	(2)	indicating having permission
		上课的时候，不可以打电话。 *Shàngkè de shíhou, bù kěyǐ dǎ diànhuà.*
	(3)	indicating a suggestion
		你如果不知道怎么做，可以问老师。
		Nǐ rúguǒ bù zhīdào zěnme zuò, kěyǐ wèn lǎoshī.

The Descriptive Pattern "Verb 得 *de* + Complement"

This pattern is used to describe an action. The complement following verb 得 *de* is usually an adverb plus adjective which modifies, describes, or comments on the verb. This pattern expresses the degree of a certain action which has been performed.

Subject + Verb + 得 *de* + Adverb + Adjective

他学得很快。　Tā xué de hěn kuài.

我昨天晚上睡得不太好。

Wǒ zuótiān wǎnshang shuì de bú tài hǎo.

If there is a "verb-object" compound involved, the verb-object compound needs to remain and the verb needs to be repeated.

▲ 昨天睡得不好。

Subject + Verb-Object + Verb + 得 *de* + Adverb + Adjective

姐姐洗澡洗得很久。　Jiějie xǐzǎo xǐ de hěn jiǔ.

弟弟吃饭吃得很慢。　Dìdi chīfàn chī de hěn màn.

When there is a "Verb-Object" compound, the object can also be moved to the front to form a noun phrase with the subject by using the particle 的 *de*.

Subject 的 *de* Object + Verb + 得 *de* + Adverb + Adjective

他的排球打得不错。　Tāde páiqiú dǎ de búcuò.

你的字写得很好。　Nǐde zì xiě de hěn hǎo.

A Comparison Pattern using the Preposition 比 *bǐ*

The preposition 比 *bǐ* is used to compare two noun phrases in the pattern "NP₁ 比 *bǐ* NP₂." What follows can be regarded as a comment on this comparison. The comment can consist of an adjective, an auxiliary verb phrase, or just a verb phrase. Note that you do not use the adverb 很 *hěn* to modify the adjective.

NP₁ + 比 *bǐ* + NP₂ + comment

哥哥比弟弟壮。　Gēge bǐ dìdi zhuàng.

小美比小文喜欢看电影。　Xiǎoměi bǐ Xiǎowén xǐhuan kàn diànyǐng.

To express that NP₁ is more or less "adjective" than NP₂, use the following pattern:

NP₁ + 比 *bǐ* + NP₂ + comment + 一点儿 *yìdiǎnr* / 得多 *de duō* / 多了 *duō le*

美国比中国大一点儿。　Měiguó bǐ Zhōngguó dà yìdiǎnr.

火车比飞机慢得多。　Huǒchē bǐ fēijī màn de duō.

这条裤子比那条好看多了。　Zhèitiáo kùzi bǐ nèitiáo hǎokàn duō le.

When sentences involve a verb-object compound, the pattern is as follows. Note that the verb-object compound can be omitted if the context is clear.

NP₁ + **Verb-Object** + **Verb** + 得 *de* + 比 *bǐ* + NP₂ + **comment**

我睡觉睡得比你少。　Wǒ shuìjiào shuì de bǐ nǐ shǎo.

他写字写得比我漂亮。　Tā xiězì xiě de bǐ wǒ piàoliang.

The Negative Comparison Pattern "没有...这么 / 那么 *méiyǒu...zhème / nàme*"

To make negative comparisons, use 没有 *méiyǒu* to compare the two noun phrases.

NP₁ + 没有 *méiyǒu* + NP₂ + **Adjective**

晚上没有中午热。　Wǎnshang méiyǒu zhōngwǔ rè.

日本没有美国大。　Rìběn méiyǒu Měiguó dà.

The adverbs 这么 *zhème* and 那么 *nàme* are typically used to intensify the degree of the following adjective. They are also used in negative comparisons to express that "one is not as 'adjective' as the other one."

NP₁ + 没有 *méiyǒu* + NP₂ + 这么 *zhème* / 那么 *nàme* + **Adjective**

妈妈没有爸爸这么高。　Māma méiyǒu bàba zhème gāo.

今天没有昨天那么冷。　Jīntiān méiyǒu zuótiān nàme lěng.

A Comparison Pattern that Shows Similarity and Disparity "跟 / 和…(不)一样 *gēn / hé...(bù) yíyàng*"

This pattern 跟 / 和…(不)一样 *gēn / hé...(bù) yíyàng* is used to compare two things. Use 跟…一样 *gēn…yíyàng* to express similarity; and 跟…不一样 *gēn… bù yíyàng to express* disparity. The preposition 跟 *gēn* can be replaced by 和 *hé*. An adjective can be added after 一样 *yíyàng* to indicate the focus of a comparison. Note that in this pattern, the second noun phrase is regarded as the "standard."

NP₁ + 跟 *gēn* / 和 *hé* + NP₂ + (不)一样 *(bù) yíyàng* + **Adjective**

这本书和那本书不一样。

Zhèiběn shū hé nèiběn shū bù yíyàng.

今天的天气跟昨天一样好。

Jīntiān de tiānqi gēn zuótiān yíyàng hǎo.

▲ 今天的天气跟昨天一样好。

🔊 **国际学生 Guójì Xuésheng** *International Student*

Wu Sen and Zhao Mei discuss a new classmate they are walking home after school.

赵梅: 这个学期班上来了一个新的国际学生。	Zhào Méi: Zhèige xuéqī bānshàng láile yíge xīnde guójì xuésheng.
吴森: 她会说中文吗?	Wú Sēn: Tā huì shuō Zhōngwén ma?
赵梅: 会是会,可是说得不太好。	Zhào Méi: Huì shì huì, kěshì shuō de bú tài hǎo.
吴森: 她长得怎么样?	Wú Sēn: Tā zhǎng de zěnmeyàng?
赵梅: 长得很漂亮,没有我这么高,比我瘦一点儿。	Zhào Méi: Zhǎng de hěn piàoliang, méiyǒu wǒ zhème gāo, bǐ wǒ shòu yìdiǎnr.
吴森: 她人怎么样?	Wú Sēn: Tā rén zěnmeyàng?
赵梅: 她很好玩儿,心地也很好。	Zhào Méi: Tā hěn hǎowánr, xīndì yě hěn hǎo.
吴森: 她跟你一样大吗?	Wú Sēn: Tā gēn nǐ yíyàng dà ma?
赵梅: 对呀,我们都十六岁。	Zhào Méi: Duì ya, wǒmen dōu shíliù suì.
吴森: 你跟她熟吗?	Wú Sēn: Nǐ gēn tā shú ma?
赵梅: 还行。	Zhào Méi: Hái xíng.
吴森: 改天找她一起去看电影怎么样?	Wú Sēn: Gǎitiān zhǎo tā yìqǐ qù kàn diànyǐng zěnmeyàng?
赵梅: 可以呀,可是她已经有男朋友了。	Zhào Méi: Kěyǐ ya, kěshì tā yǐjīng yǒu nánpéngyou le.

4 　男的还是女的?　Nánde háishì Nǚde? / *Male or Female?*

Based on the dialogue, select the gender of the new international student.

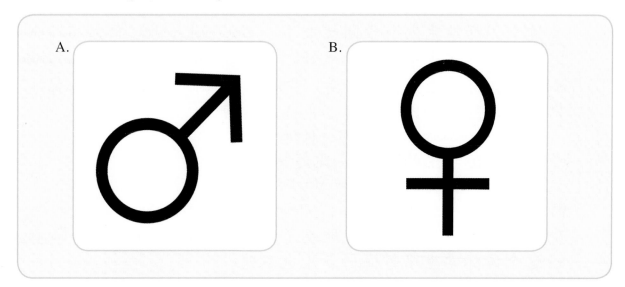

A.　　　　　　　　　　B.

5 　是谁?　Shì shéi? / *Who is the one?*

Based on the dialogue, make a logical guess and choose the image that most accurately depicts the new international student.

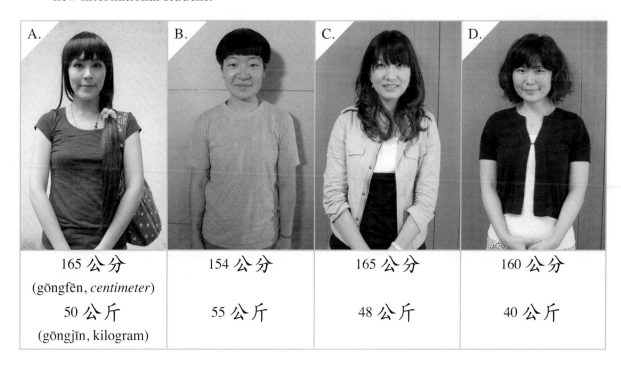

A.	B.	C.	D.
165 公分 (gōngfēn, *centimeter*)	154 公分	165 公分	160 公分
50 公斤 (gōngjīn, kilogram)	55 公斤	48 公斤	40 公斤

Read the following statements and decide if each statement is true or false. Correct any false statements.

1. 这个国际学生上个学期就来了。 Zhège guójì xuésheng shàngge xuéqī jiù láile.

2. 这个国际学生中文说得很好。 Zhège guójì xuésheng Zhōngwén shuō de hěn hǎo.

3. 这个国际学生长得很好看。 Zhège guójì xuésheng zhǎng de hěn hǎokàn.

4. 这个国际学生比赵梅矮，也比赵梅瘦。
   Zhège guójì xuésheng bǐ Zhào Méi ǎi, yě bǐ Zhào Méi shòu.

5. 这个国际学生的年纪(age)比赵梅小。
   Zhège guójì xuésheng de niánjì bǐ Zhào Méi xiǎo.

6. 这个国际学生很好玩儿。 Zhège guójì xuésheng hěn hǎowánr.

7. 这个国际学生已经有男朋友了。 Zhège guójì xuésheng yǐjīng yǒu nánpéngyou le.

8. 这个国际学生跟赵梅一点儿也不熟。
   Zhège guójì xuésheng gēn Zhào Méi yìdiǎnr yě bùshú.

文化橱窗 Wénhuà Chúchuāng
Culture Window

体校 Sports Schools

Sports schools are special institutions in China where promising young athletes are trained to become the nation's athletic stars. Different from ordinary schools, sports schools focus on students' athletic development instead of academic subjects. This allows students' athletic skills, techniques, and knowledge to improve in a short period of time. In addition to sports high schools, there are sports colleges that focus on the science of sports and athleticism through surveys, research, and experiments designed to discover new ways of pushing the human body to perform to its physical limit.

There are many specialties within sports schools, including soccer, basketball, table tennis, gymnastics, and martial arts. When a student is enrolled, the school will customize the student's curriculum according to his or her interests, physique and potential.

▲ *gymnastics*

▲ *swimming*

For example, if the student has parents who are both tall, the student may be allocated to soccer or basketball instead of gymnastics. However, students do make adjustments to their curricula as they grow and develop.

Since a sports school focuses more on physical training than academics, students from sports schools may fall behind academically. For this reason, young people in China have mixed feelings about sports schools. Most view it as an honor to be accepted, as it is proof that a person is one of the best among his or her peers. Others criticize sports schools, pointing out that the competition is so stiff that only a few students will become stars, while the rest will lack the skills to find a different career upon graduation.

The Beijing Shichahai Sports School, established in 1958, is one of the most prestigious in China. The school offers training in martial arts, gymnastics, volleyball, table tennis, and badminton, among other sports. Many famous athletes have emerged from Beijing Shichahai, including Zhang Yining, world champion in table tennis; Luo Wei, Olympic gold medalist in tae kwon do; Feng Kun, Olympic gold medalist in women's volleyball; and Jet Li, a kung fu star who has won numerous awards in martial arts.

7 文化动动脑 Wénhuà Dòngdòngnǎo / *Culture Check-up*

Choose the correct answer.

1. What subject do sports schools emphasize?
   A. Sports B. Culture C. Arts
2. What is the ultimate goal for students who attend a sports school?
   A. to become sports scientists B. to become professional athletes C. to become teachers
3. Students that go to sports colleges can also become what?
   A. sports scientists B. athletes C. PE teachers
4. If a student is petite, agile and flexible, which specialty would he/she suit best?
   A. gymnastics B. basketball C. boxing
5. Which is NOT a characteristic of sports schools?
   A. difficult training B. emphasis on academics C. stiff competition
6. In what year the Beijing Shichahai Sports School was established?
   A. 1955 B. 1985 C. 1958
7. Zhang Yining is a world champion of which sport?
   A. martial arts B. table tennis C. badminton
8. Which of the following martial artists graduated from a sports school?
   A. Jet Li B. Jackie Chan C. Bruce Lee

8 我会 **Wǒ Huì** / *I Can*

With a classmate, take turns asking and answering each other what you can and cannot do based on the following pictures. Follow the model.

Lìzi: A: 你会游泳吗?　Nǐ huì yóuyǒng ma?

B: 我会。　Wǒ huì.

Or, 我不会。　Wǒ búhuì.

1. 　2. 　3. 　4.

9 形容动作 **Xíngróng Dòngzuò** / *Describing Actions*

Describe the following actions using the pattern "Verb 得 *de*...." and the words provided.

Lìzi: 王太太说话 / 很快 Wáng tàitai shuōhuà / hěn kuài

王太太说话说得很快。　Wáng tàitai shuōhuà shuō de hěn kuài.

1. 姐姐化妆 / 很久 jiějie huàzhuāng / hěn jiǔ
2. 哥哥吃饭 / 太快 gēge chīfàn / tài kuài
3. 他们画画 / 很好看 tāmen huàhuà / hěn hǎokàn
4. 我们跳舞 / 太好了 wǒmen tiàowǔ / tài hǎole
5. 大家唱歌 / 很高兴 dàjiā chànggē / hěn gāoxìng
6. 妹妹做功课 / 很慢 mèimei zuò gōngkè / hěn màn
7. 你做这道菜 / 太辣 nǐ zuò zhèdào cài / tài là
8. 你做汤面 / 难吃死了 nǐ zuò tāngmiàn / nánchī sǐle
9. 他写中国字 / 很漂亮 tā xiě Zhōngguó zì / hěn piàoliang
10. 我今天考试 / 很不错 wǒ jīntiān kǎoshì / hěn búcuò
11. 大中打台球 / 不太好 Dàzhōng dǎ táiqiú / bú tài hǎo

▲ 大家唱歌

10 说说不同 | **Shuōshuo Bùtóng** / *Point out the Differences*

Compare the two people below using the pattern "没有...这么 / 那么 *méiyǒu...zhème / nàme*" and the photos or the information provided.

Lìzi: 郭志勇的眼睛没有罗嘉树那么大。
Guō Zhìyǒng de yǎnjīng méiyǒu Luó Jiāshù nàme dà.

姓名 xìngmíng: 郭志勇 Guō Zhìyǒng
生日 shēngrì: 1999. 8. 5
兄弟姐妹 xiōngdì-jiěmèi: 1
个性 gèxìng: 外向 wàixiàng
鞋码 xié mǎ (*foot size*): 12

姓名 xìngmíng: 罗嘉树 Luó Jiāshù
生日 shēngrì: 2002. 6. 19
兄弟姐妹 xiōngdì-jiěmèi: 4
个性 gèxìng: 内向 nèixiàng
鞋码 xié mǎ: 10.5

11 比一比 | **Bǐ Yì Bǐ** / *Make a Comparison*

Look at the following pictures and make comparisons using the preposition 比 *bǐ*. Note that you can use the words 一点儿 *yìdiǎnr*, 得多 *de duō*, or 多了 *duō le* to provide more detail.

1.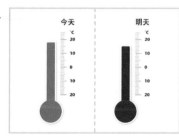

3.

5.

2.

4.

6.

12 一不一样？ **Yí Bù Yíyàng?** / *Same or Different?*

Look at the following photos and say whether the situation or the image are the same or not using the pattern "跟...(不)一样 *gēn...(bù) yíyàng*."

1.

3.
Mary   Helen

5.
Henry   Laura

2.
钱小姐   赵小姐

4.
今天   明天

6.

开口说 Kāikǒu Shuō
Communication

13 了解情况 **Liǎojiě Qíngkuàng** / *Asking About People*

Find a photograph that shows at least two of your friends. If you prefer, the photos can be cut out from a magazine. Bring the photograph to class and share it with a classmate. With your classmate, look at each others' photograph and ask questions about one of the friends shown.

1. Ask your classmate who appears in the photo.
2. Ask your classmate how they met the person.
3. Ask your classmate the name of the person.
4. Ask your classmate if the person is the same age as you.
5. Describe the look of the person and ask your classmate to describe him/her in more detail.
6. Ask your classmate to describe the person's personality.
7. Ask your classmate if he/she is close to the person.
8. Discuss with your classmate activities that their friend might enjoy.
9. Select an activity that might appeal to the person in the photo and practice how you would invite this person to join you.

自我提升 Zìwǒ Tíshēng

Raising the Bar

Vocabulary

华   huá   *n. in the flower of youth*

二八年华
èr bā nián huá
two-eights years young

▲ 二八年华

Language Note

This idiom is used to describe a young and beautiful 16-year-old girl. The two and eight in the phrase does not mean 28 years old, but two times eight (which is sixteen). The 华 *huá* in 年华 *nián huá* means beauty, and so this idiom is used to describe girls who are in the flower of their youth, especially at (but not limited to) 16 years of age.

她正当二八年华，是个高中生。

Tā zhèng dāng èr bā nián huá, shìge gāozhōngshēng.

She is two-eights years young right now and is a high school student.

In the olden days, people would always use idioms to talk about a certain ages. Below are some idioms that were used to describe young people.

1. 束*发之年 *shù fǎ zhī nián*: This idiom is used to talk about 15-year-old boys. In ancient times, boys did not cut their hair, and so by the time they reach 15, their hair would typically be long enough to tie up, symbolizing that they have become of age.

   * to bind

2. 及笄之年 *jí jī zhī nián*: This idiom is used to describe 15-year-old girls. In the olden days, once girls reached 15, she would use a hairpin (笄 *jī*) to secure their hair on top of her head, symbolizing that she has reached adulthood.

新同学

　　这个学期我的中文班来了两个新学生，一个男生，一个女生。他们是国际学生。男的是墨西哥人，女的是加拿大人。他们会说中文，而且都说得很好，可是他们的中国字写得不好，他们说他们的老师没有教他们怎么写。墨西哥来的同学黑黑壮壮的，我们全班都没有他那么高。他很害羞，是一个内向的人。我们找他一起去玩，他总是说不要。加拿大的女生长得很漂亮，身材也很苗条。她的个性很大方，所以我们常常一起出去。她比我大两岁，跟我的姐姐一样大。

Xīn Tóngxué

　　Zhège xuéqī wǒde Zhōngwén bān láile liǎngge xīn xuéshēng, yíge nánshēng, yíge nǚshēng. Tāmen shì guójì xuéshēng. Nánde shì Mòxīgērén, nǚde shì Jiā'nádàrén. Tāmen huì shuō Zhōngwén, érqiě dōu shuō de hěn hǎo, kěshì tāmen de Zhōngguó zì xiě de bùhǎo, tāmen shuō tāmen de lǎoshī méiyǒu jiāo tāmen zěnme xiě. Mòxīgē láide tóngxué hēihēi-zhuàngzhuàng de, wǒmen quán bān dōu méiyǒu tā nàme gāo. Tā hěn hàixiū, shì yíge nèixiàng de rén. Wǒmen zhǎo tā yìqǐ qù wán, tā zǒngshì shuō búyào. Jiā'nádà de nǚshēng zhǎng de hěn piàoliang, shēncái yě hěn miáotiáo. Tāde gèxìng hěn dàfāng, suǒyǐ wǒmen chángcháng yìqǐ chūqù. Tā bǐ wǒ dà liǎngsuì, gēn wǒde jiějie yíyàng dà.

14 通晓文意 **Tōngxiǎo Wényì** / *Understanding the Passage*

Complete the following sentences based on what you read in the previous passage.

1. 这个学期他的中文班来了__个__学生。
   Zhège xuéqī tāde Zhōngwénbān láile __ ge __ xuésheng.

2. 新的男同学是__人.，新的女同学是__人。
   Xīnde nán tóngxué shì __ rén, xīnde nǚ tóngxué shì __ rén.

3. 他们的中文说得__，可是中国字写得__。
   Tāmen de Zhōngwén shuō de __ , kěshì Zhōngguó zì xiě de __ .

4. 男的长得__的，他是全班__高的人。
   Nánde zhǎng de __ de, tā shì quán bān __ gāo de rén.

5. 男的个性很__，他是一个__的人。　Nánde gèxìng hěn __ , tā shì yíge __ de rén.

6. 女的长得__，身材很__。　Nǚde zhǎng de __ , shēncái hěn __ .

7. 女的个性很__，所以他们常一起出去。
   Nǚde gèxìng hěn __ , suǒyǐ tāmen cháng yìqǐ chūqù.

8. 女的比他大__，跟__一样大。　Nǚde bǐ tā dà __ , gēn __ yíyàng dà.

汉字天地 Hànzì Tiāndì

Chinese Characters

国 / 國 ■ guó ■ country; nation; state

The character 国 *guó* is a combination of radical and phonetic components. The outer part of this character—口 *wéi*—is the radical that means enclosure, and the inner part of this character—或 *huò*—is the phonetic component that gives 国 *guó* its sound. The 口 *wéi* symbolizes the boundary lines of a certain territory, the weapon (戈 *gē*) component is a symbol of defending the territory, and the mouth (口 *kǒu*) symbolizes the people living together in this territory.

Stroke Order

---

15 词汇延伸 Cíhuì Yánshēn / *Vocabulary Builder*

Below are characters that combine with 国 *guó* to create words. Match the Chinese words on the left with the appropriate English meanings on the right.

歌 gē *n. song*	庆 qìng *n. celebration*	土 tǔ *n. soil*	籍 jí *n. membership*	立 lì *v. to set up*

1. 国歌 guógē   A. national territory
2. 国庆 guóqìng   B. national; state-run
3. 国土 guótǔ   C. National Day
4. 国籍 guójí   D. national anthem
5. 国立 guólì   E. nationality

---

16 汉字侦探 Hànzì Zhēntàn / *Visual Detective*

Can you find 国 in the following pictures?

Lesson B

◀) 学校生活 (學校生活) Xuéxiào Shēnghuó *School Life*

公立学校 (公立學校)

gōnglì xuéxiào

n. public school

私立学校 (私立學校)

sīlì xuéxiào

n. private school

补习班 (補習班)

bǔxíbān

n. cram school

补习 (補習)

bǔxí

v. to take lessons after school

学长 (學長)

xuézhǎng

n. male senior (student)

学弟 (學弟)

xuédì

n. male junior (student)

学姐 (學姐)

xuéjiě

n. female senior (student)

学妹 (學妹)

xuémèi

n. female junior (student)

校友

xiàoyǒu

n. alumni

男孩
nánhái
n. boy

女孩
nǚhái
n. girl

这个学期你上了什么有意思的课?
Zhège xuéqī nǐ shàngle shénme yǒuyìsi de kè?
What interesting classes are you taking this semester?

跟上个学期一样,没什么特别有意思的。
Gēn shàngge xuéqī yíyàng, méi shénme tèbié yǒu yìsi de.
Like last semester, nothing interesting.

A: 请问你是方小姐吗? (請問你是方小姐嗎?)
Qǐngwèn nǐ shì Fāng xiǎojiě ma? *Excuse me. Are you Miss Fang?*

B: 是, 我就是。
Shì, wǒ jiù shì. *Yes, that's me.*

A: 你上高中了吗? (你上高中了嗎?)
Nǐ shàng gāozhōng le ma? *Are you in senior high school?*

B: 还没, 我还在上初中。(還沒, 我還在上初中。)
Hái méi, wǒ hái zài shàng chūzhōng. *Not yet, I'm still in junior high.*

去年跟你同班的那个日本学生回国了吗？
Qùnián gēn nǐ tóngbān de nèige Rìběn xuésheng huíguó le ma?
Did the Japanese student who was in your class last year go back to Japan?

还没，他明年才回国。
Hái méi, tā míngnián cái huíguó.
Not yet, he'll go back next year.

A: 有机会我想请你到我家来玩，这个周末怎么样？
（有機會我想請你到我家來玩。這個周末怎麼樣？）
Yǒu jīhuì wǒ xiǎng qǐng nǐ dào wǒ jiā lái wán, zhège zhōumò zěnmeyàng?
I'd like to invite you over to my house sometime. What about this weekend?

B: 不好意思，这个周末我已经有事了。
（不好意思，這個周末我已經有事了。）
Bù hǎoyìsi, zhège zhōumò wǒ yǐjīng yǒushì le.
I'm sorry, but I already have plans this weekend.

A: 这样啊，那改天吧。（這樣啊，那改天吧。）
Zhèyàng a, nà gǎitiān ba. *Oh, then maybe another day.*

· ·

这杯饮料太甜了，甜得我没办法喝。
（這杯飲料太甜了，甜得我沒辦法喝。）
Zhèbēi yǐnliào tài tiánle, tián de wǒ méi bànfǎ hē.
This drink is too sweet for me to drink.

Adjectives

同	tóng	*same; alike*
棒	bàng	*good; excellent*

Adverbs

就	jiù	*exactly; precisely*
还没有 (還沒有)	hái méiyǒu	*not yet*
非常	fēicháng	*very*
特别	tèbié	*especially; particularly*
这样 (這樣)	zhèyàng	*this way; like this*

Interjection

哦	ó	*indicating understanding or realization*

Nouns

事情	shìqing	*matter; thing; business*
文科	wénkē	*liberal arts*
理科	lǐkē	*natural sciences*
校队 (校隊)	xiàoduì	*school team*
机会 (機會)	jīhuì	*chance; opportunity*

Particle

得	de	*used between a verb or an adjective and its complement to indicate a result*

Time Word

以前	yǐqián	*before; formerly*

Verbs

参加 (參加)	cānjiā	*to join; to participate in*
请 (請)	qǐng	*to invite*

Verb-Objects

见面 (見面)	jiànmiàn	*to meet*
分班	fēnbān	*to arrange classes (based on students' academic preference)*
转学 (轉學)	zhuǎnxué	*to transfer to another school*

1 名词定义 Míngcí Dìngyì / *Definition*

Match each word with the most accurate definition.

1. 学长 xuézhǎng
2. 学弟 xuédì
3. 校友 xiàoyǒu
4. 学姐 xuéjiě
5. 学妹 xuémèi
6. 转学 zhuǎnxué

A. 年级比我大的女生 niánjí bǐ wǒ dà de nǚshēng

B. 年级比我小的男生 niánjí bǐ wǒ xiǎo de nánshēng

C. 年级比我大的男生 niánjí bǐ wǒ dà de nánshēng

D. 年级比我小的女生 niánjí bǐ wǒ xiǎo de nǚshēng

E. 到另一个学校上课 dào lìng yíge xuéxiào shàngkè

F. 已经毕业 (*to graduate*) 的同一个学校的学生 yǐjīng bìyè de tóng yíge xuéxiào de xuésheng

2 哪一科? Nǎ Yì Kē? / *Which Group?*

Identify whether the following subjects are considered liberal arts or natural science subjects. Write "A" if it is a liberal arts subject, "B" if it is a natural science subject, and "C" if it does not belong in either category.

1. 数学 shùxué
2. 美术 měishù
3. 历史 lìshǐ
4. 化学 huàxué
5. 物理 wùlǐ
6. 体育 tǐyù
7. 语文 yǔwén
8. 音乐 yīnyuè

3 个人问题 Gèrén Wèntí / *Personal Questions*

Answer the following questions in Chinese based on your own experiences and opinions.

1. 你新学期的课很有意思吗? Nǐ xīn xuéqī de kè hěn yǒu yìsi ma?
2. 你认识了新朋友吗? 多少个新朋友? Nǐ rènshi le xīn péngyou ma? Duōshǎo ge xīn péngyou?
3. 在学校里, 你跟谁特别好? 你跟他在同一个班吗? Zài xuéxiào lǐ, nǐ gēn shéi tèbié hǎo? Nǐ gēn tā zài tóng yíge bān ma?
4. 这个学期你的事情多不多? Zhège xuéqī nǐde shìqing duō bùduō?
5. 你比较喜欢文科还是理科? Nǐ bǐjiào xǐhuan wénkē háishì lǐkē?
6. 你参加校队吗? 什么校队? Nǐ cānjiā xiàoduì ma? Shénme xiàoduì?
7. 有机会你想请谁去你家玩? Yǒu jīhuì nǐ xiǎng qǐng shéi qù nǐ jiā wán?

Negate and Suspend Action with 还没(有) hái méi(yǒu)

To express that an action has not yet happened you may use the words 还没(有) hái méi(yǒu). A question that would provoke such a negative answer would usually be answered positively with a statement ending in the particle 呢 ne.

> **Subject** + **还没(有) hái méi(yǒu)** + **Verb Phrase**

饿死了，我今天还没吃东西。 È sǐ le, wǒ jīntiān hái méi chī dōngxi

A: 你做功课了吗？ Nǐ zuò gōngkè le ma?

B: 我刚刚回家，所以还没有做呢。 Wǒ gānggāng huíjiā, suǒyǐ hái méiyǒu zuò ne.

The pattern "Adjective + 得 de..." to Show the Degree of the Adjective

In the previous lesson, you learned that the pattern "Verb 得 de..." can be used to describe and show the degree of an action when it is followed by an adjective. Here, the pattern is "Adjective + 得 de..." and is followed by a sentence. It is used to tell the degree of the adjective or the effect the adjective has on the subject. Note that the subject of the attached sentence is usually omitted when it is the same as the main sentence.

> **Subject** + **Adjective** + **得 de** + **Sentence**

今天早上我累得不想起床。
Jīntiān zǎoshang wǒ lèide bùxiǎng qǐchuáng.
I was so tired this morning that I did not want to get up.

我的头疼得我没办法睡觉。
Wǒde tóu téng de wǒ méi bànfǎ shuìjiào.
I had such a headache that I could not fall asleep.

▲ 我的头疼

The Modification 的 *de*

The particle 的 *de* links modifiers and the noun that follows. The modifier can be a noun, pronoun, clause, or an adjective, and it must precede the 的 *de* before the noun. Here are some examples:

Modifier + **的** *de* + **Noun**

学生的书 xuésheng de shū (noun)

我的书 wǒde shū (pronoun)

很有意思的书 hěn yǒuyìsi de shū (adjective)

我昨天在书店买的那本书 wǒ zuótiān zài shūdiàn mǎide nèiběn shū (clause)

你常常看的那本中文书 nǐ chángcháng kànde nèiběn Zhōngwén shū

That Chinese book you're always reading

哥哥每天打球穿的那双球鞋 gēge měitiān dǎqiú chuān de nàshuāng qiúxié

The pair of tennis shoes my brother wears every day to play (tennis)

姐姐昨天去百货商店买的那件裙子真好看。

Jiějie zuótiān qù bǎihuò shāngdiàn mǎide nèijiàn qúnzi zhēn hǎokàn.

The skirt that my sister bought from the department store yesterday is very pretty.

The words 那件裙子 *nèijiàn qúnzi*, following 的 *de*, are the subject of the sentence "那件裙子真好看" meaning "That skirt is really pretty." Everything before 的 *de* tells you which skirt is implied.

他心情不好总是去的那个地方在哪儿？

Tā xīnqíng bùhǎo zǒngshì qùde nèige dìfang zài nǎr?

Where does he go when he is feeling down?

This sentence looks complex, but if you find the noun that follows 的 *de*, you should be able to work it out. The question at the end makes the sentence more difficult because in English you usually start with your question word (*where*). Since the Chinese "在哪儿 *zài nǎr*" comes at the end of the sentence, you will have to work harder to recognize questions in Chinese.

▲ 心情不好去的地方

Using the Adverb 就 *jiù* to Show Exactness

The adverb 就 *jiù* has many meanings. Here, it means "precisely; exactly." It is placed in front of a verb to indicate exactness and add emphasis.

> **Subject** + 就 *jiù* + **Verb Phrase**

虽然大家都说那部电影没有意思，可是我就想看。
Suīrán dàjiā dōu shuō nèibù diànyǐng méiyǒu yìsi, kěshì wǒ jiù xiǎng kàn.

A: 豆浆加咖啡好奇怪！ Dòujiāng jiā kāfēi hǎo qíguài.

B: 我就喜欢奇怪的饮料。 Wǒ jiù xǐhuan qíguài de yǐnliào.

Culture Note

Soy milk coffee is normal coffee with soy milk added instead of dairy milk. This style of coffee originated in the West for the lactose intolerant. Although this drink was introduced to China and Taiwan through international café chains, most Chinese people do not prefer it over regular dairy-milk coffee.

The Pattern "到...来 / 去 *dào...lái / qù*" to Show Direction

In Level 1, Unit 3, Lesson C, you were introduced to the verbs 来 *lái* and 去 *qù*, followed by a place word to indicate motion and direction. The following pattern creates the same meaning, but the place words are preceded by the preposition 到 *dào* instead.

> **Subject** + 到 *dào* + **Place** + 来 *lái* / 去 *qù*

我坐校车到学校来。 Wǒ zuò xiàochē dào xuéxiào lái.
钱小姐已经到德国去了。 Qián xiǎojiě yǐjīng dào Déguó qùle.

The Pattern "到...来 / 去 *dào...lái / qù*" to Show Purpose

A verb phrase can be added after the verb 来 *lái* / 去 *qù* to indicate purpose.

> **Subject** + 到 *dào* + **Place** + 来 *lái* / 去 *qù* + **Verb Phrase**

他们到美国来念书。 Tāmen dào Měiguó lái niànshū.
我请同学到我家来打电子游戏。 Wǒ qǐng tóngxué dào wǒ jiā lái dǎ diànzǐ yóuxì.

会话 Huìhuà

Dialogue

🔊 新学期，新生活 Xīn Xuéqī, Xīn Shēnghuó *New Semester, New Life*

Li Yunying is talking with her mom about a new friend.

妈妈：	新学期怎么样？	Māma:	Xīn xuéqī zěnmeyàng?
李云英：	我的课都很有意思。	Lǐ Yúnyīng:	Wǒde kè dōu hěn yǒuyìsi.
妈妈：	你认识了什么新朋友？	Māma:	Nǐ rènshi le shénme xīn péngyou?
李云英：	我还没认识什么新朋友。这个学期事情非常多，多得我没有时间跟朋友出去。	Lǐ Yúnyīng:	Wǒ hái méi rènshi shénme xīn péngyou. Zhèige xuéqī shìqíng fēicháng duō, duō de wǒ méiyǒu shíjiān gēn péngyou chūqù.
妈妈：	昨天来我们家的那个女孩是谁？	Māma:	Zuótiān lái wǒmen jiā de nèige nǚhái shì shéi?
李云英：	哦，她就是苏小萍，是我去年的同学，我跟她特别好。	Lǐ Yúnyīng:	Ó, tā jiùshì Sū Xiǎopíng, shì wǒ qùnián de tóngxué, wǒ gēn tā tèbié hǎo.
妈妈：	你们今年不在同一个班了吗？	Māma:	Nǐmen jīnnián búzài tóng yíge bān le ma?
李云英：	她喜欢理科，她的数学和化学都很棒，所以她去了理科班。	Lǐ Yúnyīng:	Tā xǐhuan lǐkē, tāde shùxué hé huàxué dōu hěn bàng, suǒyǐ tā qùle lǐkēbān.
妈妈：	你们现在还常见面吗？	Māma:	Nǐmen xiànzài hái cháng jiànmiàn ma?
李云英：	没有以前那么多。	Lǐ Yúnyīng:	Méiyǒu yǐqián nàme duō.
妈妈：	为什么呢？	Māma:	Wèishénme ne?
李云英：	因为这个学期她参加了游泳校队，所以很忙。	Lǐ Yúnyīng:	Yīnwèi zhèige xuéqī tā cānjiāle yóuyǒng xiàoduì, suǒyǐ hěn máng.
妈妈：	这样啊，有机会请她到我们家来吃饭。	Māma:	Zhè yàng a, yǒu jīhuì qǐng tā dào wǒmen jiā lái chīfàn.
李云英：	好啊，谢谢妈妈！	Lǐ Yúnyīng:	Hǎo a, xièxie māma!

4 她们的关系 Tāmende Guānxì / The Relationship

Based on the dialogue, identify the relationship between each character.

A.

李云英

B.

苏小萍

C.

妈妈

5 校队 Xiàoduì / School Team

Based on the dialogue, select the school team that Su Xiaoping joins this semester.

A.    B.    C.    D.

6 对还是错? Duì háishì Cuò? / True or False?

Read the following statements and decide if each statement is true or false. Correct any false statements.

1. 李云英和朋友在说话。 Lǐ Yúnyīng hé péngyou zài shuōhuà.

2. 李云英的妈妈问她新学期的事。 Lǐ Yúnyīng de māma wèn tā xīn xuéqī de shì.

3. 李云英觉得她的课没有意思。 Lǐ Yúnyīng juéde tāde kè méiyǒu yìsi.

4. 李云英认识了很多新朋友。 Lǐ Yúnyīng rènshi le hěn duō xīn péngyou.

5. 苏小萍昨天去了李云英家。 Sū Xiǎopíng zuótiān qùle Lǐ Yúnyīng jiā.

6. 苏小萍跟李云英不熟。 Sū Xiǎopíng gēn Lǐ Yúnyīng bùshú.

7. 苏小萍和李云英今年不同班，因为苏小萍去了理科班。
Sū Xiǎopíng hé Lǐ Yúnyīng jīnnián bù tóngbān, yīnwèi Sū Xiǎopíng qùle lǐkēbān.

8. 李云英的妈妈想请苏小萍吃饭。
Lǐ Yúnyīng de māma xiǎng qǐng Sū Xiǎopíng chīfàn.

International Students

Due to the recent popularity of Chinese culture around the world, more and more people would like to experience Chinese culture for themselves. Now, many famous Chinese universities take international students, including Beijing Foreign Studies University, Beijing Normal University, and Beijing University of Technology. The exchange programs vary in duration, and can be either three-month semester programs; six-month programs; or long-term programs that last over a year. These different programs have different focuses.

▲ *international students*

The short ones do not offer degrees, but provide opportunities for foreign students to experience Chinese culture and learn basic Chinese. The longer programs are equivalent to studying abroad and students will receive a degree from a Chinese university once they have completed the program. The more popular programs include Chinese language, Chinese traditional medicine, and politics.

▲ *Wudaokou, Beijing*

International students have interesting lives in China. The schools provide them with English or bilingual classes. These classes may included language courses, Chinese geography, history, or cultural studies. A special group of people is assigned to help international students adapt to their new surroundings. In addition, schools provide international students with activities to help them meet and spend time with domestic students. This allows for the opportunity for international students to join Chinese students for lunch, library trips, sporting events, and even home visits. The intention is for international students to get a feel of what life is really like for a Chinese student. During vacation periods, schools will also organize trips for international students to visit famous locations or landmarks.

International students are also encouraged to share their own cultures with their classmates. For example, in schools like Beijing Foreign Studies University where there are many international students, the school celebrates holidays and festivals from all around the world throughout the year. On those days, students will dress up; prepare each other's ethnic foods to share; and through this, experience another culture's traditions.

In the last few years, the number of international students in China has risen by 18% each year. In 2004, the total number of international students in China reached 110,800, 32,000 of which (28.9%) were studying for degrees. In 2008, this number rose to 223,000, with over 50,000 international students in Beijing alone. These international students came from over 180 countries, with South Korea at the top of the list. Near Wudaokou in Beijing, there are now many Korean stores and restaurants, forming a small Korean Town.

 文化动动脑 **Wénhuà Dòngdòngnǎo** / *Culture Check-up*

Choose the correct answer.

1. How long are the shortest exchange programs?
   A. a week
   B. three months
   C. six months

2. The short exchange programs do not include which of the following for their foreign students?
   A. experiencing the culture
   B. learning Chinese
   C. getting a degree

3. The culture link activities between international and domestic students do not include which of the following?
   A. having meals together
   B. learning together
   C. living together

4. When do schools often arrange for international students to visit famous landmarks?
   A. after class
   B. during vacations
   C. on the weekends

5. Foreign exchange students often introduce their own cultures to the Chinese through what activity?
   A. celebrating the holidays
   B. making food from their own countries
   C. providing toys from their own countries

6. Most foreign students in China come from which country?
   A. Korea
   B. Japan
   C. the United States

语言练习 Yŭyán Liànxí
Language Practice

8 还没有 Hái Méiyŏu / *Not Yet*

With a classmate, take turns asking and answering the following questions. Use the provided example as a guide.

Lìzi: A: 你去了吗？ Nǐ qùle ma?

B: 我还没（有）去。 Wǒ hái méi(yǒu) qù.

1. 你洗澡了吗？　Nǐ xǐzǎo le ma?
2. 他看病了吗？　Tā kànbìng le ma?
3. 姐姐醒了吗？　Jiějie xǐngle ma?
4. 弟弟吃药了吗？　Dìdi chīyào le ma?
5. 爷爷量体温了吗？　Yéye liáng tǐwēn le ma?
6. 你们今天锻炼了吗？　Nǐmen jīntiān duànliàn le ma?
7. 我们要出门了，你换衣服了吗？　Wǒmen yào chūmén le, nǐ huàn yīfu le ma?
8. 你买了上课要用的那本书了吗？　Nǐ mǎile shàngkè yào yòngde nèiběn shū le ma?

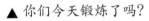
▲ 你们今天锻炼了吗？

9 描述结果 Miáoshù Jiéguŏ / *Describing Results*

Combine the sentences provided using the pattern "Adjective / Verb + 得 *de*…."

Lìzi: 妹妹吃饭吃得很慢。妈妈很不高兴。
Mèimei chīfàn chīde hěn màn. Māma hěn bù gāoxìng.
妹妹吃饭吃得很慢，慢得妈妈很不高兴。
Mèimei chīfàn chīde hěn màn, màn de māma hěn bù gāoxìng.

1. 我的腿痛。我不能走路。　Wǒde tuǐ tòng. Wǒ bùnéng zǒulù.
2. 弟弟很饿。弟弟没有精神念书。　Dìdi hěn è. Dìdi méiyǒu jīngshén niànshū.
3. 他的脚指很长。我们很惊讶。　Tāde jiǎozhǐ hěn cháng. Wǒmen hěn jīngyà.
4. 姐姐泡澡泡得很久。我生气了。　Jiějie pàozǎo pào de hěn jiǔ. Wǒ shēngqì le.
5. 奶奶非常不舒服。奶奶什么话都不想说。
Nǎinai fēicháng bù shūfu. Nǎinai shénme huà dōu bùxiǎng shuō.
6. 我流鼻涕流了一个星期了。我的鼻子痛死了。
Wǒ liú bítì liúle yíge xīngqī le. Wǒde bízi tòng sǐle.

10 形容人物 *Xíngróng Rénwù* / **Describing People**

With a classmate, take turns asking and answering who is who in each of the pictures using the pattern "…的 *de*…." Follow the model.

陈莉
Chén Lì

Lìzi: **A:** 谁是陈莉？ Shéi shì Chén Lì?

B: 在吹头发的那个人是陈莉。

Zài chuī tóufa de nèige rén shì Chén Lì

1. 钱文 Qián Wén
2. 刘大中 Liú Dàzhōng
3. 林梅芳 Lín Méifāng
4. 方玫 Fāng Méi
5. 张晴 Zhāng Qíng
6. 李武 Lǐ Wǔ

11 问答练习 **Wèn-dá Liànxí** / *Q&A Practice*

With a classmate, take turns asking each other the following questions and providing responses.

1. 校长开的车是美国车吗？ Xiàozhǎng kāide chē shì Měiguó chē ma?

2. 你自己选你每天穿的衣服吗？ Nǐ zìjǐ xuǎn nǐ měitiān chuānde yīfu ma?

3. 你常常去的那个购物中心在哪里？ Nǐ chángcháng qùde nèige gòuwù zhōngxīn zài nǎlǐ?

4. 你喜欢的衣服牌子(brand)叫什么名字？ Nǐ xǐhuan de yīfu páizi jiào shénme míngzi?

5. 下个星期你和朋友要去看的电影是什么片？
   Xiàge xīngqī nǐ hé péngyou yào qù kànde diànyǐng shì shénme piàn?

6. 上个学期中文课坐在你旁边的那个学生是男的还是女的？
   Shàngge xuéqī Zhōngwén kè zuò zài nǐ pángbiān de nèige xuésheng shì nánde háishì nǚde?

12 强调语意 Qiángdiào Yǔyì / *Emphasizing the Tone*

Answer the following questions using the adverb 就 *jiù* and the words provided.

Lìzi: 谁是你妹妹？（那个女孩）Shéi shì nǐ mèimei? (nèige nǚhái)

那个女孩就是我妹妹。 Nèige nǚhái jiù shì wǒ mèimei.

1. 哪里有书店？（学校旁边）Nǎlǐ yǒu shūdiàn? (xuéxiào pángbiān)
2. 谁是你最好的好朋友？（王平）Shéi shì nǐ zuìhǎo de hǎo péngyou? (Wang Ping)
3. 哪本书是吴老师的？（那本红色的）Něiběn shū shì Wú lǎoshī de? (nèiběn hóngsè de)
4. 哪个是抹茶口味的冰淇淋？（这个）Něige shì mǒchá kǒuwèi de bīngqílín? (zhèige)

13 合并句子 Hébìng Jùzi / *Combining Sentences*

Combine the following sentences using the pattern "到…来 / 去 *dào…lái / qù*."

Lìzi: 我哥哥去中国。我哥哥去学习。 Wǒ gēge qù Zhōngguó. Wǒ gēge qù xuéxí.

我哥哥到中国去学习。 Wǒ gēge dào Zhōngguó qù xuéxí.

1. 我要去图书馆。我要去借书。 Wǒ yào qù túshūguǎn. Wǒ yào qù jièshū.
2. 妈妈去百货商店。妈妈去买大衣。 Māma qù bǎihuò shāngdiàn. Māma qù mǎi dàyī.
3. 他爸爸来学校。他爸爸跟老师见面。 Tā bàba lái xuéxiào. Tā bàba gēn lǎoshī jiànmiàn.
4. 大明来我家。大明来我家打电子游戏。
   Dà Míng lái wǒ jiā. Dà Míng lái wǒ jiā dǎ diànzǐ yóuxì.

Kāikǒu Shuō

Communication

14 谈谈你的好朋友 Tántan nǐde hǎo péngyou / *Talk about good friends*

With a classmate, role play that one of you is a parent and the other is a child and that you are talking about a good friend. The parent should ask the following.

1. How his / her new semester is going.
2. If he / she has any new friends.
3. The name of his / her good friend.
4. How he / she got to know his / her good friend.
5. What his / her good friend likes to do for fun.
6. Suggest that he / she invite his / her good friend to come to the house some day.

Review the posters below and answer the questions that follow.

摄影社招生

爱摄影的你，快来吧！

★ 社团迎新：9/26 (日)
10:00~18:30
★ 社课时间：每周三
19:30~21:00
★ 户外摄影：每个月的第二个
星期天

还在担心照片拍不好吗？
想要学习摄影吗？马上来摄
影社吧！快打给摄影社李同
学：0935-625265

话剧社欢迎你

▲ 练习时间：每个星期一、
二、四晚上六点半到九点

社团大活动

§ 9/25(六)：迎新晚会
§ 11/16(二)：话剧比赛

如果你跟我们一样也喜
欢话剧，请你快一点儿给吴
同学打电话：0912-123321

1. 如果你想要去话剧社，应该给谁打电话？
Rúguǒ nǐ xiǎng yào qù huàjùshè, yīnggāi gěi shéi dǎ diànhuà?

2. 哪个社团每星期要练习三天？
Něige shètuán měi xīngqī yào liànxí sāntiān?

3. 哪个社团的迎新(*to greet new arrivals*)早上开始？
Něige shètuán de yíngxīn zǎoshang kāishǐ?

4. 话剧比赛是什么时候？
Huàjù bǐsài shì shénme shíhou?

5. 摄影社每个月到外面(*outside*)去摄影几次？什么时候？
Shèyǐngshè měige yuè dào wàimian qù shèyǐng jǐcì? Shénme shíhou?

Vocabulary

良	liáng	*adj.*	*good*
益	yì	*adj.*	*helpful; beneficial*

良朋益友
liángpéng-yìyǒu
a good friend

▲ 良朋益友

Language Note

This idiom describes a friend who helps to increase one's knowledge and make one a better person.

小李不但常常教我功课，而且也常常帮我，
真是我的良朋益友。

Xiǎo Lǐ búdàn chángcháng jiāo wǒ gōngkè, érqiě yě chángcháng bāng wǒ, zhēnshì wǒde liángpéng-yìyǒu.

Xiao Li not only helps me with my homework, but he often helps me in other things, too. He really is a good friend of mine.

If we have 良朋益友 *liángpéng-yìyǒu* near us, we should keep them close, but what if we have frienemies close by? 割席绝交 *gē xí jué jiāo* (to break all contact) is a Chinese idiom. It originated with the story of a person called Guan Ning who loved to learn. Once, when he was sitting on a mat and reading with a friend, a horse-drawn carriage with a passenger passed by his window. He did not look up from his book, but his friend put down his book and looked out of the window. After that moment, Guan Ning cut the mat in half so that they no longer sat together. This idiom is now used to say that one has severed all contact with one's former friend.

高二新学期

　　新学期已经开始了，这个学期我们分[1]了班。我的好朋友几乎都去了理科班。虽然我喜欢物理和化学，我也想去理科班，可是我的文科比理科好多了，所以我还是选[2]了文科班。高二开始，功课比以前多得多，多得我不能看电视。而且，我周末还得上补习班。我补外语、语文、数学、历史和地理，所以我星期六和星期天都很忙，忙得我没有时间跟朋友出去玩。高考[3]结束以后，我一定要去旅行。爸爸妈妈说了，要是我高考考得好，就带我去美国和加拿大玩一个月！

[1]分: to separate　　[2]选: to choose　　[3]高考: college entrance examination

Gāo'èr Xīn Xuéqī

　Xīn xuéqī yǐjīng kāishǐ le, zhège xuéqī wǒmen fēnle bān. Wǒde hǎo péngyou jīhū dōu qùle lǐkēbān. Suīrán wǒ xǐhuan wùlǐ hé huàxué, wǒ yě xiǎng qù lǐkēbān, kěshì wǒde wénkē bǐ lǐkē hǎo duō le, suǒyǐ wǒ háishì xuǎnle wénkēbān. Gāo'èr kāishǐ, gōngkè bǐ yǐqián duō de duō, duō de wǒ bùnéng kàn diànshì. Érqiě, wǒ zhōumò hái děi shàng bǔxíbān. Wǒ bǔ wàiyǔ, yǔwén, shùxué, lìshǐ hé dìlǐ, suǒyǐ wǒ Xīngqīliù hé Xīngqītiān dōu hěn máng, máng de wǒ méiyǒu shíjiān gēn péngyou chūqù wán. Gāokǎo jiéshù yǐhòu, wǒ yídìng yào qù lǚxíng. Bàba māma shuō le, yàoshì wǒ gāokǎo kǎo de hǎo, jiù dài wǒ qù Měiguó hé Jiā'nádà wán yíge yuè!

16 通晓文意 Tōngxiǎo Wényì / Understanding the Passage

Complete the following sentences based on what you read in the previous passage.

1. 这个学期他分了 __ 。　　Zhège xuéqī tā fēnle __.

2. 他的好朋友几乎都去了__班。　　Tāde hǎo péngyou jīhū dōu qùle __ bān.

3. 他喜欢__和__，他也想去理科班。　　Tā xǐhuan __ hé __, tā yě xiǎng qù lǐkēbān.

4. 因为他的文科比理科__，所以他选了__。
　　Yīnwèi tāde wénkē bǐ lǐkē __, suǒyǐ tā xuǎnle __.

5. __开始，功课比以前多得多，多得他__。
　　__ kāishǐ, gōngkè bǐ yǐqián duō de duō, duō de tā __.

6. 他周末得上__，所以他忙得__。　　Tā zhōumò děi shàng __, suǒyǐ tā máng de __.

7. 他说高考结束以后，他一定要去__。
　　Tā shuō gāokǎo jiéshù yǐhòu, tā yídìng yào qù __.

8. 要是他高考考得好，他的爸妈要带他去__和__，他们要去__个月。
　　Yàoshì tā gāokǎo kǎo de hǎo, tāde bà-mā yào dài tā qù __ hé __, tāmen yào qù __ ge yuè.

汉字天地 Hànzì Tiāndì

Chinese Characters

饭 ■ fàn ■ cooked rice; meal

The character 饭 *fàn* is a combination of radical and phonetic components. The 食 *shí* on the left is a radical meaning that the character has to do with food; and the character on the right, 反 *fǎn*, is the phonetic component. This character is formed to mean cooked grains, which, in the case of the Chinese, mostly means cooked rice. As rice is the staple food of the Chinese people, to have a meal can also be called "吃饭 *chīfàn*."

Stroke Order

17 词汇延伸 Cíhuì Yánshēn / Vocabulary Builder

Below are characters that combine with 饭 *fàn* to create words. Match the Chinese words on the left with the appropriate English meanings on the right.

店 diàn	厅 tīng	菜 cài	盒 hé	馆 guǎn
n. store	n. hall	n. vegetable	n. box	n. hall

1. 饭店 fàndiàn   A. hotel
2. 饭厅 fàntīng   B. lunch-box
3. 饭菜 fàncài   C. food
4. 饭盒 fànhé   D. restaurant
5. 饭馆 fànguǎn   E. dining room

Can you find 饭 in the following pictures?

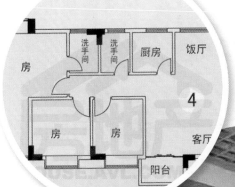

饭

词汇 Cíhuì
Vocabulary

🔊 电话用语 (電話用語) Diànhuà Yòngyǔ *Telephone Calls*

拨电话 (撥電話)
bo dianhua
v.o. to dial the phone

接电话 (接電話) jiē diànhuà
v.o. to answer the phone

挂电话 (掛電話) guà diànhuà
v.o. to hang up the phone

等一下 děng yíxià
v.+m.w. to wait a moment

留言
liúyán
v.o. to leave a message

打错了 (打錯了)
dǎcuò le
ce. to dial a wrong number

小孩
xiǎohái
n. kid; child

孩子
háizi
n. child

老人
lǎorén
n. an old person;
a senior citizen

养老院
(養老院)
yǎnglǎoyuàn
n. nursing home

孤儿院
(孤兒院)
gū'éryuàn
n. orphanage

志愿工作
(志願工作)
zhìyuàn gōngzuò
n. volunteer work

聊天
liáotiān
v.o. to chat

散步(散步)
sànbù
v. to take a walk;
to stroll

A: 喂，请问林美文在家吗？（喂，請問林美文在家嗎？）

Wéi, qǐngwèn Lín Měiwén zài jiā ma? *Hello! Is Lin Meiwen at home?*

B: 我就是。请问你是哪位？（我就是。請問你是哪位？）

Wǒ jiù shì. Qǐngwèn nǐ shì nǎwèi? *This is she. Who's speaking, please?*

or

B: 她不在，你要留言吗？（她不在，你要留言嗎？）

Tā búzài, nǐ yào liúyán ma? *She's not in. Would you like to leave a message?*

不，我不只会做中国菜，
我还会做日本菜和意大利菜。

Bù, wǒ bùzhǐ huì zuò Zhōngguó cài, wǒ hái huì zuò
Rìběn cài hé Yìdàlì cài.

No. I can not only make Chinese dishes, I can also make Japanese and Italian dishes.

你只会做中国菜吧？

Nǐ zhǐ huì zuò Zhōngguó cài ba?

You can only make Chinese dishes, right?

A: 这个故事真有意思。你再说一次，好不好？

（這個故事真有意思。你再說一次，好不好？）

Zhège gùshì zhēn yǒu yìsi. Nǐ zài shuō yícì, hǎo bùhǎo?

This story is very interesting. Can you tell it again, please?

B: 好啊。（好啊。）

Hǎo a. *Okay!*

李心今天没有来学校。她去哪里了？

Lǐ Xīn jīntiān méiyǒu lái xuéxiào. Tā qù nǎlǐ le?

Li Xin didn't come to school today. Where did she go?

我不知道她到哪里去了。

Wǒ bù zhīdào tā dào nǎlǐ qùle.

I don't know where she went.

Adverbs

常常	chángcháng	often; frequently
再	zài	again

Conjunction

不只	bùzhǐ	not only

Nouns

故事	gùshì	story
爱心（愛心）	àixīn	love and care
准备（準備）	zhǔnbèi	preparation
地方	dìfāng	place; space; part
服务（服務）	fúwù	service

Measure Word

位	wèi	polite measure word for people

Pronouns

那里（那裡）	nàlǐ	there
那儿（那兒）	nàr	there (colloquial)
这里（這裡）	zhèlǐ	here
这儿（這兒）	zhèr	here (colloquial)

Verbs

提	tí	to mention; to bring up
服务（服務）	fúwù	to serve
教	jiāo	to teach
陪	péi	to accompany
聊	liáo	to chat
叫	jiào	to ask; to advise; to tell
回	huí	to return; to answer; to reply
讲（講）	jiǎng	to speak; to say; to tell; to talk about
准备（準備）	zhǔnbèi	to prepare

Verb-Complements

提起	tíqǐ	to mention
回去	huíqù	to leave; to go back
回来（回來）	huílái	to return; to come back

Choose the appropriate phrases from the box to best complete the paragraph.

留言 liúyán	接电话 jiē diànhuà	等一下 děng yíxià
挂电话 guà diànhuà	打电话 dǎ diànhuà	

我今天下课以后给秦明 1.＿，可是没有人接，所以我就 2.＿了。然后 (then) 我给林依依打电话 3.＿的人是她姐姐，她姐姐说依依不在家，问我要不要 4.＿。我说要，所以她请我 5.＿，她得去拿纸和笔。

Wǒ jīntiān xiàkè yǐhòu gěi Qín Míng 1. ＿, kěshì méiyǒu rén jiē, suǒyǐ wǒ jiù 2. ＿le. Ránhòu, wǒ gěi Lín Yīyī dǎ diànhuà, 3. ＿de rén shì tā jiějie, tā jiějie shuō Yīyī bú zài jiā, wèn wǒ yào búyào 4. ＿. Wǒ shuō yào, suǒyǐ tā qǐng wǒ 5. ＿, tā děi qù ná zhǐ hé bǐ.

2 对还是错? Duì háishì Cuò? / True or False?

🔊 **You will hear four words. Decide if what you hear matches what is shown in the photos.**

1.

3.

2.

4.

Answer the following questions in Chinese based on your own experiences and opinions.

1. 你常常给朋友打电话吗？ Nǐ chángcháng gěi péngyou dǎ diànhuà ma?
2. 你应该怎么叫王美的爸爸？ Nǐ yīnggāi zěnme jiào Wáng Měi de bàba?
3. 你做小区(community)服务吗？ Nǐ zuò xiǎoqū fúwù ma?
4. 你喜欢讲故事吗？你讲得好不好？
   Nǐ xǐhuan jiǎng gùshi ma? Nǐ jiǎng de hǎo bù hǎo?
5. 你会不会教英文？你可以教外国学生英文吗？
   Nǐ huì búhuì jiāo Yīngwén? Nǐ kěyǐ jiāo wàiguó xuéshēng Yīngwén ma?

句型介绍 Jùxíng Jièshào
Language Patterns

Indirect Questions

Consider the following sentences:

I wonder when mom is coming home.

I don't know who that is.

These sentences contain implied questions. Rephrased they would become, "When is mom coming home?" and "Who is that?" Questions in statement form are known as indirect questions. Although you will notice that in English they involve changes in the normal word order for questions, indirect questions in Chinese do not involve word order changes. Here are some examples.

Sentence + Question

我不确定美美<u>几点到学校来</u>。 Wǒ bú quèdìng Měiměi jǐdiǎn dào xuéxiào lái.
请你帮我问问<u>这个东西多少钱</u>。 Qǐng nǐ bāng wǒ wènwen zhèige dōngxi duōshǎo qián.
那个男生很帅，我姐姐想知道<u>他是谁</u>。
Nèige nánshēng hěn shuài, wǒ jiějie xiǎng zhīdao tā shì shéi.

▲ 那个男生很帅

In Chinese, the word order of a sentence is :

Subject + **Time Word** + **Place Word** + **Verb Phrase**

You might want to ask a question about any one of the components in the sentence. To do so, in Chinese, simply place the appropriate question word into the sentence at the place where that component would normally appear. Thus the word order of a statement or a question is the same.

他昨天在书店买了这本书。 Tā zuótiān zài shūdiàn mǎile zhèiběn shū.

谁昨天在书店买了这本书？

Shéi zuótiān zài shūdiàn mǎile zhèiběn shū ?

他什么时候在书店买了这本书？

Tā shénme shíhou zài shūdiàn mǎile zhèiběn shū ?

他昨天在哪里买了这本书？ Tā zuótiān zài nǎlǐ mǎile zhèiběn shū ?

他昨天在书店买了什么？ Tā zuótiān zài shūdiàn mǎile shénme?

The Pattern "不只…还… *bùzhǐ…hái…*" to Show a Result

This pattern is similar to the pattern "不但…而且… *búdàn…érqiě…*" introduced in Level 1, Unit 6, Lesson C. The adverb 还 *hái* means "even," and it indicates that the speaker thinks the significance of the second verb phrase is greater than that of the first one. The adverb 还 *hái* can be replaced with 而且 *érqiě*.

Subject + **不只 *bùzhǐ*** + **Verb Phrase 1** + **还 *hái*** + **Verb Phrase 2**

哥哥不只会说法文，还会说中文。 Gēge bùzhǐ huì shuō Fǎwén, hái huì shuō Zhōngwén.

他病得很严重，不只咳嗽，还发烧。

Tā bìng de hěn yánzhòng, bùzhǐ késòu, hái fāshāo.

▲ 他不只咳嗽还发烧

The Verb 叫 *jiào*

The verb 叫 *jiào* means "to ask; to advise." It is a causative verb, so the subject gives an order or a suggestion and the recipient is the one who completes the action. The recipient is also the subject of the action.

Subject + 叫 *jiào* + **Recipient** + **Verb Phrase**

老师叫大家不要吵。 Lǎoshī jiào dàjiā búyào chǎo.

爸爸叫弟弟去做功课。 Bàba jiào dìdi qù zuò gōngkè.

Using the Adverb 再 *zài* to Show Repetition of an Action

The adverb 再 *zài* means "again." It indicates that the actions will be repeated in the future.

Subject + 再 *zài* + **Verb Phrase**

我好饿，我想再吃一个汉堡包。 Wǒ hǎo è, wǒ xiǎng zài chī yíge hànbǎobāo.

这个数学题我还是不懂，请你再说一次，好吗？

Zhège shùxué tí wǒ háishì bùdǒng, qǐng nǐ zài shuō yícì, hǎo ma?

Language Note

In Unit 2, Lesson B, we introduced the adverb 又 *yòu*, which also means "again." The difference between 又 *yòu* and 再 *zài* is:

又 *yòu*: refers to action that have actually repeated and actions that we know are going to happen again.

再 *zài* : refers to action that is suspected to happen in the future, but not guaranteed.

For example,

明天又是星期五了。

Míngtiān yòu shì Xīngqīwǔ le.

Tomorrow is Friday again.

那部电影很好看，所以我又看了一次。

Nèibù diànyǐng hěn hǎokàn, suǒyǐ wǒ yòu kànle yícì.

The movie was good, so I watched it again.

那部电影很好看，所以我要再看一次。

Nèibù diànyǐng hěn hǎokàn, suǒyǐ wǒ yào zài kàn yícì.

The movie is good, so I want to watch it again.

🔊 打电话 Dǎ Diànhuà *Making a Phone Call*

Qian Yongli calls his friend Dong Dade.

钱永利:	请问董大德在家吗?	Qián Yǒnglì:	Qǐngwèn Dǒng Dàdé zàijiā ma?
董妈妈:	他不在, 请问你是哪位?	Dǒng māma:	Tā búzài, qǐngwèn nǐ shì něiwèi?
钱永利:	董妈妈好。我是大德的同学, 我叫钱永利。	Qián Yǒnglì:	Dǒng māma hǎo. Wǒ shì Dàdé de tóngxué, wǒ jiào Qián Yǒnglì.
董妈妈:	永利你好, 大德常常提起你。	Dǒng māma:	Yǒnglì nǐ hǎo, Dàdé chángcháng tíqǐ nǐ.
钱永利:	您知道大德去了什么地方吗?	Qián Yǒnglì:	Nín zhīdào Dàdé qùle shénme dìfāng ma?
董妈妈:	他去养老院了, 他每个周末都去那儿服务。	Dǒng māma:	Tā qù yǎnglǎoyuàn le, tā měige zhōumò dōu qù nàr fúwù.
钱永利:	那他什么时候回家?	Qián Yǒnglì:	Nà tā shénme shíhou huíjiā?
董妈妈:	我不知道他什么时候回来。因为他不只陪那些老人聊天, 还要带他们去散步。他回家以后, 我叫他给你回电话。	Dǒng māma:	Wǒ bù zhīdào tā shénme shíhou huílai. Yīnwèi tā bùzhǐ péi nèixiē lǎorén liáotiān, háiyào dài tāmen qù sànbù. Tā huíjiā yǐhòu, wǒ jiào tā gěi nǐ huí diànhuà.
钱永利:	不用了, 我一会儿也要去孤儿院。我晚一点儿再给他打电话。	Qián Yǒnglì:	Búyòng le, wǒ yìhuǐr yě yào qù gū'éryuàn. Wǒ wǎn yìdiǎnr zài gěi tā dǎ diànhuà.
董妈妈:	你去孤儿院做什么?	Dǒng māma:	Nǐ qù gū'éryuàn zuò shénme?
钱永利:	我去那儿给小孩讲故事, 也教他们英文。	Qián Yǒnglì:	Wǒ qù nàr gěi xiǎohái jiǎng gùshi, yě jiāo tāmen Yīngwén.
董妈妈:	你们两个都是有爱心的好孩子。	Dǒng māma:	Nǐmen liǎngge dōu shì yǒu àixīn de hǎo háizi.
钱永利:	谢谢董妈妈。那么, 我得去准备了。	Qián Yǒnglì:	Xièxie Dǒng māma. Nàme, wǒ děi qù zhǔnbèi le.
董妈妈:	好, 再见, 有空来我们家玩啊。	Dǒng māma:	Hǎo, zàijiàn, yǒukòng lái wǒmen jiā wán a.
钱永利:	好的, 谢谢您, 再见。	Qián Yǒnglì:	Hǎode, xièxie nín, zàijiàn.

他们去哪里? **Tāmen qù nǎlǐ?** / *Where do they go?*

Look at the following pictures and say where Qian Yongli and Dong Dade go.

1.

2.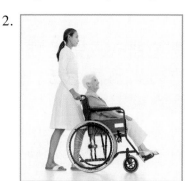

他们的活动 **Tāmen de Huódòng** / *Their Activities*

Look at the following pictures. Identify the activities Qian Yongli and Dong Dade do in their respective charity organizations.

1.

2.

3.

4.

Culture Note

In the West, people would address other people's parents by calling them Mr. or Mrs. (surname), but in China, they say (surname) 爸爸 *bàba*, (surname) 妈妈 *māma*, (surname), uncle: 伯伯 *bóbo* or 叔叔 *shūshu*, or (surname), aunt: 伯母 *bómǔ* or 阿姨 *āyí*. This is because the Chinese like to address their elders using titles they would use for their own relatives, which allows them to feel closer or more familiar.

6 | 对还是错？ **Duì háishì cuò?** *True or False?*

Read the following statements and decide if each statement is true or false. Correct any false statements.

1. 今天是星期六或是星期日。 Jīntiān shì Xīngqīliù huòshì Xīngqīrì.
2. 董大德的妈妈接电话。 Dǒng Dàdé de māma jiē diànhuà.
3. 董大德在家。 Dǒng Dàdé zài jiā.
4. 钱永利要去养老院。 Qián Yǒnglì yào qù yǎnglǎoyuàn.
5. 钱永利要董大德给他回电话。 Qián Yǒnglì yào Dǒng Dàdé gěi tā huí diànhuà.
6. 董大德的妈妈知道董大德几点回家。
   Dǒng Dàdé de māma zhīdào Dǒng Dàdé jǐdiǎn huíjiā.
7. 董大德常常跟他妈妈提起钱永利。
   Dǒng Dàdé chángcháng gēn tā māma tíqǐ Qián Yǒnglì.
8. 钱永利一会儿要出门。 Qián Yǒnglì yìhuǐr yào chūmén.

文化橱窗 Wénhuà Chúchuāng

Culture Window

Chinese Neighborhoods—Traditional Hutongs and Modern Communities

In China, there is a saying: "A distant relative does not compare to a close neighbor." (远亲不如近邻。 Yuǎn qīn bùrú jìn lín.) The proverb is a perfect expression of the Chinese belief that friendship between neighbors can sometimes be closer, or more meaningful, than that of blood relatives.

This belief has evolved from the living habits of the Chinese people over thousands of years. In the past, the Chinese lived in courtyard homes along narrow, mazelike alleys called hutongs. These traditional homes were small, and shared a common

▲ *Chinese traditional Hutong*

courtyard where people gathered to socialize. Children played together while the adults played chess and drank tea. Over time, it was not uncommon for these neighbors to become so close that they resembled a large family. Hutong neighbors typically refrained from locking their doors and would share all their facilities with one another. The relationships established in this manner lasted for a lifetime. Moreover, because the hutongs were narrow, people had to commute by bicycles or on foot, not by car, and so would have many opportunities to meet and greet their hutong neighbors.

▲ *gym in the modern community*

Today, hutongs can still be found in Chinese cities, particularly in Beijing, where several hutong neighborhoods are being preserved as historic places. With urban development, however, many of these traditional neighborhoods are being demolished to make room for high-rise apartment buildings. These structures allow for fewer and fewer opportunities for people to run into each other, but the tradition of making friends with one's neighbors still exists. Modern neighborhoods (小区 xiǎoqū) typically include public facilities such as green spaces, activity centers, schools, supermarkets and banks. Whatever its form, a good neighborhood provides a place for children to play, for the adults to shop and socialize, and for the elderly to meet, forming a large family unit made up of friendly neighbors.

7 文化动动脑 Wénhuà Dòngdòngnǎo / *Culture Check-up*

Choose the correct answer.

1. The Chinese saying "A distant relative cannot compare to a close neighbor" refers to:
   A. the friendship between neighbors
   B. the tension between relatives
   C. the distance between neighborhoods

2. Hutongs are:
   A. courtyard homes   B. narrow alleys   C. apartments

3. Traditional Chinese homes do not include:
   A. large living spaces   B. a common yard   C. shared facilities

4. People would commute to and from hutongs using:
   A. buses   B. cars   C. their own feet or bikes

5. Which Chinese city has preserved some of its historic hutongs?
   A. Beijing   B. Guangzhou   C. Shanghai

6. Now that more people live in high-rise apartment buildings rather than traditional neighborhoods, relationships between neighbors are:
   A. non-existent   B. still there, but in a different way   C. closer than before

8 句子重组 **Jùzi Chóngzǔ** / *Rewrite the Sentences*

Read the following mini-dialogues and create new sentences using the information provided and the "indirect question" pattern. Follow the model.

Lìzi: 弟弟 Dìdi: 爸爸今天几点回家？ Bàba jīntiān jǐdiǎn huíjiā?

哥哥 Gēge: 我不知道。 Wǒ bù zhīdào.

哥哥不知道爸爸今天几点回家。 Gēge bù zhīdào bàba jīntiān jǐdiǎn huíjiā.

1. 丽香 Lìxiāng: 校长家有几口人？ Xiàozhǎng jiā yǒu jǐkǒu rén?

   允武 Yǔnwǔ: 我不知道。 Wǒ bù zhīdào.

2. 亭均 Tíngjūn: 这个学期什么时候结束？ Zhèige xuéqī shénme shíhou jiéshù?

   敏莉 Mǐnlì: 我不知道。 Wǒ bù zhīdào.

3. 家容 Jiāróng: 下个星期的天气怎么样？ Xiàge xīngqī de tiānqì zěnmeyàng?

   宗纬 Zōngwěi: 我不确定。 Wǒ bú quèdìng.

4. 国强 Guóqiáng: 从美国到英国坐飞机要多久？
   Cóng Měiguó dào Yīngguó zuò fēijī yào duōjiǔ?

   力刚 Lìgāng: 我不确定。 Wǒ bú quèdìng.

5. 政钧 Zhèngjūn: 明怡最想要的生日礼物是什么？
   Míngyí zuì xiǎng yàode shēngrì lǐwù shì shénme?

   书芳 Shūfāng: 我也想知道。 Wǒ yě xiǎng zhīdào.

6. 如芬 Rúfēn: 打电话到中国一分钟要多少钱？
   Dǎ diànhuà dào Zhōngguó yì fēnzhōng yào duōshao qián?

   贞玲 Zhēnlíng: 我不知道。 Wǒ bù zhīdào.

7. 铭杰 Míngjié: 你爷爷奶奶的生日是几月几日？
   Nǐ yéye nǎinai de shēngrì shì jǐyuè jǐrì?

   诗萍 Shīpíng: 我不确定。 Wǒ bú quèdìng.

8. 东辉 Dōnghuī: 那件黑色的大衣多少钱？
   Nèijiàn hēisè de dàyī duōshǎo qián?

   孟庭 Mèngtíng: 我帮你看看。 Wǒ bāng nǐ kànkan.

▲打电话到中国多少钱？

9 出乎意料 **Chūhū Yìliào** / *Beyond Expectations*

With a classmate, take turns saying and responding to the sentences provided using the words in parentheses and the pattern "不只…还… *bùzhǐ...hái....*"

Lìzi: 我会做三明治。（煎饼）Wǒ huì zuò sānmíngzhì. (jiānbǐng)

    A: 我会做三明治。 Wǒ huì zuò sānmíngzhì.

    B: 我不只会做三明治，我还会做煎饼。
        Wǒ bùzhǐ huì zuò sānmíngzhì, wǒ hái huì zuò jiānbǐng.

1. 他会游泳。（冲浪）Tā huì yóuyǒng. (chōnglàng)
2. 李小姐很担心。（生气）Lǐ xiǎojiě hěn dānxīn. (shēngqì)
3. 吴先生很开朗。（热情）Wú xiānsheng hěn kāilǎng. (rèqíng)
4. 我有加拿大币。（人民币）Wǒ yǒu Jiā'nádàbì. (Rénmínbì)
5. 我的小腿好酸。（大腿痛）Wǒde xiǎotuǐ hǎo suān. (dàtuǐ tòng)
6. 那个病人流鼻涕。（拉肚子）Nèige bìngrén liú bítì. (lā dùzi)
7. 我昨天上课上到六点。（补习）Wǒ zuótiān shàngkè shàng dào liùdiǎn. (bǔxí)
8. 我妈妈会做德国菜。（意大利菜）Wǒ māma huì zuò Déguó cài. (Yìdàlì cài)

▲ 冲浪

10 要求他人 **Yāoqiú Tārén** / *Giving Orders*

Read and rephrase the following sentences using the verb 叫 *jiào*.

Lìzi: 吃晚饭以前，妈妈跟我说："你去洗手。"
Chī wǎnfàn yǐqián, māma gēn wǒ shuō: "nǐ qù xǐshǒu."

妈妈叫我吃晚饭以前去洗手。 Māma jiào wǒ chī wǎnfàn yǐqián qù xǐshǒu.

1. 爸爸跟哥哥说："学习的时候，别打瞌睡。"
   Bàba gēn gēge shuō: "Xuéxí de shíhou, bié dǎ kēshuì."
2. 王太太跟王先生说："你应该去锻炼锻炼。"
   Wáng tàitai gēn Wáng xiānsheng shuō: "Nǐ yīnggāi qù duànliàn duànliàn."
3. 妈妈跟爸爸说："你帮我去商店买一块肉。"
   Māma gēn bàba shuō: "Nǐ bāng wǒ qù shāngdiàn mǎi yíkuài ròu."
4. 爷爷跟我说："你帮我去图书馆借两本书。"
   Yéye gēn wǒ shuō: "Nǐ bāng wǒ qù túshūguǎn jiè liǎngběn shū."
5. 大立很害羞，老师跟他说："你应该大方一点。"
   Dà Lì hěn hàixiū, lǎoshī gēn tā shuō: "Nǐ yīnggāi dàfāng yìdiǎn."
6. 我的数学不好，爸妈跟我说："你得去上补习班。"
   Wǒde shùxué bùhǎo, bà-mā gēn wǒ shuō: "Nǐ děi qù shàng bǔxíbān."

11 再做一次 Zài zuò yícì. *Let's do it again.*

Complete the following sentences using the adverb 再 *zài*.

1. 豆浆真好喝，我要… Dòujiāng zhēn hǎo hē, wǒ yào...

2. 我的感冒还没好，我得… Wǒde gǎnmào hái méihǎo, wǒ děi...

3. 我没有收到你的电邮，请你…
   Wǒ méiyǒu shōudào nǐde diànyóu, qǐng nǐ...

4. 这几个字我写得不好看，我要…
   Zhè jǐge zì wǒ xiě de bù hǎokàn, wǒ yào...

5. 刚刚没有人接电话，所以我会…
   Gānggāng méiyǒu rén jiē diànhuà, suǒyǐ wǒ huì...

6. 你的头发没有干(dry)，你一定要…
   Nǐde tóufa méiyǒu gān, nǐ yídìng yào...

7. 这部动作片太好看了！我要…
   Zhèibù dòngzuòpiàn tài hǎokàn le! Wǒ yào...

8. 那个地方很漂亮，这个周末我想…
   Nèige dìfāng hěn piàoliang, zhèige zhōumò wǒ xiǎng...

▲ 豆浆真好喝

12 "又" 还是 "再"？ "Yòu" háishì "Zài"？ *Which "Again"?*

Read the following sentences, and decide if 又 *yòu* or 再 *zài* should be used.

1. 你的衣服已经很多了，不要__买了。
   Nǐde yīfu yǐjīng hěn duō le, búyào __ mǎile.

2. 你怎么__想睡觉，你不是刚刚才起床吗？
   Nǐ zěnme __ xiǎng shuìjiào, nǐ búshì gānggāng cái qǐchuáng ma?

3. 我喜欢话剧社，下个学期我还要__参加(join)。
   Wǒ xǐhuan huàjùshè, xiàge xuéqī wǒ hái yào __ cānjiā.

4. 吃太多快餐对身体不好，你不要__吃快餐了。
   Chī tàiduō kuàicān duì shēntǐ bùhǎo, nǐ búyào __ chī kuàicān le.

5. 奶奶的身体__不舒服了，我们要带她去医院。
   Nǎinai de shēntǐ __ bù shūfu le, wǒmen yào dài tā qù yīyuàn.

6. 这个药一天要吃三次，所以我等一下要__吃一次。
   Zhèige yào yìtiān yào chī sāncì, suǒyǐ wǒ děng yíxià yào __ chī yícì.

7. 你为什么__租(to rent)记录片？这个星期我们已经看了三部了！
   Nǐ wèishénme __ zū jìlùpiàn? Zhèige xīngqī wǒmen yǐjīng kànle sānbù le!

8. 妈妈叫弟弟学习，可是弟弟__上聊天室，所以妈妈很生气。
   Māma jiào dìdi xuéxí, kěshì dìdi __ shàng liáotiānshì, suǒyǐ māma hěn shēngqì.

開口说

13 小区服务 | **Xiǎoqū Fúwù** / *Community Service*

With a classmate, talk about the community service activities with which you are familiar and in which you have participated.

- Ask your classmate if there are any community services provided in his / her community, and if so, ask your classmate to describe them.

- Ask your classmate if he / she has been to or has taken part in any of the services he / she described.

- Ask your classmate what kind of community services he / she prefers and why.

- Ask your classmate when he / she usually volunteers for these activities.

14 福利机构 | **Fúlì Jīgòu** / *Well-being Services*

Nursing home information is displayed below. Read the information and use it to answer the questions that follow.

安心养老院 Ānxīn yǎnglǎoyuàn

◆ 服务对象 fúwù duìxiàng

1. 年满六十五岁以上之老人。
Nián mǎn liùshíwǔ suì yǐshàng zhī lǎorén.

2. 子女无法随时照顾的老人。
Zǐnǚ wúfǎ suíshí zhàogù de lǎorén.

3. 罹患慢性疾病或老人失智症者。
Líhuàn mànxìng jíbìng huò lǎorén shīzhìzhèngzhě.

4. 中风、行动不便及日常生活起居需仰赖他人协助者。
Zhòngfēng、 xíngdòng búbiàn jí rìcháng shēnghuó qǐjū xū yǎnglài tārén xiézhùzhě.

安心养老院 Ānxīn yǎnglǎoyuàn

◆ 服务内容 fúwù nèiróng

1. 二十四小时日常生活照顾。
Èrshísì xiǎoshí rìcháng shēnghuó zhàogù.

2. 专业护理人员服务。
Zhuānyè hùlǐ rényuán fúwù.

3. 每星期一、三、五有特约医师到院看病。
Měi Xīngqīyī、 sān、 wǔ yǒu tèyuē yīshī dào yuàn kànbìng.

4. 专业营养师提供营养咨询服务。
Zhuānyè yíngyǎngshī tígōng yíngyǎng zīxún fúwù.

1. 这是介绍(*to introduce*)什么的? Zhè shì jièshào shénme de?

2. 几岁以上的人是这个地方的服务对象?
Jǐsuì yǐshàng de rén shì zhèige dìfang de fúwù duìxiàng?

3. 医生一个星期去那里看几次病? 星期几?
Yīshēng yíge xīngqī qù nàlǐ kàn jǐcì bìng? Xīngqī jǐ?

Vocabulary

爱	ài	v.	to love
如	rú	v.	to be like; to be similar to
己	jǐ	n.	oneself

爱人如己
ài rén rú jǐ
Love others as you love yourself

▲ 爱人如己

Language Note

This expression means to treat others as you would like them to treat you. The complete phrase is 爱人如(爱)己 *ài rén rú (ài) jǐ*, but it is often used in the shortened form by omitting the second 爱 *ài*.

爷爷爱人如己，他把他的钱全部都捐给孤儿院。

Yéye ài rén rú jǐ, tā bǎ tāde qián quánbù dōu juān gěi gū'éryuàn.

My grandfather loves others as much as he loves himself and donated all of his money to the orphanage.

There is a similar Chinese saying: 人饥己饥，人溺己溺 *rén jī jǐ jī, rén nì jǐ nì*, which means that seeing a fellow man starving or drowning is like drowning or being starved yourself. This is a saying that is used to show sympathy toward others.

In the olden days, there was once a great flood in China that caused many people to lose their homes. A man called Dayu (大禹 *Dàyǔ*) saw how the people were suffering, and decided to try and fix the problem. To achieve his goal, he worked without returning to the comfort of his home for a period of thirteen years. So dedicated he was to his mission that he did not even see his own son. After he fixed the water system, he became known as a saint for his selfless deed.

"人饥己饥，人溺己溺 *rén jī jǐ jī, rén nì jǐ nì*" is similar to "爱人如己 *ài rén rú jǐ* (love others as you love yourself)". They are both sayings that tell people to place oneself in anothers' shoes, feel another's pain, and do what you can to help and care for those in need.

姐姐打电话

　　昨天上大学[1]的姐姐给家里打电话，爸爸妈妈不在，所以我接了电话。姐姐说她下个周末要回来看看家人，叫我记得留言给爸妈。我问她大学好不好玩儿，她说在那里除了学习以外，她还做志愿工作。她的志愿工作是教小孩做功课，她一个星期去那个小孩家三次，每次一个小时。上课以前，她还得准备准备，难怪她那么忙。我觉得姐姐很棒，什么科目都会教。我也觉得她很有爱心，因为她愿意[2]帮助别人。挂电话以后，我马上去念书，这样我上大学的时候，就也可以跟姐姐一样教小孩。

[1]大学: college; university　　[2]愿意: to be willing to

Jiějie Dǎ Diànhuà

　Zuótiān shàng dàxué de jiějie gěi jiālǐ dǎ diànhuà, bàba māma búzài, suǒyǐ wǒ jiēle diànhuà. Jiějie shuō tā xiàge zhōumò yào huílai kànkan jiārén, jiào wǒ jìde liúyán gěi bà-mā. Wǒ wèn tā dàxué hǎo bù hǎowánr, tā shuō zài nàlǐ chúle xuéxí yǐwài, tā hái zuò zhìyuàn gōngzuò. Tāde zhìyuàn gōngzuò shì jiāo xiǎohái zuò gōngkè, tā yíge xīngqī qù nèige xiǎohái jiā sāncì, měicì yíge xiǎoshí. Shàngkè yǐqián, tā hái děi zhǔnbèi zhǔnbei, nánguài tā nàme máng. Wǒ juéde jiějie hěn bàng, shénme kēmù dōu huì jiāo. Wǒ yě juéde tā hěn yǒu àixīn, yīnwèi tā yuànyì bāngzhù biérén. Guà diànhuà yǐhòu, wǒ mǎshàng qù niànshū, zhèyàng wǒ shàng dàxué de shíhou, jiù yě kěyǐ gēn jiějie yíyàng jiāo xiǎohái.

15 通晓文意 **Tōngxiǎo Wényì** / *Understand the Article*

Complete the following sentences based on what you read in the previous passage.

1. 他姐姐上＿了。　Tā jiějie shàng ＿ le.

2. 他姐姐昨天给家里＿。　Tā jiějie zuótiān gěi jiālǐ ＿.

3. 他姐姐打电话的时候，他的＿不在家，所以＿接电话。
   Tā jiějie dǎ diànhuà de shíhou, tā de ＿ bú zài jiā, suǒyǐ ＿ jiē diànhuà.

4. 他姐姐说＿要回家看家人。　Tā jiějie shuō ＿ yào huíjiā kàn jiārén.

5. 除了学习以外，他姐姐还做＿。　Chúle xuéxí yǐwài, tā jiějie hái zuò ＿.

6. 他姐姐教小孩＿，一个星期去那个小孩家＿次，每次＿个小时。
   Tā jiějie jiāo xiǎohái ＿, yíge xīngqī qù nèige xiǎohái jiā ＿ cì, měicì ＿ ge xiǎoshí.

7. 他觉得他姐姐很＿，也很＿。　Tā juéde tā jiějie hěn ＿, yě hěn ＿.

Hànzì Tiāndì

Chinese Characters

老 ▪ lǎo ▪ old

The pictograph 老 *lǎo* originally depicted an old hunchbacked man who is walking with a walking stick. Gradually, it transformed into the character in use today. It is also a common radical for words related to "the aged."

Stroke Order

16 词汇延伸 Cíhuì Yánshēn / *Vocabulary Builder*

Below are characters that combine with 老 *lǎo* to create words. Match the Chinese words on the left with the appropriate English meanings on the right.

年 nián	师 shī	大 dà	实 shí	手 shǒu
n. year	*n. teacher*	*adj. big*	*adj. true*	*n. hand*

1. 老年 lǎonián   A. honest
2. 老师 lǎoshī   B. old age
3. 老大 lǎodà   C. teacher
4. 老实 lǎoshi   D. veteran
5. 老手 lǎoshǒu   E. eldest child (in a family)

Can you find 老 in the following pictures?

Unit 4

欢迎来我家
Huānyíng Lái Wǒ Jiā

In this unit you will be able to:

- ask for and provide directions
- describe a room and a house
- discuss transportation
- make a guess
- invite friends to your home
- describe household items

Lesson A

🔊 **在马路上 Zài Mǎlù Shàng** *On the Road*

马路（馬路）mǎlù

n. road

路口 lùkǒu

n. intersection

立交桥 lìjiāoqiáo

n. overpass

天桥（天橋）tiānqiáo

n. pedestrian bridge

人行道 rénxíngdào

n. sidewalk

人行横道（人行横道）

rénxíng héngdào *n. crosswalk*

红绿灯（紅綠燈）

hónglǜdēng

n. traffic light

路灯（路燈）lùdēng

n. streetlight

行人 xíngrén

n. pedestrian

方向 Fāngxiàng Directions

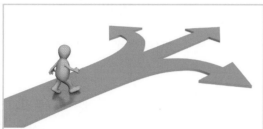

左转（左轉）zuǒ zhuǎn *v. to turn left*

右转（右轉）yòu zhuǎn *v. to turn right*

直走 zhí zǒu *v. to go straight*

往后走（往後走）wǎng hòu zǒu
v. to move backward

Language Note

拐 *guǎi* also means "to turn." It is a colloquial saying compared to 转 *zhuǎn*.
For example, 左拐 *zuǒ guǎi*, 右拐 *yòu guǎi*.

中文

方位 fāngwèi Directions / Points of the Compass

西北 xīběi
n. northwest

北 běi *n. north*

东北（東北）
dōngběi *n. northeast*

西 xī *n. west*

东（東）dōng *n. east*

东南（東南）
dōngnán
n. southeast

西南 xīnán
n. southwest

南 nán *n. south*

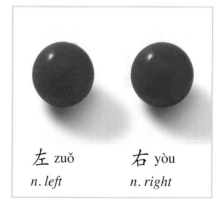

左 zuǒ
n. left

右 yòu
n. right

前 qián *n. front*

后（後）hòu *n. back*

上 shàng *n. up; above*

下 xià *n. down; under*

距离 Jùlí *Distances*		
公分 gōngfēn, 厘米 límǐ	公尺 gōngchǐ, 米 mǐ	公里 gōnglǐ
m.w. centimeter	*m.w. meter*	*m.w. kilometer*

明天会下雨。
Míngtiān huì xiàyǔ.
It is going to rain tomorrow.

那我们还是不要去爬山吧。
Nà wǒmen háishì búyào qù páshān ba.
Then let's not go climbing.

A: 你星期天想做什么？（你星期天想做什麼？）
Nǐ Xīngqītiān xiǎng zuò shénme? *What do you want to do on Sunday?*

B: 我想先去美术馆看画，再去购物中心逛逛。
（我想先去美術館看畫，再去購物中心逛逛。）
Wǒ xiǎng xiān qù měishùguǎn kànhuà, zài qù gòuwù zhōngxīn guàngguang.
I want to go to the art museum to see the paintings, and then go to the shopping mall.

我家离学校很近，你家呢？
Wǒ jiā lí xuéxiào hěn jìn, nǐ jiā ne?
My house is close to the school.
How about yours?

我家离学校有点儿远，
开车要半个小时。
Wǒ jiā lí xuéxiào yǒudiǎnr yuǎn, kāichē yào bàngè xiǎoshí.
My house is a bit far from the school. The drive takes half an hour.

A: 从这里到书店怎么走？（從這裡到書店怎麼走？）Cóng zhèlǐ dào shūdiàn zěnme zǒu?

How can I get to the bookstore from here?

B: 前面那个路口右转，直走差不多五分钟就到了。

（前面那個路口右轉，直走差不多五分鐘就到了。）

Qiánmian nèige lùkǒu yòu zhuǎn, zhí zǒu chàbùduō wǔfēn zhōng jiù dàole.

Take a right turn at the intersection ahead of you, keep walking for five minutes, and you will be there.

序数（序數）Xùshù *Ordinal Numbers*

To say ordinal numbers, just place 第 *dì* in front of numbers.

第 *dì* + Number

For example, 第一 dì-yī (*first*), 第二 dì-èr (*second*), 第十 dì-shí (*tenth*), and so on.

Adjectives

保险 (保險)	bǎoxiǎn	*safe*
远 (遠)	yuǎn	*far*
近	jìn	*near, close*
差不多	chàbuduō	*almost; nearly*

Adverbs

还是 (還是)	háishì	*had better; it's best to*
先	xiān	*first; earlier; before*
再	zài	*then (indicating that one action takes place after the completion of another)*
然后 (然後)	ránhòu	*then; afterwards; after that*
直	zhí	*directly; straight*
大概	dàgài	*probably*

Nouns

主意	zhǔyi	*idea; plan*
边 (邊)	biān	*side*
邀请 (邀請)	yāoqǐng	*invitation*

Prepositions

从 (從)	cóng	*from*
往	wǎng	*in the direction of; to; toward*
离 (離)	lí	*off; away; from*

Specifier

第	dì	(prefix for ordinal numbers)

Verbs

敢	gǎn	to dare
看	kàn	to think; to consider
过 (過)	guò	to pass; to cross
转 (轉)	zhuǎn	to turn
邀请 (邀請)	yāoqǐng	to invite

Verb-Object

做饭 (做飯)	zuòfàn	to cook

Language Note

米 *mǐ* means "meter." It is a colloquial saying compared to 公尺 *gōngchǐ*, which is the word used in the metric system.

东南西北 **Dōng-nán-xī-běi** / *All Directions*

◀)) First, draw a compass on a separate piece of paper like the one below. Then, listen to the recordings. You will hear eight directions. Match the direction you hear with the letter in the compass, write the letter next to each number.

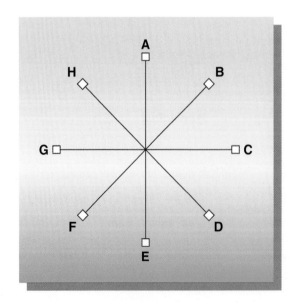

2 街景 Jiējǐng / On the Street

🔊 You will hear four sentences. Match what you hear with the corresponding pictures below.

A.  B. 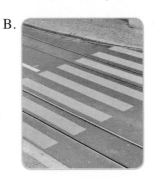 C.  D.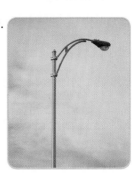

3 个人问题 Gèrén Wèntí / Personal Questions

Answer the following questions in Chinese based on your own experiences and opinions.

1. 你会做饭吗？你会做什么？ Nǐ huì zuòfàn ma? Nǐ huì zuò shénme?
2. 你喜欢邀请朋友去你家玩吗？ Nǐ xǐhuan yāoqǐng péngyou qù nǐ jiā wán ma?
3. 你家在学校的哪边？ Nǐ jiā zài xuéxiào de něibiān?
4. 你家离学校近不近？ Nǐ jiā lí xuéxiào jìn bújìn?
5. 从你家到学校怎么走？ Cóng nǐ jiā dào xuéxiào zěnme zǒu?
6. 从你家到学校要多久？ Cóng nǐ jiā dào xuéxiào yào duōjiǔ?

句型介绍 Jùxíng Jièshào
Language Patterns

The Adverb 还是 *háishì* to Indicate A Better Choice

The adverb 还是 *háishì* means "had better," and "it's best to." It indicates that the speaker makes a opinion after considering and comparing all possible choices. The particle 吧 *ba* is often added at the end to indicate a suggestion.

(Subject) + 还是 *háishì* + Verb Phrase

A: 妈妈，我想休息。 Māma, wǒ xiǎng xiūxi.
B: 如果你想玩电子游戏的话，还是快点儿写功课。
 Rúguǒ nǐ xiǎng wán diànzǐ yóuxì de huà, háishì kuài diǎnr xiě gōngkè.

那个地方太远了，我们还是开车去吧。
Nèige dìfang tài yuǎnle, wǒmen háishì kāichē qù ba.

The Pattern "先...再... *xiān...zài...*" to Show the Sequence of two Actions

The pattern 先...再... *xiān...zài...* means "first... then...." It is a correlative conjunction pattern. When there are two actions happening sequentially, this pattern is used to show the sequence of the actions.

Subject + **先 *xiān*** + **Verb Phrase 1** + **再 *zài*** + **Verb Phrase 2**

你应该先吃东西再吃药。　Nǐ yīnggāi xiān chī dōngxi zài chī yào.

爸爸叫我先洗手再吃饭。　Bàba jiào wǒ xiān xǐshǒu zài chīfàn.

The Preposition 离 *lí*

The preposition 离 *lí* means "to be apart from." It shows distance between two places. The adjectives 远 *yuǎn* and 近 *jìn* often follow 离 *lí* to describe the distance. A time expression can also be used to express distance, as illustrated in the third example below.

Place 1 + **离 *lí*** + **Place 2** + **distance / period of time**

我家离博物馆不远。　Wǒ jiā lí bówùguǎn bù yuǎn.

我家离博物馆八百米。　Wǒ jiā lí bówùguǎn bābǎimǐ

我家离博物馆走路十二分钟。　Wǒ jiā lí bówùguǎn zǒulù shí'èrfēn zhōng.

In addition to the distance between two places, the preposition 离 *lí* can also be used to show the duration of time between two events. If the first event 1 indicates "now (现在 *xiànzài*)," then it will sometimes be omitted.

Event 1 + **离 *lí*** + **Event 2** + **period of time**

现在离学期结束还有一个月。　Xiànzài lí xuéqī jiéshù hái yǒu yíge yuè.

我的生日离你的生日只有三天，我们可以一起办(to set up)生日晚会。
Wǒde shēngrì lí nǐde shēngrì zhǐ yǒu sāntiān, wǒmen kěyǐ yìqǐ bàn shēngrì wǎnhuì.

离晚饭时间只有半个钟头，你别吃东西。
Lí wǎnfàn shíjiān zhǐ yǒu bànge zhōngtóu, nǐ bié chī dōngxi.

▲ 你别吃东西。

The pattern "从...到... *cóng...dào...*"

The pattern 从...到... *cóng... dào...* means "from...to...." It indicates a range and shows the origin and the end. The terms can be place words, time words, verbs, or even pronouns.

从 *cóng* + **Term 1** + 到 *dào* + **Term 2**

从我家到篮球场，走路只要三分钟。
Cóng wǒ jiā dào lánqiúchǎng, zǒulù zhǐ yào sānfēnzhōng.
我从星期一到星期五都有中文课。
Wǒ cóng Xīngqīyī dào Xīngqīwǔ dōu yǒu Zhōngwén kè.

Topic-Comment Structure

The form of many Chinese sentences can best be described as a topic and a comment. That is to say, the first elements that appear in the sentence are not necessarily the subject, of the sentence, but could fill a number of roles. The rest of the sentence serves as a sort of comment upon the first element. In "昨天的电视节目你觉得好不好？", yesterday's TV program is not the subject of the sentence or of the verb in the sentence, but the topic, about which a question is asked. Here are some more examples.

Topic + **Comment**

饭做好了。 Fàn zuò hǎole.
衣服都洗干净(clean)了。 Yīfu dōu xǐ gānjìng le.
这个东西, 我要。 Zhèige dōngxi, wǒ yào.

▲ 饭做好了。

Keep an eye open for this type of sentence. It is much more common than in English and can easily confuse you.

The pattern "从...往... *cóng...wǎng...*"

The preposition 往 *wǎng* means "to", " toward," and it indicates the direction of an action. This pattern is used to show the starting point and the direction of movement.

从 *cóng* + **Place Word 1** + 往 *wǎng* + **Place Word 2 / Direction** + **Verb Phrase**

从这里往北开，就可以到加拿大。 Cóng zhèlǐ wǎng běi kāi, jiù kěyǐ dào Jiā'nádà.
英文要从左往右写。 Yīngwén yào cóng zuǒ wǎng yòu xiě.

会话 Huìhuà
Dialogue

🔊 **周末邀约 Zhōumò Yāoyuē** *A Weekend Appointment*

Li Yunying and her friends discuss weekend plans.

李云英:	这个星期日你们有空吗? 要不要来我家玩?	Lǐ Yúnyīng:	Zhèige Xīngqīrì nǐmen yǒukòng ma? Yào búyào lái wǒ jiā wán?
钱永利:	你要给我们做饭吗?	Qián Yǒnglì:	Nǐ yào gěi wǒmen zuòfàn ma?
李云英:	如果你们敢吃我做的饭, 我就给你们做。	Lǐ Yúnyīng:	Rúguǒ nǐmen gǎn chī wǒ zuòde fàn, wǒ jiù gěi nǐmen zuò.
吴森:	我看还是你妈妈做的比较保险。	Wú Sēn:	Wǒ kàn háishì nǐ māma zuòde bǐjiào bǎoxiǎn.
赵梅:	星期日几点呢?	Zhào Méi:	Xīngqīrì jǐdiǎn ne?
李云英:	下午四点, 怎么样? 我们可以先玩电子游戏, 再吃饭。	Lǐ Yúnyīng:	Xiàwǔ sìdiǎn, zěnmeyàng? Wǒmen kěyǐ xiān wán diànzǐ yóuxì, zài chīfàn.
钱永利:	好主意。你家在哪儿?	Qián Yǒnglì:	Hǎo zhǔyi. Nǐ jiā zài nǎr?
李云英:	我家在学校西边, 离学校不远。	Lǐ Yúnyīng:	Wǒ jiā zài xuéxiào xībiān, lí xuéxiào bùyuǎn.
吴森:	从学校到你家怎么走?	Wú Sēn:	Cóng xuéxiào dào nǐ jiā zěnme zǒu?
李云英:	先从学校往西走, 然后过三个路口, 在第四个路口往左转, 再直走三百米就到了。	Lǐ Yúnyīng:	Xiān cóng xuéxiào wǎng xī zǒu, ránhòu guò sānge lùkǒu, zài dì-sìge lùkǒu wǎng zuǒ zhuǎn, zài zhí zǒu sānbǎimǐ jiù dàole.
赵梅:	大概要走多久?	Zhào Méi:	Dàgài yào zǒu duōjiǔ?
李云英:	差不多二十分钟。	Lǐ Yúnyīng:	Chàbùduō èrshífēn zhōng.
钱永利:	云英, 谢谢你的邀请。	Qián Yǒnglì:	Yúnyīng, xièxie nǐde yāoqǐng.
李云英:	不客气, 我们星期日见。	Lǐ Yúnyīng:	Bú kèqi, wǒmen Xīngqīrì jiàn.

4 **邀请朋友** **Yāoqǐng Péngyou** / *Inviting Friends*

Based on the dialogue, choose the activities Li Yunying and her friends are going to do next Sunday.

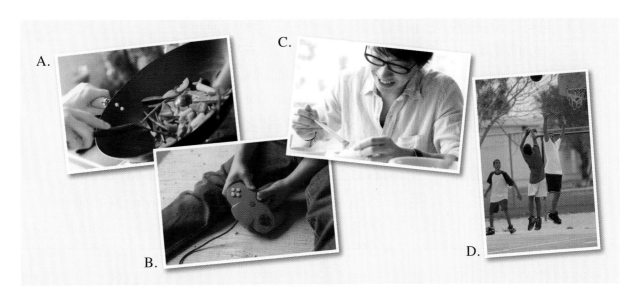

A.

C.

B.

D.

5 **李云英的家** **Lǐ Yúnyīng de Jiā** / *Li Yunying's Home*

According to the dialogue, choose the picture that best illustrates the location of Li Yunying's home in relation to the school.

A.

B.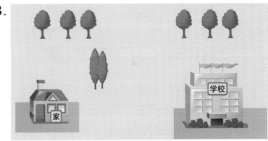

C.

D.

懂了吗?　**Dǒng le ma?** / *Do you understand?*

Answer the following questions in Chinese.

1. 谁要去李云英家玩? Shéi yào qù Lǐ Yúnyīng jiā wán?

2. 他们星期几要去李云英家玩? 几点?
   Tāmen xīngqī jǐ yào qù Lǐ Yúnyīng jiā wán? Jǐdiǎn?

3. 谁要给他们做饭? Shéi yào gěi tāmen zuòfàn?

4. 他们到李云英家以后, 要先做什么?
   Tāmen dào Lǐ Yúnyīng jiā yǐhòu, yào xiān zuò shénme?

5. 李云英家离学校远不远? Lǐ Yúnyīng jiā lí xuéxiào yuǎn bùyuǎn?

6. 从学校到李云英家怎么走? Cóng xuéxiào dào Lǐ Yúnyīng jiā zěnme zǒu?

7. 从学校到李云英家得走多久? Cóng xuéxiào dào Lǐ Yúnyīng jiā děi zǒu duōjiǔ?

文化橱窗　Wénhuà Chúchuāng
Culture Window

Hutongs (胡同 *hútóng*)

Hutongs are lanes and alleyways that connect the main streets to the residential areas. There are two types of hutongs: dead-ends and live-ends. The "dead" hutongs only have one opening with its end located inside a residential area, while the "live" hutongs connect to with two or more main streets. Hutongs are another of Beijing's cultural characteristics. The most famous hutong in Beijing is the Houhai Hutong (后海胡同 *Hòuhǎi hútóng*), where one can ride pedicabs and visit traditional siheyuans to see what Old Beijing was like. The earliest hutongs appeared in Beijing in the Yuan dynasty, and there were once as many as 6,000 hutongs in the city. The earliest recorded hutongs are the ones near Chaoyangmen. They are very organized, with the same distance between each. The north-to-south hutongs were wider and considered streets. In those days, horse carriages were popular, so the streets were also called 马路 (*mǎlù, roads*). The east-to-west hutongs were regular hutongs and thus narrower and mostly used by pedestrians. These hutongs were surrounded by siheyuans on both sides.

▲ *hutong*

Siheyuans (四合院 *sìhéyuàn*)

A siheyuan is a traditional and cultural symbol that has been around for over 3,000 years. The name literally means a courtyard surrounded by four buildings, each facing north, south, east and west to form a square shape. These residential buildings are symmetrical in appearance.

The building that locates the north is considered the main house, the building that locates the south is known as the opposite house, and the other two are known as the side houses. The main entrances into siheyuan buildings are often located in the opposite the main house that typically belongs to the master of the house with the side houses serving as guest rooms or rooms for children. The opposite house is often occupied by servants. At the corners of the siheyuan, there are often corner houses that are used for storage or used as kitchens. The southwest corner is often reserved for the toilet, and the southeast corner is often the entrance to the courtyard. Traditionally, a siheyuan houses one family only.

▲ *siheyuan*

▲ *imperial siheyuan*

Siheyuans are more popular in northern China, especially Beijing, which is home to the grandest siheyuan buildings. Smaller siheyuans may only have two north-facing rooms, but an imperial siheyuan may have up to 11 main rooms. Most of these are complexes are linked by passageways over a large area of ground. In fact, the Palace Museum is also a siheyuan.

▲ *the structure of siheyuan*

7 文化动动脑 Wénhuà Dòngdòngnǎo / *Culture Check-up*

Decide if the following statements are true or false. Correct any false statements.

1. Siheyuans have been around for about 2,000 years.
2. Siheyuan means a courtyard surrounded by four rooms.
3. The "four" in siheyuan represents north, south, east, and west.
4. The north room is the main house in a siheyuan.
5. The south room is often reserved for guests.
6. The Palace Museum is a siheyuan.
7. In Houhai, one can ride a taxi along a hutong.

8 做选择 **Zuò Xuǎnzé** / *Make a Better Choice*

With a classmate, take turns asking and answering questions using the adverb 还是 *háishì* and the hints provided. Follow the model.

Lizi: 我的膝盖有点痛，可以去健身房吗？(膝盖有问题)
Wǒde xīgài yǒudiǎn tòng, kěyǐ qù jiànshēnfáng ma? (xīgài yǒu wèntí)

A: 我的膝盖有点痛，可以去健身房吗？
Wǒ de xīgài yǒudiǎn tòng, kěyǐ qù jiànshēnfáng ma?

B: 你的膝盖可能有问题，还是不要去吧。
Nǐde xīgài kěnéng yǒu wèntí, háishì bú yào qù ba.

1. 我应该参加舞蹈社还是乐团？(你喜欢跳舞)
Wǒ yīnggāi cānjiā wǔdǎo shè háishì yuètuán? (nǐ xǐhuan tiàowǔ)

2. 我们应该走人行横道还是天桥呢？(车子很多)
Wǒmen yīnggāi zǒu rénxíng héngdào háishì tiānqiáo ne? (chēzi hěn duō)

3. 你想看纪录片呢？还是喜剧片？(我的心情不好)
Nǐ xiǎng kàn jìlùpiàn ne? Háishì xǐjùpiàn? (wǒde xīnqíng bùhǎo)

4. 去公园应该往左走还是往右走呢？(公园在右边)
Qù gōngyuán yīnggāi wǎng zuǒ zǒu háishì wǎng yòu zǒu ne? (gōngyuán zài yòubiān)

5. 我不知道要先化妆还是先换衣服。(衣服会脏(dirty))
Wǒ bù zhīdào yào xiān huàzhuāng háishì xiān huàn yīfu. (yīfu huì zāng)

6. 我的感冒还没好，不知道要不要去看病。(已经三天了)
Wǒde gǎnmào hái méihǎo, bù zhīdào yào búyào qù kànbìng. (yǐjīng sāntiān le)

7. 日本菜和墨西哥菜，你想吃哪个？(今天想吃辣的东西)
Rìběn cài hé Mòxīgē cài, nǐ xiǎng chī něige? (jīntiān xiǎng chī là de dōngxi)

8. 现在晚上八点，可是我很困，我应该睡觉吗？(累了就休息)
Xiànzài wǎnshang bādiǎn, kěshì wǒ hěn kùn, wǒ yīnggāi shuìjiào ma? (lèile jiù xiūxi)

Look at the pictures and the words provided, and make sentences using the pattern "先…再… *xiān…zài…*".

1.

我想…

Wǒ xiǎng…

2.

我想…

Wǒ xiǎng…

3.

我每次感冒都…

Wǒ měicì gǎnmào dōu…

4.

回家以后，我总是…

Huíjiā yǐhòu, wǒ zǒngshì…

5.

洗澡的时候，我…

Xǐzǎo de shíhou, wǒ…

6.

早上的时候，我…

Zǎoshang de shíhou, wǒ…

10 距离 Jùlí / Distances

Identify the distance between the two depicted places or events using the verb 离 lí. Follow the model.

Lìzi: 我家离小华家二十公里。
Wǒ jiā lí Xiǎo Huá jiā èrshí gōnglǐ.
OR, 我家离小华家很远。
Wǒ jiā lí Xiǎo Huá jiā hěn yuǎn.

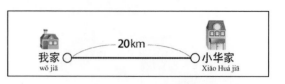

1.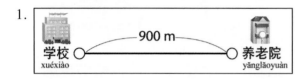

2.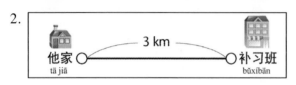

3.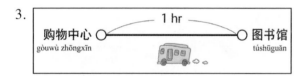

4.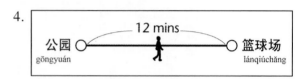

5.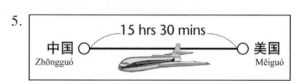

6.

11 范围 Fànwéi / Ranges

Answer the following questions using the pattern "从…到… cóng…dào…" and the words provided.

Lìzi: 你哪里不舒服？ (头→脚) Nǐ nǎlǐ bù shūfu? (tóu→jiǎo)
我从头到脚不舒服。 Wǒ cóng tóu dào jiǎo bù shūfu.

1. 李先生哪年上高中？ (1987→1990) Lǐ xiānsheng něinián shàng gāozhōng? (1987→1990)

2. 英文从左到右写，中文呢？ (左→右)
Yīngwén cóng zuǒ dào yòu xiě, Zhōngwén ne? (zuǒ→ yòu)

3. 这个东西给几岁的孩子吃？ (两岁→五岁)
Zhèige dōngxi gěi jǐsuì de háizi chī? (liǎngsuì→wǔsuì)

4. 这个学期是什么时候？ (九月初→一月中)
Zhèige xuéqī shì shénme shíhou? (Jiǔyuè chū→Yīyuè zhōng)

5. 陈小姐哪几天在西班牙？ (二十一号→二十八号)
Chén xiǎojie nǎ jǐtiān zài Xībānyá? (èrshíyī hào→èrshíbā hào)

12 往哪里? **Wăng Nălĭ?** / *To Where?*

 Listen to a conversation between two students. They happen to meet in downtown and are talking about the area. Look at the following illustration and match the stores in the box with the buildings in the illustration based on their conversation.

> A. 手机店 shŏujī diàn   B. 书店 shūdiàn   C. 电脑店 diànnăo diàn
>
> D. 中国餐厅 Zhōngguó cāntīng   E. 健身房 jiànshēnfáng

Kāikŏu Shuō

Communication

13 来我家玩吧! **Lái wŏ jiā wán ba!** / *Come to my house!*

With a classmate, take turns inviting one another to your home. Use the guide below to help steer your conversation.

- Ask your classmate when he / she is free.
- Ask your classmate if he / she wants to go to your home.
- Tell your classmate how he / she can get to your home and how long it would take he / she to reach it.
- Suggest the activities you can do together once you are there.
- Ask your classmate if he / she wants to have lunch or dinner together.
- Ask your classmate what time is good for him / her and decide on the time you would like to meet.

This is a map of Lin Mei's neighborhood. Read the map and answer the questions that follows.

1. 公园在林美家的哪边？ Gōngyuán zài Lín Měi jiā de něibiān?

2. 从鞋店到购物中心要怎么走？ Cóng xiédiàn dào gòuwù zhōngxīn yào zěnme zǒu?
   (先…然后…再…*xiān…ránhòu…zài*)

3. 从图书馆走到早餐店会经过(*to pass by*)哪些地方？
   Cóng túshūguǎn zǒu dào zǎocān diàn huì jīngguò nǎxiē dìfāng?

4. 如果林美每分钟可以走五十米，那么她从中国餐馆走到购物中心要多久？
   Rúguǒ Lín Měi měifēn zhōng kěyǐ zǒu wǔshímǐ, nàme tā cóng Zhōngcān guǎn zǒu dào gòuwù zhōngxīn yào duōjiǔ?

Vocabulary

按	àn	*v.*	*to do something according to…*
图	tú	*n.*	*picture*
索	suǒ	*v.*	*to look for*
骥	jì	*n.*	*a thoroughbred horse; steed*

按图索骥
àn tú suǒ jì
Looking for a Horse from Pictures

▲ 按图索骥

Language Note

This idiom means to "look for a good horse using a picture" and was used in a negative way to talk about someone who does not know how to react in different situations and sticks to exactly what he/she has been told. Today, however, this idiom is used to tell someone to just follow instructions to get a certain thing done.

这个实验很简单，你只要看着课本，按图索骥就可以了。

Zhèige shíyàn hěn jiǎndān, nǐ zhǐyào kànzhe kèběn, àn tú suǒ jì jiù kěyǐ le.

This experiment is very simple. Just follow what is written on the textbook.

In the very beginning, 按图索骥 *àn tú suǒ jì* had a negative connotation. In ancient China, there was a man called Bo Le who was very good at judging the quality of a horse. Those were the days of war when a good horse was in high demand so his skills were especially useful. In order to pass on to his son. Bo Le wrote a book explaining how to find a good horse just by looking at it. The book contained various illustrations of horses in different poses. Bo Le's son read the entire book and thought he had gained all of his father's knowledge. He eventually took the book out with him to search for good horses, but instead brought home a large toad. Later, this idiom evolved to describe a person who does not know how to make adjustments and can only copy the actions of others.

到朋友家玩

我们昨天晚上到李云英家去玩，大家都玩得非常高兴。李妈妈做饭做得很好吃，我们都吃得很饱[1]。回家以后，我告诉妈妈下个周末我也想请朋友到家里来，妈妈说没问题。我们家离他们的家都很近，走路就可以到，所以妈妈叫我画地图[2]给他们。爸爸做饭做得比妈妈好，所以妈妈请爸爸做他最拿手[3]的墨西哥菜，妈妈要准备水果和饮料。朋友来的时候，我们可以先吃吃水果、喝喝饮料，再一起玩游戏。爸爸说，如果天气好的话，我们还可以在外面吃饭呢！

[1] 饱: full (with hunger satisfied)　　[2] 地图: map　　[3] 拿手: good at

Dào Péngyou Jiā Wán

Wǒmen zuótiān wǎnshang dào Lǐ Yúnyīng jiā qù wán, dàjiā dōu wán de fēicháng gāoxìng. Lǐ māma zuòfàn zuò de hěn hǎochī, wǒmen dōu chī de hěn bǎo. Huíjiā yǐhòu, wǒ gàosù māma xiàge zhōumò wǒ yě xiǎng qǐng péngyou dào jiālǐ lái, māma shuō méi wèntí. Wǒmen jiā lí tāmen de jiā dōu hěnjìn, zǒulù jiù kěyǐ dào, suǒyǐ māma jiào wǒ huà dìtú gěi tāmen. Bàba zuòfàn zuò de bǐ māma hǎo, suǒyǐ māma qǐng bàba zuò tā zuì náshǒu de Mòxīgē cài, māma yào zhǔnbèi shuǐguǒ hé yǐnliào. Péngyou lái de shíhou, wǒmen kěyǐ xiān chīchi shuǐguǒ、hēhe yǐnliào, zài yìqǐ wán yóuxì. Bàba shuō, rúguǒ tiānqì hǎo dehuà, wǒmen hái kěyǐ zài wàimiàn chīfàn ne!

15 通晓文意 Tōngxiǎo Wényì / Understand the Passage

Read the above passage and answer the following questions in Chinese.

1. 他们什么时候去李云英家玩？　Tāmen shénme shíhou qù Lǐ Yúnyīng jiā wán?

2. 他们在李云英家吃哪一餐？　Tāmen zài Lǐ Yúnyīng jiā chī nǎ yìcān?

3. 他想什么时候请朋友到他家去玩？
   Tā xiǎng shénme shíhou qǐng péngyou dào tā jiā qù wán?

4. 为什么他妈妈叫他画地图给朋友们？
   Wèishénme tā māma jiào tā huà dìtú gěi péngyoumen?

5. 他们家谁做饭做得比较好？　Tāmen jiā shéi zuòfàn zuò de bǐjiào hǎo?

6. 做饭的人要做什么菜？　Zuòfàn de rén yào zuò shénme cài?

7. 谁要准备水果和饮料？　Shéi yào zhǔnbèi shuǐguǒ hé yǐnliào?

8. 天气好的话，他们可以在哪里吃饭？　Tiānqì hǎo de huà, tāmen kěyǐ zài nǎlǐ chīfàn?

汉字天地 Hànzì Tiāndì

Chinese Characters

日 ■ rì ■ the sun; day

The character 日 *rì* is a pictograph which reflects the shape of the sun. Since the rising and setting of the sun make a day, this character also means "day." It is also a common radical for words related to the sun.

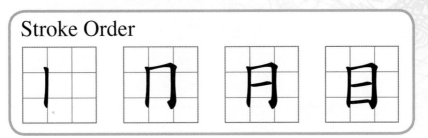

Stroke Order

16 词汇延伸 Cíhuì Yánshēn / *Vocabulary Builder*

Below are characters that combine with 日 *rì* to create words. Match the Chinese words on the left with the appropriate English meaning on the right.

落 luò	期 qī	记 jì	历 lì	出 chū
v. to fall	*n. a period of time*	*v. to write down*	*n. calendar*	*v. to go/ come out*

1. 日落 rìluò   A. diary
2. 日期 rìqī   B. sunrise
3. 日记 rìjì   C. calendar
4. 日历 rìlì   D. sunset
5. 日出 rìchū   E. date

17 汉字侦探 Hànzì Zhēntàn / *Visual Detective*

Can you find 日 in the following pictures?

Lesson B

Vocabulary

🔊 房子 Fángzi *Houses*

大楼（大樓）dàlóu

n. large building

平房 píngfáng

n. rambler

公寓 gōngyù

n. apartment

大门（大門）dàmén

n. front door

保安 bǎo'ān

n. security guard

阳台（陽台）yángtái

n. balcony

顶楼（頂樓）dǐnglóu

n. loft; attic

电梯（電梯）diàntī

n. elevator

楼梯 (樓梯) lóutī

n. stairs

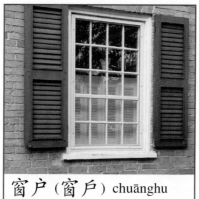

窗户 (窗戶) chuānghu

n. window

车库 (車庫) chēkù

n. garage

院子 yuànzi

n. courtyard, yard

信箱 xìnxiāng

n. mailbox

你怎么又迟到了！
(你怎麼又遲到了！)
Nǐ zěnme yòu chídào le!
How come you are late again!

对不起，下次不会了。
(對不起，下次不會了。)
Duìbùqǐ, xiàcì búhuì le.
I am sorry. I won't be late next time.

今天有籃球比賽，所以下了課，我要去籃球場。
（今天有籃球比賽，所以下了課，我要去籃球場。）
Jīntiān yǒu lánqiú bǐsài, suǒyǐ xiàle kè, wǒ yào qù lánqiúchǎng.
There is a basketball game today, so I am going to the basketball court after the class.

下课以后，你要做什么？
（下課以後，你要做什麼？）
Xiàkè yǐhòu, nǐ yào zuò shénme?
What are you going to do after class?

A: 吃快一点！我们没有时间了。（吃快一點！我們沒有時間了。）
Chī kuài yìdiǎn! Wǒmen méiyǒu shíjiān le. *Eat faster! We don't have time.*

B: 没关系，慢慢吃。我们可以坐下一班车。
（沒關係，慢慢吃。我們可以坐下一班車。）
Méi guānxi, mànmàn chī. Wǒmen kěyǐ zuò xià yìbān chē. *It's okay. Eat slowly. We can take the next bus.*

A: 你是跟谁来的？（你是跟誰來的？）

Nǐ shì gēn shéi láide? *Who did you come with?*

B: 我是跟我同学来的。（我是跟我同學來的。）

Wǒ shì gēn wǒ tóngxué láide. *I came with my classmates.*

....

A: 妈妈，这是我中文课的同学，李俊。李俊，这是我妈妈。

（媽媽，這是我中文課的同學，李俊。李俊，這是我媽媽。）

Māma, zhè shì wǒ Zhōngwén kè de tóngxué, Lǐ Jùn. Lǐ Jùn, zhè shì wǒ māma.

Mom, this is my classmate from Chinese class, Li Jun. Li Jun, this is my mom.

B: 王妈妈好。我以为你只是数学老师，没想到你还是心怡的妈妈。

（王媽媽好。我以為你只是數學老師，沒想到你還是心怡的媽媽）

Wáng māma hǎo. Wǒ yǐwéi nǐ zhǐshì shùxué lǎoshi, méi xiǎngdào nǐ háishì Xīnyí de māma.

Hi, Mrs. Wang. I know you are the math teacher, but didn't think that you are Xinyi's mom.

Language Note

When saying which floor in Chinese, just put the number in front of the noun 楼 *lóu*. For example, 一楼 *yīlóu* (1st floor), 二楼 *èrlóu* (2nd floor), 三楼 *sānlóu* (3rd floor), …, 十楼 *shílóu* (10th floor), etc.

▲ 几楼？

Adjectives

早	zǎo	*long ago; as early as; for a long time*
晚	wǎn	*not on time; late*
准时（準時）	zhǔnshí	*punctual; on time*

Adverb

终于（終於）	zhōngyú	*at last; in the end*

Common Expression

没事	méishì	*it's nothing; never mind*

Measure Words

栋（棟）	dòng	*(for buildings)*
层（層）	céng	*layer; storey; floor*

Nouns

楼（樓）	lóu	*floor*
聚会（聚會）	jùhuì	*party*

Particle

啦	la	*(the representation of the combined sounds "了 le" and "啊 a", denoting exclamation, interrogation, etc.*

Verbs

进（進）	jìn	*to enter; to come; to go into*
想	xiǎng	*to think*
以为（以為）	yǐwéi	*to think (mistakenly)*
上	shàng	*to go up; to get on*
下	xià	*to go down; to get off*

Verb-Object

迷路	mílù	*to be lost*

房屋类型 **Fángwū Lèixíng** / *House Types*

Listen to three people describing their houses. Choose the photo that best matches what they describe.

A.

B.

C.

2 住宅 **Zhùzhái** / *A Residence*

Listen to the recording. Match the places you hear with the ones in the drawing.

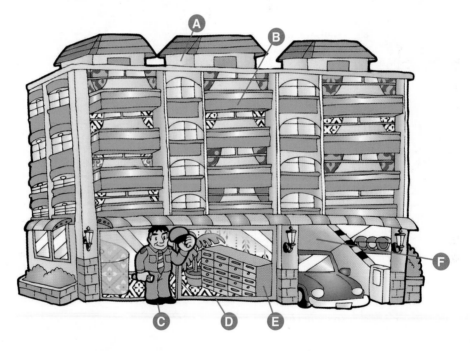

3 个人问题 **Gèrén Wèntí** / *Personal Questions*

Answer the following questions in Chinese based on your own experiences and opinions.

1. 你通常迟到还是准时？ Nǐ tōngcháng chídào háishì zhǔnshí?
2. 你容易迷路吗？ Nǐ róngyì mílù ma?
3. 你家是楼房还是平房？ Nǐ jiā shì lóufáng háishì píngfáng?
4. 你家有几层楼？ Nǐ jiā yǒu jǐcéng lóu?
5. 你家有没有电梯？ Nǐ jiā yǒu méiyǒu diàntī?

Directional Compounds with 来 *lái* and 去 *qù*

You learned in Level 1, Unit 3 Lesson C that the verb 来 *lái* (to come) indicates motion towards the speaker and the verb 去 *qù* (to go) indicates motion away from the speaker. The characters 来 *lái* or 去 *qù* can also follow some verbs and directional verbs to indicate that the direction of the action is coming towards or moving away from the speaker.

Verb / Directional Verb + 来 *lái* / 去 *qù*

上来
shànglái
to come up

上去
shàngqù
to go up

下来
xiàlái
to come down

下去
xiàqù
to go down

进来
jìnlái
to come in

进去
jìnqù
to go in

出来
chūlái
to come out

出去
chūqù
to go out

走来
zǒulái
to walk (here)

走去
zǒuqù a
to walk (there)

拿来
nálái
to bring (here)

拿去
náqù
to take (there)

骑来	开来	送来	爬来
qílái	kāilái	sònglái	pálái
to ride (here)	*to drive (here)*	*to deliver (here)*	*to crawl (here)*
骑去	开去	送去	爬去
qíqù	kāiqù	sòngqù	páqù
to ride (there)	*to drive (there)*	*to deliver (there)*	*to crawl (there)*

A: 车子呢？ Chēzi ne ?

B: 哥哥开去学校了。 Gēge kāiqù xuéxiào le.

A: 东西送来了吗？ Dōngxi sònglái le ma?

B: 还没，我再打电话问问。 Hái méi, wǒ zài dǎ diànhuà wènwen.

"是…的 *shì…de*" to Discuss Aspects of a Known Event

The 是…的 *shì…de* pattern is used to emphasize "when," "where," or "how" a PAST action occurred. Place 是 *shì* in front of the information to be emphasized and 的 *de* at the end of the information. The word 是 *shì* can be omitted when the sentence is positive, but it cannot be omitted from a negative sentence.

是 *shì* + information + 的 *de*

我是十二点钟吃中饭的。 Wǒ shì shí`èrdiǎn zhōng chī zhōngfàn de.

When 是…的 *shì…de* is used with a verb that has an object, the 的 *de* can be at the end of the sentence or between the verb and the object.

我是十二点钟吃的中饭。
Wǒ shì shí`èrdiǎn zhōng chī de zhōngfàn.

▲ 中餐馆

Here is an example:

我前天跟爸妈去中餐馆吃饭。
Wǒ qiántiān gēn bà-mā qù Zhōngcānguǎn chīfàn.

→ **Q:** 你是什么时候去中餐馆的？
   Nǐ shì shénme shíhou qù Zhōngguó cānguǎn de?

A: 我是前天去的。 Wǒ shì qiántiān qù de.

→ **Q:** 你前天是跟谁去的？ Nǐ qiántiān shì gēn shéi qùde?

A: 我是跟爸妈去的。 Wǒ shì gēn bà-mā qù de.

→ **Q:** 你前天跟爸妈是去哪里吃饭的？ Nǐ qiántiān shì gēn bàmā qù nǎlǐ chīfàn de?

A: 我们是去中餐馆吃饭的。 Wǒmen shì qù Zhōngcānguǎn chīfàn de.

→ **Q:** 你前天跟爸妈是去什么餐馆吃饭的？
   Nǐ qiántiān gēn bàmā shì qù shénme cānguǎn chīfàn de?

A: 我们是去中国餐馆吃饭的。 Wǒmen shì qù Zhōngguó cānguǎn chīfàn de.

→ **Q:** 你前天跟爸妈去中餐馆做什么？
   Nǐ qiántiān gēn bàmā qù Zhōngguó cānguǎn zuò shénme?

A: 我们是去吃饭的。 Wǒmen shì qù chīfàn de

The Pattern "从...来 / 去 cóng...lái / qù"

We were introduced to the pattern "到...来 / 去 dào...lái / qù" in Unit 3 Lesson B. Different from 到 dào which indicates motion towards a point, the word 从 cóng means "from," and it indicates motion away from some point.

Subject + 从 *cóng* + **Place** + 来 *lái* / 去 *qù*

李老师是从中国来的。 Lǐ lǎoshī shì cóng Zhōngguó lái de.

王先生是从美国到墨西哥去的。 Wáng Xiānsheng shì cóng Měiguó dào Mòxīgē qù de.

The Pattern "以为...没想到... yǐwéi...méi xiǎngdào..."

The pattern 以为...没想到... yǐwéi... méi xiǎngdào... means "...thought that..., didn't think that...." What follows 以为 yǐwéi is a mistaken thought or idea that someone previously believed that it was true, and what follows 没想到 méi xiǎngdào is the unexpected or unpredicatable truth. The pattern shows a transition between the former and latter part of a sentence.

Subject + 以为 *yǐwéi* + **mistaken thought** + 没想到 *méi xiǎngdào* + **truth**

你家在六楼，我以为有电梯，没想到只有楼梯。
Nǐ jiā zài liùlóu, wǒ yǐwéi yǒu diàntī, méi xiǎngdào zhǐ yǒu lóutī.

我以为爸爸出门了，所以我开始玩电子游戏，没想到他还在家。
Wǒ yǐwéi bàba chūmén le, suǒyǐ wǒ kāishǐ wán diànzǐ yóuxì, méi xiǎngdào tā hái zài jiā.

The pattern "S V了O, 就... S V *le* O, *jiù*..." to Show the Imminent Action

The pattern "S V了O, 就... S V *le* O, *jiù*..." is used to indicate that an action is going to happen almost immediately after the first clause (S V了 *le* O) is finished. This pattern applies to past events, habitual action, and future events. The subject can be the same or different.

(Subject 1) + **Verb** + 了 *le* + **Object** , **(Subject 2)** + 就 *jiù* + **Verb Phrase**

我昨天下了课，就去图书馆了。 Wǒ zuótiān xiàle kè, jiù qù túshūguǎn le.

我每天下了课，就去图书馆。 Wǒ měitiān xiàle kè, jiù qù túshūguǎn.

我今天下了课，就要去图书馆。 Wǒ jīntiān xiàle kè, jiù yào qù túshūguǎn.

我们出了门，就下雨了。 Wǒmen chūle mén, jiù xiàyǔ le.

爸爸到了家，妈妈就做饭。 Bàba dàole jiā, māma jiù zuòfàn.

哥哥买了车，就会开车去上课。 Gēge mǎile chē, jiù huì kāichē qù shàngkè.

🔊 拜访同学 Bàifǎng Tóngxué *Paying a Visit to Classmates*

On Sunday afternoon, Li Yunying's friends arrive at her home.

赵梅:	嘿，云英！	Zhào Méi:	Hēi, Yúnyīng!
李云英:	你们来啦，真准时！永利呢？	Lǐ Yúnyīng:	Nǐmen láila, zhēn zhǔnshí! Yǒnglì ne?
吴森:	不知道。他说有事，要自己来。	Wú Sēn:	Bù zhīdào. Tā shuō yǒushì, yào zìjǐ lái.
李云英:	没关系，你们先进来吧。	Lǐ Yúnyīng:	Méi guānxi, nǐmen xiān jìnlái ba.
赵梅:	你终于到了。	Zhào Méi:	Nǐ zhōngyú dàole.
钱永利:	对不起，对不起，我迟到了。	Qián Yǒnglì:	Duìbùqǐ, duìbùqǐ, wǒ chídào le.
李云英:	没事。你是怎么来的？	Lǐ Yúnyīng:	Méishì. Nǐ shì zěnme láide?
钱永利:	我是走路来的，可是我迷路了。	Qián Yǒnglì:	Wǒ shì zǒulù láide, kěshì wǒ mílù le.
赵梅:	你是从哪里来的？	Zhào Méi:	Nǐ shì cóng nǎlǐ láide?
钱永利:	我是从家里来的。	Qián Yǒnglì:	Wǒ shì cóng jiālǐ láide.
吴森:	你是几点出门的？	Wú Sēn:	Nǐ shì jǐdiǎn chūmén de?
钱永利:	我是两点出门的。	Qián Yǒnglì:	Wǒ shì liǎngdiǎn chūmén de.
赵梅:	两点！现在已经四点半了。我以为你会比我们早到，没想到比我们晚。	Zhào Méi:	Liǎngdiǎn! Xiànzài yǐjīng sìdiǎn bàn le. Wǒ yǐwéi nǐ huì bǐ wǒmen zǎo dào, méi xiǎngdào bǐ wǒmen wǎn.
李云英:	大家来喝饮料。慢慢喝，喝了饮料，我就带大家上楼去看看。	Lǐ Yúnyīng:	Dàjiā lái hē yǐnliào. Mànmàn hē, hēle yǐnliào, wǒ jiù dài dàjiā shàng lóu qù kànkan.

4 谁还没到？ **Shéi hái méi dào?** / *Who has not come yet?*

According to the dialogue, identify the person who has not yet arrived at Li Yunying's home.

A.

B.

C.
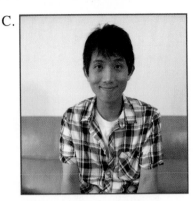

5 时间 **Shíjiān** / *Time*

Look at the following clocks, and say what happens at each displayed time based on the dialogue.

A.

B.

C.

6 懂了吗？ **Dǒng le ma?** / *Do you understand?*

Answer the following questions in Chinese.

1. 有几个人先到李云英家？他们是谁？
   Yǒu jǐge rén xiān dào Lǐ Yúnyīng jiā? Tāmen shì shéi?

2. 吴森和赵梅，谁比较早到，谁比较晚到？
   Wú Sēn hé Zhào Méi, shéi bǐjiào zǎo dào, shéi bǐjiào wǎn dào?

3. 为什么钱永利没有跟吴森和赵梅一起到？
   Wèishénme Qián Yǒnglì méiyǒu gēn Wú Sēn hé Zhào Méi yìqǐ dào?

4. 钱永利是怎么去李云英家的？ Qián Yǒnglì shì zěnme qù Lǐ Yúnyīng jiā de?

5. 为什么钱永利那么晚才到？ Wèishénme Qián Yǒnglì nàme wǎn cái dào?

6. 钱永利是从哪里来的？ Qián Yǒnglì shì cóng nǎlǐ láide?

7. 钱永利几点出门？几点到李云英家？
   Qián Yǒnglì jǐdiǎn chūmén? Jǐdiǎn dào Lǐ Yúnyīng jiā?

8. 喝了饮料以后，他们要做什么？ Hēle yǐnliào yǐhòu, tāmen yào zuò shénme?

Fengshui

Fengshui is a part of ancient Chinese traditional folk culture. Followers of the practice believe that proper alignment of our built environment can ward off bad luck and improve one's fortune. Fengshui incorporates concepts from geography, geology, astrology, meteorology, landscaping, architecture, ecology and sciences having to do with the human body. At its core, fengshui aims to understand our natural environment and harmonize our living environment with it. Fengshui would prescribe the location of one's house or workplace, its directionality, its architecture and how the furniture is arranged. This unique view of the world has followers throughout all levels of society.

Most Chinese buildings face the south. This is because China is in the northern hemisphere, so the sun shines into houses from the south throughout the year.

▲ *A Chinese compass which is used largely for fengshui related exploration.*

Houses that face the south get better sunlight and thus more warmth, which is believed to improve the occupant's luck. Fengshui also prescribes that there should be hills in front of a house and water behind a house, as this will also bring the occupant good luck. In the interior of a house, fengshui requires that bathrooms not face kitchens, because kitchens represent a water source known as "upper water," and bathrooms are where water leaves, known as "down water," so from a fengshui point of view, for the top and bottom of the water flow to form a straight line is very bad and would result in the loss of finances. From a practical point of view, having a kitchen facing a bathroom could seem unhygienic and make people feel uncomfortable.

As for interior furnishings, fengshui would say that the end of the bed should not face a window. This is also based on practical experience, because having the sun shine through the window onto one's face would make it harder to sleep well. However, in today's cities, if one is surrounded

▲ *"Lucky bamboo" is a favorite inner plant for Chinese office or house.*

by high-rises on all sides, having the end of a bed face a window would not affect one's quality of sleep. Simply put, fengshui is all about the environment we live in. If the environment is good and the interior furnishings suit the occupants' style and make them feel comfortable, that is good fengshui. However, some people think that certain objects should be placed in certain places, and those places depend on the occupant's name, time of birth, astrological sign and various other factors. For example, the placement of a fish tank can become complicated and involve the shape of the tank, the number of fish, the kind of fish and even the color of the fish themselves. Of course, how much to be believe or whether to believe any of it is left to the individual.

Fengshui has long been a part of Chinese culture, and is an ancient study. Although there are mystic elements embedded in its theories, it also contains concepts from basic science and common sense regarding the way one lives. In other words, fengshui is simply a combination of psychology, art and practical experiences about living.

▲ *A good fengshui living room*

 文化动动脑 **Wénhuà Dòngdòngnǎo** / *Culture Check-up*

Decide if each statement is true or false. Correct the false statements.

1. The Chinese word, fengshui can be translated into wind and water, and means weather.
2. Choosing the location of one's house might be based on fengshui.
3. Most Chinese buildings face the south.
4. Most of the sunshine in China comes from the north.
5. From a fengshui point of view, the kitchen and bathroom cannot face one another.
6. Fengshui is an elaborate science and should be followed to the letter.

8 动作方向 **Dòngzuò Fāngxiàng** / *The Direction of an Action*

Complete the following sentences with the words of 来 *lái* **or** 去 *qù*.

1. 拿 ___，这是给你的。 Ná ___, zhè shì gěi nǐ de.

2. 快进 ___，外面下大雪了！ Kuài jìn ___, wàimian xià dàxuě le!

3. 这本书请你送 ___ 给张老师。 Bǎ zhèiběn shū qǐng nǐ sòng ___ gěi Zhāng lǎoshī.

4. 比萨饼(*pizza*)送 ___ 了，可以吃饭了。 Bǐsàbǐng sòng ___ le, kěyǐ chīfàn le.

5. 把我的东西拿 ___，快还给我。 Bǎ wǒde dōngxi ná ___, kuài huán gěi wǒ.

6. 从这里 ___ 健身房只要三分钟。 Cóng zhèlǐ ___ jiànshēnfáng zhǐyào sānfēn zhōng.

7. 你快上 ___ 顶楼，我们都在这里，晚会已经开始了。

   Nǐ kuài shàng ___ dǐnglóu, wǒmen dōu zài zhèli, wǎnhuì yǐjīng kāishǐ le.

8. 请带狗出 ___ 好吗？诊所里不能有狗。

   Qǐng dài gǒu chū ___ hǎo ma? Gǒu bùnéng jìn ___ zhěnsuǒli.

9. 我在五楼，你在一楼等等，我马上下 ___。

   Wǒ zài wǔlóu, nǐ zài yīlóu děngdeng, wǒ mǎshàng xià ___.

10. 我一会儿要出 ___，你的车可以借给我吗？

    Wǒ yìhuǐr yào chū ___, nǐde chē kěyǐ jiè gěi wǒ ma?

9 强调重点 **Qiángdiào Zhòngdiǎn** / *Asking for Details*

With a classmate, take turns asking and answering the following questions using the pattern 是…的 *shì…de.*

1. 你是怎么来学校的？ Nǐ shì zěnme lái xuéxiào de?

2. 你是几岁上高中的？ Nǐ shì jǐsuì shàng gāozhōng de?

3. 你今天是几点起床的？ Nǐ jīntiān shì jǐdiǎn qǐchuáng de?

4. 你是几月出生(*to be born*)的？ Nǐ shì jǐyuè chūshēng de?

5. 你昨天是一个人吃晚饭的吗？ Nǐ zuótiān shì yíge rén chī wǎnfàn de ma?

6. 你穿的衣服是在哪里买的？ Nǐ chuānde yīfu shì zài nǎlǐ mǎide?

7. 你是什么时候开始学的中文？ Nǐ shì shénme shíhou kāishǐ xuéde Zhōngwén?

8. 你是在美国长大(*to grow up*)的吗？ Nǐ shì zài Měiguó zhǎngdà de ma?

The following schedules are part of a flight timetable of the Beijing Capital International Airport. With a classmate, look at the charts and take turns asking and answering questions based on the information provided. Use the pattern 从…来 / 去 *cóng…lái / qù.*

Lìzi: **A:** 早上六点零五分到北京的飞机是从哪里来的？

Zǎoshang liùdiǎn líng wǔfēn dào Běijīng de fēijī shì cóng nǎlǐ láide?

OR, EK309的飞机是从哪里来的？ EK309 de fēijī shì cóng nǎlǐ láide?

B: 是从迪拜来的。 Shì cóng Díbài láide.

计划到港 jìhuà dào gǎng (Schedule Time Arrival)	航班号 hángbān hào (Flight No.)	出发地 chūfādì (Arriving from)
06:05	EK309	迪拜 Díbài (Dubai)
06:45	AA186	芝加哥 Zhījiāgē (Chicago)
07:10	DL58	东京 Dōngjīng (Tokyo)
07:30	KA937	香港 Xiānggǎng (Hong Kong)
08:15	US5351	新加坡 Xīnjiāpō (Singapore)
08:25	KE852	首尔 Shǒu'ěr (Seoul)

Lìzi: **A:** 中午十二点的飞机从北京去哪里？

Zhōngwǔ shí'èrdiǎn de fēijī cóng Běijīng qù nǎlǐ?

Or NH160的飞机从北京去哪里？ NH160 de fēijī cóng Běijīng qù nǎlǐ?

B: 从北京去大阪。 Cóng Běijīng qù Dàbǎn.

计划离港 jìhuà lí gǎng (Schedule Time Leaving)	航班号 hángbān hào (Flight No.)	目的地 mùdìdì (Departing to)
12:00	NH160	大阪 Dàbǎn (Osaka)
12:15	DL128	西雅图 Xīyǎtú (Seattle)
13:06	BA038	伦敦 Lúndūn (London)
13:24	CI512	台北 Táiběi (Taipei)
14:10	HU7975	多伦多 Duōlúnduō (Toronto)
14:22	CA933	巴黎 Bālí (Paris)

11 出乎意料 Chūhū Yìliào / *Beyond Expectation*

Use the pattern 以为…没想到… *yǐwéi…méi xiǎngdào*…. to rephrase the following sentences into one complete sentence.

Lìzi: 我昨天想今天是晴天。 Wǒ zuótiān xiǎng jīntiān shì qíngtiān.

今天下大雨。 Jīntiān xià dà yǔ.

→ 我以为今天是晴天，没想到下大雨。
Wǒ yǐwéi jīntiān shì qíngtiān, méi xiǎngdào xià dà yǔ.

1. 我想这道菜很清淡。 Wǒ xiǎng zhèidào cài hěn qīngdàn.
   这道菜很油。 Zhèidào cài hěn yóu.

2. 我想他只是精神不好。 Wǒ xiǎng tā zhǐshì jīngshén bùhǎo.
   他生病了。 Tā shēngbìng le.

3. 我想你走楼梯。 Wǒ xiǎng nǐ zǒu lóutī.
   你坐了电梯。 Nǐ zuòle diàntī.

4. 我想他可以出门了。 Wǒ xiǎng tā kěyǐ chūmén le.
   他还没洗脸刷牙。 Tā hái méi xǐliǎn shuāyá.

5. 我想你吃了午饭了，所以没准备东西。
   Wǒ xiǎng nǐ chīle wǔfàn le, suǒyǐ méi zhǔnbèi dōngxi.
   你还没吃。 Nǐ hái méichī.

12 立即行动 Lìjí Xíngdòng / *Immediate Action*

Complete the following sentences with the pattern S V 了 O，就… S V *le* O, *jiù*… according to your own experiences and expectations.

1. 我昨天下了课，___。 Wǒ zuótiān xiàle kè, ___.
   我每天下了课，___。 Wǒ měitiān xiàle kè, ___.
   我明天下了课，___。 Wǒ míngtiān xiàle kè, ___.

2. 妈妈昨天吃了晚饭，___。 Māma zuótiān chīle wǎnfàn, ___.
   妈妈每天吃了晚饭，___。 Māma měitiān chīle wǎnfàn, ___.
   妈妈今天吃了晚饭，___。 Māma jīntiān chīle wǎnfàn, ___.

3. 爸爸昨天到了家，___。 Bàba zuótiān dàole jiā, ___.
   爸爸每天到了家，___。 Bàba měitiān dàole jiā, ___.
   爸爸今天到了家，___。 Bàba jīntiān dàole jiā, ___.

13 事件先后　**Shìjiàn Xiānhòu**／*The Ins and Outs of A Event*

Combine the following sentences using the pattern S V 了 O，就… S V *le* O, *jiù*….

1. 我们见面。　Wǒmen jiànmiàn.

   他带我去咖啡店喝饮料。　Tā dài wǒ qù kāfēidiàn hē yǐnliào.

2. 我下课。　Wǒ xiàkè.

   妈妈到学校来接(*to pick up*)我。　Māma dào xuéxiào lái jiē wǒ.

3. 李先生买车。　Lǐ xiānsheng mǎi chē.

   李先生带王小姐到海边去玩。　Lǐ xiānsheng dài Wáng xiǎojiě dào hǎibiān qù wán.

4. 我发烧。　Wǒ fāshāo.

   爸妈带我去诊所看病。　Bàmā dài wǒ qù zhěnsuǒ kànbìng.

5. 吴太太买菜回家。　Wú tàitai mǎicài huíjiā.

   吴先生帮忙做菜。　Wú xiānsheng bāngmáng zuòcài.

开口说　Kāikǒu Shuō
Communication

14 小小调查　**Xiǎoxiǎo Diàochá**／*A Survey*

 Take a survey to determine the top three activities at a party. Ask five students in your class what they like to do at a party. Use this information to create a grid like the one shown below. In the grid, write the names of the classmates you polled and the activities they like with a ranking that notes which activity they like best. Give the first activity three points, the second two points, and the third one point. At the end, calculate and find out the top three activities on your chart and share the results of your survey with the class.

Lìzi:　A: 聚会的时候，你喜欢做什么？　Jùhuì de shíhou, nǐ xǐhuan zuò shénme?

　　　　　B: 我喜欢跟朋友聊天、吃东西、玩电子游戏。

　　　　　　Wǒ xǐhuan gēn péngyou liáotiān, chī dōngxi, wán diànzǐ yóuxì.

Activities Student			
B	1.跟朋友聊天 gēn péngyou liáotiān	2.吃东西 chī dōngxi	3.玩电子游戏 wán diànzǐ yóuxì

15 聚会邀请卡 **Jùhuì Yāoqǐngkǎ** / *Party Invitation Card*

Read the following invitation card and answer the questions that follow.

亲爱的小美：

　　这个星期五是我的生日，想邀请全班同学来我家
参加我的生日派对。因为星期五大家都要上课，所以
派对是在星期六，希望你能来。

　　我妈妈会准备很多吃的和喝的东西，所以你不用带
食物来。这个派对没有主题 (*theme*)，你要穿什么衣服
都可以，所以穿你觉得舒服的就好。

　　对了，不用送我礼物，大家开心就好。

时间：九月二十八日　星期六中午十二点

地点：真棒路三十二号一楼

明伟

1. 谁邀请谁参加派对？　Shéi yāoqǐng shéi cānjiā pàiduì?
2. 为什么派对不在星期五？　Wèishénme pàiduì bú zài Xīngqīwǔ?
3. 去派对应该要穿什么？　Qù pàiduì yīnggāi yào chuān shénme?
4. 谁会准备食物？　Shéi huì zhǔnbèi shíwù?
5. 明伟家在哪里？　Míngwěi jiā zài nǎlǐ?

16 你当主人 **Nǐ Dāng Zhǔrén** / *Being A Host*

It is your turn to be a host! Refer to the invitation card in the previous activity, and write an invitation card in Chinese.

Zìwǒ Tíshēng

Raising the Bar

Vocabulary

者   zhě   *pron.*   *transforming verbs or adjectives into nouns. e.g.* 来者, *means "one who comes."*

客   kè   *n.*   *guest*

来者是客
lái zhě shì kè
Whomever Comes is a Guest

▲ 来者是客

Language Note

This idiom means that one should treat every visitor with the hospitality due an invited guest, and is a pleasantry that is often spoken to a visitor.

您别客气！来者是客，就在我家吃个饭吧！
Nín bié kèqi! Lái zhě shì kè, jiù zài wǒjiā chīge fàn ba!
Don't be so polite! You are the guest, so have dinner here!

The Chinese believe that 礼多人不怪 *lǐ duō rén bú guài* (people won't be blamed for their good manners) and would rather be polite than rude, because if one is considered rude, the thin-skinned Chinese people will lose face.

For example, compare how Westerners and Chinese might react to unexpected guests. For Westerners, it is rude to pay someone a visit when they are having a meal, but the Chinese will invite the guests in to have the meal with them and encourage them to eat more. Even if the people at the door are disliked by the hosts, they will still invite them in because 来者是客 *lái zhě shì kè*, and they will exchange pleasantries with the person. Moreover, the host will often also say 招待不周，请多包涵 *zhāodài bù zhōu, qǐng duō bāohán.* (Sorry for not being a good host)—another pleasantry—when guests leave in hopes that the guests won't say anything bad about the hosts upon leaving. From this example here, we can see that the Chinese place great emphasis on having good manners and leaving a good impression, and care very much about what others think.

家有客人

　　今天我们家有客人[1]，他是爸爸的高中同学，所以我叫他蔡伯伯。蔡伯伯是今天中午到的。爸爸以为他早上十点就到，可是等到十二点半他才到。爸爸以为他开车迷路了，没想到他是坐巴士来的。他说他家很远，所以他不想开那么久的车。妈妈以为蔡伯伯会带他的家人，所以准备了很多菜，没想到蔡伯伯是自己来的。蔡伯伯带了一只小狗，他说小狗是要送给我的。虽然小狗很可爱，可是我怕狗，而且也对狗过敏[2]，所以狗是一定不能留[3]在我家的。

[1] 客人: guest　[2] 过敏: allergic　[3] 留: to stay

Jiā Yǒu Kèrén

Jīntiān wǒmen jiā yǒu kèrén, tā shì bàba de gāozhōng tóngxué, suǒyǐ wǒ jiào tā Cài bóbo. Cài bóbo shì jīntiān zhōngwǔ dàode. Bàba yǐwéi tā zǎoshang shídiǎn jiù dào, kěshì děng dào shí'èrdiǎn bàn tā cái dào. Bàba yǐwéi tā kāichē lái mílù le, méi xiǎngdào tā shì zuò bāshì lái de. Tā shuō tā jiā hěn yuǎn, suǒyǐ tā bùxiǎng kāi nàme jiǔde chē. Māma yǐwéi Cài bóbo huì dài tāde jiārén, suǒyǐ zhǔnbèile hěnduō cài, méi xiǎngdào Cài bóbo shì zìjǐ láide. Cài bóbo dàile yìzhī xiǎogǒu, tā shuō xiǎogǒu shì yào sòng gěi wǒde. Suīrán xiǎogǒu hěn kě'ài, kěshì wǒ pà gǒu, érqiě yě duì gǒu guòmǐn, suǒyǐ gǒu shì yídìng bùnéng liú zài wǒ jiāde.

17 通晓文意 Tōngxiǎo Wényì / Understand the Passage

Read the above passage and answer the following questions in Chinese.

1. 蔡伯伯是谁？　Cài bóbo shì shéi?

2. 蔡伯伯是什么时候到的？　Cài bóbo shì shénme shíhou dào de?

3. 蔡伯伯是怎么去的？　Cài bóbo shì zěnme qù de?

4. 为什么蔡伯伯没开车？　Wèishénme Cài bóbo méi kāichē?

5. 爸爸以为蔡伯伯几点到？　Bàba yǐwéi Cài bóbo jǐ diǎn dào?

6. 为什么妈妈准备了很多菜？　Wèishénme māma zhǔnbèi le hěn duō cài?

7. 小狗是要给谁的？　Xiǎo gǒu shì yào gěi shéi de?

8. 作者(writer)要小狗吗？为什么？　Zuòzhě yào xiǎo gǒu ma? Wèishénme?

汉字天地　Hànzì Tiāndì

Chinese Characters

门 / 門 ■ mén ■ door

The traditional form of the pictograph 门 *mén* resembles a door with two panels in its original form.

Stroke Order

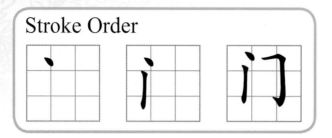

18 词汇延伸　Cíhuì Yánshēn / *Vocabulary Builder*

Below are characters that combine with 门 *mén* to create words. Match the Chinese words on the left with the appropriate English meaning on the right.

票 piào	口 kǒu	大 dà	铃 líng	牌 pái
n. ticket	*n. mouth*	*adj. big*	*n. bell*	*n. plate*

1. 门票 ménpiào   A. entrance
2. 门口 ménkǒu   B. doorbell
3. 大门 dàmén   C. doorplate
4. 门铃 ménlíng   D. entrance ticket
5. 门牌 ménpái   E. gate

19 汉字侦探 **Hànzì Zhēntàn** / *Visual Detective*

Can you find 门 in the following pictures?

门

Lesson C

🔊 房间 (房間) Fángjiān *Rooms*

客厅 (客廳) kètīng

n. living room

饭厅 (飯廳) fàntīng

n. dining room

厨房 (廚房) chúfáng

n. kitchen

卧房 (臥房) wòfáng

n. bedroom

书房 (書房) shūfáng

n. study room

客房 (客房) kèfáng

n. guest room

厕所 (廁所) cèsuǒ

n. bathroom; toilet

浴室 yùshì

n. bathroom

阁楼 (閣樓) gélóu

n. attic; loft

地下室 dìxiàshì

n. basement

贮藏室 (貯藏室) zhùcángshì

n. storage room

Language Note

In addition to 厕所 *cèsuǒ*, there are many Chinese words for "toilet." 洗手间 *xǐshǒujiān* is one of the most common.

中文

◀)) **家具 Jiājù** *Furniture*

桌子 zhuōzi *n. table; desk*
椅子 yǐzi *n. chair*

沙发 (沙發) shāfā *n. sofa*
茶几 chájī *n. coffee table*
门 (門) mén *n. door*
灯 (燈) dēng *n. lamp; light*
地板 dìbǎn *n. floor*
墙壁 (牆壁) qiángbì *n. wall*

书柜 (書櫃) shūguì

n. bookcase

垃圾桶 lājītǒng

n. garbage can

游戏机 (遊戲機)

yóuxìjī *n. video game player*

哥哥呢？他在做什么？
（哥哥呢？他在做什麼？）
Gēge ne? Tā zài zuò shénme?
Where's my big brother? What is he doing?

他正在睡觉。（他正在睡覺。）
Tā zhèngzài shuìjiào. *He's sleeping.*

A: 你今天看见他了没有？（你今天看見他了沒有？）
Nǐ jīntiān kànjiàn tā le méiyǒu? *Have you seen him today?*

B: 没有，你有急事吗？（沒有，你有急事嗎？）
Méiyǒu, nǐ yǒu jí shì ma? *No, what's up?*

你的中国字写得好漂亮。
（你的中國字寫得好漂亮。）
Nǐde Zhōngguó zì xiěde hǎo piàoliang.
Your Chinese writing is really nice!

还没有我姐姐的那么漂亮，你应该看看她写的。
（還沒有我姐姐的那麼漂亮，你應該看看她寫的。）
Hái méiyǒu wǒ jiějie de nàme piàoliang, nǐ yīnggāi kànkan tā xiěde.
It's not as good as my big sister's. You should look at her writing.

A: 我喜欢一边开车，一边听音乐。
（我喜歡一邊開車，一邊聽音樂。）
Wǒ xǐhuan yìbiān kāichē, yìbiān tīng yīnyuè.
I like listening to music when I drive.

B: 我喜欢一边开车，一边唱歌。
（我喜歡一邊開車，一邊唱歌。）
Wǒ xǐhuan yìbiān kāichē, yìbiān chànggē.
I like to sing when I drive.

▲ 我喜欢一边开车，一边唱歌。

Adverbs

正在	zhèngzài	*in the process of; during the course of*
刚刚 (剛剛)	gānggāng	*just; exactly*
一边 (一邊)	yìbiān	*(indicating two simultaneous actions) at the same time; simultaneously*
好	hǎo	*(used before certain adjectives to indicate high degree) quite*

Interjection

| 哇 | wa | *(sound of vomiting and crying)* |

Nouns

| 声音 (聲音) | shēngyīn | *sound; voice* |
| 父母 | fù-mǔ | *father and mother; parents* |

Measure Word

| 间 (間) | jiān | *room* |

Resultative Complements

好	hǎo	*(used after a verb to indicate the completion of an action)*
到	dào	*(used after a verb as a complement to indicate success)*
完	wán	*(used after a verb as a complement to indicate something ran out or was used up)*

Verbs

叫	jiào	*to call; to greet*
听 (聽)	tīng	*to listen; to hear*
完	wán	*to finish*

Verb-Object

| 放心 | fàngxīn | *to feel relieved* |

1 房屋配对 **Fángwū Pèiduì** / *House Match*

🔊 **Listen to four people describing their houses. Choose the drawing that best matches what they describe.**

A.
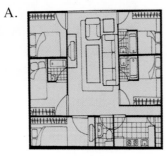

C.
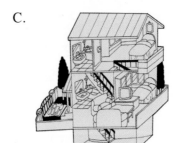

B.
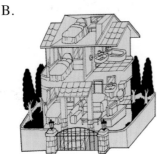

D.
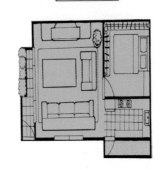

2 家具 **Jiājù** / *Furniture*

🔊 **Listen to the recording. Match the objects you hear with the corresponding picture.**

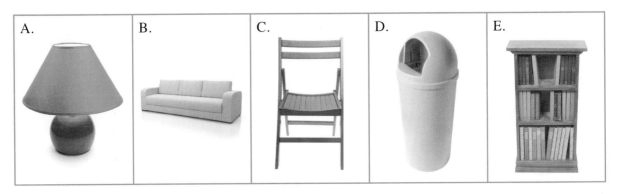

A.   B.   C.   D.   E.

3 个人问题 **Gèrén Wèntí** / *Personal Questions*

Answer the following questions in Chinese based on your own experiences and opinions.

1. 你家有几间房间？ Nǐ jiā yǒu jǐjiān fángjiān?

2. 你家有阁楼或地下室吗？ Nǐ jiā yǒu gélóu huò dìxiàshì ma?

3. 你的房间里面有沙发吗？ Nǐde fángjiān lǐmian yǒu shāfā ma?

4. 你的房间里面有浴室吗？ Nǐde fángjiān lǐmian yǒu yùshì ma?

5. 你房间的墙壁是什么颜色的？ Nǐ fángjiān de qiángbì shì shénme yánsè de?

Language Patterns

The Adverb 正在 *zhèngzài*

The adverb 正在 *zhèngzài* means "in the process of" or "during the course of." It indicates that the action is proceeding. The word 在 *zài* can be omitted.

> **Subject** + 正在 *zhèngzài* + **Verb Phrase**

爸爸正在开车，不能接电话。 Bàba zhèngzài kāi chē, bùnéng jiē diànhuà.

A: 喂，请问董文君在不在？ Wéi, qǐngwèn Dǒng Wénjūn zài búzài?

B: 她在，不过她正在洗澡。请问你是哪位？

Tā zài, búguò tā zhèngzài xǐzǎo. Qǐngwèn nǐ shì něiwèi?

The Resultative Complements (到 *dào*, 好 *hǎo*, 见 *jiàn*, 完 *wán*, 懂 *dǒng*)

In Chinese, verbs can be followed by another verb or adjective to indicate the result of the action. The verb or adjective that follows the main verb is called a resultative complement.

Resultative complements can clarify or modify the verb, for example, 吃完水果，我们玩电子游戏 *Chīwán shuǐguǒ, wǒmen wán diànzǐ yóuxì.* (We play video games after we finish eating fruit.)." They can also show a new state or change, for example, 晚饭做好了 *Wǎnfàn zuòhǎo le.* (The dinner is ready.).

In this lesson, you will learn about five of the most commonly used complements. They are the verbs 到 *dào*, 见 *jiàn*, 完 *wán*, 懂 *dǒng*, and the adjective 好 *hǎo*.

	Original Meaning as a Verb	**Extended Meaning as a Complement**
到 *dào*	to arrive	success or achievement of an action
见 *jiàn*	to see	perception of an action
完 *wán*	to finish	completion of an action
懂 *dǒng*	to understand	understanding of an action
好 *hǎo*	good	completion of an action, meaning the action is completed and in the desired manner

Language Note

The verbs that go with the complement 见 *jiàn* and 懂 *dǒng* are limited. Only verbs about vision and hearing, such as 看 *kàn*, 听 *tīng*, can have 见 *jiàn* as a complement.

Verb + **Complement** + **Object**

妈妈昨天收到一封老朋友的电邮。
Māma zuótiān shōudào yìfēng lǎo péngyou de diànyóu.

哥哥买好旅行要用的东西了。 Gēge mǎihǎo lǚxíng yào yòngde dōngxi le.

我没有听见你说的话，可以请你再说一次吗？
Wǒ méiyǒu tīngjiàn nǐ shuōde huà, kěyǐ qǐng nǐ zài shuō yícì ma?

他们打完篮球，就要回家。 Tāmen dǎwán lánqiú, jiù yào huí jiā.

The Pattern "V了没有 *V le méiyǒu*"

The pattern "V了没有 *V le méiyǒu*" is also a form for questions used to ask about a completed action. It is the same as "V了吗 *le ma*."

Subject + **Verb-Object** + 了没有 *le méiyǒu*

你刷牙了没有？ Nǐ shuāyá le méiyǒu?

A: 你做功课了没有？ Nǐ zuò gōngkè le méiyǒu?
B: 还没，我等一下就去做。 Hái méi, wǒ děng yíxià jiù qù zuò.

In some cases, the object can be moved to the front of the question, in the form of topic comment.

Object + **Subject** + **Verb** + 了没有 *le méiyǒu*

脸你洗了没有？ Liǎn nǐ xǐle méiyǒu?

A: 饭你做好了没有？ Fàn nǐ zuòhǎo le méiyǒu?
B: 色拉做好了，可是汤还没做好。 Sèlā zuòhǎo le, kěshì tāng hái méi zuòhǎo.

The Pattern "一边…一边… *yìbiān…yìbiān…*"

When two actions happen simultaneously, the pattern 一边…一边… *yìbiān…yìbiān…* is used. In some situations, based on the Temporal Sequence Principle, the verb phrase that follows the first 一边 *yìbiān* starts earlier than the verb phrase that follows the second 一边 *yìbiān*.

Subject + 一边 *yìbiān* + **Verb Phrase 1** + 一边 *yìbiān* + **Verb Phrase 2**

妹妹一边唱歌，一边跳舞。 Mèimei yìbiān chànggē, yìbiān tiàowǔ.

他一边念大学(*university*)，一边工作。 Tā yìbiān niàn dàxué, yìbiān gōngzuò

Sometimes the VP$_1$ is used as the background action while the VP$_2$ is the main action in the sentence.

小李一边走一边笑。 Xiǎo Lǐ yì biān zǒu yìbiān xiào.

王小姐一边听音乐，一边做饭。 Wáng xiǎojie yìbiān tīng yīnyuè, yìbiān zuòfàn.

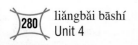

中文

会话 Huìhuà

Dialogue

你家真漂亮 Nǐ Jiā Zhēn Piàoliang *What a Beautiful House You Have*

Li Yunying takes everyone on a tour of her house.

李云英:	这里是客厅，我们家的人喜欢在这里一起看电视。
赵梅:	你们的家具真时髦！
李云英:	那里是厨房。我妈妈正在给我们做晚饭。你们放心！
李妈妈:	你们先去玩，我做好了再叫你们来饭厅吃饭。
吴森:	游戏机在客厅吗？我刚刚没看到。
李云英:	游戏机在我弟弟的房间里，他的房间就在这儿。
钱永利:	那是什么声音？大家听见了没有？

Lǐ Yúnyīng:	Zhèlǐ shì kètīng, wǒmen jiāde rén xǐhuan zài zhèlǐ yìqǐ kàn diànshì.
Zhào Méi:	Nǐmen de jiājù zhēn shímáo!
Lǐ Yúnyīng:	Nàlǐ shì chúfáng. Wǒ māma zhèngzài gěi wǒmen zuò wǎnfàn. Nǐmen fàngxīn!
Lǐ māma:	Nǐmen xiān qù wán, wǒ zuòhǎole zài jiào nǐmen lái fàntīng chīfàn.
Wú Sēn:	Yóuxìjī zài kètīng ma? Wǒ gānggāng méi kàndào.
Lǐ Yúnyīng:	Yóuxìjī zài wǒ dìdi de fángjiān lǐ, tāde fángjiān jiù zài zhèr.
Qián Yǒnglì:	Nà shì shénme shēngyīn? Dàjiā tīngjiàn le méiyǒu?

李云英：	那是我弟弟，他在浴室里一边洗澡，一边唱歌。这是我的房间。	Lǐ Yúnyīng:	Nà shì wǒ dìdi, tā zài yùshì lǐ yìbiān xǐzǎo, yìbiān chànggē. Zhè shì wǒde fángjiān.
赵梅：	哇！你的房间好大好漂亮。	Zhào Méi:	Wa! Nǐde fángjiān hǎo dà hǎo piàoliang.
李云英：	还没有我父母的那么大，他们的房间在那边。	Lǐ Yúnyīng:	Hái méiyǒu wǒ fù-mǔ de nàme dà, tāmen de fángjiān zài nàbiān.
吴森：	我们可以到客厅去玩游戏机了吗？	Wú Sēn:	Wǒmen kěyǐ dào kètīng qù wán yóuxìjī le ma?
李云英：	好。我妈妈也准备了水果，吃完水果，我们就开始玩吧。	Lǐ Yúnyīng:	Hǎo. Wǒ māma yě zhǔnbèi le shuǐguǒ. Chīwán shuǐguǒ, wǒmen jiù kāishǐ wán ba.

4 哪个没介绍? Něige méi jièshào? / *Which one has not been introduced?*

Based on the dialogue, select the room in Li Yunying's home that she did not show her friends.

A.

B.

C.

D.

5 李云英的房间 Lǐ Yúnyīng de Fángjiān / *Li Yunying's Room*

Based on the dialogue, identify the room below that is most similar to Li Yunying's room.

A.

B.

C.

6 懂了吗? **Dǒng le ma?** *Do you understand?*

Answer the following questions in Chinese.

1. 李云英的家人喜欢在客厅里做什么?
   Lǐ Yúnyīng de jiārén xǐhuan zài kètīng lǐ zuò shénme?

2. 赵梅觉得李云英家的家具怎么样?
   Zhào Méi juéde Lǐ Yúnyīng jiā de jiājù zěnmeyàng?

3. 他们在参观(*to visit*)房子的时候, 李云英的妈妈正在做什么?
   Tāmen zài cānguān fángzi de shíhou, Lǐ Yúnyīng de māma zhèngzài zuò shénme?

4. 李云英的妈妈要他们去做什么? Lǐ Yúnyīng de māma yào tāmen qù zuò shénme?

5. 游戏机在客厅里吗? Yóuxìjī zài kètīng lǐ ma?

6. 声音是从哪里来的? 那是什么声音?
   Shēngyīn shì cóng nǎlǐ láide? Nà shì shénme shēngyīn?

7. 李云英的房间跟她爸妈的房间, 哪一间大?
   Lǐ Yúnyīng de fángjiān gēn tā bà-mā de fángjiān, nǎ yìjiān dà?

文化橱窗 Wénhuà Chúchuāng
Culture Window

Filial Piety

The character 孝 *xiào* was formed by removing the bottom half of the character for old (老 *lǎo*) and combining it with the character for child (子 *zǐ*). From this, we can see that the character is in accordance with its meaning of "being good to one's parents," which is what filial piety is mostly about: a concept that in a family, the younger generation should always treat the older generation according to ethical and moral rules. To be filial—a traditional concept that has existed in the Chinese culture for thousands of years—one should serve one's parents to the best of one's ability and act according to their will.

Due to cultural differences, relationships between parents and their children are very different in the East and West. In China, a child will be cared for by his/her parents from the moment the child is born until he/she is old enough to become independent. The parents expect to provide for the child's psychological as well as material needs. In China, very

▲ *being good to parents*

few children need to take out loans to go to school, and the huge amount of schoolwork makes it nearly impossible for them to work part-time jobs, so generally, everything is provided for by a child's parents—from tutorial fees to daily necessities. For an average family with working parents, this could amount to 40 percent of a family's total expenses. Thus, in gratitude, children are expected to respect and care for their parents, especially when the parents are old and the children financially independent. Once the roles are reversed, the children are expected to thank their parents for all the hard work they put in when the children were young, by taking care of all of their parents' financial needs to ensure that they live out the second half of their lives happily.

In contrast, in Western culture, parents are not automatically expected to pay for post-secondary education. Each family decides for itself how material supports the parents will offer. The parents' finances do not belong to their children; the two are very much separate. Therefore, young people in the West are very clear that they have only themselves to depend on if they want anything once they become of age.

China's traditional agricultural society placed huge emphasis on abiding by social morals and

▲ *The children are expected to thank their parents for all the hard work they put in when the children were young.*

ethics. When the children are little, the parents would take care of them day and night without complaint, this imposes on the children, when they are grown up, the duty to act filially not just while their parents are alive, but also when they have passed away, to show thankfulness for all that their parents did for them. However, as today's society gradually shifts from an agricultural to an industrial one and the government has implemented policies regarding childbirth, the Chinese society has aged greatly. Due to the fact that many families only have one child, the tradition that the children from the same generation should take care of a family's elders together has gradually disappeared. Nowadays, a young couple must take care of two pairs of aging parents, which makes it difficult for them to take care of them as well as traditions imply they should. This dilemma, how to balance traditional values with the pressure of modern society, is a problem that the children of China's younger generation must work out for themselves.

7 文化动动脑 Wénhuà Dòngdòngnǎo / *Cultural Check-up*

Decide if the following statements are true or false. Correct any false statements.

1. The character 孝 *xiào* was formed by the character for old and the character for child.
2. Filial piety means to respect one's teachers.
3. Most Chinese students work part-time to pay for their tuition.
4. The cost of raising a child takes up roughly 40% of a family's total expenses.
5. Children show filial piety toward their parents to show gratitude for what their parents have done for them.
6. When Chinese parents grow old, they depend on institutions to care for them.
7. Having no time to work part-time jobs is a problem that the younger Chinese generation must face.

8 正在做什么？ Zhèngzài zuò shénme? / *What is been doing?*

With a classmate, look at the following photos and take turns asking and answering each other using the adverb 正在 *zhèngzài*. Follow the model.

刘杰 liú Jié

Lìzi: A: 刘杰在做什么？ Liú Jié zài zuò shénme?

B: 他正在点菜。 Tā zhèngzài diǎncài.

1.

钱玉玲 Qián Yùlíng

3.

方秀 Fāng Xiù

5.

吴宝春 Wú Bǎochūn

2.

董汉文 Dǒng Hànwén

4.

李强 Lǐ Qiáng

6.

沈佳 Shěn Jiā

9 选择补语 Xuǎnzé Bǔyǔ / *Choosing Complements*

Complete the following eight sentences with the verbs provided and add the appropriate complements. Note: for some sentences, the verbs can go with different complements.

1. 你能 ___ 印度文的书吗？（看）

   Nǐ néng ___ Yìndùwén de shū ma? (kàn)

2. 因为 ___ 好吃的东西，我很开心。（吃）

   Yīnwèi ___ hǎochī de dōngxi, wǒ hěn kāixīn. (chī)

3. 我没 ___ 他，你知道他在哪里吗？（看）

   Wǒ méi ___ tā, nǐ zhīdào tā zài nǎlǐ ma? (kàn)

4. 请你 ___ 留言以后，马上给爸爸打电话。（听）

   Qǐng nǐ ___ liúyán yǐhòu, mǎshàng gěi bàba dǎ diànhuà. (tīng)

5. 这本书 __ 以后，请你借给我，可以吗？（读）

Zhèiběn shū __ yǐhòu, qǐng nǐ jiè gěi wǒ, kěyǐ ma? (dú)

6. 你能 __ 这几句话吗？我听了几次，还是不懂。（听）

Nǐ néng __ zhè jǐjù huà ma? Wǒ tīngle jǐcì, háishì bùdǒng. (tīng)

7. 我想喝中国茶，你知道哪里可以 __ 中国茶吗？（喝）

Wǒ xiǎng hē Zhōngguó chá, nǐ zhīdào nǎlǐ kěyǐ __ Zhōngguó chá ma?

8. 这家餐厅的北京烤鸭都 __ 了，我们去那家吧。（卖 *to sell*）

Zhèjiā cāntīng de Běijīng kǎoyā dōu __ le, wǒmen qù nèijiā ba. (mài)

10 换句话说 Huàn Jù Huà Shuō / *Rephrasing the Sentences*

Rephrase the following questions using the pattern V 了没有 *V le méiyǒu*.

Lìzi: 他看病了吗？ Tā kànbìng le ma?

他看病了没有？ Tā kànbìng le méiyǒu?

1. 孩子们醒了吗？ Háizi men xǐngle ma?
2. 你们到顶楼了吗？ Tāmen dào dǐnglóu le ma?
3. 车子开进车库了吗？ Chēzi kāijìn chēkù le ma?
4. 大楼的保安来了吗？ Dàlóu de bǎo'ān láile ma?
5. 你给林心怡发短信了吗？ Nǐ gěi Lín Xīnyí fā duǎnxìn le ma?
6. 聚会的邀请卡，你都发了吗？ Jùhuì de yāoqǐngkǎ, nǐ dōu fāle ma?
7. 新家的桌子和椅子，你买了吗？ Xīn jiāde zhuōzi hé yǐzi, nǐ mǎile ma?

11 同时进行 Tóngshí Jìnxíng / *Occuring at the Same Time*

Use the pattern 一边…一边… *yìbiān…yìbiān…* to describe the following photos.

1.

2.

3.

4.

5.

6.

Kāikǒu Shuō

Communication

12 小小调查 **Xiǎoxiǎo Diàochá** / *A Survey*

Find out what your classmates' homes are like by asking five of your classmates what rooms they have in their house. Draw a table like the one shown below. In the table, write the names of the five classmates and track the types and the number of rooms they have in their homes. When you are finished, share your results with the class and note if there are any special rooms in someone's house.

Lìzi:
A: 你家有什么房间？ Nǐ jiā yǒu shénme fángjiān?

B: 我家有客厅、饭厅、厨房、三间卧房、两间厕所、两间浴室和地下室，还有一间游戏间。

Wǒ jiā yǒu kètīng, fàntīng, chúfáng, sājiān wòfáng, liǎngjiān cèsuǒ, liǎngjiān yùshì hé dìxiàshì, hái yǒu yìjiān yóuxìjiān.

Room \ Student	B				
客厅 kètīng	1				
饭厅 fàntīng	1				
厨房 chúfáng	1				
卧房 wòfáng	3				
书房 shūfáng	0				
客房 kèfáng	0				
厕所 cèsuǒ	2				
浴室 yùshì	2				
阁楼 gélóu	0				
地下室 dìxiàshì	1				
贮藏室 zhùcángshì	0				
游戏间 yóuxìjiān	1				

13 租屋广告 Zūwū Guǎnggào / House Renting Advertisement

Read the following house renting advertisement and answer the questions that follow.

1. "两厅"指(to indicate)的是什么？
   "Liǎng tīng" zhǐde shì shénme?

2. 如果在这里住一年，应该付多少钱？
   Rúguǒ zài zhèli zhù yìnián, yīnggāi fù duōshao qián?

3. 想租这个房子要联络(to contact)谁？电话号码是多少？
   Xiǎng zū zhèi ge fángzi yào liánluò shéi? Diànhuà hàomǎ shì duōshǎo?

4. 明惠和男朋友养了一只狗，他们可以租这个房子吗？为什么？
   Mínghuì hé nánpéngyou yǎngle yìzhī gǒu, tāmen kěyǐ zū zhèige fángzi ma? Wèishénme?

14 换你当房东 Huàn Nǐ Dāng Fángdōng / Being a Landlord

It is your turn to be a landlord/landlady! Refer to the advertisement in the previous activity, and write an advertisement for your own house (or an imaginary one) in Chinese.

自我提升 Zìwǒ Tíshēng

Raising the Bar

Vocabulary

朋	péng	n.	朋友 *péngyou*, friend
自	zì	*prep.*	from
远	yuǎn	*adj.*	distant
方	fāng	n.	地方 *dìfāng*, place
亦	yì	*adv.*	also
乐	lè	*adj.*	快乐 *kuàilè*, happy
乎	hū	*part.*	used to express conjecture

有朋自远方来，不亦乐乎？

Yǒu péng zì yuǎnfāng lái, bú yì lè hū?

Why wouldn't you be happy if a friend from distant places comes to visit?

▲ 有朋自远方来，不亦乐乎？

Language Note

This is a famous saying first spoken by Confucius, with the word 乎 *hū* at the end to express a question. This sentence means "isn't it a happy thing when friends come to from distant places visit?" and is now often used to welcome a friend who has come to visit from somewhere far away.

新年的时候，我的中国朋友要来我家，真的是
"有朋自远方来，不亦乐乎"啊！

Xīnnián de shíhou, wǒde Zhōngguó péngyou yào lái wǒ jiā, zhēnde shì "yǒu péng zì yuǎnfāng lái, bú yì lè hū" a!

A Chinese friend will visit me over the New Year. This really is "有朋自远方来，不亦乐乎 Yǒu péng zì yuǎnfāng lái, bú yì lè hū!"

Below are other idioms related to friendship.

良朋益友 liáng péng yì yǒu	(*a good, beneficial friend*)	A good friend
酒肉朋友 jiǔ ròu péngyou	(*a friend of wine and meat*)	A bad friend
化敌为友 huà dí wèi yǒu	(*to turn an enemy into a friend*)	For an enemy to become a friend
翻脸无情 fān liǎn wúqíng	(*to turn your face the other way and be cold*)	For a friend to become an enemy

liǎngbǎi bāshíjiǔ
Lesson C

289

买了新房子

爷爷奶奶上个星期买了新房子，在一栋十五层的大楼里。大楼有保安，所以进大门的时候，保安会请你等一下，不会让你直接[1]进去。大楼有四台电梯，所以上下楼的时候电梯很快就来了。爷爷奶奶家的客厅很大，所以他们放了一个大沙发。客厅里还有三个大书柜，因为爷爷很喜欢看书，他的书多得不得了。奶奶说有一间房间是给我的，所以我可以自己选墙壁的颜色和房间里要放的东西。我喜欢晴天，所以我想要黄色的墙壁。现在我的房间里什么都没有，只有一个垃圾桶。

[1] 直接: directly

Mǎile Xīn Fángzi

Yéye nǎinai shàngge xīngqī mǎile xīn fángzi, zhài yídòng shíwǔcéng de dàlóu lǐ. Dàlóu yǒu bǎo'ān, suǒyǐ jìn dàmén de shíhou, bǎo'ān huì qǐng nǐ děng yíxià, búhuì ràng nǐ zhíjiē jìnqù. Dàlóu yǒu sìtái diàntī, suǒyǐ shàng-xià lóu de shíhou diàntī hěn kuài jiù láile. Yéye Nǎinai jiāde kètīng hěn dà, suǒyǐ tāmen fàngle yíge dà shāfā. Kètīng li hái yǒu sānge dà shūguì, yīnwèi Yéye hěn xǐhuan kànshū, tāde shū duōde bùdéliǎo. Nǎinai shuō yǒu yìjiān fángjiān shì gěi wǒde, suǒyǐ wǒ kěyǐ zìjǐ xuǎn qiángbì de yánsè hé fángjiān li yào fàngde dōngxi. Wǒ xǐhuan qíngtiān, suǒyǐ wǒ xiǎng yào huángsè de qiángbì. Xiànzài wǒde fángjiān lǐ shénme dōu méiyǒu, zhǐyǒu yíge lājītǒng.

15 通晓文意 Tōngxiǎo Wényì / *Understanding the Passage*

Read the above passage and answer the following questions in Chinese.

1. 谁买了新房子？是什么时候买的？
   Shéi mǎile xīn fángzi? Shì shénme shíhou mǎide?

2. 那是什么样的房子？一共有几楼？
   Nà shì shénmeyàng de fángzi? Yígòng yǒu jǐlóu?

3. 他可以直接上去找爷爷奶奶吗？ Tā kěyǐ zhíjiē shàngqù zhǎo yéye nǎinai ma?

4. 坐电梯要等很久吗？为什么？ Zuò diàntī yào děng hěn jiǔ ma? Wèishénme?

5. 客厅里的书应该是谁的？ Kètīng lǐde shū yīnggāi shì shéide?

6. 他想要什么颜色的墙壁？为什么？
   Tā xiǎng yào shénme yánsè de qiángbì? Wèishénme?

7. 现在他的房间里有什么东西？ Xiànzài tāde fángjiān lǐ yǒu shénme dōngxi?

汉字天地 Hànzì Tiāndì

Chinese Characters

 ■ fáng ■ house

The character 房 *fáng* is a combination of a radical and a phonetic component and means "house" or "room." The upper part of the character is 户 *hù,* the radical, which means "door" or "household." The lower part of the character is 方 *fāng* which means "square," and it is the phonetic component that gives 房 *fáng* its sound.

Stroke Order

| 丶 | 丶 | 一 | 户 | 户 | 户 | 房 | 房 |

16 词汇延伸 Cíhuì Yánshēn / *Vocabulary Builder*

Below are characters that combine with 房 *fáng* to create new words. Match the Chinese words on the left with the appropriate English meanings on the right.

屋 wū	间 jiān	东 dōng	租 zū	产 chǎn
n. house	*n. room*	*n. owner*	*v. to rent*	*n. property*

1. 房屋 fángwū   A. real estate property
2. 房间 fángjiān   B. house
3. 房东 fángdōng   C. rent for a house
4. 房租 fángzū   D. room
5. 房产 fángchǎn   E. landlord/landlady

17 汉字侦探 Hànzì Zhēntàn / *Visual Detective*

Can you find 房 in the following pictures?

Unit 5

今天我请客

Jīntiān Wǒ Qǐngkè

In this unit you will be able to:

- write an invitation
- make a shopping list
- plan an event
- discuss and make decisions
- describe dishes
- give comments

Lesson A

◀) 超级市场 (超級市場) Chāojí Shìchǎng *Supermarket*

1. 冷冻食品 lěngdòng shípǐn *n. frozen food*

2. 乳制品 (乳製品) rǔzhìpǐn *n. dairy product*

3. 罐头 (罐頭) guàntou *n. canned good*

4. 包装食品 (包裝食品) bāozhuāng shípǐn *n. packaged food*

5. 零食 língshí *n. snack*

6. 肉类 (肉類) ròulèi *n. meat*

7. 海鲜 (海鮮) hǎixiān *n. seafood*

8. 蔬菜 shūcài *n. vegetable*

9. 熟食 shúshí *n. deli food*

◀)) **商店类型（商店類型）Shāngdiàn Lèixíng** *Types of Shops*

大型超级市场（大型超級市場）
dàxíng chāojí shìchǎng

n. superstore

超市
chāoshì

n. supermarket

Language Note

"超市 *chāoshì*" is the abbreviation of "超级市场 *chāojí shìchǎng*."

中文

便利商店
biànlì shāngdiàn
n. convenience store

杂货店（雜貨店）
záhuòdiàn
n. grocery store

菜市场（菜市場）
càishìchǎng
n. market

这家店的衣服我都不喜欢。
（這家店的衣服我不喜歡。）
Zhèijiā diànde yīfu wǒ dōu bù xǐhuan.
I don't like any of the clothing in this store.

既然你不喜欢，
我们就去下一家店吧。
（既然你不喜歡，我們就去下一家店吧。）
Jìrán nǐ bù xǐhuan, wǒmen jiù qù xià yìjiā diàn ba.
If you don't like anything here,
let's go to the next one.

A: 你唱的歌好听极了！（你唱的歌好聽極了！）
Nǐ chàng de gē hǎotīng jíle! *The songs you sing sound really great!*

B: 谢谢，我很高兴你们喜欢。（謝謝，我很高興你們喜歡。）
Xièxie, wǒ hěn gāoxìng nǐmen xǐhuan. *Thanks. I'm glad you enjoyed it.*

你今天晚上要做什么？
（你今天晚上要做什麼？）
Nǐ jīntiān wǎnshang yào zuò shénme?
What are you doing tonight?

有三个朋友会来我家看足球比赛。
（有三個朋友會來我家看足球比賽。）
Yǒu sānge péngyou huì lái wǒ jiā kàn zúqiú bǐsài.
I've got three friends coming over to watch a
soccer game.

A: 你那里有没有一百块？
(你那裡有沒有一百塊？)

Nǐ nàlǐ yǒu méiyǒu yìbǎi kuài?

Do you have 100 dollars on you?

B: 没有，我这里只有十六块。
(沒有，我這裡只有十六塊。)

Méiyǒu, wǒ zhèlǐ zhǐ yǒu shíliù kuài.

No, I only have 16 dollars.

Adjectives

有信心	yǒu xìnxīn	*confident*
新鲜 (新鮮)	xīnxiān	*fresh*
可能	kěnéng	*possible; probable*

Complement

极 (極)	jí	*extremely; exceedingly*

Movable Adverb

既然	jìrán	*since; as; now that*

Common Expression

算了	suàn le	*forget it; never mind*

Nouns

信心	xìnxīn	*confidence*
菜单 (菜單)	càidān	*menu*
决定	juédìng	*decision*
附近	fùjìn	*nearby; neighboring*

Verbs

换 (換)	huàn	*to change*
决定	juédìng	*to decide*
卖 (賣)	mài	*to sell*

Verb-Object

买菜 (買菜)	mǎicài	*to go grocery shopping*

1 买东西 Mǎi Dōngxi / Shopping

🔊 Zhenzhen is going grocery shopping. Say which department she should go to to buy the things she wants according to what you hear.

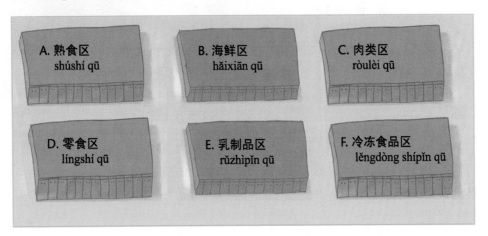

A. 熟食区 shúshí qū

B. 海鲜区 hǎixiān qū

C. 肉类区 ròulèi qū

D. 零食区 língshí qū

E. 乳制品区 rǔzhìpǐn qū

F. 冷冻食品区 lěngdòng shípǐn qū

2 对还是错? Duì háishì Cuò? / True or False?

🔊 You will hear four statements about the shops introduced in this lesson. Say if the statements are true or false.

3 个人问题 Gèrén Wèntí / Personal Questions

Answer the following questions in Chinese based on your own experiences and opinions.

1. 你常去超级市场吗? 你常去那里买什么?
   Nǐ cháng qù chāojí shìchǎng ma? Nǐ cháng qù nàlǐ mǎi shénme?

2. 你家附近有没有便利商店?
   Nǐ jiā fùjìn yǒu méiyǒu biànlì shāngdiàn?

3. 你家附近有菜市场吗?
   Nǐ jiā fùjìn yǒu càishìchǎng ma?

4. 你常常吃零食吗? 你最喜欢的零食是什么?
   Nǐ chángcháng chī língshí ma? Nǐ zuì xǐhuan de língshí shì shénme?

5. 你比较常吃冷冻食品还是新鲜的东西?
   Nǐ bǐjiào cháng chī lěngdòng shípǐn háishì xīnxiān de dōngxi?

The Pattern 既然...就... *jìrán...jiù...*

The movable adverb 既然 *jìrán* means "since." It is usually followed in a sentence by the adverbs 就 *jiù* (then), 也 *yě* or 还 *hái* (also). The pattern expresses a cause and effect relationship: *Since…, then…*.

既然 *jìrán* + **cause or reason**, + 就 *jiù* / 也 *yě* / 还 *hái* + **result or conclusion**

既然你不想去，那就不要去。

Jìrán nǐ bùxiǎng qù, nà jiù búyào qù.

我想既然他喜欢，我也给他买了一个。

Wǒ xiǎng jìrán tā xǐhuan, wǒ yě gěi tā mǎile yíge.

既然你的功课没做完，为什么还出去玩?

Jìrán nǐde gōngkè méi zuòwán, wèishénme hái chūqù wán?

"极了 *jíle*" As an Intensifying Complement for Adjectives

In Chinese, there are several intensifying complements that can be placed after adjectives to strengthen the degree or the condition of something—similar to the way *extremely* are used in English. 极了 *jíle* is one of these intensifiers.

Adjective + 极了 *jíle*

你的卧房漂亮极了。   Nǐde wòfáng piàoliang jíle.

他这次考试考得不好，难过极了。   Tā zhècì kǎoshì kǎode bùhǎo, nánguò jíle.

The Verb 有 *yǒu* Meaning Existence

You should already be familiar with the verb 有 *yǒu*, meaning "to have." When preceded by a place word, the verb 有 *yǒu* means "there is/are" and expresses the existence of what follows.

Place Word + 有 *yǒu* + **Noun**

院子里有两只狗。   Yuànzi lǐ yǒu liǎngzhī gǒu.

桌子上有好几本书。   Zhuōzi shàng yǒu hǎojǐběn shū.

▲ 院子里有两只狗。

The Place Noun Phrase Related to Specific People / Places (这里 *zhèlǐ* / 那里 *nàlǐ*)

这里 *zhèlǐ* (here) or 那里 *nàlǐ* (there), can be used after a noun to transform that noun into a place word, or after a place word to further describe that place. The use of 这里 *zhèlǐ* or 那里 *nàlǐ* will depend on the distance of the speaker from the noun or place.

Noun / Place Word + 这里 *zhèlǐ* / 那里 *nàlǐ*

For example, the following dialogue is between two friends. Person A is in Japan and person B in Germany.

A (in Japan): 德国那里有很多日本饭馆吗？
　　　　　　Déguó nàlǐ yǒu hěn duō Rìběn fànguǎn ma?

B (in Germany): 德国这里没有很多日本饭馆。
　　　　　　Déguó zhèlǐ méiyǒu hěn duō Rìběn fànguǎn.

A: 你那里有没有法文书？　Nǐ nàlǐ yǒu méiyǒu Fǎwén shū?

B: 没有，我这里只有中文书。　Méiyǒu, wǒ zhèlǐ zhǐ yǒu Zhōngwén shū.

购物中心这里有很多手机店。　Gòuwù zhōngxīn zhèlǐ yǒu hěnduō shǒujīdiàn.

李英，不要的东西拿去垃圾桶那里。　Lǐ Yīng, bú yào de dōngxi náqù lājītǒng nàlǐ.

Share and Share Alike

This pattern is used to describe each individual's portion when an amount shared. When a noun can also function as a measure word and the meaning won't be misunderstood, the measure word can be omitted, as in B's line below.

Number + **Measure Word 1** + **Noun 1** + **Number** + **Measure Word 2** + **Noun 2**

请给我们一人一杯咖啡。　Qǐng gěi wǒmen yìrén yìbēi kāfēi.

A: 妈妈，我们可以玩多久电子游戏？　Māma, wǒmen kěyǐ wán duōjiǔ diànzǐ yóuxì?

B: 一人二十分钟。　Yìrén èrshífēn zhōng.

In addition, if the context is clear, the noun can be omitted, too. However, in that case, the measure word must remain.

中国人点菜通常是有几个人点几道菜，我们四人四道菜，怎么样？
Zhōngguó rén diǎncài tōngcháng shì yǒu jǐge rén diǎn jǐdào cài, wǒmen sìrén sìdào cài, zěnmeyàng?

A: 你们家有几辆车？　Nǐmen jiā yǒu jǐliàng chē?

B: 四辆，我们一(个)人一辆(车)。　Sìliàng, wǒmen yí(ge) rén yíliàng (chē).

一起做饭吧 Yìqǐ Zuòfàn Ba *Let's Cook Together*

Wu Sen is talking with her three friends in the park.

吴森：	既然云英上周末请了我们，这个周末就换我请大家到我家来吃饭。
钱永利：	吃饭？老问题，谁要做饭？
吴森：	当然是我。每个人都说我做的饭好吃极了！
赵梅：	你那么有信心，就说一说你的菜单吧。
吴森：	我还没决定我要做什么菜。
李云英：	要是你还没决定，我们就一起做饭吧。
吴森：	这是个好主意！
李云英：	这样吧，我们一人一道菜。
吴森：	我家附近有个来来超市，所以我们可以先去买菜。
赵梅：	咦，你家那里有菜市场吗？我想菜市场的东西会更新鲜。
吴森：	有是有，不过菜市场六点就开始卖，而且东西通常到九点就卖完了。
钱永利：	算了吧，我想我们是不可能这么早起床的。

Wú Sēn:	Jìrán Yúnyīng shàng zhōumò qǐngle wǒmen, zhèige zhōumò jiù huàn wǒ qǐng dàjiā dào wǒ jiā lái chīfàn.
Qián Yǒnglì:	Chīfàn? Lǎo wèntí, shéi yào zuòfàn?
Wú Sēn:	Dāngrán shì wǒ. Měige rén dōu shuō wǒ zuòde fàn hǎochī jíle!
Zhào Méi:	Nǐ nàme yǒu xìnxīn, jiù shuō yì shuō nǐde càidān ba.
Wú Sēn:	Wǒ hái méi juédìng wǒ yào zuò shénme cài.
Lǐ Yúnyīng:	Yàoshi nǐ hái méi juédìng, wǒmen jiù yìqǐ zuòfàn ba.
Wú Sēn:	Zhè shì ge hǎo zhǔyi!
Lǐ Yúnyīng:	Zhèyàng ba, wǒmen yìrén yídào cài.
Wú Sēn:	Wǒ jiā fùjìn yǒuge Láilái chāoshì, suǒyǐ wǒmen kěyǐ xiān qù mǎi cài.
Zhào Méi:	Yí, nǐjiā nàlǐ yǒu càishìchǎng ma? Wǒ xiǎng càishìchǎng de dōngxi huì gèng xīnxiān.
Wú Sēn:	Yǒu shì yǒu, búguò càishìchǎng liùdiǎn jiù kāishǐ mài, érqiě dōngxi tōngcháng dào jiǔdiǎn jiù màiwán le.
Qián Yǒnglì:	Suànle ba, wǒ xiǎng wǒmen shì bù kěnéng zhème zǎo qǐchuáng de.

4 谁是主人? | **Shéi shì zhǔrén?** / *Who is the host?*

Based on the dialogue, say which person played the role of the host.

A.

赵梅

B.

钱永利

C.

李云英

D.

吴森

5 流程顺序 | **Liúchéng Shùnxù** / *The Correct Order*

Look at the photos and put them in the correct order according to the dialogue.

A.

B.

C.

D.

6 懂了吗? | **Dǒngle ma?** / *Do you understand?*

Answer the following questions in Chinese.

1. 这个周末他们要去谁家？ Zhèige zhōumò tāmen yào qù shéi jiā?

2. 吴森说，大家说他做的饭怎么样？
   Wú Sēn shuō, dàjiā shuō tā zuòde fàn zěnmeyàng?

3. 吴森的菜单是什么？ Wú Sēn de càidān shì shénme?

4. 谁提议(to propose)要一起做饭？ Shéi tíyì yào yìqǐ zuòfàn?

5. 他们一个人要负责几道菜？ Tāmen yíge rén yào fùzé jǐdào cài?

6. 吴森家附近的超市叫什么名字？ Wú Sēn jiā fùjìn de chāoshì jiào shénme míngzi?

7. 为什么赵梅想去菜市场买菜？ Wèishénme Zhào Méi xiǎng qù càishìchǎng mǎi cài?

8. 菜市场几点开始卖？差不多几点卖完？
   Càishìchǎng jǐdiǎn kāishǐ mài? Chàbùduō jǐdiǎn màiwán?

文化橱窗 Wénhuà Chúchuāng
Culture Window

Chinese Cooking

The culture of Chinese cuisine has existed for thousands of years. Chinese food is unique with distinct Asian flavors, and is aimed at improving health. It can be separated into eight major styles according to region: Fujian, Shandong, Sichuan, Guangdong, Jiangsu, Zhejiang, Hunan, and Anhui. These styles developed according to the types of food available in each region. For example, sheep and cattle are abundant in the grasslands of northern China, so northern dishes often contain mutton or beef. Fish and poultry are favored in southern China, and along the coast there are many seafood dishes.

The differences in flavor are mostly due to the climate of each region. Generally speaking, dishes from the cold northern regions are heavily salted so that they can be preserved for longer periods of time, while the milder climate of eastern China has produced sweeter and more savory dishes. In the southwest, where precipitation is heavy, the dishes are spicier to ward off the chill.

▲ Pearl Rice Balls, 珍珠丸 *Zhēnzhūwán*

One of the main principles of Chinese cuisine is that in addition to tasting great, food should look beautiful and smell good. However, achieving all three is no easy feat, and therefore much work goes into food preparation. The cook pays close attention to every detail—from selecting the best ingredients and condiments to expert cutting, slicing, and marinating, and from to cooking the food at the precise temperature to setting out the correct cutlery and most attractive decorations.

▲ Sweet and Sour Pork, 咕咾肉 *Gūlǎoròu*

Most Americans think of Chinese food as stir-fried, but Chinese food may be prepared in a variety of ways, including pan-frying, stir-frying, deep frying, stewing, steaming, boiling, simmering or braising (a method in which food is first seared in a hot pan and then simmered). Each method produces different results. Hunan cuisine is often deep-fried or stewed, while Jiangsu, Sichuan and Guangdong dishes are mostly steamed.

Apart from tasting good, food should also be good for our health. Because many popular Chinese dishes are fried in oil, they can be high in fat. However, light dishes can also be found on every Chinese menu. Also, every Chinese meal includes protein, vegetables (and minerals) and carbohydrates (from rice), meaning that the food is nutritionally balanced.

▲ *The dish looks colorful and smells good.*

▲ *The preparation can be complicated for Chinese food.*

7 文化动动脑 Wénhuà Dòngdòngnǎo / *Culture Check-up*

Complete each statement with an appropriate word or expression.

1. There are __ main styles of Chinese cuisine: __, Shandong, Sichuan, __, Jiangsu, __, Hunan, and Anhui.
2. The most common types of meat in northern China are __ and __.
3. Eastern China has a(n) __ climate, and the food is mostly __ and __.
4. According to the principles of Chinese cuisine, food should have all three of the following characteristics: __, __ and __.
5. Prepping before the actual cooking process involves __, __, and __.
6. Making Chinese cuisine involves using the following methods: __, stir-frying, __, stewing, __, boiling, __ and braising.
7. Every Chinese meal includes __, __ and __.

语言练习 Yǔyán Liànxí
Language Practice

8 给个建议 Gěi ge Jiànyì / Give a Suggestion

With a classmate, take turns asking and answering the following questions to make suggestions using the pattern 既然...(就 / 也 / 还...) *jìrán...(jiù / yě / hái...)* and the hints provided. Follow the model.

Lìzi: 我需要买很多汽水，可是便利商店里没有那么多。
（大型超级市场）
Wǒ xūyào mǎi hěn duō qìshuǐ, kěshì biànlì shāngdiànlǐ méiyǒu nàme duō. (dàxíng chāojí shìchǎng)

A: 我需要买很多汽水，可是便利商店里没有那么多。
Wǒ xūyào mǎi hěn duō qìshuǐ, kěshì biànlì shāngdiànlǐ méiyǒu nàme duō.

B: 既然你需要买很多，你应该到大型超级市场去买。
Jìrán nǐ xūyào mǎi hěn duō, nǐ yīnggāi dào dàxíng chāojí shìchǎng qù mǎi.

1. 我最近瘦了。（多吃一点）Wǒ zuìjìn shòule. (duō chī yìdiǎn)

2. 你要买的这件衣服真好看，我也很喜欢。（买一件）
Nǐ yào mǎide zhèijiàn yīfu zhēn hǎokàn, wǒ yě hěn xǐhuan. (mǎi yíjiàn)

3. 私立学校很贵，我家没有那么多钱。（念公立学校）
Sīlì xuéxiào hěn guì, wǒjiā méiyǒu nàme duō qián. (niàn gōnglì xuéxiào)

4. 小妹妹的体温好高，怎么办？（马上带她去诊所）
Xiǎo mèimei de tǐwēn hǎo gāo, zěnmebàn? (mǎshàng dài tā qù zhěnsuǒ)

5. 我的肩膀好疼，可是我下午有篮球练习。（休息一下）
Wǒde jiānbǎng hǎo téng, kěshì wǒ xiàwǔ yǒu lánqiú liànxí. (xiūxí yíxià)

6. 我的喉咙好痛，可是我好想吃辣的东西。（吃清淡一点的）
Wǒde hóulóng hǎo tòng, kěshì wǒ hǎo xiǎng chī làde dōngxi. (chī qīngdàn yìdiǎn de)

7. 今天功课好多，可是我想跟朋友去看电影。（先做完功课）
Jīntiān gōngkè hǎo duō, kěshì wǒ xiǎng gēn péngyou qù kàn diànyǐng. (xiān zuòwán gōngkè)

8. 等一下就要吃晚饭了，不过我现在肚子饿，想吃洋芋片。（等一等）
Děng yíxià jiù yào chī wǎnfàn le, búguò wǒ xiànzài dùzi è, xiǎng chī yángyùpiàn. (děng yì děng)

9 怎么样? **Zěnmeyàng?** / *What's it like?*

Look at the pictures and the words provided. Make sentences using 极了 *jíle* to describe the pictures.

1.

新鲜 xīnxiān

3.

有爱心 yǒu àixīn

5.

健康 jiànkāng

2.

可爱 kě'ài

4.

胖 pàng

6.

担心 dānxīn

10 有什么? **Yǒu shénme?** / *What is there?*

Look at the pictures and say what there is or are in each place, using the verb 有 *yǒu*.

1.

3.

5.

2.

4.

6.

Look at the photos and answer the questions using 这里 *zhèlǐ* or 那里 *nàlǐ*.

1.

天桥那里有人吗?

Tiānqiáo nàlǐ yǒu rén ma?

4.

林先生那里有人民币吗?

Lín xiānsheng nàlǐ yǒu Rénmínbì ma?

2.

教室那里有几个学生?

Jiàoshì nàlǐ yǒu jǐge xuéshēng?

5.

李太太那里也卖肉吗?

Lǐ tàitai nàlǐ yě mài ròu ma?

3.

你的书在桌子那里吗?

Nǐde shū zài zhuōzi nàlǐ ma?

6.

狗在房间这里吗?

Gǒu zài fángjiān zhèlǐ ma?

Answer the following questions based on the illustrations and using the "share and share" pattern to describe the amounts being distributed.

1.

他们可能怎么分
(*to share*)苹果？

Tāmen kěnéng zěnme
fēn píngguǒ?

3.

他们怎么坐？

Tāmen zěnme zuò?

5.

老师应该怎么给这
两个学生分书？

Lǎoshī yīnggāi zěnme gěi zhè
liǎngge xuésheng fēn shū?

2.

你要怎么分炸鸡给
五个小孩？

Nǐ yào zěnme fēn zhájī gěi
wǔge xiǎohái?

4.

他们去旅行，应该
怎么睡？

Tāmen qù lǚxíng, yīnggāi
zěnme shuì?

6.

他们要打扫(*to clean out*)
房间，应该怎么分
配(*to assign*)？

Tāmen yào dǎsǎo fángjiān,
yīnggāi zěnme fēnpèi?

13 拟清单 **Nǐ Qīngdān** / *Draft Your Party Menu*

Plan a dinner party with classmates. First draw a table like the one below in which you write the food choices and the names of four classmates. Ask them to choose the type of food they would like to prepare out of the three items listed. Report the results to the class.

Lizi:

A: 聚会的时候，你准备什么饮料？
Jùhuì de shíhou, nǐ zhǔnbèi shénme yǐnliào?

B: 我准备水和可乐。 Wǒ zhǔnbèi shuǐ hé kělè.

A: 你准备什么零食？ Nǐ zhǔnbèi shénme língshí?

B: 我准备洋芋片。 Wǒ zhǔnbèi yángyùpiàn.

A: 你准备什么食物？ Nǐ zhǔnbèi shénme shíwù?

B: 我准备三明治和薯条。 Wǒ zhǔnbèi sānmíngzhì hé shǔtiáo.

Items \ Students	B			
饮料 yǐnliào	1. 水 shuǐ 2. 可乐 kělè			
零食 língshí	洋芋片 yángyùpiàn			
食物 shíwù	1. 三明治 sānmíngzhì 2. 薯条 shǔtiáo			

Read the banquet menu below and answer the questions that follow.

菜单 Càidān
Menu

乳猪拼盘 Rǔzhū Pīnpán
Roast Suckling Pig

香椿煎蛋 Xiāngchūn Jiāndàn
Fried Eggs with Chopped Chinese Toon Leaves

时菜炒牛肉 Shícài chǎo Niúròu
Sautéed Beef with Seasonal Vegetable

姜葱炒龙虾 Jiāngcōng chǎo Lóngxiā
Sautéed Lobster with Ginger and Scallion

北京烤鸭 Běijīng Kǎoyā
Beijing Roast Duck

红烧狮子头 Hóngshāo Shīzitóu
Stewed Pork Ball in Brown Sauce

宫保鸡丁 Gōngbǎo Jīdīng
Kung Pao Chicken

清香荷叶饭 Qīngxiāng Héyè Fàn
Steamed Rice with Shrimps in Lotus Leaf

松茸海鲜汤 Sōngróng Hǎixiān Tāng
Clear Soup of Seafood with Fungus

甜品水果盘 Tiánpǐn Shuǐguǒ Pán
Dessert & Seasonal Fruit Plate

1. 一共有多少道菜？ Yígòng yǒu duōshǎodào cài?

2. 他们可以吃到什么肉？ Tāmen kěyǐ chī dào shénme ròu?

3. 饭和面，他们都可以吃到吗？ Fàn hé miàn, tāmen dōu kěyǐ chī dào ma?

4. 彭宇杰不吃猪肉，哪几道菜他不能吃？
   Péng Yǔjié bùchī zhūròu, nǎ jǐdào cài tā bùnéng chī?

Vocabulary

卖	mài	v.	to sell
瓜	guā	n.	melon
自	zì	n.	oneself
夸	kuā	v.	to boast

老王卖瓜，自卖自夸

Lǎo Wáng mài guā, zì mài zì kuā.

Old Wang sells melons and boasts of them himself.

▲ 老王卖瓜，自卖自夸

Language Note

The expression above describes a seller who boasts about the quality of his products. The saying is used to lightly criticize people who brag too much about themselves.

他说自己写的那本书卖得很好，真是"老王卖瓜，
自卖自夸"。

Tā shuō zìjǐ xiěde nèiběn shū màide hěnhǎo, zhēn shì "Lǎo Wáng mài guā, zì mài zì kuā".

He says that the book he wrote is selling very well. Talk about "Old Wang selling melons and boasting about them."

Modesty has always been considered a great virtue by the Chinese. In the West, when someone gives a compliment, the usual response is a simple "谢谢！我很高兴你喜欢 *Xièxie! Wǒ hěn gāoxìng nǐ xǐhuan*." (Thanks! I'm glad you like it.) But in China, it is polite to say "哪里哪里，是您不嫌弃。 *Nǎli nǎli, shì nín bù xiánqì*." (It's nothing; I'm glad you can accept it.) Many Chinese folktales teach the value of being modest. In these stories, characters are rewarded for being humble and modest, while characters who are overly self-confident meet a bad end.

一起做饭

星期日我要和朋友们一起做饭，我们决定了，一个人准备一道菜。这是我第一次做饭，所以我不知道要做什么菜。我请妈妈星期六带我去买菜，然后教我做。今天早上六点妈妈就叫我起床，她说要带我去菜市场看看。菜市场是个非常有意思的地方，跟超级市场很不一样。每个摊贩[1]卖的东西都很新鲜，也有很多有机[2]的水果和蔬菜。我看到一个卖苹果的，那里的苹果又大又漂亮。我想，做苹果派[3]应该也很不错，所以我告诉[4]妈妈，今天我想先学苹果派，明天再学做饭。

[1] 摊贩: vendor   [2] 有机: organic   [3] 苹果派: apple pie   [4] 告诉: to tell

Yìqǐ Zuòfàn

Xīngqīrì wǒ yào hé péngyoumen yìqǐ zuòfàn, wǒmen juédìng le, yíge rén zhǔnbèi yídào cài. Zhè shì wǒ dì-yīcì zuòfàn, suǒyǐ wǒ bù zhīdào yào zuò shénme cài. Wǒ qǐng māma Xīngqīliù dài wǒ qù mǎicài, ránhòu jiāo wǒ zuò. Jīntiān zǎoshang liùdiǎn māma jiù jiào wǒ qǐchuáng, tā shuō yào dài wǒ qù càishìchǎng kànkan. Càishìchǎng shìge fēicháng yǒuyìsi de dìfang, gēn chāojí shìchǎng hěn bù yíyàng. Měige tānfàn màide dōngxi dōu hěn xīnxiān, yě yǒu hěnduō yǒujī de shuǐguǒ hé shūcài. Wǒ kàndào yíge mài píngguǒ de, nàli de píngguǒ yòu dà yòu piàoliang. Wǒ xiǎng, zuò píngguǒpài yīnggāi yě hěn búcuò, suǒyǐ wǒ gàosù māma, jīntiān wǒ xiǎng xiān xué píngguǒpài, míngtiān zài xué zuòfàn.

15 通晓文意 Tōngxiǎo Wényì / *Understanding the Passage*

Read the above passage and decide if the statements are true or false. Correct any false statements.

1. 他和朋友一个人要准备一道菜。 Tā hé péngyou yíge rén yào zhǔnbèi yídào cài.

2. 他已经做了好几次饭了。 Tā yǐjīng zuòle hǎo jǐcì fàn le.

3. 他请妈妈星期六带他去买菜。 Tā qǐng māma xīngqīliù dài tā qù mǎicài.

4. 他觉得菜市场是个跟超级市场一样的地方。
   Tā juéde càishìchǎng shì ge gēn chāojí shìchǎng yíyàng de defang.

5. 在菜市场里，什么东西都是有机的。
   Zài càishìchǎng lǐ, shénme dōngxi dōu shì yǒujī de.

Hànzì Tiāndì
Chinese Characters

买 / 買 ■ mǎi ■ to buy

The character 买 *mǎi* is an ideograph: the top half of the character means "net" and the bottom half is "shell," so together, it means to use a net to gather shells. In the olden days, shells were used as coins, so now the character has come to mean "buy" or "purchase".

Stroke Order

16 **词汇延伸** **Cíhuì Yánshēn** / *Vocabulary Builder*

Below are characters that combine with 买 *mǎi* to create words. Match the Chinese words on the left with the English meaning on the right.

单 dān *n. bill*	卖 mài *v. to sell*	方 fāng *n. side*	价 jià *n. price*	气 qì *n. atmosphere*

1. 买单 mǎidān   A. purchase price
2. 买卖 mǎimài   B. trade
3. 买方 mǎifāng   C. buying
4. 买价 mǎijià   D. buyer
5. 买气 mǎiqì   E. to pay the bill

17 **汉字侦探** **Hànzì Zhēntàn** / *Visual Detective*

Can you find 买 in the following pictures?

别想歪了!

你工作得还可以，不过

你到哪买到这件裙子的

他们在巴黎上飞机。

Lesson B

词汇 Cíhuì
Vocabulary

🔊 调料（調料）**Tiáoliào** *Seasonings*

糖 táng

n. sugar

盐（鹽）yán

n. salt

橄榄油 gǎnlǎnyóu

n. olive oil

醋 cù

n. vinegar

胡椒 hújiāo

n. pepper

酱油（醬油）jiàngyóu

n. soy sauce

🔊 海鲜 (海鲜) Hǎixiān *Seafood*

鱼 (魚) yú

n. fish

虾 (蝦) xiā

n. shrimp

龙虾 (龍蝦) lóngxiā

n. lobster

蟹 xiè

n. crab

牡蛎 (牡蠣) mǔlì

n. oyster

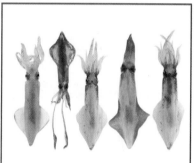

鱿鱼 (鱿鱼) yóuyú

n. squid

扇贝 (扇貝) shànbèi

n. scallops

蛤蜊 gélì

n. clam

章鱼 (章鱼) zhāngyú

n. octopus

Language Note

In addition to 牡蛎 *mǔlì*, another word for oyster is 蚝 *háo*.
贝类 (*bèilèi*, shellfish) encompasses oyster, scallop and clam. If you can not eat shellfish, you can say "我不能吃贝类。 *Wǒ bù néng chī bèilèi.*"

中文

◀)) 甜点（甜點）Tiándiǎn Desserts

蛋糕 dàngāo

n. cake

派 pài

n. pie

苹果派（蘋果派）

píngguǒ pài   *n. apple pie*

布丁 bùdīng

n. pudding

圣代（聖代）shèngdài

n. sundae

甜甜圈 tiántiánquān

n. doughnut

Language Note

To name different types of pies, just say the main ingredient or flavor plus the word 派 *pài*. For example, 巧克力派 *qiǎokèlì pài*, 柠檬派 *níngméng pài*, 牛肉派 *niúròu pài*, etc.

中文

◀)) 蔬菜 Shūcài Vegetables

芥兰（芥蘭）jièlán

n. Chinese broccoli

豆腐 dòufu

n. tofu

茄子 qiézi

n. eggplant

🔊 常见的中国菜 (常見的中國菜)
Chángjiàn de Zhōngguó cài *Popular Chinese Dishes*

糖醋鱼 (糖醋魚)
Tángcù yú
n. Sweet & Sour Fish

芥兰牛肉 (芥蘭牛肉)
Jièlán niúròu
n. Beef with Chinese Broccoli

鱼香茄子 (魚香茄子)
Yúxiāng qiézi
n. Eggplant Szechuan Style

左宗棠鸡 (左宗棠雞)
Zuǒzōngtáng jī
n. General Tsao's Chicken

蚂蚁上树 (螞蟻上樹)
Mǎyǐ shàngshù
n. Rice Noodles with Ground Pork

水煮鱼 (水煮魚)
Shuǐzhǔ yú
n. Fish Fillet in Szechuan Spicy Broth

A: 你想好下个学期要参加什么社团了吗？
(你想好下個學期要參加什麼社團了嗎？)
Nǐ xiǎnghǎo xiàge xuéqī yào cānjiā shénme shètuán le ma?
Have you decided which club you want to join next semester?

B: 还没。我想参加舞蹈社，也想参加校刊
社。唉，好难决定。
(還沒。我想參加舞蹈社，也想參加校刊
社。唉，好難決定。)
Hái méi. Wǒ xiǎng cānjiā wǔdǎo shè, yě xiǎng cānjiā xiàokān
shè. Āi, hǎo nán juédìng.
*No yet. I want to join the dance club, but I also want to join the
school paper. Oh, it's such a difficult decision.*

A: 这首歌听起来好熟，是谁唱的？（這首歌聽起來好熟，是誰唱的？）

Zhèishǒu gē tīngqǐlái hǎo shú, shì shéi chàngde? *This song sounds so familiar. Whose song is it?*

B: 我只记得他是一个很有名的人，但是我忘了他的名字。
（我只記得他是一個很有名的人，但是我忘了他的名字。）

Wǒ zhǐ jìdé tā shì yíge hěn yǒumíng de rén, dànshì wǒ wàngle tāde míngzi.
I only remember that the singer is someone famous, but I don't remember his name.

- -

A: 我要点水煮鱼。（我要點水煮魚。）

Wǒ yào diǎn shuǐzhǔyú.

I'd like to order Fish Fillet in Szechuan Spicy Broth.

B: 不要吧！你的肚子不舒服，我看
我们点清淡一点的菜比较好。
（不要吧！你的肚子不舒服，我看
我們點清淡一點的菜比較好。）

Bú yào ba! Nǐde dùzi bù shūfu, wǒ kàn wǒmen
diǎn qīngdàn yìdiǎn de cài bǐjiào hǎo.

That's not a good idea. You have an upset stomach.
Let's order something a little blander.

- -

A: 真不敢相信你会做这么多菜！（真不敢相信你會做這麼多菜！）

Zhēn bù gǎn xiāngxìn nǐ huì zuò zhème duō cài! *I can't believe you can make so many dishes!*

B: 我会做的菜还有很多呢！（我會做的菜還有很多呢！）

Wǒ huì zuòde cài hái yǒu hěn duō ne. *I can make many more!*

Adjectives

重要	zhòngyào	*important*
重	zhòng	*heavy*

Adverb

才	cái	*certainly*

Complement

得要命	de yàomìng	*to an extreme degree (lit., "to death")*

Verb-Complement

起来 (起來)	qǐlái	*to begin to; set about to*

Noun

袋子	dàizi	*bag*

Verbs

希望	xīwàng	*to hope*
少	shǎo	*to lack; to be short of*
相信	xiāngxìn	*to believe*

调料的味道 Tiáoliào de Wèidào / *Taste of Seasonings*

Match each seasoning to its taste. Some seasonings may share the same taste.

> A. 辣 là   B. 甜 tián   C. 酸 suān   D. 咸 xián

2   对还是错?   **Duì háishì cuò?** / *True or False?*

Look at the photos and listen to the statements about each one. Say true if what you hear matches the photo or false if it doesn't.

1.

2.

3.

4.

3   个人问题   **Gèrén Wèntí** / *Personal Questions*

Answer the following questions in Chinese based on your own experiences and opinions.

1. 你什么调料都喜欢吗?   Nǐ shénme tiáoliào dōu xǐhuan ma?

2. 吃薯条的时候，你加(*to add*)盐还是胡椒？还是都不加?
   Chī shǔtiáo de shíhou, nǐ jiā yán háishì hújiāo? Háishì dōu bùjiā?

3. 你吃海鲜吗?   Nǐ chī hǎixiān ma?

4. 你最喜欢的甜点是什么?   Nǐ zuì xǐhuan de tiándiǎn shì shénme?

5. 你常常吃鱼吗?   Nǐ chángcháng chī yú ma?

6. "常见的中国菜"里，你最想吃哪道菜?
   "Chángjiàn de Zhōngguó cài" li, nǐ zuì xiǎng chī něidào cài?

The Verb 看 *kàn*

You already know the verb 看 *kàn*, meaning "to look; to watch; to see." Another meaning of 看 *kàn* is "to think; to consider." What follows 看 *kàn* is a sentence which gives the speaker's opinion toward something.

> **Subject** + 看 *kàn* + **Sentence**

> A: 今天晚饭吃什么好？ Jīntiān wǎnfàn chī shénme hǎo?

> B: 我们下午会去海边，我看我们就吃海鲜吧。
> Wǒmen xiàwǔ huì qù hǎibiān, wǒ kàn wǒmen jiù chī hǎixiān ba.

> A: 今年新年我们到日本去旅行，你看怎么样？
> Jīnnián xīnnián wǒmen dào Rìběn qù lǚxíng, nǐ kàn zěnmeyàng?

> B: 日本冬天太冷了，我看去新加坡比较好。
> Rìběn dōngtiān tài lěngle, wǒ kān qù Xīnjiāpō bǐjiào hǎo.

▲ 日本冬天太冷了。

The Pattern "V起来 *V qǐlái*"

The word 起来 *qǐlái* is often used as a complement after a verb, and it can have many meanings. Here, V起来 *V qǐlái* indicates the speaker's impressions, assessment or estimation of the topic. What follows V起来 *V qǐlái* is the description or modification which flows from V起来 *V qǐlái*.

> **Verb** + 起来 *qǐlái*

There are two kinds of verbs which are often used with this structure. One is more related to the senses, such as 看 *kàn*, 听 *tīng*, 吃 *chī*, 笑 *xiào* , 闻 *wén* (*to smell*), and the other is general, such as 说 *shuō*, 做 *zuò*, 想 *xiǎng*, 穿 *chuān*, 学 *xué*, 用 *yòng*, 写 *xiě*.

他看起来很生气。 Tā kànqǐlái hěn shēngqì.

中文学起来不容易。 Zhōngwén xuéqǐlái bù róngyì.

Using the Adverb 才 *cái* to Disagree

The adverb 才 *cái* has many meanings. In Unit 1 Lesson B, we learned that it can mean "later than expected." In this lesson, 才 *cái* is used to contradict someone's statement and emphasize the certainty of one's own opinion. The particle 呢 *ne* is often added at the end of the sentence.

Topic + 才 *cái* + **Comment**

A: 美美说你的中文说得很好。 Měiměi shuō nǐde Zhōngwén shuōde hěn hǎo.

B: 不，我说得不好，她说得才好呢。 Bù, wǒ shuōde bù hǎo, tā shuōde cái hǎo ne.

A: 这个汤太清淡了。 Zhèige tāng tài qīngdàn le.

B: 这个汤才不清淡，是你吃得太咸了。
Zhèige tāng cái bù qīngdàn, shì nǐ chīde tài xiánle.

The Expression 得要命 *de yàomìng*

The expression 得要命 *de yàomìng* is used after an adjective to exaggerate the tone of a sentence. The word 命 *mìng* means "life," and the literal meaning of this expression is that something goes to the extreme, almost taking away one's life. Note that this expression is always used for unpleasant things.

Subject + **Adjective** + 得要命 *de yàomìng*

这道菜难吃得要命，我没办法吃完。
Zhèidào cài nánchī de yàomìng, wǒ méi bànfǎ chī wán.

我以为德国的夏天很舒服，没想到今年夏天热得要命。
Wǒ yǐwéi Déguó de xiàtiān hěn shūfu, méi xiǎng dào jīnnián xiàtiān rède yàomìng.

A similar expression is 得要死 *de yàosǐ*. The word 死 *sǐ* means "to die," so the expression literally means "to death."

这个音乐难听得要死，你别听了。 Zhèige yīnyuè nántīng de yàosǐ, nǐ bié tīngle.

The Verb Compound 想到 *xiǎngdào*

想到 *xiǎngdào* is a verb compound with several meanings. In Unit 4 Lesson B, we learned that it can mean to predict or to estimate, as in the phrase 没想到 *méi xiǎng dào*. In this lesson, 想到 *xiǎngdào* means to notice or to think of something.

Subject + 想到 *xiǎngdào* + **Something**

A: 看到红色的东西，会让你想到什么？
Kàndào hóngsè de dōngxi, huì ràng nǐ xiǎngdào shénme?

B: 每次看到红色的东西，我总是想到中国新年。
Měicì kàndào hóngsè de dōngxi, wǒ zǒngshì xiǎngdào Zhōngguó xīnnián.

我想到我明天要去图书馆，我要不要帮你借你想看的那本书？
Wǒ xiǎngdào wǒ míngtiān yào qù túshūguǎn, wǒ yào búyào bāng nǐ jiè nǐ xiǎng kànde nèiběn shū ?

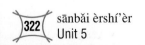

🔊 上街买菜去 **Shàngjiē Mǎicài Qù** *Going Out to Buy the Groceries*

Four friends are meeting in front of the supermarket.

赵梅：	大家都想好了要做什么菜吗？	Zhào Méi:	Dàjiā dōu xiǎng hǎole yào zuò shénme cài ma?
李云英：	我要做糖醋鱼。	Lǐ Yúnyīng:	Wǒ yào zuò Tángcù yú.
钱永利：	糖醋鱼又酸又甜，我真喜欢。	Qián Yǒnglì:	Tángcù yú yòu suān yòu tián, wǒ zhēn xǐhuan.
吴森：	我要做酸辣汤。	Wú Sēn:	Wǒ yào zuò Suānlàtāng.
钱永利：	酸辣汤又酸又辣，我也很喜欢。	Qián Yǒnglì:	Suānlàtāng yòu suān yòu là, wǒ yě hěn xǐhuan.
赵梅：	我看你没有不喜欢的菜吧。你要做什么菜？	Zhào Méi:	Wǒ kàn nǐ méiyǒu bù xǐhuan de cài ba. Nǐ yào zuò shénme cài?
钱永利：	我要做宫保鸡丁，你呢？	Qián Yǒnglì:	Wǒ yào zuò Gōngbǎo jīdīng, nǐ ne?
赵梅：	我要做芥兰牛肉。	Zhào Méi:	Wǒ yào zuò Jièlán niúròu.
李云英：	每道菜听起来都不错，希望做起来也不难。	Lǐ Yúnyīng:	Měidào cài tīngqǐlái dōu búcuò, xīwàng zuòqǐlái yě bùnán.
吴森：	我觉得，吃起来好吃才重要。	Wú Sēn:	Wǒ juéde, chīqǐlái hǎochī cái zhòngyào.
李云英：	除了鱼、鸡肉、牛肉、芥兰和豆腐，我们还需要买什么？	Lǐ Yúnyīng:	Chúle yú, jīròu, niúròu, jièlán hé dòufu, wǒmen hái xūyào mǎi shénme?
吴森：	我想到了，还少了甜点、水果和饮料。	Wú Sēn:	Wǒ xiǎngdào le, hái shǎole tiándiǎn, shuǐguǒ hé yǐnliào.

After shopping, each person is carrying two large bags.

钱永利：	这两个袋子真是重得要命啊！	Qián Yǒnglì:	Zhè liǎngge dàizi zhēnshì zhòngde yàomìng a!
赵梅：	真不敢相信我们要吃这么多东西。	Zhào Méi:	Zhēn bùgǎn xiāngxìn wǒmen yào chī zhème duō dōngxi.

4 谁做什么？ Shéi zuò shénme? / *Who is doing what?*

Match the dish to the person who is going to cook it, based on the dialogue.

1.
2.
3.
4.

A.  赵梅
B.  钱永利
C.  李云英
D.  吴森

5 什么没吃？ Shénme méi chī? / *What is not on the menu?*

Say which meat is not on the menu, according to the dialogue.

A.
B.
C.
D.

Answer the following questions in Chinese.

1. 他们在哪里见面？ Tāmen zài nǎlǐ jiànmiàn?

2. 糖醋鱼的味道(*taste*)怎么样？ 酸辣汤呢？
   Tángcùyú de wèidào zěnmeyàng? Suānlàtāng ne?

3. 谁什么菜都喜欢？ Shéi shénme cài dōu xǐhuan?

4. 吴森觉得做起来不难和吃起来好吃，哪个重要？
   Wú Sēn juéde zuòqǐlái bùnán hé chīqǐlái hǎochī, něige zhòngyào?

5. 除了鱼、肉、豆腐，他们还买了什么？
   Chúle yú, ròu, dòufu, tāmen hái mǎile shénme?

文化橱窗 Wénhuà Chúchuāng

Culture Window

Chinese Mealtime Customs

When eating a meal in China, you may notice that some customs are different than they are at home. First of all, the order that the dishes are presented is different. The typical order of dinner courses is as follows: appetizers (cold), drinks, entrees, rice or noodles, soup, and finally dessert (often fruit). Westerners usually eat their soup before a meal, but Chinese people like it afterward, believing that consuming too many liquids at the beginning of a meal spoils the appetite for the main course.

Before serving the food, servers will often bring steamed wet towels so that diners may clean their hands. (Note that the towels are not meant to be used to clean one's face.) Also, before serving foods that are eaten with the hands, such as shrimp, crab or chicken, servers may set out a dish filled with water and a lemon slice or flower petals. This water is provided so that diners may wash their hands, and is not meant to be consumed.

The Chinese cold appetizer is similar in purpose to Western appetizers: it is a small dish intended to improve one's appetite in preparation for the following entrees. Chinese appetizers are served cold

▲ *The Chinese appetizers*

so that people may feel free to relax and talk at the beginning of a meal without worrying that the food will get cold. When it comes to beverages, however, the Chinese traditionally like them warm, not cold. They believe that cold drinks can upset the stomach, and thus prefer hot tea, which aids in digestion. Today, however, cold drinks like soda and juice, which are popular with young people, are becoming more common at Chinese meals.

▲ *The waitress delivers a wet towel to the patron.*

Entrees are served when patrons have nearly finished with the appetizers. The entrees are almost always accompanied by rice, buns or noodles—staple foods in China. The hot soup is served after the entrees as a filler dish and to help digestion before dessert, usually sweets or fruit.

When Westerns go out to eat, each person typically orders his or her own entree. However, this is rare in China. Chinese meals are served family style, with large portions being shared by the entire table. All the dishes are placed in the middle of the table, usually on a revolving tray, so that each person can try the foods he or she likes. When eating at a table with a revolving tray, it is very important not to turn the tray while another person is taking food from a dish, as this is considered very impolite. It is also bad manners to use your own chopsticks or other utensils to serve yourself the food. Instead, for hygienic reasons, use the ones that are provided for serving.

▲ *A table of dishes on the revolving tray*

7 文化动动脑 Wénhuà Dòngdòngnǎo / *Cultural Check-up*

Complete each statement with an appropriate word or expression.

1. The order of courses at a Chinese meal is: ___, drinks, ___, ___, and ___, followed by ___ or fruit.
2. The steamed towels are provided so patrons can ___.
3. Appetizers serve the purpose of ___.
4. Traditionally, Chinese people like their beverages to be ___.
5. ___ is served toward the end of a meal, after the entrees and staple foods.

语言练习 Yǔyán Liànxí
Language Practice

8 给意见 **Gěi Yìjiàn** / *Giving Opinions*

With a partner, take turns asking and answering each other the following questions to give opinions, using the verb 看 *kàn* and the hints provided. Follow the model.

Lìzi: 龙虾五十块，牡蛎三十九块，我们买哪个？（我们没有很多钱）
Lóngxiā wǔshí kuài, mǔlì sānshíjiǔ kuài, wǒmen mǎi nǎige? (wǒmen méiyǒu hěn duō qián)

A: 龙虾五十块，牡蛎三十九块，我们买哪个？
Lóngxiā wǔshí kuài, mǔlì sānshíjiǔ kuài, wǒmen mǎi nǎige?

B: 我们没有很多钱，我看我们买牡蛎吧。
Wǒmen méiyǒu hěn duō qián, wǒ kàn wǒmen mǎi mǔlì ba.

1. 我们要现在过马路吗？（已经是黄灯了）
Wǒmen yào xiànzài guò mǎlù ma? (yǐjīng shì huángdēng le)

2. 我们要买熟食还是买菜回家做？（大家都很饿）
Wǒmen yào mǎi shúshí háishì mǎi cài huíjiā zuò? (dàjiā dōu hěn è)

3. 我应该买大沙发还是买椅子？（你的房间很小）
Wǒ yīnggāi mǎi dà shāfā háishì mǎi yǐzi? (nǐde fángjiān hěn xiǎo)

4. 我们走人行横道还是天桥？（这个路口太大了）
Wǒmen zǒu rénxíng héngdào háishì tiānqiáo? (zhèige lùkǒu tài dàle)

5. 我应该去便利商店还是超市买可乐？（要买五十罐）
Wǒ yīnggāi qù biànlì shāngdiàn háishì chāoshì mǎi kělè? (yào mǎi wǔshí guàn)

6. 我想看书，可是爸爸在书房做事。（客厅没有人）
Wǒ xiǎng kànshū, kěshì bàba zài shūfáng zuòshì. (kètīng méiyǒu rén)

7. 我不喜欢坐电梯，住大楼好吗？（平房或是公寓）
Wǒ bù xǐhuan zuò diàntī, zhù dàlóu hǎo ma? (píngfáng huòshì gōngyù)

8. 我给李老师打了好几次电话，可是他都不在。（给他留言）
Wǒ gěi Lǐ lǎoshī dǎle hǎo jǐcì diànhuà, kěshì tā dōu búzài. (gěi tā liúyán)

9 怎么样? **Zěnmeyàng?** / *How is it?*

Describe each picture by completing the sentences using V 起来 *V qǐlái*.

1.

他的脸…。

Tāde liǎn….

3.

这道菜…。

Zhèidào cài….

5.

这罐果汁…。

Zhèiguàn guǒzhī….

2.

王小姐…。

Wáng xiǎojie….

4.

这件连衣裙…。

Zhèijiàn liányīqún….

6.

这个东西…。

Zhèige dōngxi….

10 你的印象是什么? **Nǐde yìnxiàng shì shénme?** / *What is your impression?*

With a partner, take turns asking and answering each other the following questions.

1. 英语学起来容易吗? Yīngyǔ xuéqǐlái róngyì ma?

2. 中国字写起来难不难? Zhōngguózì xiěqǐlái nán bùnán?

3. 中国菜吃起来很清淡吗? Zhōngguócài chīqǐlái hěn qīngdàn ma?

4. 西装穿起来非常正式吗? Xīzhuāng chuānqǐlái fēicháng zhèngshì ma?

5. 你觉得法文听起来很美吗? Nǐ juéde Fǎwén tīngqǐlái hěn měi ma?

6. 运动鞋走起来比皮鞋舒服吗? Yùndòngxié zǒuqǐlái bǐ píxié shūfu ma?

11 夸张用法 Kuāzhāng Yòngfǎ / *Exaggeration*

Complete the following sentences using the expression "Adj. 得要命 *Adj. de yào mìng*" or "Adj. 得要死 *Adj. de yào sǐ*."

1. 这件衣服…，我才不要穿。 Zhèijiàn yīfu…, wǒ cái búyào chuān.

2. 你做的蛋糕糖加得太多了，…。 Nǐ zuòde dàngāo táng jiāde tài duō le, ….

3. 那个地方…，我才不要走路去。 Nèige dìfang…, wǒ cái búyào zǒulù qù.

4. 今天校车开得…，所以我迟到了。 Jīntiān xiàochē kāide…, suǒyǐ wǒ chídào le.

5. 那部浪漫爱情片…，我不想看了。 Nèibù làngmàn àiqíngpiàn…, wǒ bùxiǎng kànle.

6. 我的头…，我今天没办法去上课。 Wǒde tóu…, wǒ jīntiān méi bànfǎ qù shàngkè.

12 联想 Liánxiǎng / *Making Associations*

With a classmate, take turns asking and answering each other the following questions.

1. 说到中文，你想到什么？ Shuōdào Zhōngwén, nǐ xiǎngdào shénme?

2. 说到加拿大，你想到什么？ Shuōdào Jiā'nádà, nǐ xiǎngdào shénme?

3. 听到法文歌，你想到什么？ Tīngdào Fǎwén gē, nǐ xiǎngdào shénme?

4. 看到粉红色，你想到什么？ Kàndào fěnhóngsè, nǐ xiǎngdào shénme?

5. 说到高尔夫，你想到什么？ Shuōdào gāo'ěrfū, nǐ xiǎngdào shénme?

6. 看到黄色的车，你想到什么？ Kàndào huángsè de chē, nǐ xiǎngdào shénme?

▲ 看到这幅画(*picture*)，你想到什么？

 Kāikǒu Shuō

Communication

 拿手菜 **Náshǒucài** / *One's Special Dish*

 Think of a special dish that you would like to cook, and write down the ingredients needed to prepare it. In addition, write one or two sentences to describe how it tastes. Then, draw a table like the one shown below and in groups of three or four, ask each other about your special dishes: what is the name of the dish, what are the ingredients, and how it tastes. Record the answers in the table. Finally, one person from each group reports the information to the class.

Lìzi: **A:** 你的拿手菜(*special*)是什么？ Nǐde náshǒucài shì shénme?

B: 我的拿手菜是吉士汉堡包。 Wǒde náshǒucài shì jíshì hànbǎobāo.

A: 吉士汉堡包的材料(*ingredients*)是什么？
Jíshì hànbǎobāo de cáiliào shì shénme?

B: 它的材料是面包、牛肉、奶酪、菜。
Tāde cáiliào shì miànbāo, niúròu, nǎilào, cài.

A: 它的味道怎么样？ Tāde wèidào zěnmeyàng?

B: 很香(*appetizing*)。 Hěn xiāng.

Content \ Student	B		
菜名 càimíng (*name of dish*)	吉士汉堡包 jíshì hànbǎobāo		
材料 cáiliào (*ingredients*)	面包、牛肉、奶酪、菜 miànbāo, niúròu, nǎilào, cài		
味道 wèidào (*taste*)	很香 hěn xiāng		

Read the supermarket flyer and the menu below and answer the questions that follow referring to the flyer.

今天晚餐的菜单 jīntiān wǎncān de càidān:

- 雪菜蒸豆腐 xuěcài zhēng dòufu
- 姜葱虾仁 jiāng cōng xiārén
- 盐水大虾 yán shuǐ dàxiā
- 葱爆羊肉 cōng bào yángròu
- 海鲜南瓜汤 hǎixiān nánguā tāng
- 冰糖莲藕 bīngtáng liánǒu

1. 哪道菜是甜的？ Něidào cài shì tiánde?

2. 豆腐一斤(jin)多少钱？ Dòufu yìjīn duōshao qián?

3. 做葱爆羊肉这道菜要买什么？ Zuò cōng bào yángròu zhèidào cài yào mǎi shénme?

4. 超市里没有南瓜，哪道菜没办法做？
   Chāoshì li méiyǒu nánguā, něidào cài méi bànfǎ zuò?

Language Note

"Jin (斤 jīn)" is a Chinese unit of weight. One "jin" equals half a kilogram.
1 pound = 0.9 jin

Vocabulary

珍　　　zhēn　　　*n.*　*rare delicacy*
味　　　wèi　　　*n.*　*taste*

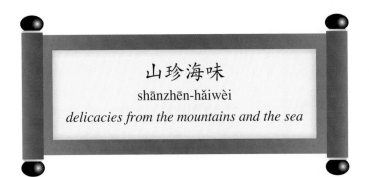

山珍海味
shānzhēn-hǎiwèi
delicacies from the mountains and the sea

▲ 山珍海味

Language Note

This idiom talks about the rare foods one might find in the mountains and in the sea—the stuff that people think of as delicacies. For the people of the past, these delicacies included bear paws, swallow nests, shark fins and sea cucumbers. Nowadays, this idiom is not only used to describe rare foods; it is also used to describe elaborate dishes.

为了庆祝我的十八岁生日，妈妈准备了一桌的山珍海味。
Wèile qìngzhù wǒde shíbā suì shēngrì, māma zhǔnbèile yìzhuō de shānzhēn-hǎiwèi.
To celebrate my 18th birthday, my mom prepared a tableful of delicious food.

Another idiom to do with food is "食指大动 *shízhǐ dà dòng* (to make one's index finger move)." There is actually a story behind this idiom. In ancient China, there was a man whose index finger would always twitch before he got to eat something delicious. One day, the man went to see the emperor with a friend, and before they left, his index finger twitched. So the man turned to his friend and said, "We'll definitely get to eat something great later on." It turned out that a neighboring country had given the emperor a huge terrapin that the emperor had just ordered the chefs to turn into a delicious dish. Thus, this idiom was first used to mean having a premonition of a great meal, but is now used to mean that the meal is delicious and it makes people feel hungry. For example: 这些好菜让人食指大动。*Zhèxiē hǎo cài ràng rén shízhǐ dà dòng.* (These great dishes make my index finger twitch.)

学做饭

　　昨天做的苹果派很成功[1]，我非常开心。今天我还想做甜点，可是妈妈说我应该要学做饭了。我和妈妈一起看了几本中国菜的食谱[2]，最后[3]我选了"蚂蚁上树"，因为我觉得这个名字很好玩儿，我的朋友一定都不知道这是什么菜。我能看懂食谱，而且我觉得食谱上写的看起来不难。不过妈妈说看懂不一定能做好，我相信妈妈说的，因为中国菜不是好做的菜。食谱上的照片[4]看起来很好吃，看得我好饿，希望我今天也能做一次就成功。

[1]成功: successful　[2]食谱: cookbook　[3]最后: in the end　[4]照片: picture

Xué Zuòfàn

　　Zuótiān zuòde píngguǒpài hěn chénggōng, wǒ fēicháng kāixīn. Jīntiān wǒ hái xiǎng zuò tiándiǎn, kěshì māma shuō wǒ yīnggāi yào xué zuòfàn le. Wǒ hé māma yìqǐ kànle jǐběn Zhōngguócài de shípǔ, zuìhòu wǒ xuǎnle "Mǎyǐ shàngshù", yīnwèi wǒ juéde zhèige míngzi hěn hǎowánr, wǒde péngyou yídìng dōu bù zhīdào zhè shì shénme cài. Wǒ néng kàn dǒng shípǔ, érqiě wǒ juéde shípǔ shàng xiěde kànqǐlái bùnán. Búguò māma shuō kàndǒng bù yídìng néng zuòhǎo, wǒ xiāngxìn māma shuōde, yīnwèi Zhōngguó cài búshì hǎo zuòde cài. Shípǔ shàngde zhàopiàn kànqǐlái hěn hǎochī, kànde wǒ hǎo è, xīwàng wǒ jīntiān yě néng zuò yícì jiù chénggōng.

15 通晓文意 **Tōngxiǎo Wényì** / *Understanding the Passage*

Read the above passage and decide if the statements are true or false. Correct any false statements.

1. 他昨天做苹果派做得不错。　Tā zuótiān zuò píngguǒpài zuòde búcuò.

2. 他和妈妈看了好几国菜的食谱。　Tā hé māma kànle hǎojǐ guó cài de shípǔ.

3. 他决定要做"蚂蚁上树"，因为这道菜很好吃。
   Tā juédìng yào zuò "Mǎyǐ shàngshù", yīnwèi zhèidào cài hěn hǎochī.

4. 他选"蚂蚁上树"是因为他的朋友都吃过这道菜。
   Tā xuǎn "Mǎyǐ shàngshù" shì yīnwèi tāde péngyou dōu chīguò zhèidào cài.

5. 他相信他妈妈说的"看懂不一定能做好"，因为他第一次做饭。
   Tā xiāngxìn tā māma shuōde "kàndǒng bù yídìng néng zuòhǎo", yīnwèi tā dìyī cì zuòfàn.

6. 食谱上的照片让他觉得很饿。
   Shípǔ shàng de zhàopiàn ràng tā juéde hěn è.

汉字天地 Hànzì Tiāndì

Chinese Characters

鱼 / 魚 ■ yú ■ fish

The character 鱼 *yú* is a pictograph. In ancient times, it was drawn in the shape of a fish. The top was a fish head and the bottom was the fish tail. Now it still retains its original shape, but in standardized strokes. The bottom part is now four dots in the traditional form, and one horizontal stroke in the simplified form. This is a common radical for words related to fish, such as 鲜 (*xiān*, fresh), 鲸 (*jīng*, whale), 鲨 (*shā*, shark) etc.

Stroke Order

16 词汇延伸 Cíhuì Yánshēn / *Vocabulary Builder*

Below are characters that combine with 鱼 *yú* to create words. Match the Chinese words on the left with the appropriate English meaning on the right.

网 wǎng	饵 ěr	竿 gān	鳞 lín	缸 gāng
n. net	*n. bait*	*n. pole*	*n. scale*	*n. big jar*

1. 鱼网 yúwǎng   A. fish tank

2. 鱼饵 yú'ěr   B. fish scales

3. 鱼竿 yúgān   C. fish bait

4. 鱼鳞 yúlín   D. fishing rod

5. 鱼缸 yúgāng   E. fishnet

Can you find 鱼 in the following pictures?

鱼类海鲜

⋯一样呢？嗯，看看

⋯有这么多

⋯的时候，保罗去钓鱼。

三味鱼⋯

钓鱼

5

40

三长江鱼馆

8小时

鱼

Lesson C

🔊 材料 Cáiliào *Ingredients*

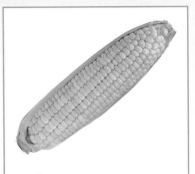

南瓜 nánguā

n. pumpkin

玉米 yùmǐ

n. corn

黄瓜 huángguā

n. cucumber

土豆 tǔdòu

n. potato

胡萝卜（胡蘿蔔）

húluóbo *n. carrot*

花菜 huācài

n. cauliflower

大白菜 dàbáicài

n. Chinese cabbage

蘑菇 mógu

n. mushroom

西红柿 xīhóngshì

n. tomato

芹菜 qíncài

n. celery

洋葱 (洋蔥) yángcōng

n. onion

蒜 suàn

n. garlic

Language Note

In addition to 土豆 *tǔdòu*, another word for potato is 马铃薯 *mǎlíngshǔ*.
西红柿 *xīhóngshì* is also called 蕃茄 *fānqié*.

中文

🔊 餐具 Cānjù *Tableware*

筷子 kuàizi

n. chopsticks

碗 wǎn

n. bowl

碟子 diézi

n. saucer

叉子 chāzi

n. fork

汤匙 (湯匙) tāngchí

n. spoon

刀子 dāozi

n. knife

盘子 (盤子) pánzi

n. plate

水杯 shuǐbēi

n. (water) cup

炒锅 (炒鍋) chǎoguō

n. wok

Language Note

The measure words for the tableware are as follows: for chopsticks, use 双 *shuāng* (一双筷子 *yìshuāng kuàizi,* "a pair of chopsticks"); for fork, knife, and spoon, use 只 *zhī* (两只叉子 *liǎngzhī chāzi,* "two forks"; 三只刀子 *sānzhī dāozi,* "three knives"; 四只汤匙 *sìzhī tāngchí* "four spoons"). For the rest, simply use 个 *ge.*

◀)) 烹调方式 Pēngtiáo Fāngshì *Food Preparation*

切 qiē

v. to cut

削 xiāo

v. to peel

烤 kǎo

v. to bake

炸 zhá

v. to fry

炒 chǎo

v. to stir-fry

煎 jiān

v. to pan-fry

煮 zhǔ

v. to cook; to boil

焖 mèn

v. to simmer

A: 你刚刚买的玉米放在哪里？

（你剛剛買的玉米放在哪裡？）

Nǐ gānggāng mǎide yùmǐ fàng zài nǎlǐ?

Where did you put the corn you just bought?

B: 我放在厨房的桌子上。

（我放在廚房的桌子上。）

Wǒ fàng zài chúfáng de zhuōzi shàng. *I put it on the kitchen table.*

A: 你别忘了，明天把书拿去图书馆还。

（你別忘了，明天把書拿去圖書館還。）

Nǐ bié wàngle, míngtiān bǎ shū ná qù túshūguǎn huán.

Don't forget to return your library books tomorrow.

B: 李明昨天已经拿去还了，不是吗？

（李明昨天已經拿去還了，不是嗎？）

Lǐ Míng zuótiān yǐjīng ná qù huánle, búshì ma? *Li Ming already returned them yesterday, didn't he?*

A: 你知道中餐的餐具怎么摆吗？（你知道中餐的餐具怎麼擺嗎？）

Nǐ zhīdào zhōngcān de cānjù zěnme bǎi ma?

Do you know how to set a Chinese dining table?

(lit: Do you know where to put different Chinese tableware on a dining table?)

B: 先放盘子，再把碗放在盘子的上面，把筷子放在盘子的右边，然后把汤匙放在筷子的右边，就好了。（先放盤子，再把碗放在盤子的上面，把筷子放在盤子的右邊，然後把湯匙放在筷子的右邊，就好了。）

Xiān fàng pánzi, zài bǎ wǎn fàng zài pánzi de shàngmian, bǎ kuàizi fàng zài pánzi de yòubiān, ránhòu bǎ tāngchí fàng zài kuàizi de yòubiān, jiù hǎole.

First set out the plates, then put the bowls on the plates, put the chopsticks to the right of the plate; put the spoons to the right of the chopsticks.

A: 唉呀，下雨了。（唉呀，下雨了。）

Āiyā, xiàyǔ le. *Uh oh, it's raining.*

B: 幸亏这里离我家很近，我们走快一点儿，应该两分钟就可以到家了。

（幸虧這裡離我家裡很近，我們走快一點兒，應該兩分鐘就可以到家了。）

Xìngkuī zhèlǐ lí wǒ jiā hěn jìn, wǒmen zǒu kuài yìdiǎnr, yīnggāi liǎngfēn zhōng jiù kěyǐ dào jiā le.

It's lucky that we're near our house. Let's walk faster; we'll be home in two minutes.

Adverb

幸亏 (幸虧)	xìngkuī	*fortunately; luckily*

Conjunction

要不然	yàobùrán	*otherwise; or*

Coverb

把	bǎ	把 *bǎ marks an object placed which precedes its verb*

Measure Words

块 (塊)	kuài	*a slice or chunk of something*
双 (雙)	shuāng	*pair of*
把	bǎ	*used for things with a handle*

Nouns

丁	dīng	*small cubes of meat or vegetable*
块 (塊)	kuài	*piece; cube; chunk*
酱料 (醬料)	jiàngliào	*sauce*
味道	wèidào	*taste*

Verbs

洗	xǐ	*to wash*
放	fàng	*to put*
收拾	shōushi	*to put in order; to tidy up*
摆 (擺)	bǎi	*to put; to place; to arrange*
加	jiā	*to add*
好像	hǎoxiàng	*to seem; to be like*

1 认识蔬菜 **Rènshì Shūcài** / *Identifying Vegetables*

Look at each photo and say what vegetable you see.

1.

2.

3.

4.

5.

6.

2 烹调方式 **Pēngtiáo Fāngshì** / *Food Preparation*

🔊 **Listen to the recording. Choose the photo that corresponds to what you hear.**

A.   B.   C.   D.

3 个人问题 **Gèrén Wèntí** / *Personal Questions*

Answer the following questions in Chinese based on your experiences and opinions.

1. 你会用筷子吗？   Nǐ huì yòng kuàizi ma?

2. 每种蔬菜你都喜欢吗？你不喜欢的蔬菜是什么？
   Měizhǒng shūcài nǐ dōu xǐhuan ma? Nǐ bù xǐhuan de shūcài shì shénme?

3. 吃饭以前，你总是帮忙摆餐具吗？
   Chīfàn yǐqián, nǐ zǒngshì bāngmáng bǎi cānjù ma?

4. 你喜欢烤的鱼还是炸的鱼？   Nǐ xǐhuan kǎode yú háishì zháde yú?

句型介绍 Jùxíng Jièshào
Language Patterns

The Preposition 在 *zài* After the Verb

We learned 在 *zài* in level 1, Unit 3 Lesson A as a verb to express the relative location of the subject. In this lesson, 在 *zài* functions as a preposition following a verb to indicate where an action took place.

> **Subject** + **Verb** + **在 *zài*** + **Place Word**

不好意思，我可以坐在你旁边吗？　Bù hǎoyìsi, wǒ kěyǐ zuò zài nǐ pángbiān ma?

这是学校的书，所以练习题(*exercises*)不可以写在书上，要写在纸上。
Zhè shì xuéxiào de shū, suǒyǐ liànxítí bù kěyǐ xiě zài shū shàng, yào xiě zài zhǐ shàng.

The Tag Question "不是吗？ *búshì ma?*"

The phrase 不是吗？ *búshì ma?* is a tag question added to the end of a sentence to ask about something the speaker is unsure of. 不是吗？ *búshì ma?* can be translated as "isn't that right?" The function is similar to the negative question pattern 不是…吗？ *búshì...ma?* which we learned in Unit 2 Lesson C.

> **Sentence** ，**不是吗？**

A: 我要点咖啡。　Wǒ yào diǎn kāfēi.

B: 我记得你以前是不喝咖啡的，不是吗？
Wǒ jìdé nǐ yǐqián shì bùhē kāfēi de, búshì ma?

A: 这个超市太大了，我不知道冰淇淋在哪里。
Zhèige chāoshì tài dàle, wǒ bù zhīdào bīngqílín zài nǎlǐ.

B: 冰淇淋在冷冻食品区呀，不是吗？　Bīngqílín zài lěngdòng shípǐn qū ya, búshì ma?

The Coverb 把 *bǎ*

The coverb 把 *bǎ* is used to bring the object before the verb, allowing the focus of the sentence to be on the object.

> **Subject** + **把 *bǎ*** + **Object** + **Verb Phrase**

请把胡椒给我，谢谢！ Qǐng bǎ hújiāo gěi wǒ, xièxie!

他们把功课写好了。 Tāmen bǎ gōngkè xiěhǎo le.

Here are more patterns with 把 *bǎ* that show different verb modifications.

> **Subject** + **把 *bǎ*** + **Object** + **Verb** + **Complement**

奶奶把药吃了。 Nǎinai bǎ yào chī le.

你应该把汤喝完。 Nǐ yīnggāi bǎ tāng hēwán.

服务员把菜送来。 Fúwùyuán bǎ cài sònglái.

哥哥把甜甜圈给弟弟。 Gēge bǎ tiántiánquān gěi dìdi.

爸爸把电脑放在桌子上。 Bàba bǎ diànnǎo fàng zài zhuōzi shàng.

李小姐把信寄到中国。 Lǐ xiǎojie bǎ xìn jì dào Zhōngguó.

你把房间收拾一下。 Nǐ bǎ fángjiān shōushí yíxià.

Language Note

There are some rules to the 把 *bǎ* pattern.

1. The object must be definite and be indicated before or known by both listener and speaker.

 (X) 我把一本书看完了。 Wǒ bǎ yìběn shū kànwán le.

 (O) 我把这一本书看完了。 Wǒ bǎ zhè yìběn shū kànwán le.

2. Negatives such as 不 *bù / bú*, 没 *méi*, 别 *bié* and 不要 *bú yào* should be placed before 把 *bǎ*.

 (X) 我把这一本书没看完。 Wǒ bǎ zhè yìběn shū méi kànwán.

 (O) 我没把这一本书看完。 Wǒ méi bǎ zhè yìběn shū kànwán.

3. Auxiliary verbs like 可以 *kěyǐ*, 想 *xiǎng*, 要 *yào*, 能 *néng* and 会 *huì* should also be placed before 把 *bǎ*.

 (X) 我把这一本书想看完。 Wǒ bǎ zhè yìběn shū xiǎng kànwán.

 (O) 我想把这一本书看完。 Wǒ xiǎng bǎ zhè yìběn shū kànwán.

4. The verb after the object cannot be a simple verb. It should be a modified verb phrase.

 (X) 我把这一本书看。 Wǒ bǎ zhè yìběn shū kàn.

 (O) 我把这一本书看了。 Wǒ bǎ zhè yìběn shū kàn le.

5. 把 *bǎ* is not used with potential complements.

 (X) 我把这一本书看得完。 Wǒ bǎ zhè yìběn shū kànde wán.

The Pattern 幸亏…要不然… *xìngkuī…yàobùrán…*

The adverb 幸亏 *xìngkuī* means "luckily." It introduces a fortunate event or circumstance. The conjunction 要不然 *yàobùrán* introduces an undesired situation which was avoided because of the good fortune. The adverb 幸好 *xìnghǎo* has the same meaning as 幸亏 *xìngkuī* and can substitute for it.

> 幸亏 *xìngkuī* + **Clause 1** ， 要不然 *yàobùrán* + **Clause 2**

A: 妈妈，这个酸辣汤怎么不酸？ Māma, zhèige suānlàtāng zěnme bùsuān?

B: 唉呀，我可能忘了放醋。幸亏你先喝了一口，要不然等一下你同学喝了，多不好意思。

 Āiya, wǒ kěnéng wàngle fàng cù. Xìngkuī nǐ xiān hēle yìkǒu, yàobùrán děngyíxià nǐ tóngxué hēle, duō bù hǎoyìsi.

我的背包不见了！幸好我的手机和钱包都没放在里面。

Wǒde bèibāo bújiànle! Xìnghǎo wǒde shǒujī hé qiánbāo dōu méifàng zài lǐmiàn.

会话 **Huìhuà**
Dialogue

🔊 做菜真好玩儿 Zuòcài Zhēn Hǎowánr *It's Fun to Cook*

Wu Sen, Qian Yongli, Zhao Mei and Li Yunying take the groceries to Wu Sen's house.

吴森:	到家了，我们开始吧！大家都先洗洗手。	Wú Sēn:	Dào jiā le, wǒmen kāishǐ ba! Dàjiā dōu xiān xǐxi shǒu.
钱永利:	吴森，你家的刀子放在哪儿？	Qián Yǒnglì:	Wú Sēn, nǐ jiāde dāozi fàng zài nǎr?
吴森:	鸡肉已经切好了，不是吗？为什么还要刀子？	Wú Sēn:	Jīròu yǐjīng qiēhǎo le, búshì ma? Wèishénme hái yào dāozi?
钱永利:	我要做"鸡丁"，所以这块鸡肉还太大，我得把它切小一点儿。	Qián Yǒnglì:	Wǒ yào zuò "jīdīng", suǒyǐ zhèikuài jīròu hái tài dà, wǒ děi bǎ tā qiē xiǎo yìdiǎnr.
赵梅:	吴森，请把炒锅给我。	Zhào Méi:	Wú Sēn, qǐng bǎ chǎoguō gěi wǒ.
吴森:	云英，糖醋鱼怎么做啊？	Wú Sēn:	Yúnyīng, tángcùyú zěnme zuò a?
李云英:	你先把鱼煎一煎，再放酱料，然后焖一下就好了。	Lǐ Yúnyīng:	Nǐ xiān bǎ yú jiānyìjiān zài fàng jiàngliào, ránhòu mèn yíxià jiù hǎ le.
吴森:	我已经把汤做好了。谁需要帮忙？	Wú Sēn:	Wǒ yǐjīng bǎ tāng zuòhǎole. Shéi xūyào bāngmáng?
李云英:	那好，你先把桌子收拾收拾，然后把餐具摆一摆吧！	Lǐ Yúnyīng:	Nà hǎo, nǐ xiān bǎ zhuōzi shōushi shōushi, ránhòu bǎ cānjù bǎi yìbǎi ba!
赵梅:	我想先喝汤。咦，为什么没有味道？	Zhào Méi:	Wǒ xiǎng xiān hē tāng. Yí, wèishénme méiyǒu wèidào?
吴森:	啊，我好像忘了加盐了。	Wú Sēn:	A, wǒ hǎoxiàng wàngle jiā yán le.
钱永利:	幸亏我们买了饮料，要不然就没东西喝了。	Qián Yǒnglì:	Xìngkuī wǒmen mǎile yǐnliào, yàoburán jiù méi dōngxi hē le.

4　他需要什么？　**Tā xūyào shénme?**　*What does he need?*

Choose which of the following Qian Yongli needs for cooking, based on the dialogue.

A.

B.

C.

5　少了什么？　**Shǎo le shénme?**　*What is missing?*

Select what is missing from the hot and sour soup, based on the dialogue.

A.　B.　C.　D.

6　懂了吗？　**Dǒngle ma?**　*Do you understand?*

Answer the following questions in Chinese.

1. 到吴森家以后，他们先做什么？　Dào Wú Sēn jiā yǐhòu, tāmen xiān zuò shénme?

2. 鸡肉已经切了吗？为什么钱永利还要刀子？
   Jīròu yǐjīng qiēle ma? Wèishénme Qián Yǒnglì hái yào dāozi?

3. 赵梅需要什么东西？　Zhàoméi xūyào shénme dōngxi?

4. 糖醋鱼怎么做？　Tángcù yú zěnme zuò?

5. 吴森做好酸辣汤以后，他做什么？
   Wú Sēn zuòhǎo suānlàtāng yǐhòu, tā zuò shénme?

6. 是谁先发现(*found*)汤没有味道的？　Shì shéi xiān fāxiàn tāng méiyǒu wèidào de?

7. 为什么汤没有味道？　Wèishénme tāng méiyǒu wèidào?

8. 如果他们不喝汤，他们还有什么可以喝？
   Rúguǒ tāmen bù hē tāng, tāmen hái yǒu shénme kěyǐ hē?

Wénhuà Chúchuāng

文化橱窗

Culture Window

Table Etiquette

Setting the Table

Eating Chinese food properly is an art all its own. It begins with setting the table. Rather than knives and forks, each table setting includes chopsticks and a large spoon. Each diner also receives a small plate or saucer for food and a bowl for rice. The bowl is placed on top of the plate or saucer and only removed when the meal begins. The chopsticks and spoons are placed on special holders or in paper sheaths, and napkins are placed in front (or on top) of the plate/saucer. In more formal situations, a cup of water is provided to the right of the plate for diners to wash their hands while eating finger foods.

▲ *Chinese table setting*

Seating Arrangements

In formal situations, certain rules must be followed when making seating arrangements. Usually, a VIP or an elder is seated at the head of the table, which is the seat facing the entrance. The host should sit in the seat nearest to the entrance. The other diners are seated according to their relationship with the person sitting at the head. Those that have a closer relationship to the person are seated closer, while those who are more distant sit farther away. Once food is served, no one may make a move until the person at the head of the table starts eating. If it is a family dinner, all the guests must wait until the eldest has started eating before picking up their own chopsticks.

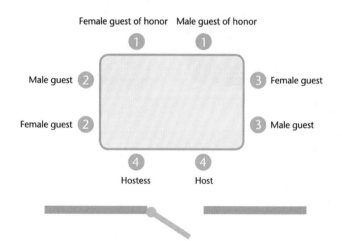

▲ *Seating arrangement. The numbers show the importance of the people at the table.*

Table Manners

As mentioned in the last lesson, Chinese food is served family-style, which means all dishes are shared. When taking food from the plates, use the chopsticks or spoon provided for serving, not your own personal utensils. Be careful not to select food from the same dish as another person at the same time—it is polite to take turns. If a dish contains liquids, move your plate or saucer close to the dish while serving yourself to prevent dripping.

There are also some basic manners regarding chopsticks. For example, it is considered very rude to point or gesture at others using chopsticks. Also avoid using your chopsticks to play with food or bang on the side of your bowl. When not using your chopsticks, lay them over the top of the bowl or place them on the chopstick holder. Never stick your chopsticks upright in a bowl of rice. This is offensive in the traditional Chinese culture because it is the way rice is offered to deceased ancestors.

▲ *Don't use your chopsticks to gesture.*

▲ *Don't touch food with your chopsticks that you are not going to eat.*

▲ *Don't stick your chopsticks into the rice.*

▲ *Don't tap your bowl with your chopsticks.*

Another unique part of Chinese dining culture is 让菜 *ràng cài*, which means to urge others to eat more or even placing food on another person's plate for them. For the Chinese, this is to show guests that they are welcome at the table. A good host will often place food on the plates of guests and pour drinks for them so that they do not have to serve themselves.

7 文化动动脑 **Wénhuà Dòngdòngnǎo** / *Culture Check-up*

Complete each statement with an appropriate word or expression.

1. Tableware used in China include ___, ___, ___ and ___.
2. The eldest or most important guest sits ___, while the host sits ___.
3. When taking food from the plate, it is polite to ___.
4. It is rude to use the chopsticks to ____ or ____.
5. 让菜 *ràng cài* means to ___.

8 在哪里？ **Zài nǎlǐ?** / *Where is it?*

Look at the pictures and answer the questions using the pattern 在… *zài*….

1.

她的脚放在哪里？

Tāde jiǎo fàng zài nǎlǐ?

3.

猫坐在哪里？

Māo zuò zài nǎlǐ?

5.

他把他的日记*(diary)*
写在哪里？

Tā bǎ tāde rìjì xiě zài nǎlǐ?

2.

碗摆在哪里？

Wǎn bǎi zài nǎlǐ?

汤匙摆在哪里？

Tāngchí bǎi zài nǎlǐ?

4.

车子停*(to park)*在哪里？

Chēzi tíng zài nǎlǐ?

6.

画挂*(to hang)*在哪里？

Huà guà zài nǎlǐ?

▲ 车子停在哪里？

Complete the following mini-dialogues using the expression 不是吗？ *búshì ma?* and the hints provided. Follow the model.

Lìzi: 大中 Dàzhōng: 这本书再借我看一次。 Zhèiběn shū zài jiè wǒ kàn yícì.

小莉 Xiǎolì: 这本书你看了四次了，不是吗？

Zhèiběn shū nǐ kànle sìcì le, búshì ma?

（大中看了四次了 Dàzhōng kànle sìcì le）

1. 孩子 háizi: 妈妈，我要买新的球鞋。 Māma, wǒ yào mǎi xīnde qiúxié.

妈妈 māma: ＿＿＿。

（现在孩子有六双球鞋 xiànzài háizi yǒu liùshuāng qiúxié）

2. 李太太 Lǐ tàitai: 下个星期就是万圣节 (Halloween) 了，我要再买几个南瓜。

Xiàge xīngqī jiù shì Wànshèngjié le, wǒ yào zài mǎi jǐge nánguā.

李先生 Lǐ xiānsheng: ＿＿＿。

（现在家里有四个南瓜 xiànzài jiāli yǒu sìge nánguā）

3. 德明 Démíng: 我想再点一只龙虾。 Wǒ xiǎng zài diǎn yìzhī lóngxiā.

梅芬 Méifēn: ＿＿＿。

（德明已经吃了四只龙虾 Démíng yǐjīng chīle sìzhī lóngxiā）

4. 小陈 Xiǎo Chén: 这个汤的味道太淡，我要再加一点盐。

Zhèige tāngde wèidao tài dàn, wǒ yào zài jiā yìdiǎn yán.

小张 Xiǎo Zhāng: ＿＿＿。

（小张觉得汤的味道刚刚好 Xiǎo Zhāng juéde tāngde wèidao gānggāng hǎo）

5. 王先生 Wáng xiānsheng: 我明天还要去打高尔夫。

Wǒ míngtiān hái yào qù dǎ gāo'ěrfū.

林小姐 Lín xiǎojie: ＿＿＿。

（王先生这个星期已经打了三次 Wáng xiānsheng zhèige xīngqī yǐjīng dǎle sāncì）

6. 妹妹 mèimei: 我要在我的圣代上再放一球 (scoop) 冰淇淋。

Wǒ yào zài wǒde shèngdài shàng zài fàng yìqiú bīngqílín.

姐姐 jiějie: ＿＿＿。

（现在妹妹的圣代上有五球冰淇淋 xiànzài mèimei de shèngdài shàng yǒu wǔqiú bīngqílín）

Unscramble the following 把 *bǎ* sentences.

Lìzi: 洗 / 她 / 把 / 了 / 衣服。

xǐ / tā / bǎ / le / yīfu.

她把衣服洗了。

▲ 她把衣服洗了。

1. 桌上的水杯 / 我 / 给 / 请 / 把。

   zhuō shàng de shuǐbēi / wǒ / gěi / qǐng / bǎ.

2. 一个 / 把 / 妈妈 / 给 / 我 / 布丁。

   yíge / bǎ / māma / gěi / wǒ / bùdīng.

3. 把 / 弟弟 / 了 / 功课 / 已经 / 做完。

   bǎ / dìdi / le / gōngkè / yǐjīng / zuòwán.

4. 你 / 把 / 手 / 洗一洗 / 要 / 先。

   nǐ / bǎ / shǒu / xǐyixi / yào / xiān.

5. 客厅 / 这个 / 游戏机 / 你 / 拿去 / 把。

   kètīng / zhèige / yóuxìjī / nǐ / náqù / bǎ.

6. 自行车 / 把 / 海边 / 妹妹 / 了 / 骑去。

   zìxíngchē / bǎ / hǎibiān / mèimei / le / qíqù.

7. 我们 / 把 / 买好 / 今天 / 菜 / 先 / 吧。

   wǒmen / bǎ / mǎihǎo / jīntiān / cài / xiān / ba.

8. 那个 / 爸爸 / 贮藏室 / 把 / 放 / 在 / 灯。

   nèige / bàba / zhùcángshì / bǎ / fàng / zài / dēng.

9. 牛肉 / 帮 / 切一切 / 我 / 把 / 你 / 这块。

   niúròu / bāng / qiēyiqie / wǒ / bǎ / nǐ / zhèikuài.

10. 你 / 这个 / 请 / 厨房 / 放到 / 把 / 花菜 / 里。

    nǐ / zhèige / qǐng / chúfáng / fàngdào / bǎ / huācài / lǐ.

11. 把 / 我们 / 那个 / 买的东西 / 先生 / 送来。

    bǎ / wǒmen / nèige / mǎide dōngxi / xiānsheng / sònglái.

With a classmate, take turns acting out the following dialogues. Use the hints and the conjunction 幸亏 *xìngkuī* to reply. Follow the model.

Lìzi: **A:** 拿去，你的南瓜在这里。别忘了留一块南瓜派给我。

Ná qù, nǐde nánguā zài zhèlǐ. Bié wàngle liú yíkuài nánguāpài gěi wǒ.

B: <u>幸亏你去了超级市场</u>，要不然我们就没有南瓜派可以吃了。

<u>Xìngkuī nǐ qùle chāojí shìchǎng</u>, yàobùrán wǒmen jiù méiyǒu nánguāpài kěyǐ chī le.

（你去了超级市场 nǐ qùle chāojí shìchǎng）

1. **A:** 我的头痛得要命，你可以帮我买药吗？

Wǒde tóu tòngde yào mìng, nǐ kěyǐ bāng wǒ mǎi yào ma?

   B: ＿＿，要不然等我买到药，你的头就痛死了。

   ＿＿, yàobùrán děng wǒ mǎidào yào, nǐde tóu jiù tòng sǐle.

   （我这里有药 wǒ zhèlǐ yǒu yào）

2. **A:** 啊，我忘了跟你说，我不吃海鲜。 A, wǒ wàngle gēn nǐ shuō, wǒ bùchī hǎixiān.

   B: ＿＿，要不然我打算(*to plan*)点鱼、虾和牡蛎。

   ＿＿, yàobùrán wǒ dǎsuàn diǎn yú, xiā hé mǔlì.

   （你点菜以前跟我说 nǐ diǎncài yǐqián gēn wǒ shuō）

3. **A:** 咦，这不是你写好的功课吗？ Yí, zhè búshì nǐ xiěhǎo de gōngkè ma?

   B: ＿＿，要不然我得再写一次。 ＿＿, yàobùrán wǒ děi zài xiě yícì.

   （你找到了 nǐ zhǎodào le）

4. **A:** 这瓶牛奶已经过期(*expired*)了，不能喝了。

Zhèipíng niúnǎi yǐjīng guòqī le, bùnéng hē le.

   B: ＿＿，要不然我喝了一定拉肚子。 ＿＿, yàobùrán wǒ hēle yídìng lā dùzi.

   （你看了日期 nǐ kànle rìqī）

5. **A:** 你饿了吧？这里有几包(*pack*)零食，拿去吧。 Nǐ èle ba? Zhèlǐ yǒu jǐbāo língshí, ná qù ba.

   B: ＿＿，要不然晚上十二点，我真不知道要去哪里买吃的东西。

   ＿＿, yàobùrán wǎnshàng shí'èrdiǎn, wǒ zhēn bù zhīdào yào qù nǎlǐ mǎi chīde dōngxi.

   （你有零食 nǐ yǒu língshí）

12 大家都爱中国菜 **Dàjiā Dōu Ài Zhōngguó Cài** / *Everyone loves Chinese food*

Search on the Internet or in a cookbook to find a recipe for a Chinese dish. Copy down the recipe, including all the ingredients and instructions. Share your recipe with the rest of the class, showing a photo of the dish if possible.

13 食谱 **Shípǔ** / *Recipe*

This is a recipe of a famous Chinese dish, Yangzhou Fried Rice. Read the recipe and answer the questions that follow.

扬州炒饭
Yángzhōu Chǎofàn

材料 cáiliào:

米饭250克(*gram*)，火腿(*ham*)30克，
鸡蛋1个，豌豆(*peas*)20克，黄瓜20克，
虾仁25克，新鲜玉米粒20克。

Mǐfàn liǎngbǎi wǔshí kè, huǒtuǐ sānshíkè,
jīdàn yíge, wāndòu èrshíkè, huángguā èrshíkè,
xiārén èrshíwǔkè, xīnxiān yùmǐ lì èrshíkè.

调味料 tiáowèiliào:

色拉油1匙，盐1匙 sèlāyóu yìchí, yán yìchí
味精和葱花(*minced green onion*) wèijīng hé cōnghuā

做法 zuòfǎ:

1. 先把豌豆、黄瓜、虾仁洗净，再把火腿、黄瓜、虾仁都切成小丁。
   Xiān bǎ wāndòu、huángguā、xiārén xǐjìng, zài bǎ huǒtuǐ、huángguā、xiārén dōu qiē chéng xiǎo dīng.

2. 鸡蛋打散以后，放入油锅中炒熟、切碎。
   Jīdàn dǎ sǎn yǐhòu, fàng rù yóu guō zhōng chǎo shú、qiē suì.

3. 在锅中放适量油，开大火烧热，然后加入葱花、火腿、豌豆、虾仁、黄瓜、玉米粒，翻炒至熟。
   Zài guō zhōng fàng shíliàng yóu, kāi dà huǒ shāo rè, jiārù cōnghuā、huǒtuǐ、wāndòu、xiārén、huángguā, yùmǐ lì, fān chǎo zhì shú.

4. 加入米饭和炒好的鸡蛋，再撒上味精、盐，翻炒均匀就可以了。
   Jiārù mǐfàn hé chǎo hǎode jīdàn, zài sǎ shàng wèijīng、yán, fān chǎo jūnyún jiù kěyǐ le.

1. 哪几个材料要切得很小？　Něi jǐge cáiliào yào qiēde hěn xiǎo?
2. 哪几个材料需要二十克？　Něi jǐge cáiliào xūyào èrshíkè?
3. 米饭什么时候放到锅子里？　Mǐfàn shénme shíhou fàng dào guōzi lǐ?
4. 鸡蛋是和米饭一起炒熟的吗？　Jīdàn shì hé mǐfàn yìqǐ chǎo shú de ma?
5. 做扬州炒饭需要什么调料？　Zuò Yángzhōu chǎofàn xūyào shénme tiáoliào?

自我提升 Zìwǒ Tíshēng

Raising the Bar

Vocabulary

大	dà	*adv.*	*greatly; fully*
显	xiǎn	*v.*	*to show; to display*
身手	shēnshǒu	*n.*	*skill; talent*

大显身手
dà xiǎn shēnshǒu
To show one's talents

▲ 大显身手

Language Note

The phrase 身手 *shēnshǒu* in this idiom does not refer to one's body and limbs—it refers to talents and special skills. The idiom is used to express the idea of displaying one's talents for all to see.

等一下的棒球比赛，你们看我大显身手吧！
Děng yíxià de lánqiú bǐsài, nǐmen kàn wǒ dà xiǎn shēnshǒu ba!
Later, when the basketball game begins, watch me show off my skills!

做中国菜

今天第一次做了中国菜，我开始对做中国菜非常有兴趣。中国菜看起来不容易做，但是如果做菜以前把材料都准备好的话，做起来其实[1]一点儿也不难。中国菜最常用的烹调方式是"炒"，炒就是在大火[2]上做菜。炒以前通常要把东西先切一切，每道菜都有不一样的切法[3]。因为东西已经切得比较小了，所以炒的时候，手得动得很快，要不然菜很容易焦[4]。炒的菜做起来很快，通常只要三到五分钟，一盘热热的菜就可以做好了。

[1]其实: in fact　[2]火: fire　[3]法: method　[4]焦: charred

Zuò Zhōngguó Cài

Jīntiān dì-yīcì zuòle Zhōngguó cài, wǒ kāishǐ duì zuò Zhōngguó cài fēicháng yǒu xìngqù. Zhōngguó cài kànqǐlái bù róngyì zuò, dànshì rúguǒ zuòcài yǐqián bǎ cáiliào dōu zhǔnbèi hǎo de huà, zuòqǐlái qíshí yìdiǎnr yě bùnán. Zhōngguó cài zuì cháng yòngde pēngtiáo fāngshì shì "chǎo", chǎo jiù shì zài dà huǒ shàng zuòcài. Chǎo yǐqián tōngcháng yào bǎ dōngxi xiān qiēyìqiē, měidào cài dōu yǒu bù yíyàng de qiēfǎ. Yīnwèi dōngxi yǐjīng qiēde bǐjiào xiǎo le, suǒyǐ chǎode shíhòu, shǒu děi dòngde hěn kuài, yàobùrán cài hěn róngyì jiāo. Chǎode cài zuòqǐlái hěn kuài, tōngcháng zhǐ yào sān dào wǔfēn zhōng, yìpán rèrè de cài jiù kěyǐ zuòhǎo le.

14 通晓文意　Tōngxiǎo Wényì ⟋ *Understanding the Passage*

Read the above passage and decide if the statements are true or false. Correct any false statements.

1. 今天是作者(*writer*)第一次做中国菜。　Jīntiān shì zuòzhě dì-yīcì zuò Zhōngguó cài.

2. 中国菜看起来不难做，但是做起来非常难。
   Zhōngguó cài kànqǐlái bù nán zuò, dànshì zuòqǐlái fēicháng nán.

3. 中国菜最常用的烹调方式是烤。
   Zhōngguó cài zuì cháng yòng de pēngtiáo fāngshì shì kǎo.

4. 炒就是在小火上慢慢煮。　Chǎo jiù shì zài xiǎo huǒ shàng mànmàn zhǔ.

5. 每道菜的切法都不一样。　Měidào cài de qiēfǎ dōu bù yíyàng.

6. 炒的时候，手得动得很快，因为怕东西焦。
   Chǎo de shíhou, shǒu děi dòng de hěn kuài, yīnwèi pà dōngxi jiāo.

手 ■ shǒu ■ hand

The character 手 *shǒu* is a pictograph. The Oracle Bones Script for hand 手 shows a person's palm with lines branching out for fingers. The modern 手 character is also a common radical for hand-related words. When 手 *shǒu* is used as a radical, it can be also written as 扌.

Stroke Order

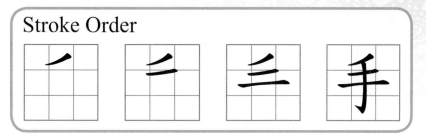

15 词汇延伸 **Cíhuì Yánshēn** / *Vocabulary Builder*

Below are characters that combine with 手 *shǒu* to create new words. Match the Chinese words on the left with the appropriate English meaning on the right.

套 tào	工 gōng	心 xīn	术 shù	势 shì
n. cover	*n. work*	*n. heart*	*n. technique*	*v. sign*

1. 手套 shǒutào   A. gesture
2. 手工 shǒugōng   B. surgical operation
3. 手心 shǒuxīn   C. handcraft
4. 手术 shǒushù   D. gloves
5. 手势 shǒu shì   E. palm

16 汉字侦探 **Hànzì Zhēntàn** / *Visual Detective*

Can you find 手 in the following pictures?

Unit 6

夏天到了

Xiàtiān Dào Le

In this unit you will be able to:

- talk about making a plan
- make comparisons and giving comments
- express a person's willingness to do something
- talk about past experiences and give examples
- express compliments and reply to other's compliments

Lesson A

🔊 邮局 Yóujú *The Post Office*

邮递员 (郵遞員)
yóudìyuán
n. mailman

信箱
xìnxiāng
n. mailbox

邮箱
yóuxiāng
n. postbox

明信片
míngxìnpiàn
n. postcard

包裹
bāoguǒ
n. parcel; package

🔊 信 Xìn *A Letter*

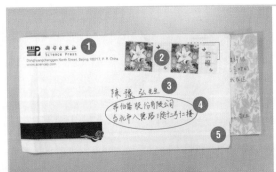

1. 寄信人地址 jìxìnrén dìzhǐ *n. sender's address*
2. 邮票 (郵票) yóupiào *n. (postage) stamp*
3. 收信人 shōuxìnrén *n. mail recipient*
4. 收信人地址 shōuxìnrén dìzhǐ *n. recipient's address*
5. 信封 xìnfēng *n. envelope*

🔊 邮件 Yóujiàn *Post / Mail*

平信	快信	挂号信 (掛號信)	航空信
píngxìn	kuàixìn	guàhàoxìn	hángkōngxìn
regular mail	*express mail*	*registered mail*	*airmail*

🔊 世界城市 Shìjiè Chéngshì *Cities Around the World*

旧金山 (舊金山)
Jiùjīnshān
n. San Francisco

洛杉矶 (洛杉磯)
Luòshānjī
n. Los Angeles

纽约 (紐約)
Niǔyuē
n. New York (City)

**华盛顿特区
(華盛頓特區)**
Huáshèngdùn Tèqū
n. Washington D.C.

伦敦 (倫敦)
Lúndūn
n. London

巴黎
Bālí
n. Paris

柏林
Bólín
n. Berlin

罗马 (羅馬)
Luómǎ
n. Rome

北京
Běijīng
n. Beijing

首尔 (首爾)
Shǒu'ěr
n. Seoul

东京 (東京)
Dōngjīng
n. Tokyo

上海
Shànghǎi
n. Shanghai

台北
Táiběi

n. Taipei

香港
Xiānggǎng

n. Hong Kong

曼谷
Màngǔ

n. Bangkok

悉尼
Xīní

n. Sydney

🔊 **住宿 Zhùsù** *Accommodation*

饭店
fàndiàn
hotel

旅馆 (旅館)
lǚguǎn
motel

**家庭旅馆
(家庭旅館)**
jiātíng lǚguǎn
*B&B (bed and
breakfast)*

**青年旅馆
(青年旅館)**
qīngnián lǚguǎn
youth hostel

Culture Note

旅馆 *lǚguǎn* is just a place for people to stay overnight and it has nothing except for a room. 饭店 *fàndiàn* is a bigger complex which has many facilities, like gyms, swimming pools, meeting rooms, and restaurants, for lodgers to use.

A: 你怎么一到家就喝冰水？（你怎麼一到家就喝冰水？）

Nǐ zěnme yí dào jiā jiù hē bīngshuǐ? *Why did you drink cold water as soon as you got home?*

B: 今天外面热得不得了，我想有一百度吧。

（今天外面熱得不得了，我想有一百度吧。）

Jīntiān wàimian rè de bùdéliǎo, wǒ xiǎng yǒu yìbǎidù ba.

It's so hot outside today. I think it must be a hundred degrees!

A: 最近蔬菜越来越贵。（最近蔬菜越來越貴。）

Zuìjìn shūcài yuè lái yuè guì. *Vegetables are getting more and more expensive lately.*

B: 为什么？最近没有大雨或大雪呀。（為什麼？最近沒有大雨或大雪呀。）

Wèishénme? Zuìjìn méiyǒu dàyǔ huò dàxuě ya.

Why? It hasn't rained or snowed a lot recently.

A: 今天是最后一科了，考完试你打算做什么？

（今天是最後一科了，考完試你打算做什麼？）

Jīntiān shì zuìhòu yīkē le, kǎo wán shì nǐ dǎsuàn zuò shénme?

We have our last final exam today, what do you plan to do after the exam?

B: 我昨天念书念到三点半，所以一考完试，我就要回家睡觉。

（我昨天念書今到三點半，所以一考完試，我就要回家睡覺。）

Wǒ zuótiān niànshū niàn dào sāndiǎn bàn, suǒyǐ yì kǎowán shì, wǒ jiùyào huíjiā shuìjiào.

I stayed up studying last night until three-thirty in the morning, so as soon as the exam is over, I'm going home to sleep.

A: 我要吃夜宵，你要不要也来一点？

（我要吃夜宵，你要不要也來一點？）

Wǒ yào chī yèxiāo, nǐ yào bú yào yě lái yìdiǎn?

I'm going to have a late-night snack. Do you want anything?

B: 不用，谢谢。我从来不在晚上十点以后吃东西。

（不用，謝謝。我從來不在晚上十點以後吃東西。）

Búyòng, xièxie. Wǒ cónglái bú zài wǎnshang shídiǎn yǐhòu chī dōngxi.

No, thanks. I never eat after 10 at night.

Adjectives

认真 (認真)	rènzhēn	serious; conscientious
用功	yònggōng	hardworking; studious; diligent
最后 (最後)	zuìhòu	last; final
不过 (不過)	búguò	but
国内 (國內)	guónèi	national; domestic
国外 (國外)	guówài	abroad; overseas
合理	hélǐ	reasonable

Adverbs

不得了	bùdéliǎo	extremely; exceedingly
从来 (從來)	cónglái	always; all along
只好	zhǐhǎo	have (no choice but) to

Measure Word

科	kē	(school) subject

Common Expressions

越来越…	yuè lái yuè…	more and more…
越…越…	yuè…yuè…	the more…, the more…

Nouns

价格 (價格)	jiàgé	price
市区 (市區)	shìqū	downtown
郊区 (郊區)	jiāoqū	suburbs; outskirts
暑假	shǔjià	summer vacation

Verbs

打算	dǎsuàn	to plan
听说 (聽說)	tīngshuō	to be told; to hear of
接近	jiējìn	to be close to; to approach
寄	jì	to send; to mail

1 环游世界 Huányóu Shìjiè / Travel Around the World

Mandy is a world traveler. Listen to her talk about the places she has visited on her travels. Then, on a separate sheet of paper, write down the city letter and the date Mandy was visiting in order from the earliest to the latest.

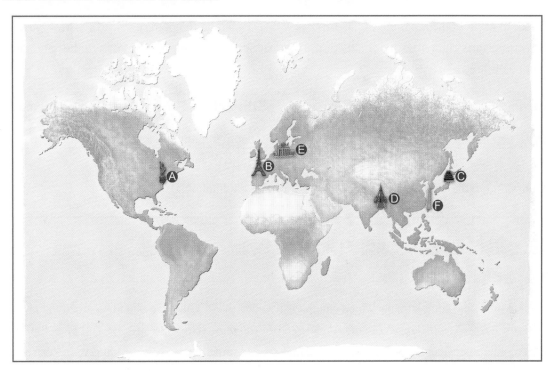

2 对还是错? Duì háishì Cuò? / True or False?

You will hear five statements related to the post office. Say if the statements are true or false.

3 个人问题 Gèrén Wèntí / Personal Questions

Answer the following questions in Chinese based on your own experiences and opinions.

1. 你家前面有邮筒吗? Nǐ jiā qiánmian yǒu yóutǒng ma?
2. 寄信的时候，你通常寄平信还是快信？
   Jì xìn de shíhou, nǐ tōngcháng jì píngxìn háishì kuàixìn?
3. 你最想去哪个城市旅行？ Nǐ zuì xiǎng qù něige chéngshì lǚxíng?
4. 你是一个用功的学生吗？ Nǐ shì yíge yònggōng de xuésheng ma?
5. 你家附近的邮局怎么走？ Nǐ jiā fùjìn de yóujú zěnme zǒu?
6. 你今年暑假打算做什么？ Nǐ jīnnián shǔjià dǎsuàn zuò shénme?

The Pattern 一...就... *yī...jiù...* to Show Imminent Action

When we want to express the meaning of "as soon as VP₁, VP₂," then the pattern 一...就... *yī...jiù...* is applied. The second action starts right after the first action. If the subjects of these two clauses are the same, either of the subjects may be omitted.

> **Subject 1** + 一 *yī* + **Verb Phrase 1** ， **Subject 2** + 就 *jiù* + **Verb Phrase 2**

爸爸一到家，妈妈就做饭。 Bàba yí dào jiā, māma jiù zuòfàn.

王太太一到上海，就给王先生打电话。
Wáng tàitai yí dào Shànghǎi, jiù gěi Wáng xiānsheng dǎ diànhuà.

不得了 *bùdéliǎo* as an Intensifying Complement for Adjectives

In Chinese, there are some complements which can intensify adjectives. You have already learned the phrases 死了 *sǐ le* (Unit 2, Lesson A), 极了 *jí le* (Unit 5 Lesson A), 得要命 *de yào mìng* (Unit 5 Lesson B), and 得要死 *de yào sǐ* (Unit 5 Lesson B). Another intensifier is 不得了 *bùdéliǎo*, which means something like "exceedingly" or "extremely."

> **Adjective** + 得 *de* + 不得了 *bùdéliǎo*

航空挂号包裹贵得不得了，我们还是别寄了。
Hángkōng guàhào bāoguǒ guìde bùdéliǎo, wǒmen háishì bié jì le.

在中国，新年的时候，火车站里人多得不得了，因为大家都要回家过年。
Zài Zhōngguó, xīnnián de shíhou, huǒchēzhàn lǐ rén duōde bùdéliǎo, yīnwèi dàjiā dōu yào huíjiā guò nián.

The Expression 越来越 *yuè lái yuè* to Describe an Increase over Time

The expression 越来越 *yuè lái yuè* is used to describe something—such as a quality or feeling—that increases with time. 越来越 *yuè lái yuè* can be translated as "more and more."

> **Subject** + 越来越 *yuè lái yuè* + **Adjective**

弟弟越来越用功了。 Dìdi yuè lái yuè yònggōng le.

夏天到了，天气越来越热。 Xiàtiān dào le, tiānqì yuè lái yuè rè.

In addition to adjectives, verbs with objects can also follow 越来越 *yuè lái yuè*. However, note that only certain verbs can be used in this way. These include 懂 *dǒng*, 爱 *ài*, 想 *xiǎng*, and 喜欢 *xǐhuan*.

Subject + 越来越 *yuè lái yuè* + **Verb** + **Object**

学生们越来越喜欢写中国字。　Xuéshengmen yuè lái yuè xǐhuan xiě Zhōngguó zì.

吃了药以后，我越来越想睡觉。　Chīle yào yǐhòu, wǒ yuè lái yuè xiǎng shuìjiào.

The Correlative Conjunctions 越...越... *yuè...yuè...*

The 越...越... *yuè...yuè...* pattern can be translated as "the more..., the more...." It indicates that as one quality or action increases, so does another. What follows 越 *yuè* can be an adjective or a verb phrase.

Subject + 越 *yuè* + **Adjective 1 / Verb Phrase 1** + 越 *yuè* +

Adjective 2 / Verb Phrase 2

通常房子越接近市区越贵。　Tōngcháng fángzi yuè jiējìn shìqū yuè guì.

这本书很有意思，我越读越喜欢。　Zhèiběn shū hěn yǒu yìsi, wǒ yuè dú yuè xǐhuan.

The pattern can also used with two different subjects.

Subject 1 + 越 *yuè* + **Adjective 1 / Verb Phrase 1** ，　**Subject 2** +

越 *yuè* + **Adjective 2 / Verb Phrase 2**

我喜欢冷的天气，所以天气越冷，我觉得越舒服。
Wǒ xǐhuan lěng de tiānqì, suǒyǐ tiānqì yuè lěng, wǒ juéde yuè shūfu.

你别买零食了，你买得越多，孩子吃得越多。
Nǐ bié mǎi língshí le, nǐ mǎide yuè duō, háizi chīde yuè duō.

The Expression 从来不 *cónglái bù*

The expression 从来不 *cónglái bù* is used to indicate something that a person never does. It can be shortened to 从不... *cóng bù*....

▲ 我喜欢冷的天气。

Subject + 从(来)不 *cóng(lái) bù* + **Verb Phrase**

奶奶不喜欢晚睡，所以她从来不在十一点以后睡觉。
Nǎinai bù xǐhuan wǎn shuì, suǒyǐ tā cónglái bú zài shíyīdiǎn yǐhòu shuìjiào.

我们家从不吃罐头。　Wǒmen jiā cóng bù chī guàntou.

◀) **准备考试 Zhǔnbèi Kǎoshì** *Preparing for Exams*

Wu Sen is reading a book in the library.

赵梅：	那么认真！我记得你一看书就想睡觉。	Zhào Méi:	Nàme rènzhēn! Wǒ jìde nǐ yí kànshū jiù xiǎng shuìjiào.
吴森：	期末考试就要到了，得用功点儿。	Wú Sēn:	Qīmò kǎoshì jiùyào dào le, děi yònggōng diǎnr.
赵梅：	你还有几科要考？	Zhào Méi:	Nǐ hái yǒu jǐkē yào kǎo?
吴森：	明天是最后一科，你呢？	Wú Sēn:	Míngtiān shì zuìhòu yìkē, nǐ ne?
赵梅：	我还有两科，比你多一科。	Zhào Méi:	Wǒ hái yǒu liǎngkē, bǐ nǐ duō yìkē.
吴森：	考完试你打算做什么？	Wú Sēn:	Kǎowán shì nǐ dǎsuàn zuò shénme?
赵梅：	一考完，我就要去旅行。	Zhào Méi:	Yì kǎowán, wǒ jiùyào qù lǚxíng.
吴森：	你要去哪儿旅行？	Wú Sēn:	Nǐ yào qù nǎr lǚxíng?
赵梅：	我要去香港。	Zhào Méi:	Wǒ yào qù Xiānggǎng.
吴森：	我听说香港的饭店贵得不得了。	Wú Sēn:	Wǒ tīngshuō Xiānggǎng de fàndiàn guì de bùdéliǎo.
赵梅：	是不便宜，而且饭店越接近市区，价格越高。不过，现在在国内旅行也越来越贵了。	Zhào Méi:	Shì bù piányi, érqiě fàndiàn yuè jiējìn shìqū, jiàgé yuè gāo. Búguò, xiànzài zài guónèi lǚxíng yě yuè lái yuè guì le.
吴森：	我觉得价钱太不合理了，所以我从来不在暑假旅行。	Wú Sēn:	Wǒ juéde jiàqián tài bù hélǐ le, suǒyǐ wǒ cónglái bú zài shǔjià lǚxíng.
赵梅：	那你等我从香港给你寄明信片吧！	Zhào Méi:	Nà nǐ děng wǒ cóng Xiānggǎng gěi nǐ jì míngxìnpiàn ba!
吴森：	也只好这样啦。	Wú Sēn:	Yě zhǐhǎo zhèyàng la.

4 贵得不得了 Guìde bùdéliǎo / *Way Too Expensive*

Pick out what Wu Sen heard is expensive in Hong Kong, according to the dialogue.

A.  B.  C.  D.

5 纪念品 Jìniànpǐn / *Souvenir*

According to the dialogue, which of the following is Zhao Mei going to send Wu Sen?

A.  B.  C.  D.

6 懂了吗? Dǒngle ma? / *Do you understand?*

Answer the following questions in Chinese.

1. 谁一看书就想睡觉? Shéi yí kànshū jiù xiǎng shuìjiào?
2. 为什么吴森说他最近得用功点儿?
   Wèishénme Wú Sēn shuō tā zuìjìn děi yònggōng diǎnr?
3. 吴森和赵梅还有几科考试? Wú Sēn hé Zhào Méi hái yǒu jǐkē kǎoshì?
4. 赵梅考完试打算做什么? Zhào Méi kǎowán shì dǎsuàn zuò shénme?
5. 赵梅要到哪里去旅行? Zhào Méi yào dào nǎlǐ qù lǚxíng?
6. 赵梅说国内旅行的价钱怎么样? Zhào Méi shuō guónèi lǚxíng de jiàqián zěnmeyàng?
7. 为什么吴森从来不在暑假旅行? Wèishénme Wú Sēn cónglái bú zài shǔjià lǚxíng?
8. 赵梅要给吴森寄什么东西? Zhào Méi yào gěi Wú Sēn jì shénme dōngxi?

Hong Kong

Situated on the southern coast of China where the Pearl River Delta meets the South China Sea, Hong Kong has long been a key port in Asia. Today it is also a powerful financial center, and, with a population of more than seven million in an area of just 1,104 square kilometers (426 square miles), one of the most densely populated regions on the planet. Visitors to the city often have the impression of being surrounded by skyscrapers—the tallest being the 88-floor International Finance Centre (IFC), standing at 416.8 meters (1367 feet). The IFC is one of Hong Kong's landmarks, and apart from being the tallest building in the city, it is also one of the tallest in the world. The majority of Hong Kong's residents are Chinese and speak Cantonese or Mandarin. However, because of Hong Kong's history as a British colony, English is also one of the official languages. It is the language spoken by the non-Chinese population, which includes Indians, Pakistanis, Canadians, Americans, Europeans, and others working in the bustling financial center.

▲ *The regional flag of the Hong Kong Special Administrative Region of the People's Republic of China stands abreast with the national flag of China.*

The British took control of Hong Kong in 1842 after defeating China in the First Opium War, and Hong Kong was not returned to Chinese rule until more than 150 years later, on July 1, 1997. Today, it is governed as a Special Administrative Region, or SAR, which means it maintains a certain amount of autonomy from the central Chinese government. Distinct from mainland China, Hong Kong has its own currency, the Hong Kong dollar (HKD), and a fully capitalist economy.

▲ *High-rise buildings are one of the characteristics of Hong Kong.*

Hong Kong today is an important financial, service and marine transport hub of Asia. Its history has transformed it from a small fishing village of 5,000 people to a metropolis known as the "Oriental Pearl." Its main industries are retail, real estate, banking and financial services, and tourism. Tourists from China and abroad are drawn to Hong Kong for shopping, dining, and sightseeing. Since products sold in the city are duty-free or taxed at a low rate, shoppers can save on high-end goods, and the many years of Western rule have greatly influenced Hong Kong's dining culture, making it one of the best places in the world to taste all kinds of international cuisine. As for sightseeing, there are not only ancient temples and museums, but also theme parks such as Disneyland and Sea World. Hong Kong's sub-tropical climate, with an average temperature of 22.8 degrees Celsius (73 degrees Fahrenheit) year-round, makes it an ideal place to visit any time of the year.

▲ *The amazing night view from the Victoria Peak.*

▲ *Hong Kong has been an important harbor city since the 19th century.*

7 文化动动脑 Wénhuà Dòngdòngnǎo / *Cultural Check-up*

On your own paper, write a short answer in English for each question.

1. Where in China is Hong Kong located?
2. What is the population of Hong Kong?
3. What are the main languages spoken in Hong Kong?
4. In what year did Hong Kong become a colony of Britain?
5. What makes Hong Kong distinct from mainland China?
6. What is a nickname for Hong Kong?
7. What are three reasons tourists are attracted to Hong Kong?

8 马上做！ **Mǎshàng Zuò!** / *Do It Right Away!*

Look at the illustrations and make sentences using the pattern 一…就… *yī…jiù….* Follow the model.

Lìzi: 林小姐一到超市就去乳制品区。

Lín xiǎojiě yí dào chāoshì jiù qù rǔzhìpǐn qū.

1.

2.

3.

4.

5.

6.

9 形容程度 **Xíngróng chéngdù** / *To Describe the Level*

Look at the pictures and complete the sentences using **Adj. + 得不得了** *de bùdéliǎo* to describe the pictures.

1.

公园里的花…。
Gōngyuán lǐ de huā….

3.

他的头…。
Tāde tóu….

5.

要考试了，她…。
Yào kǎoshì le, tā….

2.

今年冬天的雪…。
Jīnnián dōngtiān de xuě….

4.

这个小孩…。
Zhèige xiǎohái….

6.

她的宠物死了，她…。
Tāde chǒngwù sǐ le, tā….

10 程度改变 **Chéngdù gǎibiàn** / *Changes Over Time*

Say what changes in each set of pictures using the pattern 越来越… *yuè lái yuè*….

1.

2013年　2014年　2015年
$2.5　$3　$3.5

3.

十岁　十一岁　十二岁

5.

2.

四月　六月　八月

4.

6.
100km　120km　140km

11 相互影响 **Xiānghù Yǐngxiǎng** / *Mutual Influence*

Complete the following sentences using 越…越… *yuè…yuè….* Follow the model.

Lìzi: 美美很难过，我跟她说别难过，可是<u>我越说，她越难过。</u>

Měiměi hěn nánguò, wǒ gēn tā shuō bié nánguò, kěshì <u>wǒ yuè shuō, tā yuè nánguò.</u>

1. 她很生气，我跟她说别生气，可是…

   Tā hěn shēngqì, wǒ gēn tā shuō bié shēngqì, kěshì…

2. 我用电脑的时候手会痛，医生叫我最近不要用电脑，他说…

   Wǒ yòng diànnǎo de shíhou shǒu huì tòng, yīshēng jiào wǒ zuìjìn bú yào yòng diànnǎo, tā shuō…

3. 这个孩子真不听话，我叫他不要做的事，他就是要做，而且…

   Zhèige háizi zhēn bù tīnghuà, wǒ jiào tā bú yào zuò de shì, tā jiù shì yào zuò, érqiě…

4. 小狗长大了，他以前吃得不多，现在…

   Xiǎogǒu zhǎngdà le, tā yǐqián chīde bù duō, xiànzài…

5. 新的一年就要到了，大家都很兴奋。我们正在等新年倒数
   (*count down*)，大家…

   Xīn de yìnián jiù yào dào le, dàjiā dōu hěn xīngfèn. Wǒmen zhèng zài děng xīnnián dàoshǔ, dàjiā…

12 有原则 **Yǒu Yuánzé** / *Having Principles*

With a classmate, use the expression 从来不 *cónglái bù* to ask and answer the following questions.

Lìzi: 上课的时候，你从来不打瞌睡吗？

Shàngkè de shíhou, nǐ cónglái bù dǎ kēshuì ma?

A: 上课的时候，你从来不打瞌睡吗？

Shàngkè de shíhou, nǐ cónglái bù dǎ kēshuì ma?

B: 对，上课的时候，我从来不打瞌睡。

Duì, shàngkè de shíhou, wǒ cónglái bù dǎ kēshuì.

OR，不，上课的时候，我有时候打瞌睡。

Bù, shàngkè de shíhou, wǒ yǒushíhou dǎ kēshuì.

1. 你从来不吃胡萝卜吗？ Nǐ cónglái bù chī húluóbo ma?

2. 你从来不自己做饭吗？ Nǐ cónglái bú zìjǐ zuòfàn ma?

3. 你从来不写信，只打电话吗？ Nǐ cónglái bù xiě xìn, zhǐ dǎ diànhuà ma?

4. 吃薯条的时候，你从来不加盐吗？ Chī shǔtiáo de shíhou, nǐ cónglái bù jiā yán ma?

5. 考试以前，你从来不玩游戏机吗？ Kǎoshì yǐqián, nǐ cónglái bù wán yóuxì ma?

6. 感冒的时候，你从来不去诊所看病吗？

   Gǎnmào de shíhou, nǐ cónglái bú qù zhěnsuǒ kànbìng ma?

Kāikǒu Shuō

Communication

13 旅行地点大调查 **Lǚxíng Dìdiǎn Dà Diàochá** / *A Survey on Travel Destinations*

On a separate sheet of paper, draw a table like the one below. Conduct a survey to find the foreign city most of your classmates want to visit. In the table, write the names of five cities, then ask ten of your classmates for their most-wanted-visit city. Share your findings with the class.

Lìzi:

A: 你最想去哪个城市？ Nǐ zuì xiǎng qù něige chéngshì?

B: 我最想去巴黎。 Wǒ zuì xiǎng qù Bālí.

·············

A: 六个人最想去巴黎，两个人最想去伦敦，一个人最想去北京。
Liùge rén zuì xiǎng qù Bālí, liǎngge rén zuì xiǎng qù Lúndūn, yíge rén zuì xiǎng qù Běijīng.

北京 Běijīng	东京 Dōngjīng	伦敦 Lúndūn	巴黎 Bālí	罗马 Luómǎ
			B	

▲ 巴黎

Read the travel itinerary below and answer the questions that follow.

真棒旅行社

四天三夜香港游（海洋公园+自由活动）价格：2480

行程安排

第一天　北京-香港

北京首都国际机场集合，香港有名建筑——青马大桥（不下车）、
潜水湾（20分钟），海洋公园（2-3小时），
晚上到太平山看香港夜景（15分钟）

第二天　香港

游览黄大仙神祠（30分钟），珠宝及名表店（2-3小时），
九龙国际免税店（1-2小时），特别赠送：搭船游览维多利亚港（40分钟）

第三天　香港

全天自由活动

第四天　香港-北京

香港国际机场集合，回家。

1. 这是从哪里到哪里玩的行程(schedule)？　Zhè shì cóng nǎlǐ dào nǎlǐ wán de xíngchéng?

2. 第一天晚上会去哪个地方？　Dì-yītiān wǎnshang huì qù něi ge dìfang?

3. 哪一天可以去自己想去的地方？　Nǎ yìtiān kěyǐ qù zìjǐ xiǎng qù de dìfang?

4. 回家的时候在哪个机场集合(to assemble)？　Huíjiā de shíhou zài něi ge jīchǎng jíhé?

5. 参加这个行程要多少钱？　Cānjiā zhèige xíngchéng yào duōshǎo qián?

6. 这四天会坐哪些交通工具？　Zhè sìtiān huì zuò nǎxiē jiāotōng gōngjù?

7. 哪个地方大家只能在车上看？　Něige dìfang dàjiā zhǐ néng zài chē shàng kàn?

自我提升 Zìwǒ Tíshēng

Raising the Bar

Vocabulary

苦   kǔ   n. 辛苦 xīnkǔ, *hardship*

甘   gān   n. 甜 tián, *sweetness*

先苦后甘

xiān kǔ hòu gān

Bitterness before sweetness

▲ 先苦后甘

Language Note

When tea is made, the first cup always tastes bitter because the taste of tea is stronger. As more cups are brewed, the tea leaves lose their strong flavor, and each cup of tea is sweeter and milder than the last. This idiom is often used to encourage people to stay optimistic when facing the obstacles in life, because things will get better.

练习网球虽然辛苦，但是我相信"先苦后甘"，明天的比赛一定能有好成绩。

Liànxí wǎngqiú suīrán xīnkǔ, dànshì wǒ xiāngxìn "xiān kǔ hòu gān", míngtiān de bǐsài yídìng néng yǒu hǎo chéngjì.

The training I need to do for tennis is hard, but I believe that "bitterness comes before sweetness" and tomorrow's match will be in my favor.

Other idioms that use "先 *xiān*…后 *hòu*…" include the following.

1. 先人后己 *xiān rén hòu jǐ:* "Put others before oneself."
2. 先礼后兵 *xiān lǐ hòu bīng:* "Manners before violence." 礼 *lǐ* means manners, and 兵 *bīng* refers to violence. This idiom means that one should try to solve problems with others politely first before resorting to violence.

我的暑假

今年暑假我打算跟朋友一起去旅行，我们本来想去夏威夷[1]，但是因为我们找不到便宜的机票[2]，所以我们只好去近一点的城市。本来我们想去纽约，可是纽约的住宿贵得不得了，所以最后我们决定去魁北克[3]。虽然那里的消费[4]也不便宜，但是我们找到了一间又大又便宜的家庭旅馆。从我们住的地方开去魁北克只要三个小时，路上风景很美，直直的路开起来很舒服。我们在那里玩了三天，玩得非常开心，玩得我们都不想回家了呢！

[1]夏威夷: Hawaii   [2]机票: plane ticket   [3]魁北克: Quebec   [4]消费: expense

Wǒde Shǔjià

Jīnnián shǔjià wǒ dǎsuàn gēn péngyou yìqǐ qù lǚxíng, wǒmen běnlái xiǎng qù Xiàwēiyí, dànshì yīnwèi wǒmen zhǎobùdào piányi de jīpiào, suǒyǐ wǒmen zhǐhǎo qù jìn yìdiǎn de chéngshì. Běnlái wǒmen xiǎng qù Niǔyuē, kěshì Niǔyuē de zhùsù guìde bùdéliǎo, suǒyǐ zuìhòu wǒmen juédìng qù Kuíběikè. Suīrán nàlǐ de xiāofèi yě bù piányi, dànshì wǒmen zhǎodàole yījiān yòu dà yòu piányi de lǚguǎn. Cóng wǒmen zhù de dìfang kāiqù Kuíběikè zhǐ yào sānge xiǎoshí, lù shàng fēngjǐng hěn měi, zhízhí de lù kāiqilai hěn shūfu. Wǒ men zài nàlǐ wánle sāntiān, wánde fēicháng kāixīn, wánde wǒmen dōu bù xiǎng huíjiā le ne!

15 通晓文意 Tōngxiǎo Wényì / *Understanding the Passage*

Read the above passage and decide if the statements are true or false. Correct any false statements.

1. 他们没有去夏威夷是因为他们不敢坐飞机。

   Tāmen méiyǒu qù Xiàwēiyí shì yīnwèi tāmen bù gǎn zuò fēijī.

2. 因为要去近一点的城市，所以他们去了纽约。

   Yīnwèi yào qù jìn yìdiǎn de chéngshì, suǒyǐ tāmen qùle Niǔyuē.

3. 纽约的住宿价格非常高。   Nǔyuē de zhùsù jiàgé fēicháng gāo.

4. 他们最后去了魁北克，因为那里的消费很便宜。

   Tmen zuìhòu qù le Kuíběikè, yīnwèi nàlǐ de xiāofèi hěn piányi

5. 他们在魁北克住的地方是一间又大又便宜的家庭旅馆。

   Tāmen zài Kuíběikè zhù de dìfang shì yìjiān yòu dà yòu piányi de jiātíng lǚguǎn.

6. 从他们的家开车去魁北克要三个小时。

   Cóng tāmen de jiā kāiqù Kuíběikè yào sānge xiǎoshí.

汉字天地 Hànzì Tiāndì

Chinese Characters

行 ■ xíng ■ to walk

The character 行 *xíng* is a pictograph. In ancient times, it was drawn as a crossroads. Its original meaning was road, but as people walk on roads, the meaning of 行 *xíng* was extended to represent "to walk," and "to travel."

Stroke Order

16 词汇延伸 Cíhuì Yánshēn / *Vocabulary Builder*

Below are some characters that can be combined with 行 *xíng* to create words. Match the Chinese words on the left with the English meaning on the right.

人 rén *n. people*	礼 lǐ *n. courtesy*	期 qī *n. date*	动 dòng *v. to move*	政 zhèng *n. politics*

1. 行人 xíngrén   A. date of departure
2. 行礼 xínglǐ   B. pedestrian
3. 行期 xíngqī   C. administration
4. 行动 xíngdòng   D. action
5. 行政 xíngzhèng   E. to salute

17 汉字侦探 Hànzì Zhēntàn / *Visual Detective*

Can you find 行 in the following pictures?

Lesson B

词汇 Cíhuì
Vocabulary

🔊 **暑期工作和活动 Shǔqī Gōngzuò hé Huódòng**
Works and Activities in Summer Vacation Time

看孩子 kān háizi
v.o. to look after kids

实习（實習）shíxí
v. to intern

实习生（實習生）
shíxíshēng   *n. intern*

露营（露營）
lùyíng
v./n. to camp; camping

夏令营（夏令營）
xiàlìngyíng

n. summer camp

游学（遊學）yóuxué
v. to study abroad

游学团（遊學團）
yóuxuétuán

n. overseas study group

度假
dùjià

v. to go on vacation

🔊 在快餐店 Zài Kuàicāndiàn *In a Fast-Food Restaurant*

玉米汤 (玉米湯)
yùmǐtāng
n. corn soup

鸡块 (雞塊)
jīkuài
n. chicken nugget

洋葱圈
yángcōngquān
n. onion ring

百吉饼 (百吉餅)
bǎijíbǐng
n. bagel

松饼 (鬆餅)
sōngbǐng
n. muffin

煎饼
jiānbǐng
n. pancake

威化饼 (威化餅)
wēihuàbǐng
n. waffle

比萨饼 (比薩餅)
bǐsàbǐng
n. pizza

蕃茄酱 (蕃茄醬)
fānqiéjiàng
n. ketchup

辣椒油
làjiāoyóu
n. Tabasco sauce

餐巾纸 (餐巾紙)
cānjīnzhǐ
n. napkin

吸管
xīguǎn
n. straw

打包袋
dǎbāodài
n. doggie bag

餐盘 (餐盤)
cānpán
n. tray

快餐盒
kuàicānhé
n. to-go box

塑料袋
sùliàodài
n. plastic bag

A: 你去过法国吗？（你去過法國嗎？）

Nǐ qù guò Fǎguó ma? *Have you been to France?*

B: 我从来没去过。去年我朋友从法国寄了一张明信片给我，好美！有机会我真想去看看。（我從來沒去過。去年我朋友從法國寄了一張明信片給我，好美！有機會我真想去看看。）

Wǒ cónglái méi qù guò. Qùnián wǒ péngyou cóng Fǎguó jìle yìzhāng míngxìnpiàn gěi wǒ, hǎo měi! Yǒu jīhuì wǒ zhēn xiǎng qù kànkan.

I've never been there. My friend sent me a postcard from France last year, and it was so beautiful! I really want to go if I ever get the chance.

....

A: 别念了，已经十一点了，去睡觉吧。（别念了，已經十一點了，去睡覺吧。）

Bié niàn le, yǐjīng shíyītdiǎn le, qù shuìjiào ba.

Stop studying; it's already 11 p.m. Go to bed.

B: 不要，在没有把这一课念完以前，我是不会去睡觉的。（不要，在沒有把這一課念完以前，我是不會去睡覺的。）

Bú yào, zài méiyǒu bǎ zhè yí kè niàn wán yǐqián, wǒ shì bú huì qù shuìjiào de.

No, I don't want to go to bed until I finish this lesson.

....

A: 你喜欢吃什么海鲜？（你喜歡吃什麼海鮮？）

Nǐ xǐhuan chī shénme hǎixiān? *What seafood do you like?*

B: 三文鱼、龙虾、蚝什么的，我都喜欢。
（三文魚、龍蝦、蚝什麼的，我都喜歡。）

Sānwényú, lóngxiā, háo shénme de, wǒ dōu xǐhuan.

Salmon, lobster, oyster and so on—I like them all!

....

A: 不用问他了，他对电影没兴趣。
（不用問他了，他對電影沒興趣。）

Búyòng wèn tā le, tā duì diànyǐng méi xìngqù.

Don't bother to invite him. He's not interested in movies.

B: 还是问问吧。这部剧情片是今年最棒的电影，他一定会想看的。
（還是問問吧。這部劇情片是今年最棒的電影，他一定會想看的。）

Háishì wènwen ba. Zhè bù jùqíngpiàn shì jīnnián zuì bàng de diànyǐng, tā yídìng huì xiǎng kàn de.

Let's ask him anyway. This drama is the best movie of the year. He'll definitely want to see it.

Nouns

假	jià	holiday; vacation
计划 (計畫)	jìhuà	plan
邻居 (鄰居)	línjū	neighbor
工作	gōngzuò	work

Particle

过 (過)	guò	indicates an action completed or a past experience

Verbs

看	kān	to look after; to take care of
看	kàn	to see; to visit
例如	lìrú	for example; such as
工作	gōngzuò	to work

Verb-Object

放假	fàngjià	to have a holiday or vacation; to have a day off

1 点餐时间 **Diǎncān Shíjiān** / *Time to Order*

🔊 **Four people are ordering their food. As you listen to the recording, write down the menu items they order and calculate how much the order will cost. Follow the model.**

> **Lìzi:** A(1 order), C(2 orders) = 十一块钱 shíyīkuài qián

A. $5

C. $3

E. $6

G. $4.2

B. $4.5

D. $9

F. $2.5

H. $3.5

对还是错? **Duì háishì Cuò?** / *True or False?*

🔊 You will hear four statements related to fast food restaurants. Say if the statements are true or false.

3

个人问题 **Gèrén Wèntí** / *Personal Questions*

Answer the following questions in Chinese based on your own experiences and opinions.

1. 你喜欢暑假吗? 为什么? Nǐ xǐhuan shǔjià ma? Wèishénme?

2. 你看过孩子吗? 如果看过, 你觉得看孩子很有意思吗?
   Nǐ kān guò háizi ma? Rúguǒ kān guò, nǐ juéde kān háizi hěn yǒuyìsi ma?

3. 你知道怎么跟孩子玩吗? Nǐ zhīdào zěnme gēn háizi wán ma?

4. 你在快餐店打过工吗? 你做了多久?
   Nǐ zài kuàicāndiàn dǎ guò gōng ma? Nǐ zuò le duōjiǔ?

5. 你吃快餐吗? Nǐ chī kuàicān ma?

6. 你喜欢吃炸的东西吗? 你特别喜欢什么?
   Nǐ xǐhuan chī zhá de dōngxi ma? Nǐ tèbié xǐhuan shénme?

句型介绍 Jùxíng Jièshào
Language Patterns

The Expression 从来没V过 *cónglái méi V guò*

In the previous lesson, we learned how to use the expression 从来不 *cónglái bù* to talk about something a person never does. In this lesson, 从来没V过 *cónglái méi V guò* is introduced. It means that a person has never had the experience of doing something.

> **Subject** + 从来没 *cónglái méi* + **Verb** + 过 *guò* + **something**

他们从来没打过高尔夫。 Tāmen cónglái méi dǎguò gāo'ěrfū.

我从来没用过筷子, 所以我第一次去中国餐厅吃饭的时候很紧张。
Wǒ cónglái méi yòngguò kuàizi, suǒyǐ wǒ dì-yīcì qù Zhōngguó cāntīng chīfàn de shíhou hěn jǐnzhāng.

The Expression 在没有...以前 *zài méiyǒu...yǐqián*

This expression is used to talk about things a person has never done before and is now doing for the first time. Follow the examples below.

> 在没有 *zài méiyǒu* + **Verb Phrase** + 以前 *yǐqián*, **Sentence**

在没有考完试以前，我不会出去玩。

Zài méiyǒu kǎowán shì yǐqián, wǒ bú huì chūqù wán.

在没有吃中国菜以前，林小姐不知道中国菜这么好吃。

Zài méiyǒu chī Zhōngguó cài yǐqián, Lín xiǎojie bù zhīdào Zhōngguó cài zhème hǎochī.

The Pattern 会...的 *huì...de* to Show Certainty

The auxiliary verb 会 *huì* here indicates future possibility. With the use of 的 *de* at the end of the sentence, it adds a tone of certainty. This pattern is used to talk about something that the speaker thinks will surely happen in the future.

Subject + 会 *huì* + **Adjective / Verb Phrase** + 的 *de*

那本书很有意思，我想你会喜欢的。

Nèiběn shū hěn yǒuyìsi, wǒ xiǎng nǐ huì xǐhuan de.

这么晚了，你别打电子游戏，妈妈会生气的。

Zhème wǎn le, nǐ bié dǎ diànzǐ yóuxì, māma huì shēngqì de.

▲ 你别打电子游戏

The Expression 什么的 *shénme de* to Give Examples

Similar to the word 'etcetera' in English, 什么的 *shénme de* is used at the end of a list of several adjectives, nouns, verbs, or parallel phrases to indicate that more examples could be given. Note that it is a very informal expression.

Adjectives / Nouns / Verbs / Phrases + 什么的 *shénme de*

你喜欢什么运动？ Nǐ xǐhuan shénme yùndòng?

冲浪，瑜珈，有氧运动什么的，我都喜欢。

Chōnglàng, yújiā, yǒuyǎng yùndòng shénme de, wǒ dōu xǐhuan.

吃薯条的时候，我不加调味料，所以盐，蕃茄酱什么的，我都不加。

Chī shǔtiáo de shíhou, wǒ bù jiā tiáowèiliào, suǒyǐ yán, fānqiéjiàng shénme de, wǒ dōu bù jiā.

The Expression 特别是 *tèbié shì* to Create Emphasis

The expression 特别是 *tèbié shì*, similar to the word *especially* in English, is used to introduce things the speaker wants to emphasize. In this pattern, the speaker begins by making a general statement, and then uses 特别是 *tèbié shì* to highlight a particular example.

Statement，特别是 *tèbié shì* + **Nouns / Verbs / Phrases**

泰国一年四季都很热，特别是四月。 Tàiguó yìnián sìjì dōu hěn rè, tèbié shì Sìyuè.

我感冒了，全身都不舒服，特别是喉咙。

Wǒ gǎnmào le, quán shēn dōu bù shūfu, tèbié shì hóulóng.

会话 Huìhuà

Dialogue

🔊 暑假计划 Shǔjià jìhuà *Summer Vacation Plans*

Qian Yongli and Li Yunying talk while waiting for the bus.

钱永利:	放假了！	Qián Yǒnglì:	Fàngjià le!
李云英:	对呀，真开心。	Lǐ Yúnyīng:	Duì ya, zhēn kāixīn.
钱永利:	你有什么暑假计划？	Qián Yǒnglì:	Nǐ yǒu shénme shǔjià jìhuà?
李云英:	我要打工，今年我要帮邻居看孩子，你看过孩子吗？	Lǐ Yúnyīng:	Wǒ yào dǎgōng, jīnnián wǒ yào bāng línjū kān háizi, nǐ kānguò háizi ma?
钱永利:	我从来没看过孩子，我不知道怎么跟孩子玩。	Qián Yǒnglì:	Wǒ cónglái méi kānguò háizi, wǒ bù zhīdào zěnme gēn háizi wán.
李云英:	一点也不难。在没有看过孩子以前，我也不知道怎么跟他们玩，现在就容易多了。你呢？你找了工作了吗？	Lǐ Yúnyīng:	Yìdiǎn yě bù nán. Zài méiyǒu kānguò háizi yǐqián, wǒ yě bù zhīdào zěnme gēn tāmen wán, Xiànzài jiù róngyì duō le. Nǐ ne? Nǐ zhǎole gōngzuò le ma?
钱永利:	我要去快餐店打工，有空来吃吃东西、看看我。	Qián Yǒnglì:	Wǒ yào qù kuàicāndiàn dǎgōng, yǒu kòng lái chīchi dōngxi, kànkan wǒ.
李云英:	看你是可以，但是我是不会吃快餐的。	Lǐ Yúnyīng:	Kàn nǐ shì kěyǐ, dànshì wǒ shì bú huì chī kuàicān de.
钱永利:	所以汉堡、鸡块、玉米汤什么的，你都不吃？	Qián Yǒnglì:	Suǒyǐ hànbǎo, jīkuài, yùmǐtāng shénme de, nǐ dōu bù chī?
李云英:	是的，我不吃，特别是那些炸的东西，例如炸鸡、薯条、洋葱圈。	Lǐ Yúnyīng:	Shì de, wǒ bù chī, tèbié shì nèixiē zhá de dōngxi, lìrú zhájī, shǔtiáo yángcōngquān.
钱永利:	看起来你的暑假会很健康。	Qián Yǒnglì:	Kàn qǐlái nǐde shǔjià huì hěn jiànkāng.
李云英:	没错，希望你的也一样。暑假快乐！	Lǐ Yúnyīng:	Méicuò, xīwàng nǐde yě yíyàng. Shǔjià kuàilè!
钱永利:	暑假快乐！	Qián Yǒnglì:	Shǔjià kuàilè!

4 李云英的暑假工作　**Lǐ Yúnyīng de Shǔjià Gōngzuò** / *Li Yunying's Summer Job*

Pick out what Li Yunying will do as a part-time job in summer based on the dialogue.

A.

B.

C.

5 钱永利的暑假工作　**Qián Yǒnglì de Shǔjià Gōngzuò** / *Qian Yongli's Summer Job*

Pick out what Qian Yongli will do as a part-time job in summer based on the dialogue.

A.

B.

C.

6 懂了吗？　**Dǒngle ma?** / *Do you understand?*

Answer the following questions in Chinese.

1. 他们放假了吗？　Tāmen fàngjià le ma?

2. 李云英有什么暑假计划？　Lǐ Yúnyīng yǒu shénme shǔjià jìhuà?

3. 钱永利知道怎么跟孩子玩吗？李云英呢？
   Qián Yǒnglì zhīdào zěnme gēn háizi wán ma? Lǐ Yúnyīng ne?

4. 钱永利暑假打算做什么？　Qián Yǒnglì shǔjià dǎsuàn zuò shénme?

5. 李云英吃不吃快餐？特别是哪些东西？
   Lǐ Yúnyīng chī bù chī kuàicān? Tèbié shì něixiē dōngxi?

6. 为什么钱永利说李云英的暑假会很健康？
   Wèishénme Qián Yǒnglì shuō Lǐ Yúnyīng de shǔjià huì hěn jiànkāng?

Wénhuà Chúchuāng

Culture Window

Part-Time Jobs in China

Because of the demands of schoolwork, Chinese teenagers rarely work during the academic year. However, some take part-time jobs during summer and winter vacation. Winter vacation is celebrated around the time of the Chinese New Year, usually from late January until the end of February. Summer vacation lasts all of July and August.

There are many ways for students to find jobs in China. For example, there are websites dedicated to recruiting students as temporary workers. Students can also find jobs through a paid agent or through a job ad posted in an employment agency.

Part-time jobs in China are similar to those in the United States. They typically require little or no experience and offer low pay but flexible hours. Young people may work part-time in restaurants as servers, hosts or dishwashers or in retail stores selling such things as clothes or electronics. They may also conduct

▲ *An advertisement for recruiting waiters/ waitresses.*

surveys online or by phone. However, there are some differences between part-time jobs in the U.S. and China. For example, American students often find work delivering pizza or other food, but in China this job is almost nonexistent because few Chinese students own cars and most Chinese restaurants do not offer delivery services. Another difference is that Chinese patrons do not leave tips at restaurants, so a student working in a restaurant receives his or her hourly wages and nothing more.

▲ *Waitress is serving food.*

There are also some jobs that pay better, but naturally, these jobs also require more of their applicants. For instance, students with exceptional academic achievement may be able to tutor during summer vacation. Or, with the right skills, they can model, perform in concerts, or act as tour guides for English-speaking foreigners.

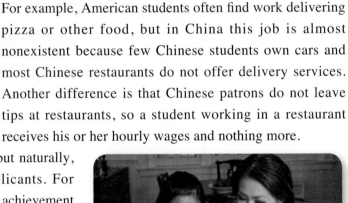

▲ *Tutoring is a popular part-time job for college students.*

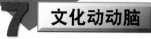

7 文化动动脑 **Wénhuà Dòngdòngnǎo** / *Culture Check-up*

On your own paper, write a short answer in English for each question.

1. During what time of year do most Chinese students work part-time?
2. What are some ways Chinese students can find part-time jobs?
3. What are some popular jobs for students in China?
4. What is one part-time job that Chinese students do not do, and why?
5. Why can't Chinese students earn much money working at a restaurant?
6. What types of part-time jobs have better pay? What requirements are there for such jobs?

语言练习 Yǔyán Liànxí

Language Practice

8 个人经验 **Gèrén Jīngyàn** / *Personal Experience*

With a classmate, take turns asking and answering whether you have ever done the activities pictured below. Depending on your experience, use either the particle 过 *guò* or the expression 从来没V过 *cónglái méi V guò* in your answer. Follow the model.

Lìzi: **A:** 你骑过摩托车吗？ Nǐ qí guò mótuōchē ma?

B: 我骑过。 Wǒ qí guò.

OR, 我从来没骑过。 Wǒ cónglái méi qí guò.

1.

2.

3.

4.

5.

6.

9 说说经验 **Shuōshuo Jīngyàn** / *Talking about Past Experiences*

With a classmate, talk about your past experiences using the expression 在没有…以前 *zài méiyǒu…yǐqián*. Follow the model.

Lìzi: 数学课怎么样？ Shùxuékè zěnmeyàng?

A: 你觉得数学课怎么样？ Nǐ juéde shùxuékè zěnmeyàng?

B: 在没有上数学课以前，我觉得数学很难。但是上了课以后，我觉得数学很有意思。
Zài méiyǒu shàng shùxuékè yǐqián, wǒ juéde shùxué hěn nán. Dànshì shàngle kè yǐhòu, wǒ juéde shùxué hěn yǒuyìsi.

1. 洋葱好吃吗？ Yángcōng hǎochī ma?

2. 做饭难不难？ Zuòfàn nán bù nán?

3. 筷子容易用 (to use) 吗？ Kuàizi róngyì yòng ma?

4. 中文学起来怎么样？ Zhōngwén xuéqǐlái zěnmeyàng?

5. 罐头食物吃起来怎么样？ Guàntou shíwù chīqǐlái zěnmeyàng?

6. 古典乐 (classical music) 听起来怎么样？ Gǔdiǎnyuè tīngqǐlái zěnmeyàng?

10 会怎么样？ **Huì zěnmeyàng?** / *What will it be?*

Complete the following sentences using the pattern 会…的 *huì…de* and the words provided.

1. 这个药不…，你快一点吃。（苦）
Zhèige yào bù…, nǐ kuài yìdiǎn chī. (kǔ)

2. 这个汤面很好吃，你一定…。（喜欢）
Zhèige tāngmiàn hěn hǎochī, nǐ yídìng….(xǐhuan)

3. 外面阴阴的，等一下一定…。（下雨）
Wàimiàn yīnyīn de, děng yíxià yídìng ….(xiàyǔ)

4. 已经八点了，你再不起床，…。（迟到）
Yǐjīng bādiǎn le, nǐ zài bù qǐchuáng, ….(chídào)

5. 你吃得那么少，两个钟头以后一定…。（饿）
Nǐ chīde nàme shǎo, liǎngge zhōngtóu yǐhòu yídìng ….(è)

6. 天气那么冷，你只穿吊带衫和短裤出门，…。（感冒）
Tiānqì nàme lěng, nǐ zhǐ chuān diàodàishān hé duǎnkù chūmén, ….(gǎnmào)

Look at the photos and answer the questions using the expression 什么的 *shénme de*. **Follow the model.**

Lìzi: 你有什么症状？ Nǐ yǒu shénme zhèngzhuàng?

咳嗽，喉咙痛，流鼻涕什么的，我都有。
Késòu, hóulóng tòng, liú bítì shénme de, wǒ dōu yǒu.

1.

他不吃什么蔬菜？
Tā bù chī shénme shūcài?

3.

张先生不能吃海鲜吗？

Zhāng xiānsheng bù néng chī hǎixiān ma?

5.

这个家庭旅馆的房间里面有什么家具？

Zhèige jiātíng lǚguǎn de fángjiān lǐmiàn yǒu shénme jiājù?

2.

他去过哪些城市？
Tā qù guò něixiē chéngshì?

4.

你家附近有什么店？
Nǐ jiā fùjìn yǒu shénme diàn?

6.

你喜欢看什么片？
Nǐ xǐhuan kàn shénme piàn?

Look at the photos and answer the questions using the expression 特别是 *tèbié shì.*

1.

吴晴文喜欢文科还是理科？

Wú Qíngwén xǐhuan wénkē háishì lǐkē?

3.

这个小姐漂亮吗？

Zhèige xiǎojiě piàoliang ma?

5.

这四个男人都很高吗？

Zhèi sìge nánrén dōu hěn gāo ma?

2.

她哪里不舒服？

Tā nǎlǐ bù shūfu?

4.

这三件连衣裙的价钱怎么样？

Zhèi sānjiàn liányīqún de jiàqián zěnmeyàng?

6.

姐姐每天都有很多课吗？

Jiějie měitiān dōu yǒu hěn duō kè ma?

▲ 姐姐每天都有很多课。

13 暑期工作调查 / **Shǔqī gōngzuò diàochá** / *Summer Jobs Survey*

Conduct a survey to learn about your classmates' summer jobs. First, draw a table like the one below. Write five summer jobs in the first column, and then ask eight of your classmates which job they plan to take. Share your findings with the class.

Lìzi:

A: 你暑假要做什么工作? Nǐ shǔjià yào zuò shénme gōngzuò?

B: 我要教邻居的小孩数学。 Wǒ yào jiāo línjū de xiǎohái shùxué.

....

A: 五个人要当 *(to be)* 保姆，三个人要当服务生，两个人要当家教。

Wǔge rén yào dāng bǎomǔ, sānge rén yào dāng fúwùshēng, liǎngge rén yào dāng jiājiào.

Jobs \ Student	B							
保姆 bǎomǔ								
家教 jiājiào	✗							
店员 diànyuán								
服务生 fúwùshēng								
其他 qítā (others)								

Read the employment advertisement below and answer the questions that follow.

快餐店招聘暑期服务员

性别要求：男女皆可

工作地点：真棒快餐店

工作时间：六月底至九月初

工作时数：每日6-8小时

工作经验：不限

年龄要求：18-35岁

工资待遇：5.7-8元/小时

需求人数：15人

联系人：王小姐

联系电话：1521-2567878

1. 如果钱永利想去这家快餐店打工，他应该怎么做？
   Rúguǒ Qián Yǒnglì xiǎng qù zhèijiā kuàicāndiàn dǎgōng, tā yīnggāi zěnme zuò?

2. 这家快餐店需要多少个服务员？ Zhèijiā kuàicāndiàn xūyào duōshǎo ge fúwùyuán?

3. 这个打工只有男生可以去吗？ Zhèige dǎgōng zhǐyǒu nánshēng kěyǐ qù ma?

4. 李小兰今年十七岁，她可以去这家快餐店打工吗？为什么？
   Lǐ Xiǎolán jīnnián shíqīsuì, tā kěyǐ qù zhèijiā kuàicāndiàn dǎgōng ma? Wèishénme?

5. 张苹六月十号开始放假，她最快什么时候可以去工作？
   Zhāng Píng Liùyuè shíhào kāishǐ fàngjià, tā zuìkuài shénme shíhou kěyǐ qù gōngzuò?

6. 钱永利七月和八月在快餐店打工，他一个小时拿六块钱。如果他每天打工六个小时，一个月只休息四天，那他的薪水一共是多少？
   Qián Yǒnglì Qīyuè hé Bāyuè zài kuàicāndiàn dǎgōng, tā yíge xiǎoshí ná liùkuài qián. Rúguǒ tā měitiān dǎgōng liùge xiǎoshí, yíge yuè zhǐ xiūxi sìtiān, nà tāde xīnshuǐ yígòng shì duōshǎo?

自我提升 Zìwǒ Tíshēng

Raising the Bar

Vocabulary

从...中   cóng...zhōng   *prep. from*

从做中学
cóng zuò zhōng xué
learning from doing

▲ 从做中学

Language Note

This idiom is often used when talking about education. It suggests that students must learn by doing things themselves, rather than just by listening to a teacher or reading a textbook.

最好的学习方法是从做中学，老师应该多给学
生练习的机会。

Zuìhǎo de xuéxí fāngfǎ shì cóng zuò zhōng xué, lǎo shī yīnggāi duō gěi xuésheng liànxí de jīhuì.

The best way to learn is to learn through doing. Teachers should provide students with more opportunities to practice (what they have learned).

The Chinese educational system tends to stress learning by rote. Students are taught to memorize what is written in their textbooks and are inclined to focus on mathematics and scientific research. In the West, learning is more hands-on. Emphasis is placed on critical and creative thinking, and students are encouraged to come up with their own answers. In recent years, however, as more academic interaction is taking place, teachers in the East are adopting some Western educational methods. Now, more and more classes in China allow opportunities for hands-on learning.

暑假打工

去年夏天我参加了夏令营，过了一个开心的暑假。今年夏天我想开始做一些认真的事，所以我到购物中心的服饰[1]店去打工。我选服饰店是因为我对流行[2]的东西很有兴趣，而且我觉得我做得很不错，例如：每次朋友要参加聚会，不知道要穿什么衣服的时候，我都可以帮他们选出最适合他们的衣服。来店里的客人[3]都很喜欢我，特别是年轻的女生。虽然这只是一份打工的工作，但是我学到了很多东西。我希望以后有机会能开[4]一家自己的店！

[1]服饰: dress and personal adornment [2]流行: fashion [3]客人: customer [4]开: to open

Shǔjià Dǎgōng

Qùnián shǔjià wǒ cānjiāle xiàlìngyíng, guòle yíge kāixīn de shǔjià. Jīnnián xiàtiān wǒ xiǎng kāishǐ zuò yìxiē rènzhēn de shì, suǒyǐ wǒ dào gòuwù zhōngxīn de fúshìdiàn qù dǎgōng. Wǒ xuǎn fúshìdiàn shì yīnwèi wǒ duì liúxíng de dōngxi hěn yǒu xìngqù, érqiě wǒ juéde wǒ zuò de hěn búcuò, lìrú: měicì péngyou yào cānjiā jùhuì, bù zhīdào yào chuān shénme yīfu de shíhou, wǒ dōu kěyǐ bāng tāmen xuǎn chū zuì shìhé tāmen de yīfú. Lái diànlǐ de kèrén dōu hěn xǐhuan wǒ, tèbié shì niánqīng de nǚshēng. Suīrán zhè zhǐ shì yìfèn dǎgōng de gōngzuò, dànshì wǒ xué dào le hěnduō dōngxi. Wǒ xīwàng yǐhòu yǒu jīhuì néng kāi yìjiā zìjǐ de diàn.

15 通晓文意 Tōngxiǎo Wényì / *Understanding the Passage*

Read the passage above and fill in the blanks.

1. 去年夏天他去了＿＿，今年夏天他去了＿＿。

   Qùnián xiàtiān tā qùle＿＿, jīnnián xiàtiān tā qùle＿＿.

2. 他选这个工作是因为他对＿＿的东西很有兴趣。

   Tā xuǎn zhèige gōngzuò shì yīnwèi tā duì＿＿de dōngxi hěn yǒu xìngqù.

3. 他觉得他做这个工作做得＿＿。 Tā juéde tā zuò zhèige gōngzuò zuò de＿＿.

4. 他的朋友要参加＿＿的时候，他可以帮他们选出最适合他们的衣服。

   Tāde péngyou yào cānjiā＿＿de shíhou, tā kěyǐ bāng tāmen xuǎn chū zuì shìhé tāmende yīfu.

5. 去他们店里的客人都很喜欢他，特别是＿＿。

   Qù tāmén diànlǐ de kèrén dōu hěn xǐhuan tā, tèbié shì＿＿.

6. 他希望以后可以＿＿。 Tā xīwàng yǐhòu kěyǐ＿＿

Hànzì Tiāndì

Chinese Characters

子 ■ zǐ ■ son

The character 子 *zǐ* is a pictograph of a baby with its arms outstretched. The original meaning of 子 *zǐ* was "infant," but it can also be interpreted as "son." 子 *zǐ* is found as a radical in words related to children such as 孩 (*hái*, child), 孙 (*sūn*, grandchild), 孕 (*yùn*, pregnancy), 学 (*xué*, to study).

Stroke Order

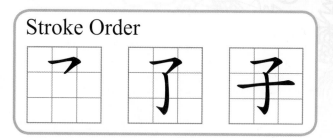

16 词汇延伸 **Cíhuì Yánshēn** / *Vocabulary Builder*

Below are some characters that can be combined with 子 *zǐ* to create words. Match the Chinese words on the left with the English meaning on the right.

女 nǚ	音 yīn	孙 sūn	句 jù	公司 gōngsī
n. daughter; girl	*n. sound*	*n. grandchild*	*n. sentence*	*n. company*

1. 子女 zǐnǚ   A. clause
2. 子音 zǐyīn   B. consonant
3. 子孙 zǐsūn   C. children
4. 子句 zǐjù   D. subsidiary company
5. 子公司 zǐgōngsī   E. descendants

17 汉字侦探 **Hànzì Zhēntàn** / *Visual Detective*

Can you find 子 in the following pictures?

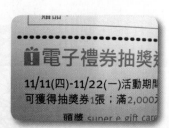

Lesson C

◀)) 苏州著名景点 **Sūzhōu Zhùmíng Jǐngdiǎn**
Famous Scenic Spots Around Suzhou

拙政园（拙政園）
Zhuózhèng Yuán
n. Humble Administrator's Garden

网师园（網師園）
Wǎngshī Yuán
n. Garden of the Master of the Nets

虎丘
Hǔqiū
n. Tiger Hill

周庄（周莊）
Zhōuzhuāng
n. Zhouzhuang (a historic "water town" built on a system of canals)

城市
chéngshì
n. city

乡下（鄉下）
xiāngxià
n. countryside

中国著名景点 Zhōngguó Zhùmíng Jǐngdiǎn
Famous Tourist Destinations in China

长城 (長城)
Cháng Chéng
n. The Great Wall of China

故宫 (故宫)
Gù Gōng
n. National Palace Museum

圆明园 (圆明園)
Yuánmíng Yuán
n. Old Summer Palace

颐和园 (頤和園)
Yíhéyuán
n. Summer Palace

九寨沟 (九寨溝)
Jiǔzhàigōu
n. Jiuzhaigou Valley

西湖 (西湖)
Xīhú
n. West Lake

长江三峡 (長江三峽)
Chángjiāng Sānxiá
n. Yangtze River Three Gorges

泰山
Tài Shān
n. Mount Tai

兵马俑 (兵馬俑)
Bīngmǎyǒng
n. Terracotta Army

照片 / 相片

zhàopiàn / xiàngpiàn

n. photograph

风景 (風景)

fēngjǐng

n. scenery

旅游 (旅遊)

lǚyóu

n. traveling

旅客 / 游客 (遊客)

lǚkè / yóukè

n. traveler

观光客 (觀光客)

guānguāngkè

n. tourist

摄影　shèyǐng

v. to take photograph

摄影师 shèyǐngshī

n. photographer

摄像 shèxiàng

v. to shoot a film

摄像机 shèxiàngjī

n. video camera

照相

zhàoxiàng

v.o. to take photos

照相机 (照相機)

zhàoxiàngjī

n. camera

A: 你暑假要做什么？（你暑假要做什麼？）

Nǐ shǔjià yào zuò shénme? *What are you doing over summer vacation?*

B: 本来我想到纽约去旅行，可是纽约的住宿贵得要命，所以我想去附近的城市玩玩就好。（本來我想到紐約去旅行，可是紐約的住宿貴得要命，所以我想去附近的城市玩玩就好。）

Běnlái wǒ xiǎng dào Niǔyuē qù lǚxíng, kěshì Niǔyuē de zhùsù guì de yào mìng, suǒyǐ wǒ xiǎng qù fùjìn de chéngshì wánwan jiù hǎo.

I wanted to go to New York, but the accommodation is really expensive there, so now I just want to visit cities nearby.

- -

A: 我受不了了！这几天下大雨，都不能出门，在家又没有事情做。（我受不了了！這幾天下大雨，都不能出門，在家又沒有事情做。）

Wǒ shòubùliǎo le! Zhè jǐtiān xià dà yǔ, dōu bùnéng chūmén, zàijiā yòu méiyǒu shìqíng zuò.

I can't stand it anymore! It's been raining these past few days so I can't go out and there's nothing to do at home.

B: 家里不是有很多书吗？你可以把没看过的书读一读啊。（家裡不是有很多書嗎？你可以把沒看過的書讀一讀啊。）

Jiā lǐ búshì yǒu hěn duō shū mā? Nǐ kěyǐ bǎ méi kàn guò de shū dú yì dú a. *Don't you have a lot of books? You can read the ones you haven't read yet.*

- -

A: 比赛才半个钟头，这个队就赢二十分了。（比賽才半個鐘頭，這個隊就贏二十分了。）

Bǐsài cái bàngè zhōngtóu, zhèige duì jiù yíng èrshí fēn le.

It's only half an hour into the game and this team is already leading by 20 points.

B: 这个队本来就会赢，只是赢得多或赢得少。（這個隊本來就會贏，只是贏得多或贏得少。）

Zhèige duì běnlái jiù huì yíng, zhǐshì yíng de duō huò yíng de shǎo.

This team was going to win anyway. The question was always by how much.

- -

A: 你们是同学吗？（你們是同學嗎？）

Nǐmen shì tóngxué ma? *Are you classmates?*

B: 我们只是同校，也没有一起上课，所以不算同学。（我們只是同校，也沒有一起上課，所以不算同學。）

Wǒmen zhǐ shì tóng xiào, yě méiyǒu yìqǐ shàngkè, suǒyǐ bú suàn tóngxué.

Not really. We just went to the same school, but didn't have the same classes.

Adjectives

够	gòu	*enough*
得意	déyì	*proud or pleased with oneself*

Adverbs

又	yòu	*also; and (indicates additional ideas or an afterthought)*
本来 (本來)	běnlái	*originally*
才	cái	*only*
就	jiù	*at once; right away*

Complements

了	liǎo	*indicates possibility*
下去	xiàqù	*indicates the continuation of an action*

Common Expression

受不了	shòubùliǎo	*not able to bear or tolerate*

Measure Words

些	xiē	*some; a little*
句	jù	*sentence*

Number + Measure Words

一些	yìxiē	*some; a few*

Nouns

郊外	jiāowài	*the countryside around a city; the outskirts of town*
园 (園)	yuán	*garden*
丘	qiū	*mound; hill*
庄 (莊)	zhuāng	*village*
句	jù	*sentence*

Pronouns

这些 (這些)	zhèixiē	*these*
那些	nèixiē	*those*

Verbs

受	shòu	*to stand; to endure; to bear*
住	zhù	*to live*
待	dāi	*to stay*
继续 (繼續)	jìxù	*to continue*
传 (傳)	chuán	*to pass (something) on*
算	suàn	*to count*
夸 (誇)	kuā	*to praise*

Verb-Complement

睡着 (睡著)	shuìzháo	*to fall asleep*

中国游记 Zhōngguó Yóujì / *China Travel Journal*

Sam kept a journal while traveling in China. Read the following entry from Sam's journal and fill in the blanks with the names of the tourist destinations he visited.

A. 圆明园 Yuánmíng Yuán	B. 拙政园 Zhuózhèng Yuán
C. 故宫 Gù Gōng	D. 长城 Cháng Chéng

这是我第一次到中国来玩，我好兴奋。第一天，我在北京市区走走，我去看了1.__，那里有很多以前的东西，皇帝(emperor)也住在这里。第二天我去了2.__，那个地方大得不得了，我走了一天还走不完。虽然腿很酸，但是我第三天还是去爬了3.__，真不知道以前的人是怎么盖(to build)起来的。第四天，我往南到了苏州，那里有很多很美的花园(garden)。我去了4.__，它在苏州博物馆的旁边。中国南方的建筑(building)和北方不太一样，小小的，很精致(exquisite)。

Zhèi shì wǒ dì-yī cì dào Zhōngguó lái wán, wǒ hǎo xīngfèn. Dì-yī tiān, wǒ zài Běijīng shìqū zǒuzou, wǒ qù kànle 1. __ , nàlǐ yǒu hěn duō yǐqián de dōngxi, huángdì yě zhù zài zhèlǐ. Dì-èr tiān wǒ qùle 2. __ , nèige dìfang dà de bùdéliǎo, wǒ zǒule yìtiān hái zǒu bù wán. Suīrán tuǐ hěn suān, dànshì wǒ dì-sān tiān háishì qù pále 3. __ , zhēn bù zhīdào yǐqián de rén shì zěnme gài qǐlái de. Dì-sì tiān, wǒ wǎng nán dàole Sūzhōu, nàlǐ yǒu hě nduō hěn měi de huāyuán. Wǒ qùle 4. __ , tā zài Sūzhōu Bówùguǎn de pángbiān. Zhōngguó nánfāng de jiànzhù hé běifāng bú tài yíyàng, xiǎoxiǎode, hěn jīngzhì.

2 对还是错？ Duì háishì Cuò? / True or False?

🔊 Listen to the recording and decide whether what you hear matches the photos. If the photo matches what you hear, say true. If it does not match, say false.

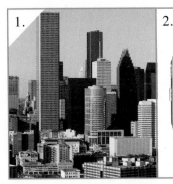   

3 个人问题 Gèrén Wèntí / Personal Questions

Answer the following questions in Chinese based on your own experiences and opinions.

1. 你喜欢住在城市还是乡下？ Nǐ xǐhuan zhù zài chéngshì háishì xiāngxià?
2. 你喜不喜欢照相？ Nǐ xǐ bù xǐhuan zhàoxiàng?
3. 你家的客厅有很多照片吗？ Nǐ jiā de kètīng yǒu hěn duō zhàopiàn ma?
4. 你家附近风景美不美？ Nǐ jiā fùjìn fēngjǐng měi bù měi?
5. 你最想去哪个中国景点看看？ Nǐ zuì xiǎng qù něige Zhōngguó jǐngdiǎn kànkan?

句型介绍 Jùxíng Jièshào

Language Patterns

Using 得 *de* or 不 *bù* / *bú* to Show Possibility

The words 得 *de* and 不 *bù* / *bú* can be used after a verb to indicate the result of an action. 得 *de* indicates a result that is possible; 不 *bù* / *bú* indicates a result that is not possible.

> **Subject** + **Verb** + 得 *de* / 不 *bù, bú* + **result**
>
> 今天老师教的，我们都听得懂。 Jīntiān lǎoshī jiāo de, wǒmen dōu tīng de dǒng.
>
> 这份餐太多了，妹妹吃不完。 Zhèi fèn cān tài duō le, mèimei chī bù wán.
>
> **A:** 你看得见黑板上的字吗？ Nǐ kàn de jiàn hēibǎn shàng de zì ma?
>
> **B:** 我看不见，字太小了。 Wǒ kàn bú jiàn, zì tài xiǎo le.

得 *de* and 不 *bù* / *bú* can also be added to give directions about something that should or should not be done or that can or cannot be done.

Subject + Verb + 得 *de* / 不 *bù, bú* + Directional Compound

书柜里只放了几本书，这五本书应该还放得进去。
Shūguì lǐ zhǐ fàngle jǐ běn shū, zhè wǔběn shū yīnggāi hái fàng de jìnqù.

他不够高，这些盘子他放不上去。
Tā bú gòu gāo, zhèixiē pánzi tā fàng bú shàngqù.

If there is a place word, then the place word should be inserted between the directional verb and 来 *lái* or 去 *qù*.

Subject + Verb + 得 *de* / 不 *bù, bú* + Directional Verb + 来 *lái* / 去 *qù*

A: 你想那个沙发放得进客厅去吗？ Nǐ xiǎng nèige shāfā fàng de jìn kètīng qù ma?

B: 第一，门那么小，那个沙发一定拿不进客厅去。第二，客厅已经有太多东西了，一定放不下去。
Dì-yī, mén nàme xiǎo, nèige shāfā yídìng ná bú jìn kètīng qù. Dì-èr, kètīng yǐjīng yǒu tài duō dōngxi le, yídìng fàng bú xiàqù.

Using 得了 *de liǎo* and 不了 *bù liǎo* to Show Possibility

The word 了 *liǎo* here indicates the possibility of an action or a change about to occur. Note that either 不 *bù* or 得 *de* must come before 了 *liǎo* in this pattern. 了 *liǎo* cannot follow the verb by itself.

Verb + 得 *de* / 不 *bù* + 了 *liǎo*

你一个人吃得了这么多东西吗？ Nǐ yíge rén chī de liǎo zhème duō dōngxi ma?

因为七月和八月我都得打工，所以你们今年夏天的旅行我去不了。
Yīnwèi Qīyuè hé Bāyuè wǒ dōu děi dǎgōng, suǒyǐ nǐmen jīnnián xiàtiān de lǚxíng wǒ qù bù liǎo.

下去 *xiàqù* to Indicate Continuing Action

下去 *xiàqù* literally means "go down." However, when placed after a verb, it can also indicate an action or situation that is continuing or ongoing, as in the examples below.

Verb + 下去 *xiàqù*

你别说话，让他说下去。
Nǐ bié shuōhuà, ràng tā shuō xiàqù.

这个工作很有意思，虽然很累，但是我还是想做下去。
Zhèige gōngzuò hěn yǒu yìsi, suīrán hěn lèi, dànshì wǒ háishì xiǎng zuò xiàqù.

▲ 这个工作很有意思。

The Adverb 本来 *běnlái*

The movable adverb 本来 *běnlái* means "originally" or "at first." It is used to indicate a situation, state of being, or action that has changed from what it was at first.

> **Subject** + 本来 *běnlái* + **Verb Phrase**

今天下大雨，本来我们打算去海边，现在只好待在家。

Jīntiān xià dà yǔ, běnlái wǒmen dǎsuàn qù hǎibiān, xiànzài zhǐhǎo dāi zài jiā.

我本来不喜欢胡萝卜，但是吃了你做的"胡萝卜炒蛋"以后，我觉得胡萝卜很好吃。

Wǒ běnlái bù xǐhuan húluóbo, dànshì chīle nǐ zuò de "húluóbo chǎo dàn" yǐhòu, wǒ juéde húluóbo hěn hǎochī.

The Adverb 才 *cái* Meaning "Only"

The adverb 才 *cái* here means "only." It is used to indicate things that are small or low in quantity or degree.

> **Subject** + 才 *cái* + **quantity / degree of things**

他才六岁，拿不了这么重的东西。

Tā cái liùsuì, ná bù liǎo zhème zhòng de dōngxi.

今天才三度，出门的时候多穿一点衣服。

Jīntiān cái sāndù, chūmén de shíhou duō chuān yìdiǎn yīfu.

▲ 今天才三度。

The Pattern 才...就... *cái...jiù...*

The adverb 才 *cái* indicates a small quantity or low degree, while the adverb 就 *jiù* that follows indicates the result is greater than expected. This pattern shows a contrast between low expectations and big results. Note that the subjects of the two clauses can be different.

> **Subject** + 才 *cái* + **quantity / degree of things**, **Subject** + 就 *jiù* + **result**

他才学了一年的中文，就看得懂这本故事书了。

Tā cái xuéle yìnián de Zhōngwén, jiù kàn de dǒng zhèiběn gùshìshū le.

我才唱第一句，他就知道这首歌叫什么名字。

Wǒ cái chàng dì-yījù, tā jiù zhīdào zhèishǒu gē jiào shénme míngzi.

🔊 假期生活 Jiàqī Shēnghuó *Summer Break Life*

Zhao Mei calls Li Yunying while she is babysitting.

赵梅:	云英，你在做什么？	Zhào Méi:	Yúnyīng, nǐ zài zuò shénme?
李云英:	我在看孩子。你在哪儿？	Lǐ Yúnyīng:	Wǒ zài kān háizi. Nǐ zài nǎr?
赵梅:	我在乡下，在我外公家。	Zhào Méi:	Wǒ zài xiāngxià, zài wǒ wàigōng jiā.
李云英:	你外公家在哪儿？	Lǐ Yúnyīng:	Nǐ wàigōng jiā zài nǎr?
赵梅:	在苏州郊外。这儿热死了，我外公家又没空调，我晚上都睡不着，快受不了了。	Zhào Méi:	Zài Sūzhōu jiāowài. Zhèr rè sǐ le, wǒ wàigōng jiā yòu méi kōngtiáo, wǒ wǎnshang dōu shuì bù zháo, kuài shòu bù liǎo le.
李云英:	听起来你好像住不下去了，你打算继续在那儿待多久？	Lǐ Yúnyīng:	Tīng qǐlái nǐ hǎoxiàng zhù bú xiàqù le, nǐ dǎsuàn jìxù zài nàr dāi duōjiǔ?
赵梅:	本来我想住一个月，现在我想早点儿回去。今天才第五天，我想再待两天吧，住一个星期够了。	Zhào Méi:	Běnlái wǒ xiǎng zhù yí ge yuè, xiànzài wǒ xiǎng zǎo diǎnr huíqù. Jīntiān cái dì wǔ tiān, wǒ xiǎng zài dāi liǎng tiān ba, zhù yí ge xīngqī gòu le.
李云英:	你这几天去哪儿玩了？	Lǐ Yúnyīng:	Nǐ zhè jǐ tiān qù nǎr wán le?
赵梅:	去了拙政园、网师园、虎丘，还去了周庄。	Zhào Méi:	Qùle Zhuózhèng Yuán, Wǎngshī Yuán, Hǔ Qiū, hái qùle Zhōuzhuāng.
李云英:	这些地方我都没去过，听说风景很美。你不是上过摄影课吗？传一些照片来看看吧。	Lǐ Yúnyīng:	Zhèxiē dìfang wǒ dōu méi qùguò, tīngshuō fēngjǐng hěn měi. Nǐ bú shì shàngguo shèyǐngkè ma? Chuán yìxiē zhàopiàn lái kànkan ba.
赵梅:	对，我现在可以算是半个摄影师了呢。	Zhào Méi:	Duì, wǒ xiànzài kěyǐ suànshì bàn ge shèyǐngshī le ne.
李云英:	才夸你一句，你就这么得意，我等你的照片啰。	Lǐ Yúnyīng:	Cái kuā nǐ yíjù, nǐ jiù zhème déyì, wǒ děng nǐde zhàopiàn luō.

4 外公有没有？ Wàigōng yǒu méiyǒu? / *Does grandpa have it?*

Select what Zhao Mei needs when she is at her grandfather's house, based on the dialogue.

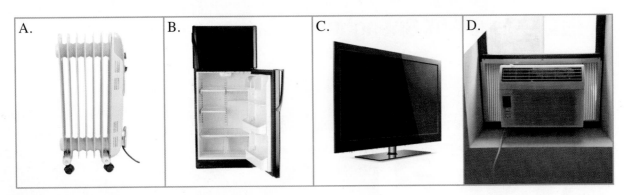

5 她要什么？ Tā yào shénme? / *What does she want?*

Pick out what Li Yunying wants Zhao Mei to send her, according to the dialogue.

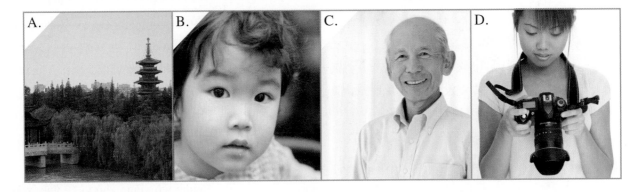

6 懂了吗？ Dǒngle ma? / *Do you understand?*

Answer the following questions in Chinese.

1. 赵梅给李云英打电话的时候，李云英在做什么？
   Zhào Méi gěi Lǐ Yúnyīng dǎ diànhuà de shíhou, Lǐ Yúnyīng zài zuò shénme?

2. 赵梅那个时候在哪里？她在那里多久了？
   Zào Méi nèige shíhou zài nǎlǐ? Tā zài nàlǐ duōjiǔ le?

3. 赵梅的外公家在哪里？ Zhào Méi de wàigōng jiā zài nǎlǐ?

4. 为什么赵梅晚上睡不着？ Wèishénme Zhào Méi wǎnshang shuìbùzháo?

5. 赵梅本来想在她外公家待多久？现在呢？
   Zhào Méi běnlái xiǎng zài tā wàigōng jiā dāi duōjiǔ? Xiànzài ne?

6. 为什么李云英要赵梅传照片给她？
   Wèishénme Lǐ Yúnyīng yào Zhào Méi chuán zhàopiàn gěi tā?

文化橱窗 Wénhuà Chúchuāng

Culture Window

The Classical Gardens of Suzhou and the West Lake of Hangzhou

Suzhou and Hangzhou are China's most famous historical cities. An ancient saying, "There's heaven up above and Suzhou, Hangzhou down below," alludes to the beauty that the two cities offer.

Suzhou is renowned for its classical Chinese gardens, which originate as far back as 2,500 years ago when the state of Wu was established there in 514 B.C. Located in eastern China near Shanghai, Suzhou has a temperate subtropical climate with lots of rainfall, making it an ideal place for plants

▲ *Lion Grove Garden*

to grow. Over the centuries, the imperial court and other nobles added to the gardens, until in the sixteenth century, there were as many as 100 throughout the city. Fortunately, many of these survive today in their original form—a rare thing in and of itself. The most praised gardens in Suzhou are the Great Wave Pavilion (Sung Dynasty, 960–1276 A.D.), Lion's Grove Garden (Yuan Dynasty, 1271–1368 A.D.), the Humble Administrator's Garden (Ming Dynasty, 1368–1644 A.D.) and Lingering Garden (Qing Dynasty, 1644–1911 A.D.). These four gardens are representative of the styles of their respective dynasties. The smallest garden in the city is the Garden of the Master of Nets. Although tiny, some say it is the most beautiful. These gardens are not only a piece of history, but also a representation of Chinese philosophy and culture, as reflected in the names of the gardens, the placement of the rocks, the sculptures, and the plants themselves.

The city of Hangzhou is situated about 100 miles to the southwest of Suzhou. Its most famous spot is

▲ *Lingering Garden*

West Lake, named for its location in the west of the city. West Lake is also known as "heaven on Earth" due to its beautiful scenery and the ancient temples built on its shores. Its shape is an almost symmetrical polygon, divided into five smaller areas by the Su Ti and Bai Ti causeways. The five areas are linked with bridges but the waters cannot flow from one area to another, resulting in differences among the five bodies of water. The West Lake covers 5.593 square kilometers in area, and has an overall volume of 110 million cubic meters with an average depth of 1.97 meters. West

Lake's scenery is different at different times of year. In spring, the willows lining the causeways are dressed in a delicate pale green; in summer, lotus flowers bloom over the lake. In the fall, people often go to the lake to drink tea under a yellow harvest moon, and in winter, when the the trees and pagodas around it are dusted with snow, West Lake transforms once more. West Lake is not only beautiful and surrounded by architectural relics, but is also the place of myths, making it a fusion of nature, culture, history, and art.

▲ *West Lake*

 7 **文化动动脑** **Wénhuà Dòngdòngnǎo** / *Culture Check-up*

On your own paper, write a short answer in English for each question.

1. What are the names of the two most famous historical cities in China?
2. Which city is famous for its classical gardens?
3. The classical gardens have a history of how many years?
4. Where is Hangzhou's location in relationship to Suzhou, and what is the distance between the two cities?
5. What is Hangzhou's most famous scenic spot?
6. What can be seen on the West Lake in summer?

▲ *West Lake shoreside*

8 做不做得到? Zuò bú zuò dé dào? / *Can you do it?*

Complete the following sentences using the the verb-complement provided and 得 *de* **or** 不 *bù/ bú*.

Lìzi: 这么一大盘菜,你肯定___。(吃完)

Zhème yí dàpán cài, nǐ kěndìng ___. (chī wán)

这么一大盘菜,你肯定吃不完。

Zhème yí dàpán cài, nǐ kěndìng chī bù wán.

1. 北京有名的景点一天___。(玩完)

Běijīng yǒumíng de jǐngdiǎn yìtiān ___ . (wánwán)

2. 天气太热了,热得我___。(睡着)

Tiānqì tài rè le, rè de wǒ ___ . (shuìzháo)

3. 这个药苦得不得了,我___。(吃下去)

Zhèige yào kǔ de bùdéliǎo, wǒ ___ . (chīxiàqù)

4. 档案(*file*)这么多,半个小时 ___ 吗?(传完)

Dàng'àn zhème duō, bàngè xiǎoshí ___ ma? (chuánwán)

5. 我 ___ 了!你们别欺负(*to bully*)他了。(看下去)

Wǒ ___ le! Nǐmen bié qīfù tā le. (kànxiàqù)

6. 不能上网的时候,你还___ 电子邮件吗?(收到)

Bù néng shàngwǎng de shíhou, nǐ hái ___ diànzǐ yóujiàn ma? (shōudào)

7. 购物中心里的书店___ 这本中文课本吗?(买到)

Gòuwù zhōngxīn lǐ de shūdiàn ___ zhèiběn Zhōngwén kèběn ma? (mǎidào)

8. 这部悲剧片太惨了,我现在___,我等一等再看。(看下去)

Zhèibù bēijùpiàn tài cǎn le, wǒ xiànzài ___ , wǒ děng yì děng zài kàn. (kànxiàqù)

With a classmate, take turns asking and answering the following questions using the pattern Verb + 得 *de* or Verb + 不 *bù* / *bú*. Follow the model.

Lìzi: **A:** 老师刚刚说的，你听得懂吗？ Lǎoshī gānggāng shuō de, nǐ tīng de dǒng ma?

B: 我听得懂。你呢？ Wǒ tīng de dǒng. Nǐ ne?

OR, 我听不懂。你呢？ Wǒ tīng bù dǒng. Nǐ ne?

A: 我（也）听得懂。 Wǒ (yě) tīng de dǒng.

OR, 我（也）听不懂。 Wǒ (yě) tīng bù dǒng.

1. 黑板上的字，你都看得见吗？ Hēibǎn shàng de zì, nǐ dōu kàndejiàn ma?
2. 你吃得完快餐店的一份餐吗？ Nǐ chīdewán kuàicāndiàn de yífèn cān ma?
3. 华氏零度的冬天，你受得了吗？ Huáshì língdù de dōngtiān, nǐ shòudeliǎo ma?
4. 从你家到学校，走路走得到吗？ Cóng nǐ jiā dào xuéxiào, zǒulù zǒudedào ma?
5. 这本课本放得进你的背包去吗？ Zhèiběn kèběn fàngdejìn nǐde bēibāo qù ma?
6. 课本里的每个中国字，你都写得出来吗？
   Kèběn lǐ de měige Zhōngguó zì, nǐ dōu xiědechūlái ma?

7. 晚饭以后，给你一大块巧克力蛋糕，你吃得完吗？
   Wǎnfàn yǐhòu, gěi nǐ yí dà kuài qiǎokèlì dàngāo, nǐ chīdewán ma?

Complete the following sentences using the verb provided and 得了 *de liǎo* or 不了 *bù liǎo*.

Lìzi: 我上学就要迟到了，吃不了早饭了。（吃）
Wǒ shàngxué jiùyào chídào le, chī bù liǎo zǎofàn le. (chī)

1. 那家面包店的面包贵死了，难怪一天__几个。（卖）
   Nèijiā miànbāodiàn de miànbāo guì sǐ le, nánguài yìtiān __ jǐge. (mài)
2. 他总是很冷淡，我想只有喜欢他的人__他吧。（受）
   Tā zǒngshì hěn lěngdàn, wǒ xiǎng zhǐyǒu xǐhuan tā de rén ___ tā ba. (shòu)
3. 这么大杯的饮料，我一个人__，你也喝一点吧。（喝）
   Zhème dà bēi de yǐnliào, wǒ yíge rén __, nǐ yě hē yìdiǎn ba. (hē)
4. 他不喜欢做功课，每次__几个字，他就说他累。（写）
   Tā bù xǐhuan zuò gōngkè, měicì __ jǐge zì, tā jiù shuō tā lèi. (xiě)
5. 没问题，我七月打工，所以八月的旅行我还是__。（去）
   Méiwèntí, wǒ Qīyuè dǎgōng, suǒyǐ Bāyuè de lǚxíng wǒ háishì __ . (qù)

Answer the following questions using the complement 下去 *xiàqù.*

Lìzi: 你已经游泳两个小时了，还要游下去吗？
Nǐ yǐjīng yóuyǒng liǎngge xiǎoshí le, hái yào yóu xiàqù ma?

我游得下去。 Wǒ yóu de xiàqù.

OR, 我游不下去。 Wǒ yóu bù xiàqù.

1. 你学中文已经学了两年了，你还想学下去吗？
   Nǐ xué Zhōngwén yǐjīng xuéle liǎngnián le, nǐ hái xiǎng xuéxiàqù ma?

2. 如果你等公交车等了一个小时，车没有来，你会等下去吗？
   Rúguǒ nǐ děng gōngjiāochē děngle yíge xiǎoshí, chē méiyǒu lái, nǐ huì děngxiàqù ma?

3. 今天功课特别多，已经十一点半了还没写完，你会继续写下去吗？
   Jīntiān gōngkè tèbié duō, yǐjīng shíyī diǎn bàn le háiméi xiěwán, nǐ huì jìxù xiěxiàqù ma?

4. 你第一次开车到一个地方去旅行，路上没有车也没有人，你会继续开下去吗？
   Nǐ dì-yī cì kāichē dào yíge dìfang qù lǔxíng, lùshàng méiyǒu chē yě méiyǒu rén, nǐ huì jìxù kāixiàqù ma?

5. 你打算在青年旅馆住十天，可是同一个房间的人打呼(to snore)打了三天，你会住下去吗？
   Nǐ dǎsuàn zài qīngnián lǔguǎn zhù shítiān, kěshì tóng yíge fángjiān de rén dǎhū dǎle sāntiān, nǐ huì zhùxiàqù ma?

6. 你跟朋友在聊天室聊了三个小时了，你们聊得很开心，可是已经晚上十二点了，明天要上课，你会聊下去吗？
   Nǐ gēn péngyou zài liáotiānshì liáole sānge xiǎoshí le, nǐmen liáo de hěn kāixīn, kěshì yǐjīng wǎnshang shí'èr diǎn le, míngtiān yào shàngkè, nǐ huì liáoxiàqù ma?

▲ 和朋友在聊天室聊天。

12 改变发生 **Gǎibiàn Fāshēng** / *There Is a Change*

Connect the following phrases to make complete sentences using the adverb 本来 *běnlái*.
Follow the model.

 Lìzi: 爬山／下大雪／在家看电视 páshān / xià dà xuě / zài jiā kàn diànshì

我本来要爬山，可是下大雪，所以我在家看电视。
Wǒ běn lái yào páshān, kěshì xià dà xuě, suǒyǐ wǒ zài jiā kàn diànshì.

1. 吃甜点／晚饭吃太多了／喝茶
   chī tiándiǎn / wǎnfàn chī tài duō le / hē chá

2. 爬长城／冬天风太大／逛故宫
   pá Cháng Chéng / dōngtiān fēng tài dà / guàng Gù Gōng

3. 做糖醋鱼／鱼卖完了／做牛肉面
   zuò Tángcùyú / yú màiwán le / zuò niúròumiàn

4. 走人行横道／路口太大／走天桥
   zǒu rénxíng héngdào / lùkǒu tài dà / zǒu tiānqiáo

5. 跟哥哥打网球／哥哥手痛／踢足球
   gēn gēge dǎ wǎngqiú / gēge shǒu tòng / tī zúqiú

6. 寄信给你／找不到邮筒／寄电子邮件
   jìxìn gěi nǐ / zhǎobúdào yóutǒng / jì diànzǐ yóujiàn

▲ 踢足球

13 加强语气 **Jiāqiáng Yǔqì** / *Adding Emphasis*

Read the following sentences and put the adverb 才 *cái* in the correct place to add emphasis to the
sentences. Follow the model.

Lìzi: 明天考一课，你别担心。 Míngtiān kǎo yíkè, nǐ bié dānxīn.

明天才考一课，你别担心。 Míngtiān cái kǎo yíkè, nǐ bié dānxīn.

1. 这块蛋糕一块五分，好便宜！ Zhèikuài dàngāo yíkuài wǔfēn, hǎo piányi!

2. 我要买十罐汽水，这里八罐。 Wǒ yào mǎi shíguàn qìshuǐ, zhèlǐ bāguàn.

3. 哇！你认识好多人，你不是来学校两天吗？
   Wa! Nǐ rènshi hǎo duō rén, nǐ bú shì lái xuéxiào liǎngtiān ma?

4. 奇怪，你吃一个布丁，怎么这么饱*(full)*？
   Qíguài, nǐ chī yíge bùdīng, zěnme zhème bǎo?

5. 我好饿，你为什么给我一个松饼？
   Wǒ hǎo è, nǐ wèishénme gěi wǒ yíge sōngbǐng?

6. 这么难的数学问题，他算了两分钟，真行！
   Zhème nán de shùxué wèntí, tā suànle liǎngfēnzhōng, zhēn xíng!

14 反差 Fǎnchā / *Contrasts*

Combine the two phrases given into one sentence using the pattern 才...就... *cái...jiù....* Follow the model.

Lìzi: 这个小孩一岁 / 会说很长的句子 zhèige xiǎohái yísuì / huì shuō hěn cháng de jùzi

这个小孩才一岁，就会说很长的句子。
Zhèige xiǎohái cái yísuì, jiù huì shuō hěn cháng de jùzi.

1. 他吃完感冒药 / 他睡着了 tā chīwán gǎnmàoyào / tā shuìzháo le

2. 一个数学小考 / 让你那么紧张 yíge shùxué xiǎokǎo / ràng nǐ nàme jǐnzhāng

3. 妈妈刚刚出门 / 孩子哭 *(to cry)* 了 māma gānggāng chūmén / háizi kū le

4. 他不太累，他睡了四个小时 / 他起床
tā bú tài lèi, tā shuìle sìge xiǎoshí / tā qǐchuáng

5. 她心情不好，她喝一点儿汤 / 她不喝了
tā xīnqíng bù hǎo, tā hē yìdiǎnr tāng / tā bù hē le

6. 英国的东西好贵，买一个三明治 / 要八块英镑
Yīngguó de dōngxi hǎo guì, mǎi yíge sānmíngzhì / yào bākuài Yīngbàng

7. 今天的功课很容易，孩子写了半个钟头 / 孩子写完了
jīntiān de gōngkè hěn róngyì, háizi xiěle bàngе zhōngtóu / háizi xiěwán le

8. 这里的游客多得我没办法照相，我照了一张相 / 我回家了
zhèlǐ de yóukè duō de wǒ méibànfǎ zhàoxiàng, wǒ zhàole yìzhāng xiàng / wǒ huíjiā le

Kāikǒu Shuō
Communication

15 照片分享 Zhàopiàn Fēnxiǎng / *Photo Story*

Bring three of your favorite vacation photos to class. If you prefer you can cut out photos from a magazine. With a classmate, tell each other the story behind each photo. Include the following information in your stories:

- Where and when the photo was taken.
- Who you were with.
- What you did there.
- Why the photo is so special to you.

Below is a letter Wu Sen wrote to Li Yunying. Read it and answer the questions that follow.

云英：

暑假快乐！暑假已经差不多过了一半了，你每天都做
些什么呢？我记得你说过要帮邻居看孩子，会不会
很累呢？我现在在山上外婆家，这里的天气不太热也
不太冷，凉凉的，很舒服。而且，跟城市很不一样的
是，这里的空气新鲜极了。我每天都会陪外婆出去散步，
看到这里美丽的风景，就让人心情很好。我有时候
也照照相，才来一个礼拜，我已经照了四百多张照片了。
这两张照片是我在山上照的，给你看看。美极了，
不是吗？以后有机会你一定要来这里玩玩！

吴森　七月二十八日

1. 这封信是谁写给谁的？　Zhèi fēng xìn shì shéi xiěgěi shéi de?

2. 暑假过了多久了？　Shǔjià guòle duōjiǔ le?

3. 吴森的外婆家在哪里？吴森在那里待了多久了？
   Wú Sēn de wàipó jiā zài nǎlǐ? Wú Sēn zài nàlǐ dāile duōjiǔ le?

4. 吴森外婆家的天气怎么样？　Wú Sēn wàipó jiā de tiānqì zěnmeyàng?

5. 吴森知不知道云英暑假要做什么？
   Wú Sēn zhī bù zhīdào Yúnyīng shǔjià yào zuò shénme?

6. 吴森在外婆家每天都做什么事？
   Wú Sēn zài wàipó jia měitiān dōu zuò shénme shì?

自我提升 Zìwǒ Tíshēng

Raising the Bar

Vocabulary

静	jìng	*adv.*	*calm*
自然	zìrán	*adv.*	*in due course; naturally*

心静自然凉
xīnjìng zìrán liáng
If you are calm, you will feel cool.

▲ 心静自然凉

Language Note

心静 *xīn jìng* refers to calmness of the mind—a natural peacefulness. This idiom means that as long as your mental state is calm, you will not feel hot and bothered.

俗话说：“心静自然凉”，你这样走来走去，当然会觉得热。

Súhuà shuō: "xīn jìng zìrán liáng", nǐ zhèyàng zǒu lái zǒu qù, dāngrán huì juéde rè.

There's a saying: peace of mind leads to coolness. Your pacing will of course make you feel hot.

When things aren't going well, it is human nature to feel stressed. Sometimes even when things have blown over, we still ruminate over the matter. The Chinese believe that as long as one has peace of mind, many problems will naturally resolve themselves. This belief stems from the importance placed on the power of the mind in ancient Chinese philosophy.

Human desire is endless. Whether we desire money, friendship, family or power, it will inevitably lead to frustration. The urge to gain without loss creates bitter conflict in our society. Therefore, the Chinese have traditionally placed great importance on cultivating a tranquil mind as a way to elevate people to a higher plane of existence.

周庄介绍

周庄是中国第一的水乡，它也是世界文化遗产[1]。有一句话说"上有天堂[2]，下有苏杭，中间还有一个周庄"，说的就是周庄的美。周庄的历史很久，很多有名的人住过这里。周庄离上海很近，坐车只要九十分钟，而且在上海体育馆旁边的旅游中心就有车可以到。除了历史和地理的因素[3]以外，让周庄有名起来的，其实是一幅画。1984年10月，那幅美丽的画在纽约展出[4]，大家很惊讶[5]中国有这么漂亮的地方。越来越多人到周庄旅游，而周庄也就越来越有名了。

[1]遗产: heritage [2]天堂: heaven [3]因素: factor [4]展出: to exhibit [5]惊讶: surprise

Zhōuzhuāng Jièshào

Zhōuzhuāng shì Zhōngguó dì-yī de shuǐxiāng, tā yě shì shìjiè wénhuà yíchǎn. Yǒu yíjù huà shuō "Shàng yǒu tiāntáng, xià yǒu Sū Háng, zhōngjiān hái yǒu yíge Zhōuzhuāng", shuō de jiù shì Zhōuzhuāng de měi. Zhōuzhuāng de lìshǐ hěn jiǔ, hěn duō yǒumíng de rén zhù guò zhèlǐ. Zhōuzhuāng lí Shànghǎi hěn jìn, zuò chē zhǐ yào jiǔshí fēnzhōng, érqiě zài Shànghǎi Tǐyùguǎn pángbiān de lǚyóu zhōngxīn jiù yǒu chē kěyǐ dào. Chúle lìshǐ hé dìlǐ de yīnsù yǐwài, ràng Zhōuzhuāng yǒumíng qǐlái de, qíshí shì yìfú huà. Yī jiǔ bā sì nián Shíyuè, nèifú měilì de huà zài Niǔyuē zhǎnchū, dàjiā hěn jīngyà Zhōngguó yǒu zhème piàoliang de dìfang. Yuè lái yuè duō rén dào Zhōuzhuāng lǚyóu, ér Zhōuzhuāng yě jiù yuè lái yuè yǒumíng le.

17 通晓文意 Tōngxiǎo Wényì / Understanding the Passage

Read the above passage and decide if the statements are true or false. Correct any false statements.

1. "上有天堂，下有苏杭，中间还有一个周庄"，这句话的意思是，周庄没有苏州和杭州那么漂亮。
   "Shàng yǒu tiāntáng, xià yǒu Sū Háng, zhōngjiān hái yǒu yíge Zhōuzhuāng", zhèijù huà de yìsi shì, Zhōuzhuāng méiyǒu Sū Zhōu hé Háng Zhōu nàme piàoliang.

2. 周庄离上海开车差不多九十分钟。
   Zhōuzhuāng lí Shànghǎi kāichē chàbùduō jiǔshífēn zhōng.

3. 你可以在上海体育馆买到去周庄的车票(ticket)。
   Nǐ kěyǐ zài Shànghǎi Tǐyùguǎn mǎi dào qù Zhōuzhuāng de chēpiào

4. 周庄开始有名是因为一幅画。 Zhōuzhuāng kāishǐ yǒumíng shì yīnwèi yìfú huà.

汉字天地 Hànzì Tiāndì

Chinese Characters

月 ■ yuè ■ the moon; month

The character 月 *yuè* is a pictograph. In its earliest form, the character was in the shape of a half moon. Later, a dot was added in the middle to make it seem more like a concrete object. With the passing of time, the dot and the line on the left turned into the two strokes in the middle.

Stroke Order

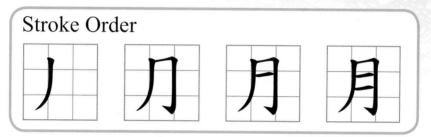

18 词汇延伸 **Cíhuì Yánshēn** / *Vocabulary Builder*

Below are some characters that can be combined with 月 *yuè* to create new words. Match the Chinese words on the left with the English meaning on the right.

光 guāng	票 piào	台 tái	食 shí	蜜 mì
n. light	*n. ticket*	*n. stage*	*v. to eat*	*adj. honey*

1. 月光 yuèguāng   A. honeymoon
2. 月票 yuèpiào   B. lunar eclipse
3. 月台 yuètái   C. platform
4. 月食 yuèshí   D. monthly pass
5. 蜜月 mìyuè   E. moonlight

19 汉字侦探 **Hànzì Zhēntàn** / *Visual Detective*

Can you find 月 in the following pictures?

句型介绍 Language Patterns

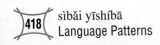

Unit 1, Lesson C

Unit 2, Lesson A

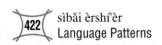

Unit 4, Lesson C

Unit 5, Lesson A

Unit 6, Lesson B

Unit 6, Lesson C

拼音索引 Pinyin to Chinese and English Vocabulary

Each entry lists the Pinyin, simplified character, traditional character, part of speech, English meaning, unit and lesson.

A

| ǎi | 矮 | 矮 | *Adj.* | short | U3A |
| àixīn | 爱心 | 愛心 | *N.* | love and care | U3C |

B

ba	吧	吧	*P.*	used at the end of a sentence to indicate doubt or conjecture	U2B
bǎ	把	把	*M.W.*	a measure word for knives	U5C
			CV.	把 *bǎ* marks an object placed which precedes its verb	
bǎi	摆	擺	*V.*	to put; to place; to arrange	U5C
bǎijíbǐng	百吉饼	百吉餅	*N.*	bagel	U6B
Bālí	巴黎	巴黎	*N.*	Paris	U6A
bān	班	班	*N.*	class	U3A
bāng	帮	幫	*V.*	to help	U2B
bàng	棒	棒	*Adj.*	good; excellent	U3B
bǎo'ān	保安	保安	*N.*	security guard	U4B
bāoguǒ	包裹	包裹	*N.*	parcel; package	U6A
bǎomǔ	保姆	保姆	*N.*	baby-sitter	U2B
bǎoxiǎn	保险	保險	*Adj.*	safe	U4A
bāozhuāng shípǐn	包装食品	包裝食品	*N.*	packaged food	U5A
běi	北	北	*N.*	north	U4A
bèi	背	背	*N.*	back	U1A
Běijīng	北京	北京	*N.*	Beijing	U6A
bēijùpiàn	悲剧片	悲劇片	*N.*	tragedy	U2C
bèilèi	贝类	貝類	*N.*	shellfish	U5B
běnlái	本来	本來	*Adv.*	originally	U6C
bǐ	比	比	*Prep.*	used to indicate a difference in manner or degree through comparison	U3A
biān	边	邊	*N.*	side	U4A

biànlì shāngdiàn	便利商店	便利商店	*N.*	convenience store	U5A
bié	别	别	*Adv.*	do not (used in imperative sentences)	U1B
Bīngmǎyǒng	兵马俑	兵馬俑	*N.*	Terracotta Army	U6C
bìngrén	病人	病人	*N.*	patient	U1C
bǐsàbǐng	比萨饼	比薩餅	*N.*	pizza	U6B
bísāi	鼻塞	鼻塞	*Adj.*	(a) stuffed nose	U1C
bízi	鼻子	鼻子	*N.*	nose	U1C
bō diànhuà	拨电话	撥電話	*V.O.*	to dial (a phone)	U3C
bókè	博客	博客	*N.*	blog	U1B
Bólín	柏林	柏林	*N.*	Berlin	U6A
bózi	脖子	脖子	*N.*	neck	U1A
bù	部	部	*M.W.*	used for films or a volume of books	U2C
bù shūfu	不舒服	不舒服	*Adj.*	uncomfortable	U1B
bùdéliǎo	不得了	不得了	*Adv.*	extremely; exceedingly	U6A
bùdīng	布丁	布丁	*N.*	pudding	U5B
búguò	不过	不過	*Adj.*	but	U6A
bǔxí	补习	補習	*V.*	to take lessons after school	U3B
bǔxíbān	补习班	補習班	*N.*	cram school	U3B
bùzhǐ	不只	不只	*Conj.*	not only	U3C
cái	才	才	*Adv.*	(used before a verb to indicate that something happened later than was expected)	U1B
				certainly	U5B
				only	U6C
càidān	菜单	菜單	*N.*	menu	U5A
cáiliào	材料	材料	*N.*	ingredient	U5C
càishìchǎng	菜市场	菜市場	*N.*	market	U5A
cānjiā	参加	參加	*V.*	to join; to participate in	U3B
cānjīnzhǐ	餐巾纸	餐巾紙	*N.*	napkin	U6B
cānjù	餐具	餐具	*N.*	tableware	U5C
cānpán	餐盘	餐盤	*N.*	tray	U6B
céng	层	層	*M.W.*	layer; storey; floor	U4B

cèsuǒ	厕所	廁所	*N.*	bathroom; toilet	U4C
chàbuduō	差不多	差不多	*Adj.*	almost; nearly	U4A
chájī	茶几	茶几	*N.*	coffee table	U4C
chángcháng	常常	常常	*Adv.*	often; frequently	U3C
Cháng Chéng	长城	長城	*N.*	The Great Wall of China	U6C
Chángjiāng Sānxiá	长江三峡	長江三峡	*N.*	Yangtze River Three Gorges	U6C
chǎo	炒	炒	*V.*	to stir-fry	U5C
chǎoguō	炒锅	炒鍋	*N.*	wok	U5C
chāojí shìchǎng	超级市场	超級市場	*N.*	supermarket	U5A
chāoshì	超市	超市	*N.*	supermarket	U5A
chāzi	叉子	叉子	*N.*	fork	U5C
chē	车	車	*N.*	car; vehicle	U2A
chēkù	车库	車庫	*N.*	garage	U4B
chéngshì	城市	城市	*N.*	city	U6C
chī zǎofàn	吃早饭	吃早飯	*V.O.*	to have breakfast	U2A
chídào	迟到	遲到	*V.*	to arrive late; to be late	U2A
chāojí shìchǎng	超级市场	超級市場	*N.*	supermarket	U5A
chuán	船	船	*N.*	boat; ship	U2A
	传	傳	*V.*	to pass (something) on	U6C
chuānghu	窗户	窗戶	*N.*	window	U4B
chúfáng	厨房	廚房	*N.*	kitchen	U4C
chuī tóufa	吹头发	吹頭髮	*V.O.*	to blow-dry hair	U2A
chúle...yǐwài, dōu/ yě	除了...以外,都/也...	除了…以外,都/也…	*I.E.*	except for; besides	U2C
chūmén	出门	出門	*V.*	to go out	U2A
chūqù	出去	出去	*V.C.*	to go out	U2B
chūzūchē	出租车	出租車	*N.*	taxi; cab	U2A
cì	次	次	*M.W.*	times	U1C
cóng	从	從	*Prep.*	from	U4A
cónglái	从来	從來	*Adv.*	always; all along	U6A
cù	醋	醋	*N.*	vinegar	U5B

D					
dā	搭	搭	V.	to take a ride from someone; to travel by	U2A
dà	大	大	Adj.	old (age-wise)	U3A
dǎ diànhuà	打电话	打電話	V.O.	to make a phone call	U2B
dǎ kēshuì	打瞌睡	打瞌睡	V.	to doze; to nod off	U1B
dǎ pēntì	打喷嚏	打噴嚏	V.O.	to sneeze	U1C
dàbáicài	大白菜	大白菜	N.	Chinese cabbage	U5C
dǎbāodài	打包袋	打包袋	N.	doggie bag	U6B
dǎcuò le	打错了	打錯了	C.E.	to dial a wrong number	U3C
dàfāng	大方	大方	Adj.	natural and poised	U3A
dàgài	大概	大概	Adv.	probably	U4A
dǎgōng	打工	打工	V.O.	to have a part-time job	U2B
dāi	待	待	V.	to stay	U6C
dài	戴	戴	V.	to wear; to put on	U1A
dàizi	袋子	袋子	N.	bag	U5B
dàlóu	大楼	大樓	N.	large building	U4B
dàmén	大门	大門	N.	front door	U4B
dàngāo	蛋糕	蛋糕	N.	cake	U5B
dànshì	但是	但是	Conj.	but	U2B
dānxīn	担心	擔心	Adj.	worried	U1B
			V.	to worry	U1B
dào	到	到	R.C.	(used after a verb as a complement to indicate success)	U4C
dāozi	刀子	刀子	N.	knife	U5C
dǎsuàn	打算	打算	V.	to plan	U6A
dàtuǐ	大腿	大腿	N.	thigh	U1A
dàxíng chāojí shìchǎng	大型超级市场	大型超級市場	N.	superstore	U5A
de	得	得	P.	used between a verb or an adjective and its complement to indicate degree	U3A
				used between a verb or an adjective and its complement to indicate result	U3B
de yàomìng	得要命	得要命	C.	to an extreme degree (lit., "to death")	U5B
dēng	灯	燈	N.	lamp; light	U4C

děng	等	等	*V.*	to wait	U2A
děng yíxià	等一下	等一下	*V.+M.W.*	to wait a moment	U3C
déyì	得意	得意	*Adj.*	proud or pleased with oneself	U6C
dī	低	低	*Adj.*	low	U1A
dì	第	第	*Sp.*	(prefix for ordinal numbers)	U4A
diàntī	电梯	電梯	*N.*	elevator	U4B
diǎnxīn	点心	點心	*N.*	snacks	U2A
diànyǐng fēnlèi	电影分类	電影分類	*N.*	film genres	U2C
diànyóu	电邮	電郵	*N.*	email (the short form of 电子邮件 *diànzǐ yóujiàn*)	U2C
diànyuán	店员	店員	*N.*	sales clerk	U2B
dìbǎn	地板	地板	*N.*	floor	U4C
diézi	碟子	碟子	*N.*	saucer	U5C
dìfang	地方	地方	*N.*	place; space; part	U3C
dīng	丁	丁	*N.*	small cube of meat or vegetable	U5C
dǐnglóu	顶楼	頂樓	*N.*	loft; attic	U4B
díquè	的确	的確	*Adv.*	indeed; really	U2B
dìxiàshì	地下室	地下室	*N.*	basement	U4C
dōng	东	東	*N.*	east	U4A
dòng	栋	棟	*M.W.*	(for buildings)	U4B
dōngběi	东北	東北	*N.*	northeast	U4A
Dōngjīng	东京	東京	*N.*	Tokyo	U6A
dōngnán	东南	東南	*N.*	southeast	U4A
dòngzuòpiàn	动作片	動作片	*N.*	action film	U2C
dòufu	豆腐	豆腐	*N.*	tofu	U5B
duǎnxìn	短信	短信	*N.*	text message	U2C
duì	对	對	*Prep.*	to; toward	U2C
dùjià	度假	度假	*V.O.*	to go on vacation	U6B
duō	多	多	*Adv.*	more; a lot	U1C
duōjiǔ	多久	多久	*Q.W.*	how long	U1A

E

ěrduo	耳朵	耳朵	*N.*	ear	U1C

F

fā	发	發	*V.*	to send; to distribute	U2C
fàndiàn	饭店	飯店	*N.*	hotel	U6A
fàng	放	放	*V.*	to put	U5C
fàngjià	放假	放假	*V.O.*	to have a holiday or vacation; to have a day off	U6B
fángjiān	房间	房間	*N.*	room	U4C
fāngwèi	方位	方位	*N.*	direction; points of the compass	U4A
fāngxiàng	方向	方向	*N.*	direction	U4A
fàngxīn	放心	放心	*V.O.*	to feel relieved	U4C
fàngxué	放学	放學	*V.*	to finish school	U2B
fángzi	房子	房子	*N.*	house	U4B
fānqié	蕃茄	蕃茄	*N.*	tomato	U5C
fānqiéjiàng	蕃茄酱	蕃茄醬	*N.*	ketchup	U6B
fàntīng	饭厅	飯廳	*N.*	dining room	U4C
fāshāo	发烧	發燒	*V.O.*	to have a fever	U1C
fēicháng	非常	非常	*Adv.*	very	U3B
fēijī	飞机	飛機	*N.*	plane	U2A
fēnbān	分班	分班	*V.O.*	to arrange classes (based on students' academic preference)	U3B
fēng	封	封	*M.W.*	used for letters, emails	U2C
fēngjǐng	风景	風景	*N.*	scenery	U6C
fēnzhōng	分钟	分鐘	*M.W.*	minute	U1A
fùjìn	附近	附近	*N.*	nearby; neighboring	U5A
fù-mǔ	父母	父母	*N.*	father and mother; parents	U4C
fúwù	服务	服務	*N.*	service	U3C
			V.	to serve	U3C
fúwùyuán	服务员	服務員	*N.*	waiter; waitress	U2B

G

gǎitiān	改天	改天	*Adv.*	another day; some other day	U3A
gǎn	敢	敢	*V.*	to dare	U4A
gānggāng	刚刚	剛剛	*Adv.*	just; exactly	U4C

gǎnlǎnyóu	橄榄油	橄欖油	*N.*	olive oil	U5B
gǎnmào	感冒	感冒	*V.*	to have a cold	U1C
gāo	高	高	*Adj.*	high	U1A
				tall	U3A
gēbo	胳膊	胳膊	*N.*	arm	U1A
gěi	给	給	*Prep.*	for	U2B
gélí	蛤蜊	蛤蜊	*N.*	clam	U5B
gélóu	阁楼	閣樓	*N.*	attic; loft	U4C
gèxìng	个性	個性	*N.*	personality	U3A
gōngchǐ	公尺	公尺	*M.W.*	meter	U4A
gōngfēn	公分	公分	*M.W.*	centimeter	U4A
gōngfupiàn	功夫片	功夫片	*N.*	kung-fu film	U2C
gōngjiāochē	公交车	公交車	*N.*	bus	U2A
gōngkè	功课	功課	*N.*	homework	U2B
gōnglǐ	公里	公里	*M.W.*	kilometer	U4A
gōnglì xuéxiào	公立学校	公立學校	*N.*	public school	U3B
gōngyù	公寓	公寓	*N.*	apartment house	U4B
gōngzuò	工作	工作	*N.*	job; work	U6B
			V.	to work	U6B
gòu	够	夠	*Adj.*	enough	U6C
gū'éryuàn	孤儿院	孤兒院	*N.*	orphanage	U3C
guà diànhuà	挂电话	掛電話	*V.O.*	to hang up (the phone)	U3C
guàhàoxìn	挂号信	掛號信	*N.*	registered mail	U6A
guǎi	拐	拐	*V.*	to turn	U4A
guānguāngkè	观光客	觀光客	*N.*	tourist	U6C
guàntou	罐头	罐頭	*N.*	canned good	U5A
Gù Gōng	故宫	故宮	*N.*	National Palace Museum	U6C
guò	过	過	*V.*	to pass; to go through	U1C
				to pass; to cross	U4A
			P.	indicates an action completed or a past experience	U6B
guójì	国际	國際	*Adj.*	international	U3A
guónèi	国内	國內	*Adj.*	national; domestic	U6A
guówài	国外	國外	*Adj.*	abroad; overseas	U6A

gùshi	故事	故事	*N.*	story	U3C
gùzhí	固执	固執	*Adj.*	stubborn	U3A

H

hái méi	还没	還沒	*Adv.*	not yet	U3B
háishì	还是	還是	*Adv.*	had better; it's best to	U4A
hǎixiān	海鲜	海鮮	*N.*	seafood	U5A
hàixiū	害羞	害羞	*Adj.*	shy	U3A
háizi	孩子	孩子	*N.*	child	U3C
hángkōngxìn	航空信	航空信	*N.*	airmail	U6A
háo	蚝	蠔	*N.*	oyster	U5B
hǎo	好	好	*Adv.*	so (used before certain adjectives to indicate high degree)	U1A
				very	U1B
				(used before certain adjectives to indicate high degree) quite	U4C
			Adj.	in good health; to get well	U1C
			R.C.	(used after a verb to indicate the completion of an action)	U4C
hǎoxiàng	好像	好像	*V.*	to seem; to be like	U5C
héchàngtuán	合唱团	合唱團	*N.*	chorus	U2B
hélǐ	合理	合理	*Adj.*	reasonable	U6A
hónglǜdēng	红绿灯	紅綠燈	*N.*	traffic light	U4A
hóulóng tòng	喉咙痛	喉嚨痛	*N.*	(a) sore throat	U1C
huà	话	話	*N.*	word; remark	U1B
huācài	花菜	花菜	*N.*	cauliflower	U5C
huàjù	话剧	話劇	*N.*	drama	U2B
huàn	换	換	*V.*	to change	U5A
huàn yīfu	换衣服	換衣服	*V.O.*	to change clothes	U2A
huángguā	黄瓜	黃瓜	*N.*	cucumber	U5C
Huáshèngdùn Tèqū	华盛顿特区	華盛頓特區	*N.*	Washington D.C.	U6A
huàzhuāng	化妆	化妝	*V.O.*	to put on makeup	U2A
huí	回	回	*V.*	to return; to answer; to reply	U3C
huì	会	會	*A.V.*	can; to know how to; to be able to	U3A

huílái	回来	回來	*V.C.*	to return; to come back	U3C
huíqù	回去	回去	*V.C.*	to leave; to go back	U3C
hújiāo	胡椒	胡椒	*N.*	pepper	U5B
húluóbo	胡萝卜	胡蘿蔔	*N.*	carrot	U5C
huò	后	後	*N.*	back	U4A
huǒchē	火车	火車	*N.*	train	U2A
huódòng	活动	活動	*N.*	activity	U6B
Hǔqiū	虎丘	虎丘	*N.*	Tiger Hill	U6C
hùshì	护士	護士	*N.*	nurse	U1C

J

jí	急	急	*Adj.*	anxious; in a hurry	U2A
			Adv.	extremely; exceedingly	U5A
jì	寄	寄	*V.*	to send; to mail	U6A
jiā	加	加	*V.*	to add	U5C
jià	假	假	*N.*	holiday; vacation	U6B
jiàgé	价格	價格	*N.*	price	U6A
jiājiào	家教	家教	*N.*	tutor	U2B
jiājù	家具	傢俱	*N.*	furniture	U4C
jiān	间	間	*M.W.*	room	U4C
	煎	煎	*V.*	to pan-fry	U5C
jiānbǎng	肩膀	肩膀	*N.*	shoulder	U1A
jiānbǐng	煎饼	煎餅	*N.*	pancake	U6B
jiǎng	讲	講	*V.*	to speak; to say; to tell; to talk about	U3C
jiàngliào	酱料	醬料	*N.*	sauce	U5C
jiàngyóu	酱油	醬油	*N.*	soy sauce	U5B
jiànkāng	健康	健康	*Adj.*	healthy	U1C
			N.	health	U1C
jiànmiàn	见面	見面	*V.O.*	to meet	U3B
jiànshēnfáng	健身房	健身房	*N.*	gym	U1A
jiāo	教	教	*V.*	to teach	U3C
jiǎo	脚	腳	*N.*	foot	U1A
jiào	叫	叫	*V.*	to ask; to advise; to tell	U3C
				to call; to greet	U4C

jiāoqū	郊区	郊區	*N.*	suburbs; outskirts	U6A
jiāotōng gōngjù	交通工具	交通工具	*N.*	transportation	U2A
jiāowài	郊外	郊外	*N.*	the countryside around a city; the outskirts of town	U6C
jiǎozhǐ	脚指	腳指	*N.*	toe	U1A
jiātíng lǚguǎn	家庭旅馆	家庭旅館	*N.*	B&B (bed and breakfast)	U6A
jìde	记得	記得	*V.*	to remember	U2B
jiē diànhuà	接电话	接電話	*V.O.*	to answer the phone	U3C
jiējìn	接近	接近	*V.*	to be close to; to approach	U6A
jièlán	芥兰	芥蘭	*N.*	Chinese broccoli	U5B
Jièlán niúròu	芥兰牛肉	芥蘭牛肉	*N.*	Beef with Chinese Broccoli	U5B
jiēshi	结实	結實	*Adj.*	fit; firm	U3A
jīhū	几乎	幾乎	*Adv.*	almost	U1A
jìhuà	计划	計畫	*N.*	plan	U6B
jīhuì	机会	機會	*N.*	chance; opportunity	U3B
jīkuài	鸡块	雞塊	*N.*	chicken nugget	U6B
jìlù	记录	記錄	*V.*	to record	U1B
jìlùpiàn	记录片	記錄片	*N.*	documentary	U2C
jìn	近	近	*Adj.*	near; close	U4A
	进	進	*V.*	to enter; to come; to go into	U4B
jīngshén	精神	精神	*N.*	spirit	U1B
jīngshén bù hǎo	精神不好	精神不好	*Adj.*	not energetic	U1B
jīngshén hǎo	精神好	精神好	*Adj.*	energetic	U1B
jīngyà	惊讶	驚訝	*Adj.*	surprised	U1B
jǐnzhāng	紧张	緊張	*Adj*	nervous	U1B
jìrán	既然	既然	*M.A.*	since; as; now that	U5A
jiǔ	久	久	*Adj.*	long	U1A
jiù	就	就	*Adv.*	just; only	U1A
				(used before a verb to indicate that something happened earlier than was expected)	U1B
				exactly; precisely	U3B
				at once; right away	U6C
Jiùjīnshān	旧金山	舊金山	*N.*	San Francisco	U6A
jiùyào	就要	就要	*Adv.*	be about to; be going to	U2A

Jiǔzhàigōu	九寨沟	九寨溝	N.	Jiuzhaigou Valley	U6C
jìxìnrén dìzhǐ	寄信人地址	寄信人地址	N.	sender's address	U6A
jìxù	继续	繼續	V.	to continue	U6C
jù	句	句	M.W.	sentence	U6C
			N.	sentence	U6C
juédìng	决定	決定	N.	decision	U5A
			V.	to decide	U5A
jùhuì	聚会	聚會	N.	party	U4B
jùqíngpiàn	剧情片	劇情片	N.	drama	U2C

K

kāi	开	開	V.	to drive	U2A
kāichē	开车	開車	V.O.	to drive a car	U2A
kāilǎng	开朗	開朗	Adj.	out-going	U3A
kāishǐ	开始	開始	V.	to begin	U1A
kāixīn	开心	開心	Adj.	happy	U1B
kān	看	看	V.	to look after; to take care of	U6B
kàn	看	看	V.	to think; to consider	U4A
				to see; to visit	U6B
kān háizi	看孩子	看孩子	V.O.	to look after kids	U6B
kànbìng	看病	看病	V.O.	(of a patient) to see a doctor; (of a doctor) to see a patient	U1C
kǎo	烤	烤	V.	to bake	U5C
kǎtōngpiàn	卡通片	卡通片	N.	animation; cartoon	U2C
kē	科	科	M.W.	(school) subject	U6A
kèfáng	客房	客房	N.	guest room	U4C
kēhuànpiàn	科幻片	科幻片	N.	sci-fi film	U2C
kěnéng	可能	可能	Adj.	possible; probable	U5A
késòu	咳嗽	咳嗽	V.	to cough	U1C
kètīng	客厅	客廳	N.	living room	U4C
kèwài huódòng	课外活动	課外活動	N.	extracurricular activities	U2B
kèzhōng	刻钟	刻鐘	M.W.	quarter hour	U1A
kòng	空	空	N.	free time	U2B
kǒngbùpiàn	恐怖片	恐怖片	N.	horror film	U2C

kuā	夸	誇	*V.*	to praise	U6C
kuài	块	塊	*M.W.*	a slice or chunk of something	U5C
			N.	piece; cube; chunk	U5C
kuàicāndiàn	快餐店	快餐店	*N.*	fast-food restaurant	U6B
kuàicānhé	快餐盒	快餐盒	*N.*	to-go box	U6B
kuàixìn	快信	快信	*N.*	express mail	U6A
kuàizi	筷子	筷子	*N.*	chopsticks	U5C
kùn	困	睏	*Adj.*	sleepy	U1B
la	啦	啦	*P.*	(the representation of the combined sounds "了 *le*" and "啊 *a*", denoting exclamation, interrogation, etc.)	U4B
lā dùzi	拉肚子	拉肚子	*V.O.*	to suffer from diarrhea	U1C
làjiāoyóu	辣椒油	辣椒油	*N.*	Tabasco sauce	U6B
lājītǒng	垃圾桶	垃圾桶	*N.*	dustbin; garbage can	U4C
lǎn	懒	懶	*Adj.*	lazy	U1B
làngmàn àiqíngpiàn	浪漫爱情片	浪漫愛情片	*N.*	romance	U2C
lǎorén	老人	老人	*N.*	an old person; a senior citizen	U3C
le	了	了	*P.*	(used after a verb to indicate completion of action)	U1A
				used to indicate a change of status	U1B
lèi	累	累	*Adj.*	tired	U1B
lěngdàn	冷淡	冷淡	*Adj.*	aloof	U3A
lěngdòng shípǐn	冷冻食品	冷凍食品	*N.*	frozen food	U5A
lí	离	離	*Prep.*	off; away; from	U4A
lì	粒	粒	*M.W.*	pill	U1C
lián	连	連	*Conj.*	even	U2A
liǎn	脸	臉	*N.*	face	U1C
liáng	量	量	*V.*	to measure	U1C
liánluò gōngjù	联络工具	聯絡工具	*N.*	communication tools	U2C
liànxí	练习	練習	*V.*	to practice	U1A
liáo	聊	聊	*V.*	to chat	U3C
liǎo	了	了	*C.*	indicating possibility	U6C

liáotiān	聊天	聊天	*V.O.*	to chat	U3C
liáotiānshì	聊天室	聊天室	*N.*	chat room	U2C
lìjiāoqiáo	立交桥	立交橋	*N.*	overpass	U4A
lǐkē	理科	理科	*N.*	natural sciences	U3B
límǐ	厘米	釐米	*M.W.*	centimeter	U4A
língshí	零食	零食	*N.*	snack	U5A
línjū	邻居	鄰居	*N.*	neighbor	U6B
lìrú	例如	例如	*V.*	for example; such as	U6B
liú bítì	流鼻涕	流鼻涕	*V.O.*	to have a runny nose	U1C
liúyán	留言	留言	*V.O.*	to leave a message	U3C
lóngxiā	龙虾	龍蝦	*N.*	lobster	U5B
lóu	楼	樓	*N.*	floor	U4B
lóutī	楼梯	樓梯	*N.*	stairs	U4B
lù	路	路	*N.*	road; path; way	U1A
lùdēng	路灯	路燈	*N.*	streetlight	U4A
lǚguǎn	旅馆	旅館	*N.*	hotel	U6A
lǚkè	旅客	旅客	*N.*	traveler	U6C
lùkǒu	路口	路口	*N.*	intersection	U4A
Lúndūn	伦敦	倫敦	*N.*	London	U6A
lùntán	论坛	論壇	*N.*	bulletin board system (BBS)	U2C
Luómǎ	罗马	羅馬	*N.*	Rome	U6A
Luòshānjī	洛杉矶	洛杉磯	*N.*	Los Angeles	U6A
lùyíng	露营	露營	*V.*	to camp	U6B
			N.	camping	U6B
lǚyóu	旅游	旅遊	*N.*	traveling	U6C

M

mài	卖	賣	*V.*	to sell	U5A
mǎicài	买菜	買菜	*V.O.*	to go grocery shopping	U5A
mǎlíngshǔ	马铃薯	馬鈴薯	*N.*	potato	U5C
mǎlù	马路	馬路	*N.*	road	U4A
máng	忙	忙	*Adj.*	busy	U2B
Màngǔ	曼谷	曼谷	*N.*	Bangkok	U6A
Mǎyǐ shàngshù	蚂蚁上树	螞蟻上樹	*N.*	Rice Noodles with Ground Pork	U5B

měi	每	每	*Pron.*	every; each	U1A
méi bànfǎ	没办法	沒辦法	*C.E.*	can not do anything.	U1B
méi shénme	没什么	沒什麼	*C.E.*	nothing; don't mention it	U2C
méiguānxi	没关系	沒關係	*C.E.*	it's okay	U2A
méimáo	眉毛	眉毛	*N.*	eyebrow	U1C
méishì	没事	沒事	*C.E.*	it's nothing; never mind	U4B
méiyǒu	没有	沒有	*Adv.*	did not; have not	U2C
mén	门	門	*N.*	door	U4C
mèn	焖	燜	*V.*	to simmer	U5C
mǐ	米	米	*M.W.*	meter	U4A
miáotiáo	苗条	苗條	*Adj.*	slender; slim	U3A
miǎozhōng	秒钟	秒鐘	*M.W.*	second	U1A
mílù	迷路	迷路	*V.O.*	to be lost	U4B
míngxìnpiàn	明信片	明信片	*N.*	postcard	U6A
mógu	蘑菇	蘑菇	*N.*	mushroom	U5C
mótuōchē	摩托车	摩托車	*N.*	scooter; motorcycle	U2A
mǔlì	牡蛎	牡蠣	*N.*	oyster	U5B

N

nàlǐ	那里	那裡	*Pron.*	there	U3C
nàme	那么	那麼	*Adv.*	that, so	U1A
nán	男	男	*Adj.*	male	U3A
			N.	male	U3A
	南	南	*N.*	south	U4A
nánde	男的	男的	*N.*	male	U3A
nánguā	南瓜	南瓜	*N.*	pumpkin	U5C
nánguài	难怪	難怪	*Conj.*	no wonder	U2A
nánguò	难过	難過	*Adj*	sad	U1B
nánhái	男孩	男孩	*N.*	boy	U3B
nánpéngyou	男朋友	男朋友	*N.*	boyfriend	U3A
nánrén	男人	男人	*N.*	man	U3A
nánshēng	男生	男生	*N.*	boy	U3A
nàr	那儿	那兒	*Pron.*	there (colloquial)	U3C

ne	呢	呢	*P.*	a final particle used at the end of an interrogative sentence	U1B
nèixiàng	内向	內向	*Adj.*	introverted	U3A
nèixiē	那些	那些	*Pron.*	those	U6C
néng	能	能	*A.V.*	can; to be able to; to have the opportunity to	U1A
Niǔyuē	纽约	紐約	*N.*	New York (City)	U6A
nǚ	女	女	*Adj.*	female	U3A
			N.	female	U3A
nǚde	女的	女的	*N.*	female	U3A
nǚhái	女孩	女孩	*N.*	girl	U3B
nǚpéngyou	女朋友	女朋友	*N.*	girlfriend	U3A
nǚrén	女人	女人	*N.*	woman	U3A
nǚshēng	女生	女生	*N.*	girl	U3A

O

ō	喔	喔	*P.*	a final particle used in imperative sentences to remind the listener to pay attention to what is said	U1B
ó	哦	哦	*Intj.*	indicating understanding or realization	U3B

P

pá	爬	爬	*V.*	to crawl; to climb	U1A
pà	怕	怕	*V.*	to be afraid of	U1C
pài	派	派	*N.*	pie	U5B
pàng	胖	胖	*Adj.*	fat	U3A
pánzi	盘子	盤子	*N.*	plate	U5C
pàozǎo	泡澡	泡澡	*V.O.*	to take a soak in the tub	U2A
péi	陪	陪	*V.*	to accompany	U3C
pēngtiáo fāngshì	烹调方式	烹調方式	*N.*	food preparation	U5C
píngfáng	平房	平房	*N.*	rambler	U4B
píngguǒ pài	苹果派	蘋果派	*N.*	apple pie	U5B
píngxìn	平信	平信	*N.*	regular mail	U6A

Q

qí	骑	騎	*V.*	to ride	U2A
qí mótuōchē	骑摩托车	騎摩托車	*V.O.*	to ride a motorcycle	U2A
qí zìxíngchē	骑自行车	騎自行車	*V.O.*	to ride a bicycle	U2A
qián	前	前	*N.*	front	U4A
qiángbì	墙壁	牆壁	*N.*	wall	U4C
qǐchuáng	起床	起床	*V.*	to get up	U2A
qiē	切	切	*V.*	to cut	U5C
qiézi	茄子	茄子	*N.*	eggplant	U5B
qǐlái	起来	起來	*V.C.*	to begin to; set about to	U5B
qíncài	芹菜	芹菜	*N.*	celery	U5C
qǐng	请	請	*V.*	to invite	U3B
qīngnián lǚguǎn	青年旅馆	青年旅館	*N.*	youth hostel	U6A
qíngxù	情绪	情緒	*N.*	emotion	U1B
qíshí	其实	其實	*Adv.*	in fact; actually	U2C
qiū	丘	丘	*N.*	mound; hill	U6C
qiúduì	球队	球隊	*N.*	team	U1B
quán	全	全	*Adj.*	whole; all over	U1A
quán shēn wú lì	全身无力	全身無力	*Adj.*	to feel weak all over	U1C
quèdìng	确定	確定	*V.*	to determine; to confirm	U1A

R

ràng	让	讓	*V.*	to let; to allow	U2B
ránhòu	然后	然後	*Adv.*	then; afterwards; after that	U4A
rén	人	人	*N.*	person	U3A
rénxíng héngdào	人行横道	人行橫道	*N.*	crosswalk	U4A
rénxíngdào	人行道	人行道	*N.*	sidewalk	U4A
rènzhēn	认真	認真	*Adj.*	serious; conscientious	U6A
rèqíng	热情	熱情	*Adj.*	passionate	U3A
rìcháng shēnghuó	日常生活	日常生活	*N.*	daily life	U2A
ròulèi	肉类	肉類	*N.*	meat	U5A

róumá	肉麻	肉麻	Adj.	disgusting	U2C
rúguǒ	如果	如果	Conj.	if	U2B
rǔzhìpǐn	乳制品	乳製品	N.	dairy product	U5A

S

sànbù	散步	散步	V.	to take a walk; to stroll	U3C
sāngdiàn lèixíng	商店类型	商店類型	N.	types of shops	U5A
shāfā	沙发	沙發	N.	sofa	U4C
shànbèi	扇贝	扇貝	N.	scallop	U5B
shànbiàn	善变	善變	Adj.	fickle	U3A
shàng	上	上	N.	up; above	U4A
			V.	to go up; to get on	U4B
shàng cèsuǒ	上厕所	上廁所	V.O.	to use the toilet	U2A
Shànghǎi	上海	上海	N.	Shanghai	U6A
shàngxué	上学	上學	V.	to go to school	U2B
shǎo	少	少	V.	to lack; to be short of	U5B
shēn	身	身	N.	body	U1A
shēncái	身材	身材	N.	(body) figure	U3A
shēngbìng	生病	生病	V.	to be sick	U1C
shèngdài	圣代	聖代	N.	sundae	U5B
shēnglǐ gǎnjué	生理感觉	生理感覺	N.	feeling	U1B
shēngqì	生气	生氣	Adj.	angry	U1B
			V.O.	to get angry	U1B
shēngyīn	声音	聲音	N.	sound; voice	U4C
shēntǐ	身体	身體	N.	body	U1A
shètuán	社团	社團	N.	club	U2B
shèyǐng	摄影	攝影	N.	photography	U2B
			V.	to take a photograph	U6C
shèxiàngjī	摄像机	攝像機	N.	video camera	U6C
shèyǐngshī	摄影师	攝影師	N.	photographer	U6C
shī	湿	濕	Adj.	wet	U2A
shì	是	是	V.	used to express emphasis and to indicate certainty	U2B

shíjiān	时间	時間	*N.*	time	U2A
shìpín	视频	視頻	*N.*	video chat	U2C
shìqing	事情	事情	*N.*	matter; thing; business	U3B
shìqū	市区	市區	*N.*	downtown	U6A
shíxí	实习	實習	*V.*	to intern	U6B
shíxíshēng	实习生	實習生	*N.*	intern	U6B
shǒu	手	手	*N.*	hand	U1A
shòu	瘦	瘦	*Adj.*	thin	U3A
	受	受	*V.*	to stand; to endure; to bear	U6C
Shǒu'ěr	首尔	首爾	*N.*	Seoul	U6A
shòubùliǎo	受不了	受不了	*C.E.*	not able to bear or tolerate	U6C
shōudào	收到	收到	*V.C.*	to receive; to get	U2C
shōushi	收拾	收拾	*V.*	to put in order; to tidy up	U5C
shōuxìnrén	收信人	收信人	*N.*	mail recipient	U6A
shōuxìnrén dìzhǐ	收信人地址	收信人地址	*N.*	recipient's address	U6A
shǒuzhǐ	手指	手指	*N.*	finger	U1A
shū	输	輸	*V.*	to lose	U1B
shú	熟	熟	*Adj.*	familiar	U3A
shuāng	双	雙	*M.W.*	pair of	U5C
shuāyá	刷牙	刷牙	*V.O.*	to brush one's teeth	U2A
shūcài	蔬菜	蔬菜	*N.*	vegetable	U5A
shūfáng	书房	書房	*N.*	study room	U4C
shūfu	舒服	舒服	*Adj.*	comfortable	U1A
shūguì	书柜	書櫃	*N.*	bookcase	U4C
shuì	睡	睡	*V.*	to sleep	U1B
shuǐbēi	水杯	水杯	*N.*	(water) cup	U5C
shuǐguǒ	水果	水果	*N.*	fruit	U1C
shuìzháo	睡着	睡著	*V.C.*	to fall asleep	U6C
shuǐzhǔyú	水煮鱼	水煮魚	*N.*	Fish Fillet in Sichuan Spicy Broth	U5B
shǔjià	暑假	暑假	*N.*	summer vacation	U6A
shuō	说	說	*V.*	to say; to speak; to talk	U1B
shúshí	熟食	熟食	*N.*	deli food	U5A
sǐ	死	死	*Adv.*	extremely	U2A

sīlì xuéxiào	私立学校	私立學校	*N.*	private school	U3B
sōngbǐng	松饼	鬆餅	*N.*	muffin	U6B
suān	酸	酸	*Adj.*	sore	U1A
suàn	蒜	蒜	*N.*	garlic	U5C
	算	算	*V.*	to count	U6C
suàn le	算了	算了	*C.E.*	forget it; never mind	U5A
suíhé	随和	隨和	*Adj.*	easy-going	U3A
suīrán	虽然	雖然	*Conj.*	although	U2B
sùliàodài	塑料袋	塑料袋	*N.*	plastic bag	U6B
Sūzhōu	苏州	蘇州	*N.*	Suzhou	U6C

T

Tài Shān	泰山	泰山	*N.*	Mount Tai	U6C
Táiběi	台北	台北	*N.*	Taipei	U6A
táng	糖	糖	*N.*	sugar	U5B
tāngchí	汤匙	湯匙	*N.*	spoon	U5C
Tángcùyú	糖醋鱼	糖醋魚	*N.*	Sweet & Sour Fish	U5B
tèbié	特别	特別	*Adv.*	especially; particularly	U3B
téng	疼	疼	*Adj.*	aching; achy	U1A
tí	提	提	*V.*	to mention; to bring up	U3C
tiándiǎn	甜点	甜點	*N.*	dessert	U5B
tiānqiáo	天桥	天橋	*N.*	pedestrian bridge	U4A
tiántiánquān	甜甜圈	甜甜圈	*N.*	doughnut	U5B
tiáo	条	條	*M.W.*	used for text messages	U2C
tiáoliào	调料	調料	*N.*	seasoning	U5B
tīng	听	聽	*V.*	to listen; to hear	U4C
tīngshuō	听说	聽說	*V.*	to be told; to hear of	U6A
tíqǐ	提起	提起	*V.C.*	to mention	U3C
tǐwēn	体温	體溫	*N.*	body temperature	U1C
tǐwēnjì	体温计	體溫計	*N.*	thermometer	U1C
tóng	同	同	*Adj.*	same; alike	U3B
tòng	痛	痛	*V.*	to ache	U1A
tóngzǐjūn	童子军	童子軍	*N.*	scouts	U2B

tóu	头	頭	*N.*	head	U1A
tóufa	头发	頭髮	*N.*	hair	U1A
tóutòng	头痛	頭痛	*N.*	headache	U1C
tóuyūn	头晕	頭暈	*Adj.*	dizzy	U1C
tǔdòu	土豆	土豆	*N.*	potato	U5C

W

wa	哇	哇	*Intj.*	(sound of vomiting and crying)	U4C
wàixiàng	外向	外向	*Adj.*	extroverted	U3A
wán	完	完	*R.C.*	(used after a verb as a complement to indicate something ran out or used up)	U4C
			V.	to finish	U4C
wǎn	碗	碗	*N.*	bowl	U5C
	晚	晚	*Adj.*	late	U2A
				not on time; late	U4B
wǎncān	晚餐	晚餐	*N.*	dinner	U2A
wǎnfàn	晚饭	晚飯	*N.*	dinner	U2A
wǎng	往	往	*Prep.*	in the direction of; to; toward	U4A
wǎng hòu zǒu	往后走	往後走	*V.*	to move backward	U4A
wàngjì	忘记	忘記	*V.*	to forget	U2B
Wǎngshī Yuán	网师园	網師園	*N.*	Garden of the Master of the Nets	U6C
wèi	位	位	*M.W.*	polite measure word for people	U3C
wèidào	味道	味道	*N.*	taste	U5C
wēihuàbǐng	威化饼	威化餅	*N.*	waffle	U6B
wénkē	文科	文科	*N.*	liberal arts	U3B
wèntí	问题	問題	*N.*	problem; question	U2C
wòfáng	卧房	臥房	*N.*	bedroom	U4C
wǔcān	午餐	午餐	*N.*	lunch	U2A
wǔdǎo	舞蹈	舞蹈	*N.*	dance	U2B
wǔfàn	午饭	午飯	*N.*	lunch	U2A
xuéxiào shēnghuó	学校生活	學校生活	*N.*	school life	U3B

xī	西	西	*N.*	west	U4A
xǐ	洗	洗	*V.*	to wash	U5C
xiā	虾	蝦	*N.*	shrimp	U5B
xià	下	下	*N.*	down; under	U4A
			V.	to go down; to get off	U4B
xiàlìngyíng	夏令营	夏令營	*N.*	summer camp	U6B
xiān	先	先	*Adv.*	first; earlier; before	U4A
xiǎng	想	想	*V.*	to think	U4B
Xiānggǎng	香港	香港	*N.*	Hong Kong	U6A
xiàngpiàn	相片	相片	*N.*	photograph	U6C
xiāngxià	乡下	鄉下	*N.*	countryside	U6C
xiāngxìn	相信	相信	*V.*	to believe	U5B
xiāo	削	削	*V.*	to peel	U5C
xiàochē	校车	校車	*N.*	school bus	U2A
xiàoduì	校队	校隊	*N.*	school team	U3B
xiǎohái	小孩	小孩	*N.*	kid; child	U3C
xiàokān	校刊	校刊	*N.*	school paper	U2B
xiǎoshí	小时	小時	*N.*	hour	U1A
xiǎotuǐ	小腿	小腿	*N.*	calf	U1A
xiàoyǒu	校友	校友	*N.*	alumni	U3B
xiàqù	下去	下去	*C.*	indicates the continuation of an action	U6C
xīběi	西北	西北	*N.*	northwest	U4A
xiē	些	些	*M.W.*	some; a little	U6C
xiě	写	寫	*V.*	to write	U1B
xiè	蟹	蟹	*N.*	crab	U5B
xīgài	膝盖	膝蓋	*N.*	knee	U1A
xīguǎn	吸管	吸管	*N.*	straw	U6B
xīhóngshì	西红柿	西红柿	*N.*	tomato	U5C
Xīhú	西湖	西湖	*N.*	West Lake	U6C
xǐjùpiàn	喜剧片	喜劇片	*N.*	comedy	U2C
xǐliǎn	洗脸	洗臉	*V.O.*	to wash one's face	U2A
xìn	信	信	*N.*	letter	U6A

xīnán	西南	西南	*N.*	southwest	U4A
xīndì	心地	心地	*N.*	heart (metaphorical)	U3A
xìnfēng	信封	信封	*N.*	envelope	U6A
xǐng	醒	醒	*V.*	to wake up	U2A
xīngfèn	兴奋	興奮	*Adj.*	excited	U1B
xìngkuī	幸亏	幸虧	*Adv.*	fortunately; luckily	U5C
xìngqù	兴趣	興趣	*N.*	interest	U2C
xíngrén	行人	行人	*N.*	pedestrian	U4A
Xīní	悉尼	悉尼	*N.*	Sydney	U6A
xīnqíng	心情	心情	*N.*	mood	U1B
xīnqíng bù hǎo	心情不好	心情不好	*Adj.*	in a bad mood	U1B
xīnqíng hǎo	心情好	心情好	*Adj.*	in a good mood	U1B
xīnxiān	新鲜	新鮮	*Adj.*	fresh	U5A
xìnxiāng	信箱	信箱	*N.*	mailbox	U4B
xìnxīn	信心	信心	*N.*	confidence	U5A
xǐshǒujiān	洗手间	洗手間	*N.*	bathroom; toilet	U4C
xiūxi	休息	休息	*V.*	to rest	U1C
xīwàng	希望	希望	*V.*	to hope	U5B
xǐzǎo	洗澡	洗澡	*V.O.*	to take a shower; to have a bath	U2A
xuédì	学弟	學弟	*N.*	male junior (student)	U3B
xuéjiě	学姐	學姐	*N.*	female senior (student)	U3B
xuémèi	学妹	學妹	*N.*	female junior (student)	U3B
xuéxí	学习	學習	*V.*	to study	U2B
xuéxiào	学校	學校	*N.*	school	U2A
xuézhǎng	学长	學長	*N.*	male senior (student)	U3B

Y

ya	呀	呀	*P.*	used after short answers to soften the tone	U3A
yáchǐ	牙齿	牙齒	*N.*	tooth	U1C
yán	盐	鹽	*N.*	salt	U5B
yángcōng	洋葱	洋蔥	*N.*	onion	U5C
yángcōngquān	洋葱圈	洋蔥圈	*N.*	onion ring	U6B
yǎnglǎoyuàn	养老院	養老院	*N.*	nursing home	U3C

yángtái	阳台	陽台	*N.*	balcony	U4B
yǎnjīng	眼睛	眼睛	*N.*	eye	U1C
yánzhòng	严重	嚴重	*Adj.*	serious	U1C
yào	药	藥	*N.*	medicine; medication	U1C
yàobùrán	要不然	要不然	*Conj.*	otherwise; or	U5C
yāoqǐng	邀请	邀請	*N.*	invitation	U4A
			V.	to invite	U4A
yàoshì	要是	要是	*Conj.*	if	U2B
yèxiāo	夜宵	夜宵	*N.*	late-night snack	U2A
yí	咦	咦	*Intj.*	(indicating surprise) well; why; what	U2A
yìbiān	一边	一邊	*Adv.*	(indicating two simultaneous actions) at the same time; simultaneously	U4C
yídìng	一定	一定	*Adv.*	must	U1B
Yíhé Yuán	颐和园	頤和園	*N.*	Summer Palaces	U6C
yìhuǐr	一会儿	一會兒	*T.W.*	a moment	U1B
yíng	赢	赢	*V.*	to win	U1B
yǐqián	以前	以前	*T.W.*	before; formerly	U3B
yīshēng	医生	醫生	*N.*	doctor	U1C
yìshù	艺术	藝術	*N.*	art	U2B
yǐwéi	以为	以為	*V.*	to think (mistakenly)	U4B
yìxiē	一些	一些	*Num.+M. W.*	some; a few	U6C
yíyàng	一样	一樣	*Adj.*	the same	U3A
yīyuàn	医院	醫院	*N.*	hospital	U1C
yǐzi	椅子	椅子	*N.*	chair	U4C
yònggōng	用功	用功	*Adj.*	hardworking; studious; diligent	U6A
yòu	又	又	*Adv.*	again	U2B
				also; and (indicates additional ideas or an afterthought)	U6C
	右	右	*N.*	right	U4A
yóu chāi	邮差	郵差	*N.*	mailman	U6A
yòu guǎi	右拐	右拐	*V.*	to turn right	U4A
yǒu xìnxīn	有信心	有信心	*Adj.*	confident	U5A
yòu zhuǎn	右转	右轉	*V.*	to turn right	U4A

yóujú	邮局	郵局	*N.*	post office	U6A
yóukè	游客	遊客	*N.*	traveler	U6C
yóupiào	邮票	郵票	*N.*	(postage) stamp	U6A
yóuxiāng	邮箱	郵箱	*N.*	mailbox	U6A
yóuxìjī	游戏机	遊戲機	*N.*	video game player	U4C
yóuxué	游学	遊學	*V.*	to study abroad	U6B
yóuxuétuán	游学团	遊學團	*N.*	overseas study group	U6B
yóuyú	鱿鱼	鱿魚	*N.*	squid	U5B
yú	鱼	魚	*N.*	fish	U5B
yuán	园	園	*N.*	garden	U6C
yuǎn	远	遠	*Adj.*	far	U4A
Yuánmíngyuán	圆明园	圓明園	*N.*	Old Summer Palace	U6C
yuànzi	院子	院子	*N.*	courtyard; yard	U4B
yuè lái yuè…	越来越…	越來越…	*C.E.*	more and more…	U6A
yuè…yuè…	越…越…	越…越…	*C.E.*	the more…, the more…	U6A
yuètuán	乐团	樂團	*N.*	band	U2B
yùmǐ	玉米	玉米	*N.*	corn	U5C
yùmǐtāng	玉米汤	玉米湯	*N.*	corn soup	U6B
yūn	晕	暈	*V.*	to feel dizzy; to faint	U1C
yùndòng	运动	運動	*N.*	sports	U2B
yùshì	浴室	浴室	*N.*	bathroom	U4C
Yúxiāng qiézi	鱼香茄子	魚香茄子	*N.*	Eggplant Sichuan Style	U5B

Z

záhuòdiàn	杂货店	雜貨店	*N.*	grocery store	U5A
zài	再	再	*Adv.*	again	U3C
				then (indicating that one action takes place after the completion of another)	U4A
zánmen	咱们	咱們	*Pron.*	we; us	U1A
zǎo	早	早	*Adj.*	early	U2A
				long ago; as early as; for a long time	U4B
zǎocān	早餐	早餐	*N.*	breakfast	U2A
zěnme	怎么	怎麼	*Q.W.*	why; how	U1A
zěnme le	怎么了	怎麼了	*C.E.*	What's up? What's wrong?	U2C

zhá	炸	炸	V.	to fry	U5C
zhǎng	长	長	V.	to grow	U3A
zhāngyú	章鱼	章魚	N.	octopus	U5B
zhǎo	找	找	V.	to call on; to invite; to look for	U3A
zhàogù	照顾	照顧	V.	to take care (of sb.)	U2B
zhàopiàn	照片	照片	N.	photograph	U6C
zhàoxiàng	照相	照相	V.O.	to take photos	U6C
zhàoxiàngjī	照相机	照相機	N.	camera	U6C
zhèixiē	这些	這些	Pron.	these	U6C
zhèlǐ	这里	這裡	Pron.	here	U3C
zhème	这么	這麼	Adv.	this, so	U1A
zhèngzài	正在	正在	Adv.	in the process of; during the course of	U4C
zhèngzhuàng	症状	症狀	N.	symptom	U1C
zhěnsuǒ	诊所	診所	N.	clinic	U1C
zhèr	这儿	這兒	Pron.	here (colloquial)	U3C
zhèyàng	这样	這樣	Adv.	this way; like this	U3B
zhí	直	直	Adv.	directly; straight	U4A
zhí zǒu	直走	直走	V.	to go straight	U4A
zhǐ	只	只	M.W.	a measure word for utensils like spoons and forks	U5C
zhǐhǎo	只好	只好	Adv.	have (no choice but) to	U6A
zhǐshì	只是	只是	Adv.	merely; simply; just; only	U2C
zhìyuàn gōngzuò	志愿工作	志願工作	N.	volunteer work	U3C
zhìyuànzhě	志愿者	志願者	N.	volunteer	U2B
zhòng	重	重	Adj.	heavy	U5B
zhōngcān	中餐	中餐	N.	lunch	U2A
zhōngfàn	中饭	中飯	N.	lunch	U2A
zhōngtóu	钟头	鐘頭	N.	hour	U1A
zhòngyào	重要	重要	Adj.	important	U5B
zhōngyú	终于	終於	Adv.	at last; in the end	U4B
Zhōuzhuāng	周庄	周莊	N.	Zhouzhuang (a historic "water town" built on a system of canals)	U6C
zhǔ	煮	煮	V.	to cook; to boil	U5C
zhù	住	住	V.	to live	U6C

zhuǎn	转	轉	*V.*	to turn	U4A
zhuāng	庄	莊	*N.*	village	U6C
zhuàng	壮	壯	*Adj.*	strong	U3A
zhuǎnxué	转学	轉學	*V.O.*	to transfer to another school	U3B
zhùcángshì	贮藏室	貯藏室	*N.*	storage room	U4C
zhǔnbèi	准备	準備	*N.*	preparation	U3C
			V.	to prepare	U3C
zhǔnshí	准时	準時	*Adj.*	punctual; on time	U4B
Zhuózhèng Yuán	拙政园	拙政園	*N.*	Humble Administrator's Garden	U6C
zhuōzi	桌子	桌子	*N.*	table; desk	U4C
zhùsù	住宿	住宿	*N.*	accommodation	U6A
zhǔyi	主意	主意	*N.*	idea; plan	U4A
zhùyì	注意	注意	*V.*	to pay attention to	U1C
zìxíngchē	自行车	自行車	*N.*	bicycle	U2A
zǒngshì	总是	總是	*Adv.*	always	U1A
zǒulù	走路	走路	*V.O.*	to walk	U1A
zuǐba	嘴巴	嘴巴	*N.*	mouth	U1C
zuìhǎo	最好	最好	*Adv.*	had better; it would be best if	U1C
zuìhòu	最后	最後	*Adj.*	last; final	U6A
zuìjìn	最近	最近	*Adv.*	recently; lately	U2C
zuò	座	座	*M.W.*	(used for mountains or buildings)	U1A
	坐	坐	*V.*	to go by; to travel by	U2A
	左	左	*N.*	left	U4A
zuò gōngkè	做功课	做功课	*V.O.*	to do homework	U2A
zuǒ guǎi	左拐	左拐	*V.*	to turn left	U4A
zuǒ zhuǎn	左转	左轉	*V.*	to turn left	U4A
zuòfàn	做饭	做飯	*V.O.*	to cook	U4A
Zuǒzōngtáng jī	左宗棠鸡	左宗棠雞	*N.*	General Tsao's chicken	U5B

Each entry lists the English meaning, simplified character, traditional character, Pinyin, part of speech, unit and lesson.

A

English	Simplified	Traditional	Pinyin	Part of Speech	Unit
(indicating two simultaneous actions) at the same time; simultaneously	一边	一邊	yìbiān	*Adv.*	U4C
a final particle used at the end of an interrogative sentence	呢	呢	ne	*P.*	U1B
a final particle used in imperative sentences to remind the listener to pay attention to what is said	喔	喔	ō	*P.*	U1B
a moment	一会儿	一會兒	yíhuǐr	*T.W.*	U1B
a slice or chunk of something	块	塊	kuài	*M.W.*	U5C
abroad; overseas	国外	國外	guówài	*Adj.*	U6A
accommodation	住宿	住宿	zhùsù	*N.*	U6A
to accompany	陪	陪	péi	*V.*	U3C
to ache	痛	痛	tòng	*V.*	U1A
aching; achy	疼	疼	téng	*Adj.*	U1A
action film	动作片	動作片	dòngzuòpiàn	*N.*	U2C
activity	活动	活動	huódòng	*N.*	U6B
to add	加	加	jiā	*V.*	U5C
again	又	又	yòu	*Adv.*	U2B
	再	再	zài	*Adv.*	U3C
airmail	航空信	航空信	hángkōngxìn	*N.*	U6A
almost	几乎	幾乎	jīhū	*Adv.*	U1A
almost; nearly	差不多	差不多	chàbuduō	*Adj.*	U4A
aloof	冷淡	冷淡	lěngdàn	*Adj.*	U3A
also; and (indicates additional ideas or an afterthought)	又	又	yòu	*Adv.*	U6C
although	虽然	雖然	suīrán	*Conj.*	U2B
alumni	校友	校友	xiàoyǒu	*N.*	U3B
always	总是	總是	zǒngshì	*Adv.*	U1A
always; all along	从来	從來	cónglái	*Adv.*	U6A
to an extreme degree (lit., "*to death*")	得要命	得要命	de yàomìng	*C.*	U5B
an old person; a senior citizen	老人	老人	lǎorén	*N.*	U3C

angry	生气	生氣	shēngqì	*Adj.*	U1B
animation; cartoon	卡通片	卡通片	kǎtōngpiàn	*N.*	U2C
another day; some other day	改天	改天	gǎitiān	*Adv.*	U3A
to answer the phone	接电话	接電話	jiē diànhuà	*V.O.*	U3C
anxious; in a hurry	急	急	jí	*Adj.*	U2A
apartment house	公寓	公寓	gōngyù	*N.*	U4B
apple pie	苹果派	蘋果派	píngguǒ pài	*N.*	U5B
arm	胳膊	胳膊	gēbo	*N.*	U1A
to arrange classes (based on students' academic preference)	分班	分班	fēnbān	*V.O.*	U3B
to arrive late; to be late	迟到	遲到	chídào	*V.*	U2A
art	艺术	藝術	yìshù	*N.*	U2B
to ask; to advise; to tell	叫	叫	jiào	*V.*	U3C
at last; in the end	终于	終於	zhōngyú	*Adv.*	U4B
at once; right away	就	就	jiù	*Adv.*	U6C
attic; loft	阁楼	閣樓	gélóu	*N.*	U4C

B

B&B (bed and breakfast)	家庭旅馆	家庭旅館	jiātíng lǚguǎn	*N.*	U6A
把 *bǎ* marks an object placed which precedes its verb	把	把	bǎ	*CV.*	U5C
baby-sitter	保姆	保姆	bǎomǔ	*N.*	U2B
back	背	背	bèi	*N.*	U1A
	后	後	huò	*N.*	U4A
bag	袋子	袋子	dàizi	*N.*	U5B
bagel	百吉饼	百吉餅	bǎijíbǐng	*N.*	U6B
to bake	烤	烤	kǎo	*V.*	U5C
balcony	阳台	陽台	yángtái	*N.*	U4B
band	乐团	樂團	yuètuán	*N.*	U2B
Bangkok	曼谷	曼谷	Màngǔ	*N.*	U6A
basement	地下室	地下室	dìxiàshì	*N.*	U4C
bathroom	浴室	浴室	yùshì	*N.*	U4C
bathroom; toilet	厕所	廁所	cèsuǒ	*N.*	U4C
	洗手间	洗手間	xǐshǒujiān	*N.*	

be about to; be going to	就要	就要	jiùyào	*Adv.*	U2A
to be afraid of	怕	怕	pà	*V.*	U1C
to be close to; to approach	接近	接近	jiējìn	*V.*	U6A
to be lost	迷路	迷路	mílù	*V.O.*	U4B
to be sick	生病	生病	shēngbìng	*V.*	U1C
to be told; to hear of	听说	聽說	tīngshuō	*V.*	U6A
bedroom	卧房	臥房	wòfáng	*N.*	U4C
Beef with Chinese Broccoli	芥兰牛肉	芥蘭牛肉	jièlán niúròu	*N.*	U5B
before; formerly	以前	以前	yǐqián	*T.W.*	U3B
to begin	开始	開始	kāishǐ	*V.*	U1A
to begin to; set about to	起来	起來	qǐlái	*V.C.*	U5B
Beijing	北京	北京	Běijīng	*N.*	U6A
to believe	相信	相信	xiāngxìn	*V.*	U5B
Berlin	柏林	柏林	Bólín	*N.*	U6A
bicycle	自行车	自行車	zìxíngchē	*N.*	U2A
blog	博客	博客	bókè	*N.*	U1B
to blow-dry hair	吹头发	吹頭髮	chuī tóufa	*V.O.*	U2A
boat; ship	船	船	chuán	*N.*	U2A
body	身体	身體	shēntǐ	*N.*	U1A
	身	身	shēn	*N.*	
body temperature	体温	體溫	tǐwēn	*N.*	U1C
bookcase	书柜	書櫃	shūguì	*N.*	U4C
bowl	碗	碗	wǎn	*N.*	U5C
boy	男生	男生	nánshēng	*N.*	U3A
	男孩	男孩	nánhái	*N.*	U3B
boyfriend	男朋友	男朋友	nánpéngyou	*N.*	U3A
breakfast	早餐	早餐	zǎocān	*N.*	U2A
to brush one's teeth	刷牙	刷牙	shuāyá	*V.O.*	U2A
bulletin board system (BBS)	论坛	論壇	lùntán	*N.*	U2C
bus	公交车	公交車	gōngjiāochē	*N.*	U2A
busy	忙	忙	máng	*Adj.*	U2B
but	但是	但是	dànshì	*Conj.*	U2B
	不过	不過	búguò	*Adj.*	U6A

cake	蛋糕	蛋糕	dàngāo	N.	U5B
calf	小腿	小腿	xiǎotuǐ	N.	U1A
to call on; to invite; to look for	找	找	zhǎo	V.	U3A
to call; to greet	叫	叫	jiào	V.	U4C
camera	照相机	照相機	zhàoxiàngjī	N.	U6C
to camp	露营	露營	lùyíng	V.	U6B
camping	露营	露營	lùyíng	N.	U6B
can not do anything.	没办法	沒辦法	méi bànfǎ	C.E.	U1B
can; to be able to; to have the opportunity to	能	能	néng	A.V.	U1A
can; to know how to; to be able to	会	會	huì	A.V.	U3A
canned good	罐头	罐頭	guàntou	N.	U5A
car; vehicle	车	車	chē	N.	U2A
carrot	胡萝卜	胡蘿蔔	húluóbo	N.	U5C
cauliflower	花菜	花菜	huācài	N.	U5C
celery	芹菜	芹菜	qíncài	N.	U5C
centimeter	公分	公分	gōngfēn	M.W.	U4A
	厘米	釐米	límǐ	M.W.	
certainly	才	才	cái	Adv.	U5B
chair	椅子	椅子	yǐzi	N.	U4C
chance; opportunity	机会	機會	jīhuì	N.	U3B
to change	换	換	huàn	V.	U5A
to change clothes	换衣服	換衣服	huàn yīfu	V.O.	U2A
to chat	聊天	聊天	liáotiān	V.O.	U3C
	聊	聊	liáo	V.	U3C
chat room	聊天室	聊天室	liáotiānshì	N.	U2C
chicken nugget	鸡块	雞塊	jīkuài	N.	U6B
child	孩子	孩子	háizi	N.	U3C
Chinese broccoli	芥兰	芥蘭	jièlán	N.	U5B
Chinese cabbage	大白菜	大白菜	dàbáicài	N.	U5C
chopsticks	筷子	筷子	kuàizi	N.	U5C
chorus; choir	合唱团	合唱團	héchàngtuán	N.	U2B
city	城市	城市	chéngshì	N.	U6C

clam	蛤蜊	蛤蜊	gélí	N.	U5B
class	班	班	bān	N.	U3A
clinic	诊所	診所	zhěnsuǒ	N.	U1C
club	社团	社團	shètuán	N.	U2B
coffee table	茶几	茶几	chájī	N.	U4C
comedy	喜剧片	喜劇片	xǐjùpiàn	N.	U2C
comfortable	舒服	舒服	shūfu	Adj.	U1A
communication tools	联络工具	聯絡工具	liánluò gōngjù	N.	U2C
confidence	信心	信心	xìnxīn	N.	U5A
confident	有信心	有信心	yǒu xìnxīn	Adj.	U5A
to continue	继续	繼續	jìxù	V.	U6C
convenience store	便利商店	便利商店	biànlì shāngdiàn	N.	U5A
to cook	做饭	做飯	zuòfàn	V.O.	U4A
to cook; to boil	煮	煮	zhǔ	V.	U5C
corn	玉米	玉米	yùmǐ	N.	U5C
corn soup	玉米汤	玉米湯	yùmǐtāng	N.	U6B
to cough	咳嗽	咳嗽	késòu	V.	U1C
to count	算	算	suàn	V.	U6C
countryside	乡下	鄉下	xiāngxià	N.	U6C
courtyard; yard	院子	院子	yuànzi	N.	U4B
crab	蟹	蟹	xiè	N.	U5B
cram school	补习班	補習班	bǔxíbān	N.	U3B
to crawl; to climb	爬	爬	pá	V.	U1A
crosswalk	人行横道	人行横道	rénxíng héngdào	N.	U4A
cucumber	黄瓜	黃瓜	huángguā	N.	U5C
(water) cup	水杯	水杯	shuǐbēi	N.	U5C
to cut	切	切	qiē	V.	U5C

D

daily life	日常生活	日常生活	rìcháng shēnghuó	N.	U2A
dairy product	乳制品	乳製品	rǔzhìpǐn	N.	U5A
dance	舞蹈	舞蹈	wǔdǎo	N.	U2B

English	Simplified	Traditional	Pinyin	Type	Unit
to dare	敢	敢	gǎn	V.	U4A
to decide	决定	決定	juédìng	V.	U5A
decision	决定	決定	juédìng	N.	U5A
deli food	熟食	熟食	shúshí	N.	U5A
dessert	甜点	甜點	tiándiǎn	N.	U5B
to determine; to confirm	确定	確定	quèdìng	V.	U1A
to dial (a phone)	拨电话	撥電話	bō diànhuà	V.O.	U3C
to dial a wrong number	打错了	打錯了	dǎcuò le	C.E.	U3C
did not; have not	没有	沒有	méiyǒu	Adv.	U2C
dining room	饭厅	飯廳	fàntīng	N.	U4C
dinner	晚饭	晚飯	wǎnfàn	N.	U2A
	晚餐	晚餐	wǎncān	N.	U2A
direction	方向	方向	fāngxiàng	N.	U4A
direction; points of the compass	方位	方位	fāngwèi	N.	U4A
directly; straight	直	直	zhí	Adv.	U4A
disgusting	肉麻	肉麻	ròumá	Adj.	U2C
dizzy	头晕	頭暈	tóuyūn	Adj.	U1C
to do homework	做功课	做功課	zuò gōngkè	V.O.	U2A
do not (used in imperative sentences)	别	別	bié	Adv.	U1B
doctor	医生	醫生	yīshēng	N.	U1C
documentary	记录片	記錄片	jìlùpiàn	N.	U2C
doggie bag	打包袋	打包袋	dǎbāodài	N.	U6B
door	门	門	mén	N.	U4C
doughnut	甜甜圈	甜甜圈	tiántiánquān	N.	U5B
down; under	下	下	xià	N.	U4A
downtown	市区	市區	shìqū	N.	U6A
to doze; to nod off	打瞌睡	打瞌睡	dǎ kēshuì	V.	U1B
drama	话剧	話劇	huàjù	N.	U2B
	剧情片	劇情片	jùqíngpiàn	N.	U2C
to drive	开	開	kāi	V.	U2A
to drive a car	开车	開車	kāichē	V.O.	U2A
dustbin; garbage can	垃圾桶	垃圾桶	lājītǒng	N.	U4C

E

English	Simplified	Traditional	Pinyin	Part	Unit
ear	耳朵	耳朵	ěrduo	*N.*	U1C
early	早	早	zǎo	*Adj.*	U2A
east	东	東	dōng	*N.*	U4A
easy-going	随和	隨和	suíhé	*Adj.*	U3A
eggplant	茄子	茄子	qiézi	*N.*	U5B
Eggplant Sichuan Style	鱼香茄子	魚香茄子	Yúxiāng qiézi	*N.*	U5B
elevator	电梯	電梯	diàntī	*N.*	U4B
email (the short form of 电子邮件 *diànzǐ yóujiàn*)	电邮	電郵	diànyóu	*N.*	U2C
emotion	情绪	情緒	qíngxù	*N.*	U1B
energetic	精神好	精神好	jīngshén hǎo	*Adj.*	U1B
enough	够	夠	gòu	*Adj.*	U6C
to enter; to come; to go into	进	進	jìn	*V.*	U4B
envelope	信封	信封	xìnfēng	*N.*	U6A
especially; particularly	特别	特別	tèbié	*Adv.*	U3B
even	连	連	lián	*Conj.*	U2A
every; each	每	每	měi	*Pron.*	U1A
exactly; precisely	就	就	jiù	*Adv.*	U3B
except for; besides	除了…以外, 都/也…	除了…以外, 都/也…	chúle…yǐwài, dōu/ yě	*I.E.*	U2C
excited	兴奋	興奮	xīngfèn	*Adj.*	U1B
express mail	快信	快信	kuàixìn	*N.*	U6A
extracurricular activities	课外活动	課外活動	kèwài huódòng	*N.*	U2B
extremely	死	死	sǐ	*Adv.*	U2A
extremely; exceedingly	极	極	jí	*Adv.*	U5A
	不得了	不得了	bùdéliǎo	*Adv.*	U6A
extroverted	外向	外向	wàixiàng	*Adj.*	U3A
eye	眼睛	眼睛	yǎnjīng	*N.*	U1C
eyebrow	眉毛	眉毛	méimáo	*N.*	U1C

F

English	Simplified	Traditional	Pinyin	Part	Unit
(body) figure	身材	身材	shēncái	*N.*	U3A
face	脸	臉	liǎn	*N.*	U1C

to fall asleep	睡着	睡著	shuìzháo	*V.C.*	U6C
familiar	熟	熟	shú	*Adj.*	U3A
far	远	遠	yuǎn	*Adj.*	U4A
fast-food restaurant	快餐店	快餐店	kuàicāndiàn	*N.*	U6B
fat	胖	胖	pàng	*Adj.*	U3A
father and mother; parents	父母	父母	fù-mǔ	*N.*	U4C
to feel dizzy; to faint	晕	暈	yūn	*V.*	U1C
to feel relieved	放心	放心	fàngxīn	*V.O.*	U4C
to feel weak all over	全身无力	全身無力	quán shēn wú lì	*Adj.*	U1C
feeling	生理感觉	生理感覺	shēnglǐ gǎnjué	*N.*	U1B
female	女	女	nǚ	*Adj.*	U3A
			nǚ	*N.*	U3A
	女的	女的	nǚde	*N.*	U3A
female junior (student)	学妹	學妹	xuémèi	*N.*	U3B
female senior (student)	学姐	學姐	xuéjiě	*N.*	U3B
fickle	善变	善變	shànbiàn	*Adj.*	U3A
film genres	电影分类	電影分類	diànyǐng fēnlèi	*N.*	U2C
finger	手指	手指	shǒuzhǐ	*N.*	U1A
to finish	完	完	wán	*V.*	U4C
to finish school	放学	放學	fàngxué	*V.*	U2B
first; earlier; before	先	先	xiān	*Adv.*	U4A
fish	鱼	魚	yú	*N.*	U5B
Fish Fillet in Sichuan Spicy Broth	水煮鱼	水煮魚	Shuǐzhǔyú	*N.*	U5B
fit; firm	结实	結實	jiēshi	*Adj.*	U3A
floor	楼	樓	lóu	*N.*	U4B
	地板	地板	dìbǎn	*N.*	U4C
food preparation	烹调方式	烹調方式	pēngtiáo fāngshì	*N.*	U5C
foot	脚	腳	jiǎo	*N.*	U1A
for	给	給	gěi	*Prep.*	U2B
for example; such as	例如	例如	lìrú	*V.*	U6B
to forget	忘记	忘記	wàngjì	*V.*	U2B
forget it; never mind	算了	算了	suàn le	*C.E.*	U5A
fork	叉子	叉子	chāzi	*N.*	U5C
fortunately; luckily	幸亏	幸虧	xìngkuī	*Adv.*	U5C

free time	空	空	kòng	*N.*	U2B
fresh	新鲜	新鮮	xīnxiān	*Adj.*	U5A
from	从	從	cóng	*Prep.*	U4A
front	前	前	qián	*N.*	U4A
front door	大门	大門	dàmén	*N.*	U4B
frozen food	冷冻食品	冷凍食品	lěngdòng shípǐn	*N.*	U5A
fruit	水果	水果	shuǐguǒ	*N.*	U1C
to fry	炸	炸	zhá	*V.*	U5C
furniture	家具	傢俱	jiājù	*N.*	U4C

G

garage	车库	車庫	chēkù	*N.*	U4B
garden	园	園	yuán	*N.*	U6C
Garden of the Master of the Nets	网师园	網師園	Wǎngshī Yuán	*N.*	U6C
garlic	蒜	蒜	suàn	*N.*	U5C
General Tsao's chicken	左宗棠鸡	左宗棠雞	Zuǒzōngtáng jī	*N.*	U5B
to get angry	生气	生氣	shēngqì	*V.O.*	U1B
to get up	起床	起床	qǐchuáng	*V.*	U2A
girl	女生	女生	nǚshēng	*N.*	U3A
	女孩	女孩	nǚhái	*N.*	U3B
girlfriend	女朋友	女朋友	nǚpéngyou	*N.*	U3A
to go by; to travel by	坐	坐	zuò	*V.*	U2A
to go down; to get off	下	下	xià	*V.*	U4B
to go grocery shopping	买菜	買菜	mǎicài	*V.O.*	U5A
to go on vacation	度假	度假	dùjià	*V.O.*	U6B
to go out	出门	出門	chūmén	*V.*	U2A
	出去	出去	chūqù	*V.C.*	U2B
to go straight	直走	直走	zhí zǒu	*V.*	U4A
to go to school	上学	上學	shàngxué	*V.*	U2B
to go up; to get on	上	上	shàng	*V.*	U4B
good; excellent	棒	棒	bàng	*Adj.*	U3B
grocery store	杂货店	雜貨店	záhuòdiàn	*N.*	U5A
to grow	长	長	zhǎng	*V.*	U3A

guest room	客房	客房	kèfáng	N.	U4C
gym	健身房	健身房	jiànshēnfáng	N.	U1A

H

had better; it would be best if	最好	最好	zuìhǎo	Adv.	U1C
had better; it's best to	还是	還是	háishì	Adv.	U4A
hair	头发	頭髮	tóufa	N.	U1A
hand	手	手	shǒu	N.	U1A
to hang up (the phone)	挂电话	掛電話	guà diànhuà	V.O.	U3C
happy	开心	開心	kāixīn	Adj.	U1B
hardworking; studious; diligent	用功	用功	yònggōng	Adj.	U6A
have (no choice but) to	只好	只好	zhǐhǎo	Adv.	U6A
to have a cold	感冒	感冒	gǎnmào	V.	U1C
to have a fever	发烧	發燒	fāshāo	V.O.	U1C
to have a holiday or vacation; to have a day off	放假	放假	fàngjià	V.O.	U6B
to have a part-time job	打工	打工	dǎgōng	V.O.	U2B
to have a runny nose	流鼻涕	流鼻涕	liú bítì	V.O.	U1C
to have breakfast	吃早饭	吃早飯	chī zǎofàn	V.O.	U2A
head	头	頭	tóu	N.	U1A
headache	头痛	頭痛	tóutòng	N.	U1C
health	健康	健康	jiànkāng	N.	U1C
healthy	健康	健康	jiànkāng	Adj.	U1C
heart (metaphorical)	心地	心地	xīndì	N.	U3A
heavy	重	重	zhòng	Adj.	U5B
to help	帮	幫	bāng	V.	U2B
here	这里	這裡	zhèlǐ	Pron.	U3C
here (colloquial)	这儿	這兒	zhèr	Pron.	U3C
high	高	高	gāo	Adj.	U1A
holiday; vacation	假	假	jià	N.	U6B
homework	功课	功課	gōngkè	N.	U2B
Hong Kong	香港	香港	Xiānggǎng	N.	U6A
to hope	希望	希望	xīwàng	V.	U5B
horror film	恐怖片	恐怖片	kǒngbùpiàn	N.	U2C

hospital	医院	醫院	yīyuàn	*N.*	U1C
hotel	饭店	飯店	fàndiàn	*N.*	U6A
	旅馆	旅館	lǚguǎn	*N.*	U6A
hour	小时	小時	xiǎoshí	*N.*	U1A
	钟头	鐘頭	zhōngtóu	*N.*	U1A
house	房子	房子	fángzi	*N.*	U4B
how long	多久	多久	duōjiǔ	*Q.W.*	U1A
Humble Administrator's Garden	拙政园	拙政園	Zhuózhèng Yuán	*N.*	U6C

idea; plan	主意	主意	zhǔyi	*N.*	U4A
if	要是	要是	yàoshì	*Conj.*	U2B
	如果	如果	rúguǒ	*Conj.*	U2B
important	重要	重要	zhòngyào	*Adj.*	U5B
in a bad mood	心情不好	心情不好	xīnqíng bù hǎo	*Adj.*	U1B
in a good mood	心情好	心情好	xīnqíng hǎo	*Adj.*	U1B
in fact; actually	其实	其實	qíshí	*Adv.*	U2C
in good health; to get well	好	好	hǎo	*Adj.*	U1C
in the direction of; to; toward	往	往	wǎng	*Prep.*	U4A
in the process of; during the course of	正在	正在	zhèngzài	*Adv.*	U4C
indeed; really	的确	的確	díquè	*Adv.*	U2B
indicates an action completed or a past experience	过	過	guò	*P.*	U6B
indicates the continuation of an action	下去	下去	xiàqù	*C.*	U6C
indicating possibility	了	了	liǎo	*C.*	U6C
indicating understanding or realization	哦	哦	ó	*Intj.*	U3B
ingredient	材料	材料	cáiliào	*N.*	U5C
interest	兴趣	興趣	xìngqù	*N.*	U2C
intern	实习	實習	shíxí	*V.*	U6B
to intern	实习生	實習生	shíxíshēng	*N.*	U6B
international	国际	國際	guójì	*Adj.*	U3A
intersection	路口	路口	lùkǒu	*N.*	U4A
introverted	内向	內向	nèixiàng	*Adj.*	U3A

invitation	邀请	邀請	yāoqǐng	*N.*	U4A
to invite	请	請	qǐng	*V.*	U3B
	邀请	邀請	yāoqǐng	*V.*	U4A
it's nothing; never mind	没事	沒事	méishì	*C.E.*	U4B
it's okay	没关系	沒關係	méiguānxi	*C.E.*	U2A

J

Jiuzhaigou Valley	九寨沟	九寨溝	Jiǔzhàigōu	*N.*	U6C
job; work	工作	工作	gōngzuò	*N.*	U6B
to join; to participate in	参加	參加	cānjiā	*V.*	U3B
just; exactly	刚刚	剛剛	gānggāng	*Adv.*	U4C
just; only	就	就	jiù	*Adv.*	U1A

K

ketchup	蕃茄酱	蕃茄醬	fānqiéjiàng	*N.*	U6B
kid; child	小孩	小孩	xiǎohái	*N.*	U3C
kilometer	公里	公里	gōnglǐ	*M.W.*	U4A
kitchen	厨房	廚房	chúfáng	*N.*	U4C
knee	膝盖	膝蓋	xīgài	*N.*	U1A
knife	刀子	刀子	dāozi	*N.*	U5C
kung-fu film	功夫片	功夫片	gōngfupiàn	*N.*	U2C

L

to lack; to be short of	少	少	shǎo	*V.*	U5B
lamp; light	灯	燈	dēng	*N.*	U4C
large building	大楼	大樓	dàlóu	*N.*	U4B
last; final	最后	最後	zuìhòu	*Adj.*	U6A
late	晚	晚	wǎn	*Adj.*	U2A
late-night snack	夜宵	夜宵	yèxiāo	*N.*	U2A
layer; storey; floor	层	層	céng	*M.W.*	U4B
lazy	懒	懶	lǎn	*Adj.*	U1B
to leave a message	留言	留言	liúyán	*V.O.*	U3C
to leave; to go back	回去	回去	huíqù	*V.C.*	U3C

left	左	左	zuǒ	*N.*	U4A
to let; to allow	让	讓	ràng	*V.*	U2B
letter	信	信	xìn	*N.*	U6A
liberal arts	文科	文科	wénkē	*N.*	U3B
to listen; to hear	听	聽	tīng	*V.*	U4C
to live	住	住	zhù	*V.*	U6C
living room	客厅	客廳	kètīng	*N.*	U4C
lobster	龙虾	龍蝦	lóngxiā	*N.*	U5B
loft; attic	顶楼	頂樓	dǐnglóu	*N.*	U4B
London	伦敦	倫敦	Lúndūn	*N.*	U6A
long	久	久	jiǔ	*Adj.*	U1A
long ago; as early as; for a long time	早	早	zǎo	*Adj.*	U4B
to look after kids	看孩子	看孩子	kān háizi	*V.O.*	U6B
to look after; to take care of	看	看	kān	*V.*	U6B
Los Angeles	洛杉矶	洛杉磯	Luòshānjī	*N.*	U6A
to lose	输	輸	shū	*V.*	U1B
love and care	爱心	愛心	àixīn	*N.*	U3C
low	低	低	dī	*Adj.*	U1A
lunch	午饭	午飯	wǔfàn	*N.*	U2A
	中饭	中飯	zhōngfàn	*N.*	U2A
	午餐	午餐	wǔcān	*N.*	U2A
	中餐	中餐	zhōngcān	*N.*	U2A

M

mail recipient	收信人	收信人	shōuxìnrén	*N.*	U6A
mailbox	信箱	信箱	xìnxiāng	*N.*	U4B
	邮箱	郵箱	yóuxiāng	*N.*	U6A
mailman	邮差	郵差	yóu chāi	*N.*	U6A
to make a phone call	打电话	打電話	dǎ diànhuà	*V.O.*	U2B
male	男	男	nán	*Adj.*	U3A
	男	男	nán	*N.*	U3A
	男的	男的	nánde	*N.*	U3A
male junior (student)	学弟	學弟	xuédì	*N.*	U3B
male senior (student)	学长	學長	xuézhǎng	*N.*	U3B

man	男人	男人	nánrén	N.	U3A
market	菜市场	菜市場	càishìchǎng	N.	U5A
matter; thing; business	事情	事情	shìqing	N.	U3B
to measure	量	量	liáng	V.	U1C
a measure word for buildings	栋	棟	dòng	M.W.	U4B
a measure word for knives	把	把	bǎ	M.W.	U5C
a measure word for mountains or buildings	座	座	zuò	M.W.	U1A
a measure word for rooms	间	間	jiān	M.W.	U4C
a measure word for utensils like spoons and forks	只	只	zhǐ	M.W.	U5C
meat	肉类	肉類	ròulèi	N.	U5A
medicine; medication	药	藥	yào	N.	U1C
to meet	见面	見面	jiànmiàn	V.O.	U3B
to mention	提起	提起	tíqǐ	V.C.	U3C
to mention; to bring up	提	提	tí	V.	U3C
menu	菜单	菜單	càidān	N.	U5A
merely; simply; just; only	只是	只是	zhǐshì	Adv.	U2C
meter	公尺	公尺	gōngchǐ	M.W.	U4A
	米	米	mǐ	M.W.	U4A
minute	分钟	分鐘	fēnzhōng	M.W.	U1A
mood	心情	心情	xīnqíng	N.	U1B
more and more...	越来越…	越來越…	yuè lái yuè...	C.E.	U6A
more; a lot	多	多	duō	Adv.	U1C
mound; hill	丘	丘	qiū	N.	U6C
Mount Tai	泰山	泰山	Tài Shān	N.	U6C
mouth	嘴巴	嘴巴	zuǐba	N.	U1C
to move backward	往后走	往後走	wǎng hòu zǒu	V.	U4A
muffin	松饼	鬆餅	sōngbǐng	N.	U6B
mushroom	蘑菇	蘑菇	mógu	N.	U5C
must	一定	一定	yídìng	Adv.	U1B

N

napkin	餐巾纸	餐巾紙	cānjīnzhǐ	N.	U6B
National Palace Museum	故宫	故宫	Gù Gōng	N.	U6C

national; domestic	国内	國內	guónèi	*Adj.*	U6A
natural and poised	大方	大方	dàfāng	*Adj.*	U3A
natural sciences	理科	理科	lǐkē	*N.*	U3B
near; close	近	近	jìn	*Adj.*	U4A
nearby; neighboring	附近	附近	fùjìn	*N.*	U5A
neck	脖子	脖子	bózi	*N.*	U1A
neighbor	邻居	鄰居	línjū	*N.*	U6B
nervous	紧张	緊張	jǐnzhāng	*Adj*	U1B
New York (City)	纽约	紐約	Niǔyuē	*N.*	U6A
no wonder	难怪	難怪	nánguài	*Conj.*	U2A
north	北	北	běi	*N.*	U4A
northeast	东北	東北	dōngběi	*N.*	U4A
northwest	西北	西北	xīběi	*N.*	U4A
nose	鼻子	鼻子	bízi	*N.*	U1C
not able to bear or tolerate	受不了	受不了	shòubùliǎo	*C.E.*	U6C
not energetic	精神不好	精神不好	jīngshén bù hǎo	*Adj.*	U1B
not on time; late	晚	晚	wǎn	*Adj.*	U4B
not only	不只	不只	bùzhǐ	*Conj.*	U3C
not yet	还没	還沒	hái méi	*Adv.*	U3B
nothing; don't mention it	没什么	沒什麼	méi shénme	*C.E.*	U2C
nurse	护士	護士	hùshì	*N.*	U1C
nursing home	养老院	養老院	yǎnglǎoyuàn	*N.*	U3C

O

octopus	章鱼	章魚	zhāngyú	*N.*	U5B
off; away; from	离	離	lí	*Prep.*	U4A
often; frequently	常常	常常	chángcháng	*Adv.*	U3C
old (age-wise)	大	大	dà	*Adj.*	U3A
Old Summer Palace	圆明园	圓明園	Yuánmíng Yuán	*N.*	U6C
olive oil	橄榄油	橄欖油	gǎnlǎnyóu	*N.*	U5B
onion	洋葱	洋蔥	yángcōng	*N.*	U5C
onion ring	洋葱圈	洋蔥圈	yángcōngquān	*N.*	U6B
only	才	才	cái	*Adv.*	U6C
originally	本来	本來	běnlái	*Adv.*	U6C

orphanage	孤儿院	孤兒院	gū'éryuàn	*N.*	U3C
otherwise; or	要不然	要不然	yàobùrán	*Conj.*	U5C
out-going	开朗	開朗	kāilǎng	*Adj.*	U3A
overpass	立交桥	立交橋	lìjiāoqiáo	*N.*	U4A
overseas study group	游学团	遊學團	yóuxuétuán	*N.*	U6B
oyster	牡蛎	牡蠣	mǔlì	*N.*	U5B
	蚝	蠔	háo	*N.*	U5B

P

packaged food	包装食品	包裝食品	bāozhuāng shípǐn	*N.*	U5A
pair of	双	雙	shuāng	*M.W.*	U5C
pancake	煎饼	煎餅	jiānbǐng	*N.*	U6B
to pan-fry	煎	煎	jiān	*V.*	U5C
parcel; package	包裹	包裹	bāoguǒ	*N.*	U6A
Paris	巴黎	巴黎	Bālí	*N.*	U6A
party	聚会	聚會	jùhuì	*N.*	U4B
to pass (something) on	传	傳	chuán	*V.*	U6C
to pass; to cross	过	過	guò	*V.*	U4A
to pass; to go through	过	過	guò	*V.*	U1C
passionate	热情	熱情	rèqíng	*Adj.*	U3A
patient	病人	病人	bìngrén	*N.*	U1C
to pay attention to	注意	注意	zhùyì	*V.*	U1C
pedestrian	行人	行人	xíngrén	*N.*	U4A
pedestrian bridge	天桥	天橋	tiānqiáo	*N.*	U4A
to peel	削	削	xiāo	*V.*	U5C
pepper	胡椒	胡椒	hújiāo	*N.*	U5B
person	人	人	rén	*N.*	U3A
personality	个性	個性	gèxìng	*N.*	U3A
photograph	照片	照片	zhàopiàn	*N.*	U6C
	相片	相片	xiàngpiàn	*N.*	
photographer	摄影师	攝影師	shèyǐngshī	*N.*	U6C
photography	摄影	攝影	shèyǐng	*N.*	U2B
pie	派	派	pài	*N.*	U5B

English	Simplified	Traditional	Pinyin	Type	Unit
piece; cube; chunk	块	塊	kuài	N.	U5C
pill	粒	粒	lì	M.W.	U1C
pizza	比萨饼	比薩餅	bǐsàbǐng	N.	U6B
place; space; part	地方	地方	dìfang	N.	U3C
plan	计划	計畫	jìhuà	N.	U6B
to plan	打算	打算	dǎsuàn	V.	U6A
plane	飞机	飛機	fēijī	N.	U2A
plastic bag	塑料袋	塑料袋	sùliàodài	N.	U6B
plate	盘子	盤子	pánzi	N.	U5C
polite measure word for people	位	位	wèi	M.W.	U3C
possible; probable	可能	可能	kěnéng	Adj.	U5A
post office	邮局	郵局	yóujú	N.	U6A
postcard	明信片	明信片	míngxìnpiàn	N.	U6A
potato	土豆	土豆	tǔdòu	N.	U5C
	马铃薯	馬鈴薯	mǎlíngshǔ	N.	U5C
to practice	练习	練習	liànxí	V.	U1A
to praise	夸	誇	kuā	V.	U6C
(prefix for ordinal numbers)	第	第	dì	Sp.	U4A
preparation	准备	準備	zhǔnbèi	N.	U3C
to prepare	准备	準備	zhǔnbèi	V.	U3C
price	价格	價格	jiàgé	N.	U6A
private school	私立学校	私立學校	sīlì xuéxiào	N.	U3B
probably	大概	大概	dàgài	Adv.	U4A
problem; question	问题	問題	wèntí	N.	U2C
proud or pleased with oneself	得意	得意	déyì	Adj.	U6C
public school	公立学校	公立學校	gōnglì xuéxiào	N.	U3B
pudding	布丁	布丁	bùdīng	N.	U5B
pumpkin	南瓜	南瓜	nánguā	N.	U5C
punctual; on time	准时	準時	zhǔnshí	Adj.	U4B
to put	放	放	fàng	V.	U5C
to put in order; to tidy up	收拾	收拾	shōushi	V.	U5C
to put on makeup	化妆	化妝	huàzhuāng	V.O.	U2A
to put; to place; to arrange	摆	擺	bǎi	V.	U5C

Q

| quarter hour | 刻钟 | 刻鐘 | kèzhōng | *M.W.* | U1A |

R

rambler	平房	平房	píngfáng	*N.*	U4B
reasonable	合理	合理	hélǐ	*Adj.*	U6A
to receive; to get	收到	收到	shōudào	*V.C.*	U2C
recently; lately	最近	最近	zuìjìn	*Adv.*	U2C
recipient's address	收信人地址	收信人地址	shōuxìnrén dìzhǐ	*N.*	U6A
to record	记录	記錄	jìlù	*V.*	U1B
registered mail	挂号信	掛號信	guàhàoxìn	*N.*	U6A
regular mail	平信	平信	píngxìn	*N.*	U6A
to remember	记得	記得	jìde	*V.*	U2B
(the representation of the combined sounds "了 *le*" and "啊 *a*", denoting exclamation, interrogation, etc.)	啦	啦	la	*P.*	U4B
to rest	休息	休息	xiūxi	*V.*	U1C
to return; to answer; to reply	回	回	huí	*V.*	U3C
to return; to come back	回来	回來	huílái	*V.C.*	U3C
Rice Noodles with Ground Pork	蚂蚁上树	螞蟻上樹	Mǎyǐ shàngshù	*N.*	U5B
to ride	骑	騎	qí	*V.*	U2A
to ride a bicycle	骑自行车	騎自行車	qí zìxíngchē	*V.O.*	U2A
to ride a motorcycle	骑摩托车	騎摩托車	qí mótuōchē	*V.O.*	U2A
right	右	右	yòu	*N.*	U4A
road	马路	馬路	mǎlù	*N.*	U4A
road; path; way	路	路	lù	*N.*	U1A
romance	浪漫爱情片	浪漫愛情片	làngmàn àiqíngpiàn	*N.*	U2C
Rome	罗马	羅馬	Luómǎ	*N.*	U6A
room	房间	房間	fángjiān	*N.*	U4C

S

| sad | 难过 | 難過 | nánguò | *Adj* | U1B |
| safe | 保险 | 保險 | bǎoxiǎn | *Adj.* | U4A |

sales clerk	店员	店員	diànyuán	N.	U2B
salt	盐	鹽	yán	N.	U5B
same; alike	同	同	tóng	Adj.	U3B
San Francisco	旧金山	舊金山	Jiùjīnshān	N.	U6A
sauce	酱料	醬料	jiàngliào	N.	U5C
saucer	碟子	碟子	diézi	N.	U5C
to say; to speak; to talk	说	說	shuō	V.	U1B
scallop	扇贝	扇貝	shànbèi	N.	U5B
scenery	风景	風景	fēngjǐng	N.	U6C
school	学校	學校	xuéxiào	N.	U2A
school bus	校车	校車	xiàochē	N.	U2A
school life	学校生活	學校生活	xéxiào shēnghuó	N.	U3B
school paper	校刊	校刊	xiàokān	N.	U2B
school team	校队	校隊	xiàoduì	N.	U3B
sci-fi film	科幻片	科幻片	kēhuànpiàn	N.	U2C
scooter; motorcycle	摩托车	摩托車	mótuōchē	N.	U2A
scouts	童子军	童子軍	tóngzǐjūn	N.	U2B
seafood	海鲜	海鮮	hǎixiān	N.	U5A
seasoning	调料	調料	tiáoliào	N.	U5B
second	秒钟	秒鐘	miǎozhōng	M.W.	U1A
security guard	保安	保安	bǎo'ān	N.	U4B
(of a patient) to see a doctor; (of a doctor) to see a patient	看病	看病	kànbìng	V.O.	U1C
to see; to visit	看	看	kàn	V.	U6B
to seem; to be like	好像	好像	hǎoxiàng	V.	U5C
to sell	卖	賣	mài	V.	U5A
to send; to distribute	发	發	fā	V.	U2C
to send; to mail	寄	寄	jì	V.	U6A
sender's address	寄信人地址	寄信人地址	jìxìnrén dìzhǐ	N.	U6A
sentence	句	句	jù	M.W.	U6C
			jù	N.	U6C
Seoul	首尔	首爾	Shǒu'ěr	N.	U6A
serious	严重	嚴重	yánzhòng	Adj.	U1C
serious; conscientious	认真	認真	rènzhēn	Adj.	U6A

to serve	服务	服務	fúwù	*V.*	U3C
service	服务	服務	fúwù	*N.*	U3C
Shanghai	上海	上海	Shànghǎi	*N.*	U6A
shellfish	贝类	貝類	bèilèi	*N.*	U5B
short	矮	矮	ǎi	*Adj.*	U3A
shoulder	肩膀	肩膀	jiānbǎng	*N.*	U1A
shrimp	虾	蝦	xiā	*N.*	U5B
shy	害羞	害羞	hàixiū	*Adj.*	U3A
side	边	邊	biān	*N.*	U4A
sidewalk	人行道	人行道	rénxíngdào	*N.*	U4A
to simmer	焖	燜	mèn	*V.*	U5C
since; as; now that	既然	既然	jìrán	*M.A.*	U5A
to sleep	睡	睡	shuì	*V.*	U1B
sleepy	困	睏	kùn	*Adj.*	U1B
slender; slim	苗条	苗條	miáotiáo	*Adj.*	U3A
small cube of meat or vegetable	丁	丁	dīng	*N.*	U5C
snack	零食	零食	língshí	*N.*	U5A
snacks	点心	點心	diǎnxīn	*N.*	U2A
to sneeze	打喷嚏	打噴嚏	dǎ pēntì	*V.O.*	U1C
so (used before certain adjectives to indicate high degree)	好	好	hǎo	*Adv.*	U1A
sofa	沙发	沙發	shāfā	*N.*	U4C
some; a few	一些	一些	yìxiē	*Num.* + *M.W.*	U6C
some; a little	些	些	xiē	*M.W.*	U6C
sore	酸	酸	suān	*Adj.*	U1A
(a) sore throat	喉咙痛	喉嚨痛	hóulóng tòng	*N.*	U1C
(sound of vomiting and crying)	哇	哇	wa	*Intj.*	U4C
sound; voice	声音	聲音	shēngyīn	*N.*	U4C
south	南	南	nán	*N.*	U4A
southeast	东南	東南	dōngnán	*N.*	U4A
southwest	西南	西南	xīnán	*N.*	U4A
soy sauce	酱油	醬油	jiàngyóu	*N.*	U5B
to speak; to say; to tell; to talk about	讲	講	jiǎng	*V.*	U3C

spirit	精神	精神	jīngshén	*N.*	U1B
spoon	汤匙	湯匙	tāngchí	*N.*	U5C
sports	运动	運動	yùndòng	*N.*	U2B
squid	鱿鱼	鱿魚	yóuyú	*N.*	U5B
stairs	楼梯	樓梯	lóutī	*N.*	U4B
(postage) stamp	邮票	郵票	yóupiào	*N.*	U6A
to stand; to endure; to bear	受	受	shòu	*V.*	U6C
to stay	待	待	dāi	*V.*	U6C
to stir-fry	炒	炒	chǎo	*V.*	U5C
storage room	贮藏室	貯藏室	zhùcángshì	*N.*	U4C
story	故事	故事	gùshi	*N.*	U3C
straw	吸管	吸管	xīgu ǎn	*N.*	U6B
streetlight	路灯	路燈	lùdēng	*N.*	U4A
strong	壮	壯	zhuàng	*Adj.*	U3A
stubborn	固执	固執	gùzhí	*Adj.*	U3A
to study	学习	學習	xuéxí	*V.*	U2B
to study abroad	游学	遊學	yóuxué	*V.*	U6B
study room	书房	書房	shūfáng	*N.*	U4C
(a) stuffed nose	鼻塞	鼻塞	bísāi	*Adj.*	U1C
(school) subject	科	科	kē	*M.W.*	U6A
suburbs; outskirts	郊区	郊區	jiāoqū	*N.*	U6A
to suffer from diarrhea	拉肚子	拉肚子	lā dùzi	*V.O.*	U1C
sugar	糖	糖	táng	*N.*	U5B
summer camp	夏令营	夏令營	xiàlìngyíng	*N.*	U6B
Summer Palaces	颐和园	頤和園	Yíhéyuán	*N.*	U6C
summer vacation	暑假	暑假	shǔjià	*N.*	U6A
sundae	圣代	聖代	shèngdài	*N.*	U5B
supermarket	超级市场	超級市場	chāojí shìchǎng	*N.*	U5A
	超市	超市	chāoshì	*N.*	U5A
supermarket	超级市场	超級市場	chāojí shìchǎng	*N.*	U5A
superstore	大型超级市场	大型超級市場	dàxíng chāojí shìchǎng	*N.*	U5A
surprised	惊讶	驚訝	jīngyà	*Adj.*	U1B
Sūzhōu	苏州	蘇州	Suzhou	*N.*	U6C

Sweet & Sour Fish	糖醋鱼	糖醋魚	tángcùyú	N.	U5B
Sydney	悉尼	悉尼	Xīní	N.	U6A
symptom	症状	症狀	zhèngzhuàng	N.	U1C

Tabasco sauce	辣椒油	辣椒油	làjiāoyóu	N.	U6B
table; desk	桌子	桌子	zhuōzi	N.	U4C
tableware	餐具	餐具	cānjù	N.	U5C
Taipei	台北	台北	Táiběi	N.	U6A
to take a photograph; to shoot a film	摄影	攝影	shèyǐng	V.	U6C
to take a ride from someone; to travel by; to go by	搭	搭	dā	V.	U2A
to take a shower; to have a bath	洗澡	洗澡	xǐzǎo	V.O.	U2A
to take a soak in the tub	泡澡	泡澡	pàozǎo	V.O.	U2A
to take a walk; to stroll	散步	散步	sànbù	V.	U3C
to take care (of sb.)	照顾	照顧	zhàogù	V.	U2B
to take lessons after school	补习	補習	bǔxí	V.	U3B
to take photos	照相	照相	zhàoxiàng	V.O.	U6C
tall	高	高	gāo	Adj.	U3A
taste	味道	味道	wèidào	N.	U5C
taxi; cab	出租车	出租車	chūzūchē	N.	U2A
to teach	教	教	jiāo	V.	U3C
team	球队	球隊	qiúduì	N.	U1B
Terracotta Army	兵马俑	兵馬俑	Bīngmǎyǒng	N.	U6C
text message	短信	短信	duǎnxìn	N.	U2C
that, so	那么	那麼	nàme	Adv.	U1A
the countryside around a city; the outskirts of town	郊外	郊外	jiāowài	N.	U6C
The Great Wall of China	长城	長城	Cháng Chéng	N.	U6C
the more..., the more...	越…越…	越…越…	yuè...yuè...	C.E.	U6A
the same	一样	一樣	yíyàng	Adj.	U3A
then (indicating that one action takes place after the completion of another)	再	再	zài	Adv.	U4A
then; afterwards; after that	然后	然後	ránhòu	Adv.	U4A
there	那里	那裡	nàlǐ	Pron.	U3C

there (colloquial)	那儿	那兒	nàr	*Pron.*	U3C
thermometer	体温计	體溫計	tǐwēnjì	*N.*	U1C
these	这些	這些	zhèixiē	*Pron.*	U6C
thigh	大腿	大腿	dàtuǐ	*N.*	U1A
thin	瘦	瘦	shòu	*Adj.*	U3A
to think	想	想	xiǎng	*V.*	U4B
to think (mistakenly)	以为	以為	yǐwéi	*V.*	U4B
to think; to consider	看	看	kàn	*V.*	U4A
this way; like this	这样	這樣	zhèyàng	*Adv.*	U3B
this, so	这么	這麼	zhème	*Adv.*	U1A
those	那些	那些	nèixiē	*Pron.*	U6C
Tiger Hill	虎丘	虎丘	Hǔqiū	*N.*	U6C
time	时间	時間	shíjiān	*N.*	U2A
times	次	次	cì	*M.W.*	U1C
tired	累	累	lèi	*Adj.*	U1B
to; toward	对	對	duì	*Prep.*	U2C
toe	脚指	腳指	jiǎozhǐ	*N.*	U1A
tofu	豆腐	豆腐	dòufu	*N.*	U5B
to-go box	快餐盒	快餐盒	kuàicānhé	*N.*	U6B
Tokyo	东京	東京	Dōngjīng	*N.*	U6A
tomato	西红柿	西红柿	xīhóngshì	*N.*	U5C
	蕃茄	蕃茄	fānqié	*N.*	U5C
tooth	牙齿	牙齒	yáchǐ	*N.*	U1C
tourist	观光客	觀光客	guānguāngkè	*N.*	U6C
traffic light	红绿灯	紅綠燈	hónglǜdēng	*N.*	U4A
tragedy drama	悲剧片	悲劇片	bēijùpiàn	*N.*	U2C
train	火车	火車	huǒchē	*N.*	U2A
to transfer to another school	转学	轉學	zhuǎnxué	*V.O.*	U3B
transportation	交通工具	交通工具	jiāotōng gōngjù	*N.*	U2A
traveler	旅客	旅客	lǚkè	*N.*	U6C
	游客	遊客	yóukè	*N.*	U6C
traveling	旅游	旅遊	lǚyóu	*N.*	U6C
tray	餐盘	餐盤	cānpán	*N.*	U6B
to turn	拐	拐	guǎi	*V.*	U4A

to turn	转	轉	zhuǎn	*V.*	U4A
to turn left	左转	左轉	zuǒ zhuǎn	*V.*	U4A
	左拐	左拐	zuǒ guǎi	*V.*	
to turn right	右转	右轉	yòu zhuǎn	*V.*	U4A
	右拐	右拐	yòu guǎi	*V.*	
tutor	家教	家教	jiājiào	*N.*	U2B
types of shops	商店类型	商店類型	sāngdiàn lèixíng	*N.*	U5A

U

uncomfortable	不舒服	不舒服	bù shūfu	*Adj.*	U1B
up; above	上	上	shàng	*N.*	U4A
to use the toilet	上厕所	上廁所	shàng cèsuǒ	*V.O.*	U2A
(used after a verb as a complement to indicate something ran out or used up)	完	完	wán	*R.C.*	U4C
(used after a verb as a complement to indicate success)	到	到	dào	*R.C.*	U4C
(used after a verb to indicate completion of action)	了	了	le	*P.*	U1A
(used after a verb to indicate the completion of an action)	好	好	hǎo	*R.C.*	U4C
used after short answers to soften the tone	呀	呀	ya	*P.*	U3A
used at the end of a sentence to indicate doubt or conjecture	吧	吧	ba	*P.*	U2B
(used before a verb to indicate that something happened earlier than was expected)	就	就	jiù	*Adv.*	U1B
(used before a verb to indicate that something happened later than was expected)	才	才	cái	*Adv.*	U1B
(used before certain adjectives to indicate high degree) quite	好	好	hǎo	*Adv.*	U4C
used between a verb or an adjective and its complement to indicate degree	得	得	de	*P.*	U3A
used between a verb or an adjective and its complement to indicate result	得	得	de	*P.*	U3B
used for films or a volume of books	部	部	bù	*M.W.*	U2C
used for letters, emails	封	封	fēng	*M.W.*	U2C

used for text messages	条	條	tiáo	*M.W.*	U2C
used to express emphasis and to indicate certainty	是	是	shì	*V.*	U2B
used to indicate a change of status	了	了	le	*P.*	U1B
used to indicate a difference in manner or degree through comparison	比	比	bǐ	*Prep.*	U3A

V

vegetable	蔬菜	蔬菜	shūcài	*N.*	U5A
very	好	好	hǎo	*Adv.*	U1B
	非常	非常	fēicháng	*Adv.*	U3B
video camera	摄影机	攝影機	shèyǐngjī	*N.*	U6C
video chat	视频	視頻	shìpín	*N.*	U2C
video game player	游戏机	遊戲機	yóuxìjī	*N.*	U4C
village	庄	莊	zhuāng	*N.*	U6C
vinegar	醋	醋	cù	*N.*	U5B
volunteer	志愿者	志願者	zhìyuànzhě	*N.*	U2B
volunteer work	志愿工作	志願工作	zhìyuàn gōngzuò	*N.*	U3C

W

waffle	威化饼	威化餅	wēihuàbǐng	*N.*	U6B
to wait	等	等	děng	*V.*	U2A
to wait a moment	等一下	等一下	děng yíxià	*V.+M.W.*	U3C
waiter / waitress	服务员	服務員	fúwùyuán	*N.*	U2B
to wake up	醒	醒	xǐng	*V.*	U2A
to walk	走路	走路	zǒulù	*V.O.*	U1A
wall	墙壁	牆壁	qiángbì	*N.*	U4C
to wash	洗	洗	xǐ	*V.*	U5C
to wash one's face	洗脸	洗臉	xǐliǎn	*V.O.*	U2A
Washington D.C.	华盛顿特区	華盛頓特區	Huáshèngdùn Tèqū	*N.*	U6A
we; us	咱们	咱們	zánmen	*Pron.*	U1A
to wear; to put on	戴	戴	dài	*V.*	U1A

(indicating surprise) well; why; what	咦	咦	yí	*Intj.*	U2A
west	西	西	xī	*N.*	U4A
West Lake	西湖	西湖	Xīhú	*N.*	U6C
wet	湿	濕	shī	*Adj.*	U2A
What's up? What's wrong?	怎么了	怎麼了	zěnme le	*C.E.*	U2C
whole; all over	全	全	quán	*Adj.*	U1A
why; how	怎么	怎麼	zěnme	*Q.W.*	U1A
to win	赢	赢	yíng	*V.*	U1B
window	窗户	窗戶	chuānghu	*N.*	U4B
wok	炒锅	炒鍋	chǎoguō	*N.*	U5C
woman	女人	女人	nǚrén	*N.*	U3A
word; remark	话	話	huà	*N.*	U1B
to work	工作	工作	gōngzuò	*V.*	U6B
worried	担心	擔心	dānxīn	*Adj.*	U1B
to worry	担心	擔心	dānxīn	*V.*	U1B
to write	写	寫	xiě	*V.*	U1B

Y

Yangtze River Three Gorges	长江三峡	長江三峡	Chángjiāng Sānxiá	*N.*	U6C
youth hostel	青年旅馆	青年旅館	qīngnián lǚguǎn	*N.*	U6A

Z

Zhouzhuang (a historic "water town" built on a system of canals)	周庄	周莊	Zhōuzhuāng	*N.*	U6C

主题索引 Index of Topics

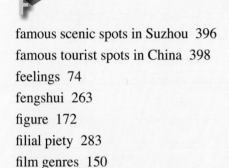

照片与实物提供者　Photo and Realia Credits

All photos and realia in 真棒! *Zhēn Bàng!* Level 2 textbook not supplied by LiveABC Interactive Corporation have been provided by the following: